CW01213395

The Drawing Room

ENGLISH COUNTRY HOUSE DECORATION

Jeremy Musson
Foreword by Julian Fellowes

The Drawing Room

ENGLISH COUNTRY HOUSE DECORATION

Photography by Paul Barker
and *Country Life*

Rizzoli
NEW YORK

New York · Paris · London · Milan

To Penelope Lady Sitwell, and to the memory of the late Sir Reresby Sitwell, Bt., with thanks for their unforgettable hospitality at Renishaw Hall.

First published in the United States of America in 2014
by Rizzoli International Publications, Inc.
300 Park Avenue South, New York, NY 10010

www.rizzoliusa.com

© 2014 by Jeremy Musson
Photographs © 2014 by Paul Barker
Introduction photographs © 2014 by *Country Life*
Foreword © 2014 by Julian Fellowes

All rights reserved. No part of this publication may be reproduced, stored in a retrieval system, or transmitted in any form or by any means, electronic, mechanical, photocopying, recording, or otherwise, without prior consent of the publishers.

2014 2015 2016 2017 / 10 9 8 7 6 5 4 3 2 1

Distributed in the US trade by Random House, New York

ISBN 978 0 8478 4333 6

Library of Congress Cataloging-in-Publication Data

Musson, Jeremy, author.

The drawing room : English country house decoration / Jeremy Musson ; foreword by Julian Fellowes ; photography by Paul Barker and Country Life.

pages cm

Includes bibliographical references and index.

ISBN 978-0-8478-4333-6 (alk. paper)

1. Interior decoration--England--Themes, motives. 2. Drawing rooms--England. 3. Country homes--England. I. Barker, Paul, 1952- illustrator. II. Fellowes, Julian, writer of supplementary textual content. III. Country life (London, England) IV. Title.

NK2117.D7M87 2014

747'.8880942--dc23

2014005913

Designed by Robert Dalrymple
Typeset in Elena and Quadraat
Printed in China

Endpapers: *Dashwood*, hand block printed design, c.1780 Hamilton Weston Wallpapers Ltd.
Binding: A detail of a door at Kedleston, Derbyshire
Page 2: The drawing room at Deene Park, Northamptonshire
Page 6: A detail of the Henry Holland–designed chimneypiece at Althorp

CONTENTS

Foreword *Julian Fellowes* 7

Introduction: Enter the Drawing Room 9

I EVOLUTION
The Sixteenth to Eighteenth Centuries

Loseley Park 25

South Wraxall Manor 33

Chillingham Castle 41

Newby Hall 49

Kedleston Hall 57

Althorp 65

Broadlands 73

II ELEGANCE
The Early Nineteenth Century

Oakly Park 81

Attingham Park 89

Renishaw Hall 97

Felbrigg Hall 105

III OPULENCE
The Later Nineteenth Century

Eastnor Castle 113

Knebworth 121

Alnwick Castle 129

Hutton in the Forest 137

Madresfield Court 145

IV TASTEMAKERS
The Twentieth Century

Hilles House 153

Dyrham Park 161

The Yellow Room 167

Deene Park 175

Lypiatt Park 183

Cholmondeley Castle 191

The Grove 199

V CONTINUITY
The Timeless Drawing Room

Stanway House 207

Bradley Court 215

Wormington Grange 223

Whithurst House 231

Aynhoe Park 237

Thame Park 245

Knepp Castle 251

The Temple 259

Acknowledgements 265

Select Bibliography and Sources 266

Notes and References 268

Index 271

GEORGIANA COUNTESS SPENCER
1737 ———— 1814
LADY GEORGIANA SPENCER AFTERWARDS
DUCHESS OF DEVONSHIRE
1757 ———— 1806
SIR JOSHUA REYNOLDS P.R.A
23 ———— 1792
154

THE DRAWING ROOM · ENGLISH COUNTRY HOUSE DECORATION

Foreword

I am grateful to the culture of the English country house, not only because it has provided me with a living over quite a few years, but also because it seems to me to encapsulate the best of British in many ways. And at the centre of this tradition is the drawing room, the scene of confidence and intrigue, of secrets and grand display. It is a room that was designed to be the province of the ladies and, as such, has been the background of many schemes, romantic and otherwise, over the centuries. Men might claim the library or the dining room as their province, but in the drawing room, the lady was always Queen. And anyone doubting this has only to turn to the novels of every writer from Jane Austen to Galsworthy and beyond. I am a believer in petticoat influence, as it used to be called, in both public and private life, which has been much stronger than many suppose from long before the political liberation of women and which has almost invariably been an influence for the good. The drawing room was the backdrop for much of it, and it is only right that a handsome book should celebrate this part of our national life.

Jeremy Musson and Paul Barker have given us a ravishing study of more than thirty drawing rooms from many of our greatest houses, which shows us just what important chambers they have been and indeed still are. They are trumpets of status, certainly, filled with art and furniture of importance, worked on by the greatest designers, bedecked with collections gathered on the Grand Tour and from all around the world, so much of which we used to govern, but what I love most is that they were designed for pleasure, too, for comfort and delight, for intimacy as well as splendour. I am lucky enough to know quite a number of the rooms illustrated here, and I have seen how they work as part of what is essentially a performance art, entertaining in a great house, which the reader can enjoy vicariously, in the safe hands of Jeremy and Paul, the perfect companions for this armchair tour.

The drawing room evolved into something like the room we enjoy now in the eighteenth century, but every age has made its changes to how it was decorated or used, with new fashions and new dreams to include, and this book, by bringing together so many of the finest examples, from splendid ducal palaces to those smaller manor houses which are perhaps more envied by most of us, restores my faith in the survival of the good taste and glamour of the English country house, which somehow, even in this altered and more challenging age, is still going strong.

JULIAN FELLOWES

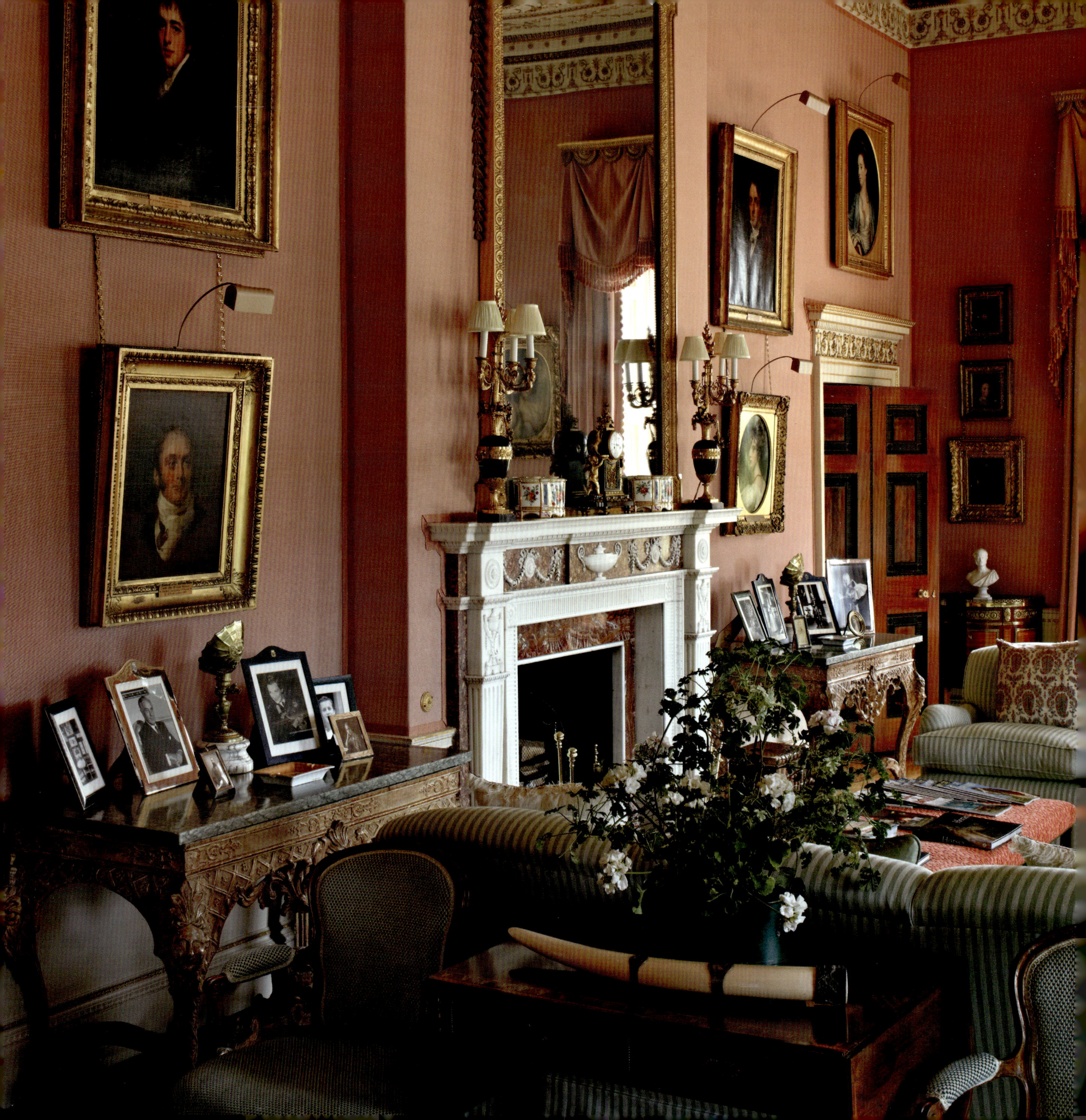

INTRODUCTION · THE BIOGRAPHY OF A ROOM

Enter the Drawing Room

The drawing room is one of the defining spaces of the English country house. The name immediately evokes a grand space in which the finest decoration and furnishing is found. But where did this room come from, how did it get its name, and what made it such an important part of the country house?

The central role the drawing room plays in the social functioning of the country house is well illustrated by familiar scenes in Jane Austen's novels, published in the early 1800s: such as the evening in *Pride and Prejudice* when Lizzie Bennet is at Netherfield Park and joins her hosts. On entering the drawing room, she finds the whole party at cards but declines joining them in favour of reading, to the astonishment of Mr. Hurst, but the admiration of Mr. Darcy. This prompts the dreaded Miss Bingley to begin her great commentary on the accomplishments of a lady, many of which were associated with the drawing room: music, singing, and drawing.[1]

In Austen's *Sense and Sensibility* the widowed Mrs. Dashwood arrives, in reduced circumstances, to take up residence in modest Barton Cottage. She blithely speaks of how she could improve the inadequate "parlours" she finds there, remarking brightly how "a new drawing-room … may be easily added" and showing how significant such a room was to a woman of her class.[2] No new drawing room is forthcoming however. It is also in the drawing room, waiting for the men to join the ladies after dinner, that Emma has her most difficult time with the maddening Mrs. Weston.[3] In Austen's novels the "drawing room" is often juxtaposed with the "dining-parlour."[4]

By Jane Austen's time, the drawing room was usually found as the significant pairing to the dining room, on either side of a hall (additional parlours might still be used for more informal reception and dining). The later eighteenth-century dining room and drawing room were designed to balance each other in proportion and significance, often forming part of the defining symmetry of the country houses on a classical model.[5] The dining room was entirely dedicated to formal meals, with the drawing room as the place for receiving visitors, conversation, entertainment, and, most important, the service of tea and coffee following a meal.

Even in the late eighteenth century, these rooms were overtly spoken of as the realms of the different sexes: the dining room was seen as masculine, and the drawing room feminine. This gender zoning was, in part at least, political, as architect Robert Adam asserted in the 1770s, the generation before Austen.[6] In his account of his work at Syon House for the 1st Duke of Northumberland, Adam wrote, "To understand thoroughly the art of living, it is necessary to have passed some time amongst the French, and to have studied the customs of that social and conversible people. In one particular, however, our manners prevent us from imitating them. Their eating rooms seldom or never constitute a piece in their great apartments, but lie out of the suite, and in fitting them up, little attention is paid to beauty or decoration. The reason for this is obvious: the French meet there only at meals, when they trust to the display of the table for show and magnificence, not to the decoration of the apartment; and as soon as the entertainment is over, they immediately retire to the rooms of company."

Adam argued: "It is not so with us. Accustomed by habit, or induced by the nature of our climate, we indulge more largely in the enjoyment of the bottle. Every person of rank here is either a member of legislation, or entitled by his condition to take part in the political arrangements of his country, and to enter with ardour into those discussions to which they give rise; these circumstances lead men to live more with one another, and more detached from the society of the ladies."

The significance of this for Adam was that the eating rooms were therefore "considered as the apartments of conversation, in which we are to pass a great part of our time. This renders it desirable to have them fitted up with elegance and splendour,

⬅ *Comfort and elegance together: the drawing room at Broadlands in Hampshire.*

➡ *An Edwardian fantasy: the aesthetically arranged drawing room of fifteenth-century Herstmonceux Castle, which had been restored from 1912 for the connoisseur, army officer, and conservative politician Colonel Claude Lowther.*

but in a style different from other apartments. Instead of being hung with damask, tapestry, &c. they are always finished with stucco, and adorned with statues and paintings, that they may not retain the smell of victuals."

The fitting-up to which Adam refers is intriguing evidence of the practicalities of design and decoration in the mind of any wealthy Georgian patron, hostess, architect, and decorator.[7] But the social habits expressed in his eloquent account had a much older political significance, as the drawing-room circle of the ladies began to be more and more significant from the late seventeenth century onwards.

The political settlement by which William III and Mary came to the throne, in 1688, known as the Glorious Revolution, included the establishment of a constitutional monarchy, and assured the primacy of parliament. Thus from this period, the landowning male (connected either through the House of Lords or through the House of Commons, MPs for the shires were subject to a property qualification) found his outlets at the London coffee house, club, and dining table, while the aristocratic female asserted her influence (political, social, and familial) through the drawing room in both her town and country house. So Robert Adam was, after all, describing well-developed social conventions of English country house life that can be traced back to almost a century before.[8]

By Adam's time, and beyond, drawing rooms, like dining rooms, were, in essence, functional spaces, always centred on a substantial fireplace to provide warmth and tall windows for daylight and (in the country) prospect over the land. The drawing room was connected to other rooms of reception, such as halls, saloons (the grandest rooms of reception aligned on the hall), and libraries, with doors arranged so that servants (butlers and footmen) could serve those occupying the rooms. Above all, the drawing room belonged to a series of rooms designed for sociability, with the comfort and elegance necessary when the English landowner and his wife were entertaining their peers. Thus it was also the repository of fine art and significant portraits, expensive furniture, exotic cabinets, fine textiles, and upholstery.[9]

The richness of decoration was often calibrated to heighten the experience of the guests as they passed from lesser spaces into the more important rooms of the house.[10] From the late eighteenth century, the English country house drawing room was the elegant stage for well-developed rituals of visiting and entertaining, a place to assemble before or after dinner, and thus for the art of conversation and the pursuit and display of culture: the discussion of art, history, and travel; the inspection of paintings; and the performance of music.

THE ORIGINS OF THE DRAWING ROOM: THE HISTORICAL PICTURE

The evolution of the drawing room to the condition described by Adam is not a simple, linear story, but the result of a merging and separating out of the key room functions and names that went before. To dig deeper into the evolutionary story of the drawing room for just a moment, it is important to note the transition of country house social life from the public ritual and display of the medieval and Tudor household to a more controlled, refined environment: where the success of social events depended not on the public impact but on the enjoyment of your immediate peers as guests.

In the medieval house, the principal division in a great house was between the double-height great hall and the first-floor great chamber, a bed-sitting room of the lord and lady of the house. The hall was where public rituals were enacted in front of a full household and visitors. In time, the bed was moved to an adjoining privy chamber, and by the Tudor period, great chambers had become effectively the principal room of state, regularly used for formal dining and splendid entertainment.

Parlours were also provided, on the same storey as the great hall, and used primarily for more informal dining and reception. (In the seventeenth century there was often more than one: a Little Parlour and a Great Parlour or a Winter Parlour and a Summer Parlour.)[11]

The "withdrawing" room began as a smaller anteroom between the great chamber and the bedchamber. The word "withdraughte" can be traced to the fifteenth century and seemed then to relate to any smaller room leading off a chamber of importance.[12] Originally more associated with the bedchamber and used for a variety of ancillary purposes, the withdrawing room comes to service the Great Parlour, which had really become the significant social room of the house by the second quarter of the seventeenth century—as in the "compact" double-pile style of country house, set over a half-basement.[13] Only in the grandest state apartments did the withdrawing room still relate to the bedchamber.

The Great Parlour was still used both for dining and general reception, but with an increasing emphasis on dining. In the mid-seventeenth century withdrawing rooms were still generally modestly proportioned square rooms and seem to have been used for the most intimate socializing or as a space for the owner and guests to retire to while the Great Parlour was being prepared for a meal, or after a meal for dancing or other entertainments.[14]

Both the uses and the name of the drawing room were clearly somewhat fluid in the seventeenth century. In the 1660s gentleman architect Sir Roger Pratt wrote about his plan for an ideal country house and referred to it having "The little Parlour with its closets at the end next the kitchen, then the

Great Parlour and afterwards the with-drawing-room with its conveniences like a bedchamber and so to be used in time of need ... the little parlour may be used as a Drawing-room, when the drawing room is a bedchamber."[15] Roger North, another gentleman amateur who wrote on architecture, referred in this period to his admiration for one Norfolk house and how "it had one great perfection, which is that the withdrawing room, serves both the Great and the Little Parlour; a thing much to be desired in any house."[16]

But by the end of the seventeenth century, the drawing room had, except in the case of the grandest and fully expressed "state apartments," become the expensively appointed pendant to the Great Parlour, or the dining room. The pairing of these rooms becomes natural, such as in Celia Fiennes's journal to Lowther Castle in the 1690s, in which she wrote of going "thence into a dininge room and drawing-roome well wainscoated of oake large panels."[17] Drawing rooms were often lavishly decorated, originally with tapestries, and then with hangings of silk and velvet in the seventeenth century.

The significance of the drawing room had increased with the fashionable and expensive ritual of drinking tea and coffee after meals, from the 1670s onwards.[18] The hostesses would retire to brew these drinks themselves, after which the gentlemen, who had continued drinking at the table, would join them and the party carried on.[19] The interval grew longer as time went on, and in the later eighteenth century, French aristocrat La Rochefoucauld on visiting England recorded the women retiring from the table: "at the end of two or three hours a servant announces [to the men] that tea is ready and conducts the gentlemen from their drinking, to join the ladies in the drawing-room, where they are usually employed making tea and coffee. After making tea, one generally plays whist, and at midnight there is cold meat for those who are hungry."[20]

THE NAMING OF THE DRAWING ROOM

But the question still remains why "drawing room" came to be the accepted name. A clue may come from Samuel Johnson's 1755 *Dictionary*, which defines a drawing room as "The room in which company assembles at court."[21] The importance and prestige of the court "drawing room" cannot be underestimated.[22] In the 1630s Charles I's French queen, Henrietta Maria, had instituted a weekly social event whereby select courtiers, both men and women, were invited to her presence chamber of state apartment, for informal conversation. This was revived after the Commonwealth. Charles II's queen, Catherine of Braganza, developed the idea of this social gathering and moved it from the presence chamber to the withdrawing room of her own State Bedchamber (and thus removing it from the control of the Lord Chamberlain). She would receive visitors while sitting near the door of her withdrawing room. The king and the Duke of York enjoyed the opportunity to socialise on less formal terms with favourite courtiers. The custom was adopted by Queen Anne.

The event itself became known simply as "a drawing room" — distinct from the court "levee" which was only attended by men. The significance of the "drawing room" as a social event was reflected in the creation of the new "great east front drawing room" at Hampton Court, built between 1698 and 1705 as well as in the fitting out of St. James's Palace for Queen Anne, for whom a new and magnificent drawing room was created there in the main enfilade.[23]

Some of the flavour of the later-eighteenth-century court "drawing room" as an event is given in the frequent references in Lady Mary Coke's letters. For instance, on March 8, 1769: "Lady Greenwich called on me at one O'clock to go to the Drawing room. We found the Duchess of Douglass waiting in one of the outward rooms. Ly Lothian, Ly Jane Scott, Ly Mary, & the Duchess of Queensberry, & Ly Betty Mackenzie joined us. We stood altogether. Their Majesties were very civil."[24]

The "drawing room" was a well-established social ritual, which remained central to court life until the mid-twentieth century, as it was at a court "drawing room" that young debutantes were "presented" at court to the monarch, the event becoming more and more formal during the nineteenth century—its significance has been largely forgotten now.[25] So it may be that the eighteenth-century habit of naming the principal room of reception in country houses as the "drawing room" is a reflection of this court usage. Whether or not this is the case, certainly in the arena of the country house, by the mid-eighteenth century the drawing room had been chosen by social habit as the key room for the formal reception of visitors by the hostess, and the removal (or "withdrawing") of ladies from the dining table to allow men time for political discussion—and for drinking.

The practicality of this is evidenced in the planning of larger country houses in the mid-eighteenth century. During the building of Hagley Hall, in Worcestershire, the patron, 1st Lord Lyttleton, advised his architect that "Lady Lyttleton wishes for a room of separation between the eating room and the drawing room, to hinder the ladies from the noise and talk of the men when left to their bottle, which must sometimes happen, even at Hagley."[26] The drawing room at Hagley, hung with Soho tapestry and with fine upholstered parcel-gilt seat furniture, is also one of the supreme examples of the aristocratic fashion for French style in the English drawing room, which coincided with the increased importance of the room type itself.[27]

Elegant upholstered chairs would be "set in prim form around the room" (as Mrs. Delany described the arrangement at Bulstrode in Buckinghamshire). Furniture was supplied in sets: six armchairs and two settees for the long walls. If not hung with fashionable tapestry, drawing rooms would often be hung with silk velvet or crimson damask and have, according to one contemporary, Mrs. Lybbe Powys, a certain "delicateness."[28] The comfort of the upholstered seat furniture reflected the need for comfort for the room in which the ladies might converse for hours at a time.

THE DRAWING ROOM AS WE KNOW IT

At the very end of the eighteenth century, and beginning of the nineteenth, there was a notable shift in taste away from the formality of the grand eighteenth-century set-piece state drawing rooms, as at Hagley, Newby Hall, and Kedleston, towards something less formal, at least to modern eyes. Humphry Repton, in *Collected Fragments* published in 1819, wrote, "the most recent modern custom is, to use the library as the general living room; and that sort of state room, formerly called the best parlour, and of late years the drawing room, is now a melancholy apartment, when entirely shut up, and only opened to give visitors a formal cold reception." Repton thought the library had become the favoured modern living room, "but if such a room opens into an adjoining one and the two are fitted up with the same curtains carpets etc. they become in some degree one room, and the comfort of that which is books, or musical instruments, is extended into its space which has only sofas, chairs and card tables."[29]

Repton may have been trying to promote his own ends as a fashionable designer in this observation, but the description evokes the English country house drawing room as we now think of it: a substantial room arranged for a mixture of informal comfort and grandeur at the same time, which can also be the setting for all those social accomplishments mentioned above.[30] This comfortable, but less formal elegance (which was the sort Jane Austen would have known at her brother's Kentish seat of Godmersham Park, the model for Mansfield Park) could be quite startling to some used to more formal arrangements.

An acute American visitor, Louis Simond, wrote of his

1810 visit to Osterley Park, then the home of Sarah Sophia, Countess of Jersey: "Tables, sofas and chairs were studiously arranged about the fire-places and in the middle of the rooms, as if the family had just left them. Such is the modern fashion of placing furniture carried to an extreme, as fashions always are, that the apartments of a fashionable house look like an upholsterer's or a cabinet-maker's shop."[31] It rendered them more comfortable but at the same time less flexible than the eighteenth-century versions.

How the conventional and well-appointed country house drawing room was used in the early and mid-nineteenth century is suggested by the letters written by a young American woman, Anna Maria Fay, attending a dinner party at Oakly Park in Shropshire in 1852. Her account gives a vivid picture of how the rooms of the house, as redesigned in the 1820s by Cockerell, were used and enjoyed. On arrival, the family was greeted by "two footmen in red plush breeches and blue coats and silver buttons and the groom of the chambers, in black."[32] The guests were led through the staircase hall and into a "large and beautiful library ... [where] an elegant circle of ladies and gentlemen rose to meet us." The party then makes a little procession into the dining room.

14 | THE BIOGRAPHY OF A ROOM

← *Unmistakably feminine and delicate in detail: a 1915 view of the Tapestry Drawing Room at Hagley Hall, Worcestershire, created in the 1750s and sparking a fashion for elegant rooms hung with decorative tapestry, with seat furniture upholstered to match the tapestry. The room remains intact today.*

↙ *Early Georgian refinement: the Tapestry Drawing Room at Ditchley Park, Oxfordshire, as photographed in the early 1930s, hung with tapestry and provided with upholstered seat furniture in the French style.*

↓ *The 1760s stately drawing room at Syon House, designed by Robert Adam as part of a sequence of entertaining rooms for the 1st Duke of Northumberland. The ceiling roundels were painted by Cipriani.*

After the meal, at a signal from Lady Harriet Clive, the ladies withdrew to the drawing room, "coffee was brought in and some of the ladies sat down to their beautiful worsted work, while others disposed themselves around the room." Watercolours of Italy and lithographs of Middle Eastern subjects were discussed, and when the gentlemen joined the ladies, Lady Harriet entertained them with pieces on the piano. The drawing room was an essential stage for accomplishment and conversation. Indeed, as a glance at any library catalogue will show, from this era there are numerous publications that appear to cater for drawing room entertainments, songs, poems, readings, and plays.

Anyone who has visited a Victorian country house will have been struck by the obvious significance of the drawing room (illustrated in this book by those at Alnwick Castle, Knebworth, and Madresfield Court). This significance is also clear from one of the key nineteenth-century treatises on country house design, Robert Kerr's *The Gentleman's House*, first published in the 1860s, in which he tried to capture all the details of country house planning in a "system." The drawing room in his account remained planned firmly in relation to the dining room, often separated from it by a hall.

Kerr made it quite explicit that the drawing room was usually the domain of the lady of the house but also the general sitting room of family and guests: "This is the Lady's apartment essentially ... If a Morning-room be not provided, it is properly the only Sitting-room of the family. In it also in any case the ladies receive calls throughout the day, and the family and guests assemble before dinner. After dinner, the ladies withdraw to it, and are joined by the gentleman for the evening. It is also the Reception-room for evening parties."[33]

Kerr noted that these essential requirements were true for the house of a duchess and that of "the simplest gentlewoman." Kerr thought that the character to be aimed at in a drawing room was "especial cheerfulness, refinement of elegance, and what is called lightness as opposed to massiveness. Decoration and furniture ought therefore to be comparatively delicate." A dining room could be quite different and indeed quite

THE DRAWING ROOM | 15

masculine. He advised putting a drawing room on the southeast corner of the house so the room would be made "cheerful" by the morning sun before it comes into use, and would have sufficient shade in the afternoon. In its relationship to the dining room, he argued for the desirability of there being at least an anteroom in between the two rooms. Kerr also noted that in most houses the drawing room was also the music room.[34] Throughout the nineteenth century, the style of decoration followed the changing historicist fashions for Gothic, old English, Jacobean, French, or Italian, as the patron and designer chose.

J. J. Stevenson, an architect of the younger Queen Anne revival generation, followed a broadly similar line to Kerr in his book *House Architecture*, published in 1880.[35] He noted the drawing room's use as a retiring room for the ladies through history but observed more pointedly, "with us this is still its use, in accordance with our custom, which Continental nations consider barbarous, of the ladies retiring to it after dinner, and leaving the gentlemen to drink by themselves." As well as being the ladies' sitting room and a reception room for callers, Stevenson thought it "takes the position of the hall of old houses as the place for evening entertainments, for dancing, music and receptions." The best width of room, for such purposes was, he argued, at least twenty feet, and the length could be anything up to a hundred feet "in which case it may be broken into compartments by pillars or wide openings."

Stevenson also felt a drawing room should be "cheerful" and sunny, and that if "the house affords a good view of scenery, the drawing-room has a better claim to other rooms to the benefit

16 | THE BIOGRAPHY OF A ROOM

← *Regency stateliness: the drawing room at Broughton Hall, Yorkshire, in the 1950s, part of the alterations to that house by William Atkinson in 1809–14 for the Tempest family, as photographed in the 1950s.*

→ *High Victorian: the 1860s Brodsworth Hall, Yorkshire, has a well-preserved drawing room of typical nineteenth-century exuberance, in this case decorated in an eighteenth-century French spirit: the crimson silk hangings and Axminster carpet were supplied by Lapworth Brothers.*

of them." Stevenson was more aware of the need for physical space for furniture than Kerr, and remarked on the necessity of "providing sufficient wall-space for the quantity of bulky furniture which a drawing-room usually contains, such as sofas and couches, console-tables, a grand piano, cabinets for curiosities, a quantity of statuary, stands for folios of engravings, or a bookcase for books on works of art." He also referred to the habit of placing a round table in the centre of the room where books could be left.

Stevenson, from a younger generation than Kerr, and probably thinking more of the affluent professional than the landowner, concluded his discussion with something of a diatribe against the stiff formality of the English drawing room: "often one of the most uncomfortable rooms in the house ... much too fine for daily use, the furniture too flimsy or the coverings too costly for wear." He thought that "except on rare occasions, the room remains unused, in dignified and dismal desolations, all the more cheerless that it is kept in perfect order." In a complete reverse of Adam's analysis in the eighteenth century, Stevenson looked to the French system of building houses with two day rooms only: "a *salon* to live in, and an eating-room" which he thought much more sensible and comfortable. He even looked to the simpler old English custom of "one good-sized *hall*, with space for games or a dance when the tables were cleared away after meals, with its little drawing room for retirement or for seeing of occasional callers."

← The huge decorative hearth at Lord Armstrong's Cragside in Northumberland—designed by W. R. Lethaby while working for Richard Norman Shaw for the top-lit drawing room—evokes the hearths of seventeenth-century houses, which were considered symbolic of the secure pleasures of the home.

Architects usually focused on writing about the layout of the room. But the proliferation of published works of advice on interior decoration is proof in itself of the interest and expenditure on decoration and furnishing. In Charles Eastlake's provocative *Hints on Household Taste*, 1868, he reserved some of his most damning remarks on the degeneracy of taste for the drawing room furniture of his day. For instance, he noted that an ancient sofa from Knole in Kent had been depicted in a painting by Royal Academician Marcus Stone, but also that most of the sofas of his period would only be fit, in the twenty-first century, for a "Chamber of Horrors" exhibition on bad taste to be held at the South Kensington Museum.[36]

He continued: "How often do we see in fashionable drawing-rooms a couch which seems to be composed of nothing but cushions ... I do not wish to be ungallant in my remarks, but I fear there is a large class of young ladies who look upon this sort of furniture as 'elegant.' Now if elegance means nothing more than a milliner's idea of the beautiful, which changes every season—so that a bonnet which is pronounced 'lovely' in 1868 becomes 'a fright' in 1869—then no doubt this sofa ... is elegant indeed."

The self-consciously artistic approach to decoration had taken hold by the next decade, as well as the interest in collecting antiques, and in 1878, Mrs. Orrinsmith brought out a book: *The Drawing-Room: Its Decoration and Furniture*. This subject she thought had only been touched on by a recent volume on *House Decoration*, by Miss Garrett, associated with the newly popular Queen Anne taste. These ladies are both champions of the new Aesthetic Movement approach to decoration, and follow Eastlake in chafing at the English habit of having houses "crowded with ugly shapes disguised by meretricious ornament." Mrs. Orrinsmith exhorts patrons and designers alike to be aware that "it cannot be too strongly insisted that the most trivial details of decoration in the surroundings of our daily life are important."[37]

Mrs. Orrinsmith looked in turn at each of the major elements of drawing room decoration: papers, for which she advised the kind of "suggestive floral decoration," which is now associated with William Morris's design, with harmonious colour and no strong contrasts "to fatigue the eye." She added: "If expense is not an object, and the drawing room is large or in an old picturesque house, or one newly designed with artistic knowledge, more elaborate schemes for wall-decoration might easily suggest themselves"—such as a wooden dado with a surbase of a chair rail. Paint colours "should never be vivid; quiet olives and blue-greens make an excellent dressing for walls." Silk hangings were recommended if they could be afforded, and Mrs. Orrinsmith rejected the late Georgian fashion (adapted from the French) for the tall, grand overmantel mirrors in favour of the multipart overmantel mirror, with brackets, and shelves for ornament.[38]

Curiously, given the hiving off of the dining role into the dining room earlier in its history, a new meal emerged in the drawing room in the 1830s and 1840s.[39] By about 1840, afternoon tea had become a feature of the English country house day, probably related to the main meal of the day having moved to the evening from the middle of the day during the course of the eighteenth century. The sporting exertions of the country-house party may well have added to the attractions of this small (and sometimes not-so-small) afternoon meal. It is also linked to the tradition of coffee and tea being served to guests by the mistress of the household, as this was also in effect a meal taken without the hovering presence of servants. In the early twentieth century afternoon tea was described as the "hour of flirtation" by Lady Muriel Beckwith, daughter of the Duke of Richmond at Goodwood.[40]

The spectacle of tea in these great country houses in its Edwardian heyday was clearly memorable. One Lady Jeune wrote, "Who does not know the aspect of a magnificently furnished drawing room at 5.30, with its well-shrouded lamps and candles throwing a subdued light over a scheme as brilliant as any evening entertainment, where the brocade silks and lace and flashing jewels make all observers rub their eyes, and wonder whether this fairy scene is not a dream."[41]

The significance of afternoon tea is obvious even from printed social manuals, for instance, *Lady Troubridge's Book of Etiquette* summed up the character of afternoon tea in the 1920s: "tea is placed in the drawing-room and poured out by the hostess or her daughter. The help of a servant is not required." She also observed, "In country houses, where energetic exercise is the order of the day, tea is often quite a substantial meal."[42] A more formal "At Home" was also fashionable until the mid-twentieth century, with invitations sent out on cards for afternoon tea in the drawing room (some afternoon parties also included a musical performance or lecture). Injunctions for the best way to receive callers—or how to use the drawing room for assembling before dinner, and withdrawing for coffee and entertainment afterwards—were also outlined in detail by Lady Troubridge.

Some sense of the role and practice of the drawing room throughout the nineteenth century is revealed in Mrs. Beeton's famous *Household Management*. The butler, according to Mrs. Beeton, supervised the presentation of the table for dinner, "and announces in the drawing room that dinner is on the table."[43] After the service of the dessert, "He now proceeds to the drawing-room, arranges the fireplace and sees to the lights; he then returns to his pantry, prepared to answer his bell, and attend to the company … At tea he again attends. At bedtime he appears with the candles." The footman likewise might be called on to carry the trays and serve tea and coffee, cakes and biscuits. It was this cycle of activity and detailed preparation that underscored all the experience of hospitality in a great house.

When there was a special reception or evening party, the footman, under the direction of the butler, prepared the drawing room for after-dinner activity: "the card-tables laid out with cards and counters, and other such arrangements as are necessary made for the reception of the company, the rooms should be lighted up as the hour appointed approaches." This detail was important but so was the deft action of the servants: "Attendants in the drawing room even more than in the dining-room, should move about actively but noiselessly; no creaking of shoes, which is an abomination."

In the early morning, the housemaid would be up to clear the ashes, black the grates, and lay the new fires. The footmen, under the direction of the butler—or in some larger houses "the groom of the chambers," a kind of upper footman charged with finessing the presentation of the rooms of reception—would be responsible for polishing the best furniture and cleaning the gilt-framed pictures and mirror-glasses. This procedure, in the grandest houses, persisted well into the mid-twentieth century, but did not long survive the 1950s.

THE DRAWING ROOM IN THE TWENTIETH CENTURY AND BEYOND

The Edwardian drawing room still retained its distinction as the realm of the lady of the house, continuing to fascinate (or, in some cases, horrify) Continental observers. In the early 1900s, German cultural attaché and architectural critic Hermann Muthesius was intrigued by the Englishman's habit of referring to the drawing room as his wife's room so that the English gentleman seemed almost to be his wife's guest when he was in his own house.[44] Muthesius thought, "The drawing-room is the most important of the reception-rooms in the English house. It is difficult to find a German term for this room, for we have no room that is precisely equivalent to it."

Muthesius dug deep into the significance of the room as a woman's room: "drawing room, the mistress's throne-room, is the rallying-point of the whole life of the house, the room in which one talks, reads and spends idle hours, the room in which the occupants assemble before meals and amuse themselves afterwards with conversation and play."[45] He struggled to find a directly comparable German equivalent and observed how the drawing room compared to three different rooms in the German country house: the *wohnzimmer* (living room), the *empfangszimmer* (reception room), and the lady of the house's personal and private sitting room.

The English country house drawing room was expected to "be bright, to produce a light, pleasing impression and a general air of 'joie-de-vivre,' and a south-easterly aspect to be preferred." Although he admired the English drawing room in architectural terms, he was harsh about how the "deliberate informality [of furnishing] all too often degenerates into confusion" and wrote sniffily about framed and unframed photographs.[46]

The debate as to formality and comfort persisted into the next decade and is reflected in the writing of novelist Edith Wharton and architect Ogden Codman, who collaborated in 1915 on *The Decoration of Houses*. In this book, they went to some length to explore the evolution of the drawing room: "Pains have been taken to trace as clearly as possible the mixed ancestry of the modern drawing-room, in order to show that it is the result of two distinct influences—that of the gala apartment and that of the family sitting room."[47] They also saw the American and English drawing room as too often "still considered sacred to gilding and discomfort."

But this concentration on comfort and elegance was all part of the modern era's idealization of the very idea of "home." This is picked up in Virginia Woolf's piquant satire on the changing constitution of England in *Orlando*: "Stealthily and imperceptibly ... the constitution of England was altered and nobody knew it. Everywhere the effects were felt. The hardy country gentleman, who had sat down gladly to a meal of ale and beef in a room designed, perhaps by the brothers Adam, with classic dignity, now felt chilly. Rugs appeared; beards were grown; trousers were fastened tight under the instep. The chill which he felt in his legs the country gentleman soon transferred to his house; furniture was muffled; walls and tables were covered; nothing was left bare ... Coffee supplanted the after-dinner port, and as coffee led to a drawing-room in which to drink it, and a drawing-room to glass cases, and the glass, and glass cases to artificial flowers, and artificial flowers to mantelpieces to pianofortes, and pianofortes to drawing-room ballads (skipping a stage or two) to innumerable little dogs, mats, china ornaments, the home—which had become extremely important—was completely altered."[48]

Both Woolf and Wharton were writing in an age defined less by new design than the inspiration of the past, and by an intense interest in antiques, antique collecting, and thus in decorating rooms in the styles of the past, especially the Georgian era. Country house drawing rooms were steadily refurnished with antiques, and connoisseurship was fashionable in aristocratic circles.[49] Writer Henry Shapland produced a manual of advice for those keen to furnish rooms well in consistent styles, *Style Schemes in Antique Furnishing* (1909), in which he observed of the Georgian drawing room: "it will be noted that there is in this interior an absence of that over-crowded effect which is the bane of the modern living room ... the general impression of a room furnished in the manner indicated would be very refined in colour, suggestive of the Georgian period, and would be very far removed from the commonplace, a characteristic which people of culture so much appreciate provided the effect is not obtained by bizarre methods."[50]

Another curious feature of the late Victorian and Edwardian

↓ The understated interwar elegance of the drawing room at Biddesden in Wiltshire, as photographed in 1938.

↓ The drawing room at Biddesden in Wiltshire, as furnished by the Guinness family in the 1930s, exemplifies this sense of stylish simplicity and restraint.

country house is the spread of the drawing room functions throughout the house, both in the renaming of rooms, and especially in the "living hall" or drawing room use of the great hall, suitable for big house parties. The architect Goodhart-Rendel recalled from his youth: "the strange Edwardian fashion ... of sitting not in one's sitting rooms but in the hall outside them ... however invitingly it might be furnished with sofas, screens, palm trees and perhaps a grand piano."[51]

In the mid-twentieth century, the tradition in country houses of the drawing room as the place of assembly before a dinner, and a place to which the ladies withdrew to give the men some time over their port, continued without a tremor. Beverley Nichols recalled the 1930s dinners at Polesden Lacey in Surrey when Churchill would hold forth: "his 'finest hour' was after dinner, when the ladies had left the table, with more than usually earnest entreaties that we should not be too long over our port, for they knew with bitter experience that when Winston was at the dinner table with a good cigar in one hand and a better Armagnac in the other, the chances were that they would be left without cavaliers until nearly bedtime, and would have to spend the rest of the evening hissing at each other across acres of Aubusson."[52]

In decorative terms, a distinctive stylistic restraint entered into the furnishing of even historic drawing rooms. This is especially evident when comparing many crowded pre–First World War interiors in *Country Life* with the appearance of the same rooms in the magazine in the 1920s and 1930s. It has even been suggested that the attentions of *Country Life* photographers influenced this taste by thinning out the furniture so that pieces of interest could be clearly seen.[53] Yet it was also a continuation of the "artistic" decorative approach that had been informed both by modernist idea and the subtle orientalism seen in

22 | THE BIOGRAPHY OF A ROOM

the paintings of Whistler. The drawing room at Biddesden in Wiltshire, as furnished in 1929–30 by Diana Mitford when newly married to the Hon. Bryan Guinness, exemplifies this sense of stylish simplicity and restraint.[54]

The essential historic functions of such rooms persist, for gathering before and after meals, but for a younger generation living in historic country houses, a lighter, more informal flavour was created within a framework of considered elegance: rooms yet sparser than those illustrated by Wharton. Often inspired by the eighteenth century, the result was something quite different from the historic Georgian model where furniture would have been arranged around the walls. This interwar approach still dominated the drawing rooms featured in 1950s and 1960s *Country Life* articles, and those in other parallel publications, *Homes and Gardens*, *Vogue*, and *Tatler*. The institution of the grand afternoon tea in the drawing room had faded out, but the drawing room remained — and remains in most privately owned houses — the room for pre-dinner drinks and post-dinner conversation, where bridge might be played and where the best paintings can be seen.

In the most Modernist postwar country houses, and in the majority of new homes built in the early twenty-first century, a sitting/living room is likely to be a much more fluid space, open to and engaged with the other living areas of the house. But in the lived-in historic country houses featured in this volume, and in new country houses of traditional design, the drawing room remains an indefatigably "Valhalla" kind of room: one from which to enjoy the view of the garden and park in the day; and a good fire and good company in the evening. In old houses, it may well not be a room in everyday use, but it is a room from which to contemplate the ambitions of previous generations, while current generations work to preserve its spirit, or renew and revive it for modern life.

The drawing rooms chosen for this book belong to many of the great historic houses of England. Many are inherited homes of the aristocracy, and all have been shaped by artists and designers of interest. Some are deeply personal, some newly made or furnished. These rooms, seen through the lens of Paul Barker's camera, give us a tour through many of the most interesting and beautiful social spaces in the kingdom. In most cases, the drawing rooms featured in this book are still used as rooms in which to spend time with friends and family, especially in the evening; to drink, to chat, and to savour companionship and conversation (or watch television, listen to music, or read). In the twenty-first century, the English country house drawing room remains, although in subtly altered guise, what Robert Adam asserted so amusingly in the eighteenth century, "*a salle de compagnie*," where guests may be entertained, good conversation cultivated, and the fine possessions of a house presented and enjoyed.

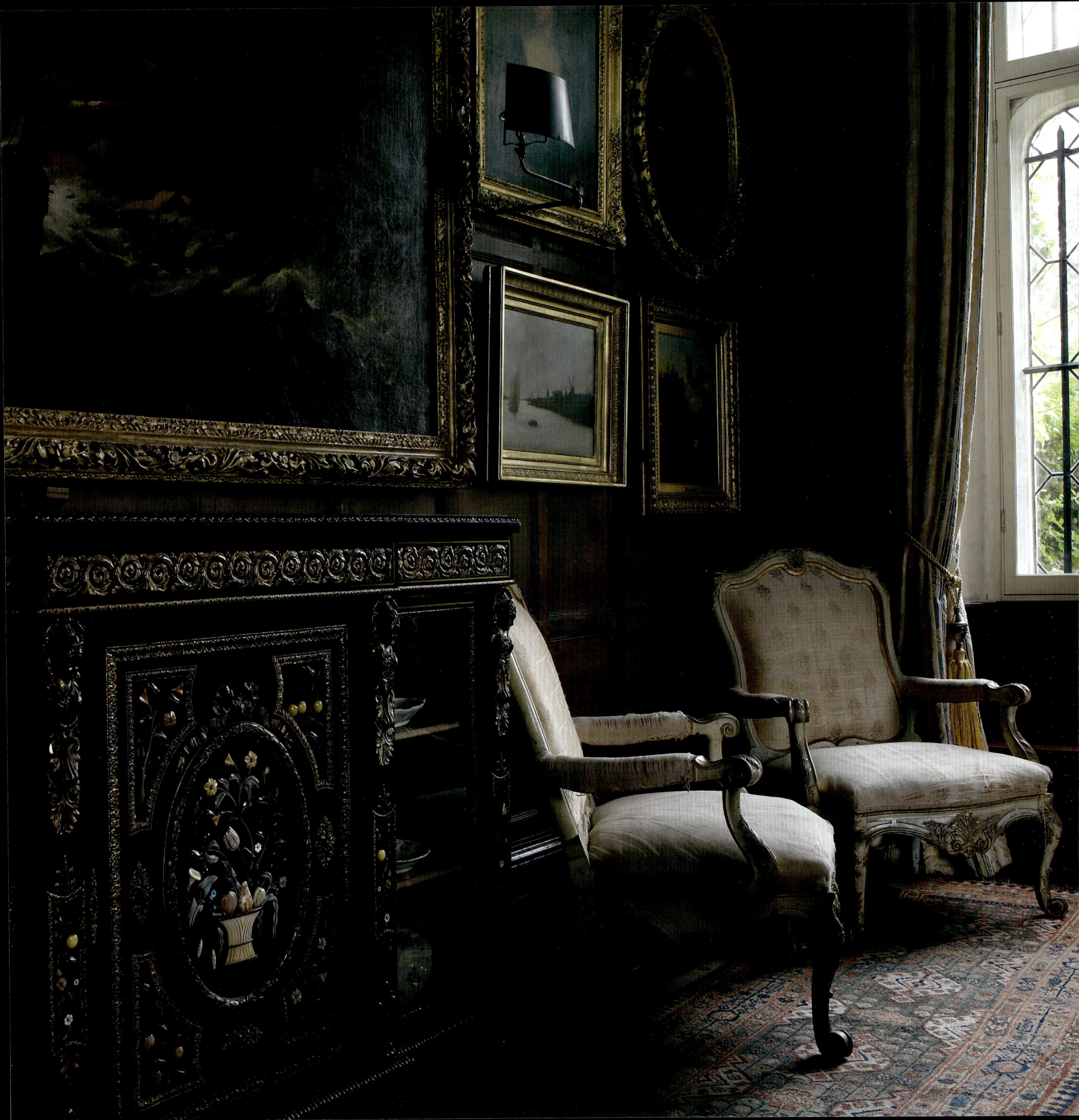

I · EVOLUTION · THE SIXTEENTH TO EIGHTEENTH CENTURIES

Loseley Park

Elizabethan grandeur: the sixteenth-century Great Chamber becomes the principal drawing room.

Loseley Park in Surrey was built in 1562–68 by Sir William More MP, close ally of Lord Burghley and faithful servant of Queen Elizabeth I. The project was an ambitious one, and the craftsmen who worked on the house were well regarded, having worked on other important houses such as Cowdray House in Sussex. Sir William More was highly educated and had an extensive library, including works in Italian, French, Latin, and Greek. He entertained Queen Elizabeth at the house several times and at one moment was advised in memorable fashion that Loseley should be fit for the honour: "sweet and meet" to receive his queen.[1] Sir William More was also executor for his friend Sir Thomas Cawarden, Master of the Kings Revels and Tents, which explains the presence in the house of a series of captivating 1540s painted canvases in the Italian manner, which now hang in the gallery of the Great Hall and may once have been used for temporary banqueting houses. Something of the same spirit of celebration and visual delight informed the taste of Sir William in the fitting out of his house and especially in his Great Chamber—which has become in later times the drawing room.

Loseley House was handsomely extended by his son, Sir George More ("little of stature but of great abilities," an MP, High Sheriff, and treasurer to Prince Henry). Sir George added a west wing in the early 1600s with a long gallery and chapel, and entertained James I at the house. He also moved in a world of high culture, and Loseley was touched by the stories of two poets during his lifetime, as Sir George was the guardian of Lord Herbert of Cherbury—soldier, philosopher, and poet. His own daughter, Anne, married—secretly—the poet John Donne. The elegant west wing fell into disuse by the end of the eighteenth century and was demolished in the early nineteenth century. A certain amount of romantic redecoration was carried out in the main house in the later nineteenth century, and a nursery wing was also added in 1877.[2]

The handsomely proportioned drawing room at Loseley Park is a well-preserved and panelled ground-floor room situated beyond the dais end of the Great Hall, separated by the library. The drawing room, perhaps the best-preserved room in the house, is dominated by a superb carved chalk chimneypiece that immediately arrests the view of anyone entering the room. It frames the families' painted coats of arms, which are significant, but the glory of the piece is in the rippling, multi-faceted detailing of the decoration. There is certainly no other surviving chimneypiece in chalk of this scale—although it is clearly a close cousin to many fine plasterwork and carved stone ensembles of the period.

The historian Anthony Wells-Cole traced the several different printed sources for the sculptural atlantid figures and rich ornamental work of the overmantel and surrounds of the chimneypiece, including engravings by Virgil Solis and Du Cerceau, and shows how such printed and engraved material aided the passage of image and design in this period.[3] This spread of visual ideas is also illustrated by the vast lion's paw volute—the main mullion of the north window—which is taken straight from Serlio's Doric chimneypiece from his famous treatise on architecture, first published in 1537. The paw is surprisingly and delightfully echoed in this room by the carved and gilded feet of the curious part-eighteenth-century marble-topped table standing beneath it—of which the longer history is unknown.

The original plasterwork ceiling is divided into a typical Elizabethan geometric pattern of interlaced ribs and decorated pendants. The moorhens, cockatrices, and mulberry trees ornamenting the frieze and ceiling are all references to

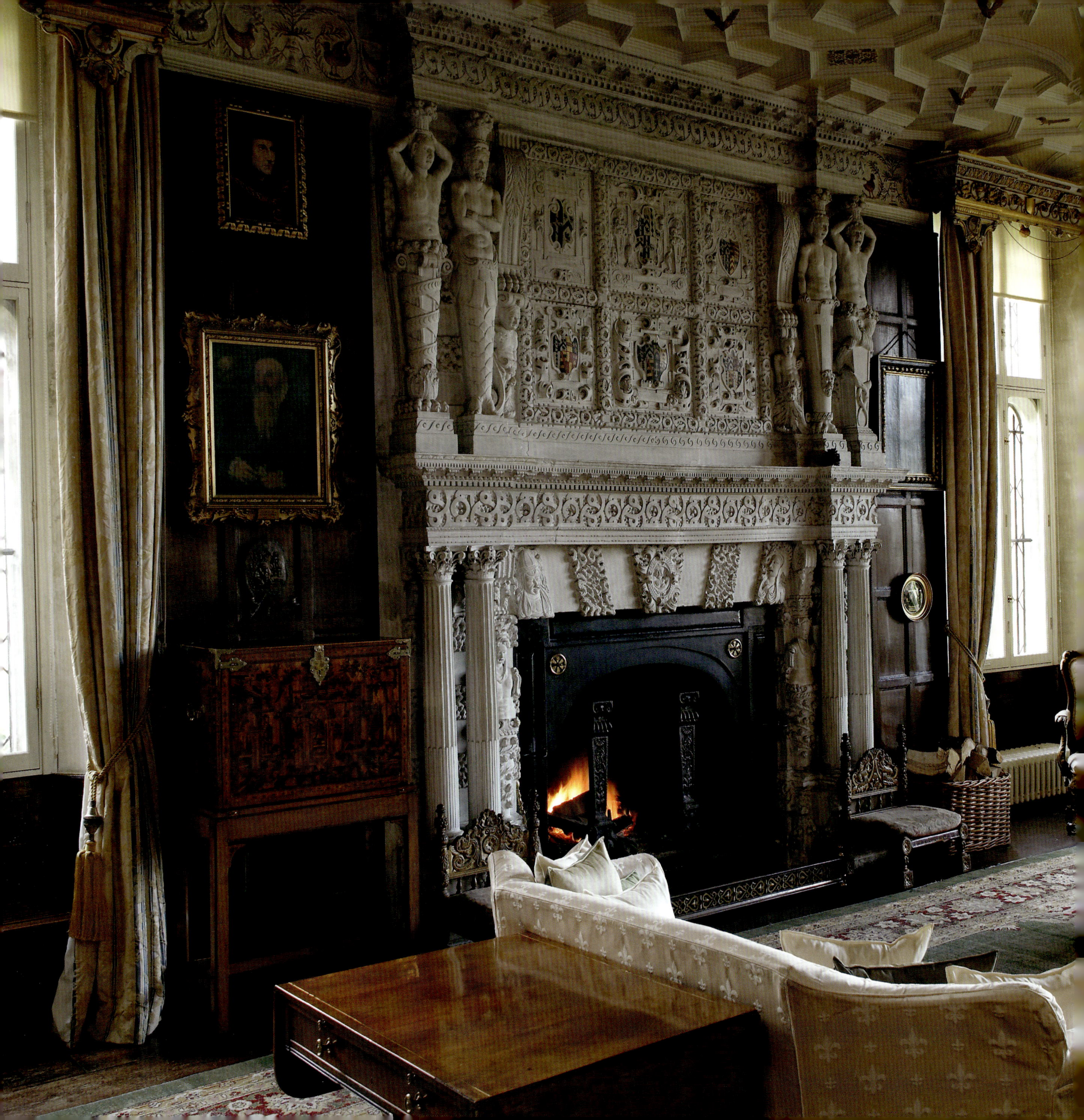

← The drawing room of Loseley Park, originally thought to be the Great Chamber. The ornament of the ornately carved overmantel is derived from published engravings by Virgil Solis and Du Cerceau.

↓ The carved chalk ornament of the chimneypiece is framed by crisp architectural detail.

The contrasts found in a house which has passed through many generations can be surprising, such as this detail of the early-eighteenth-century carved table of unknown origin in the panelled drawing room.

the family's crest and name. The motto appearing on the frieze, "Morus tarde moriens morum cito moriturum" or, in English, "the mulberry tree dying slowly, the fruit about to die quickly," refers to the family, like the tree, surviving for a long time, while individuals, like the fruit of the mulberry, will have a relatively short existence. There is an ancient mulberry tree preserved and cherished in the walled garden at Loseley.

As in most houses that have passed by descent through one family, the furnishings and paintings in the drawing room belong to many periods, and the arrangement of furniture is inevitably a response to this sense of inheritance.[4] The portraits in the room include Sir George More, by Cornelius Janssen, and Sir Thomas More, the famous Lord Chancellor and author of *Utopia*, painted in the manner of Hans Holbein. Sir Thomas was a relation of the Loseley Mores by marriage. The eighteenth-century portraits include a full-length portrait facing the chimneypiece of Elizabeth Lowndes-Stone, a cousin of the More-Molyneuxs, after Gainsborough's original portrait now in the Gulbenkian in Lisbon, which shows a graceful young woman in a salmon pink dress against a backdrop of trees. There is also a portrait of the Duchess of Chandos. The large, dramatic ship painting on the south wall is by Willem Van der Velde and is dated 1696.

There are some fine eighteenth-century side tables and a lacquered cabinet on stand. To the left of the chimneypiece is a very rare sixteenth-century *wrangelschranck* inlaid cabinet of highly intricate workmanship. There is also a pair of ornate low stools, sixteenth century in date, with rare surviving needlework cushions that have been said by long family tradition to be the work of the lady-attendants of Queen Elizabeth I on her visits here, or even by the queen herself. It is a happy legend that adds to the romance of this handsome room. The house, which has passed by descent from the builder and is the home of Michael and Sarah More-Molyneux, is much admired for the mellow atmosphere of its many panelled rooms, not least of these the atmospheric drawing room.

28 | LOSELEY PARK

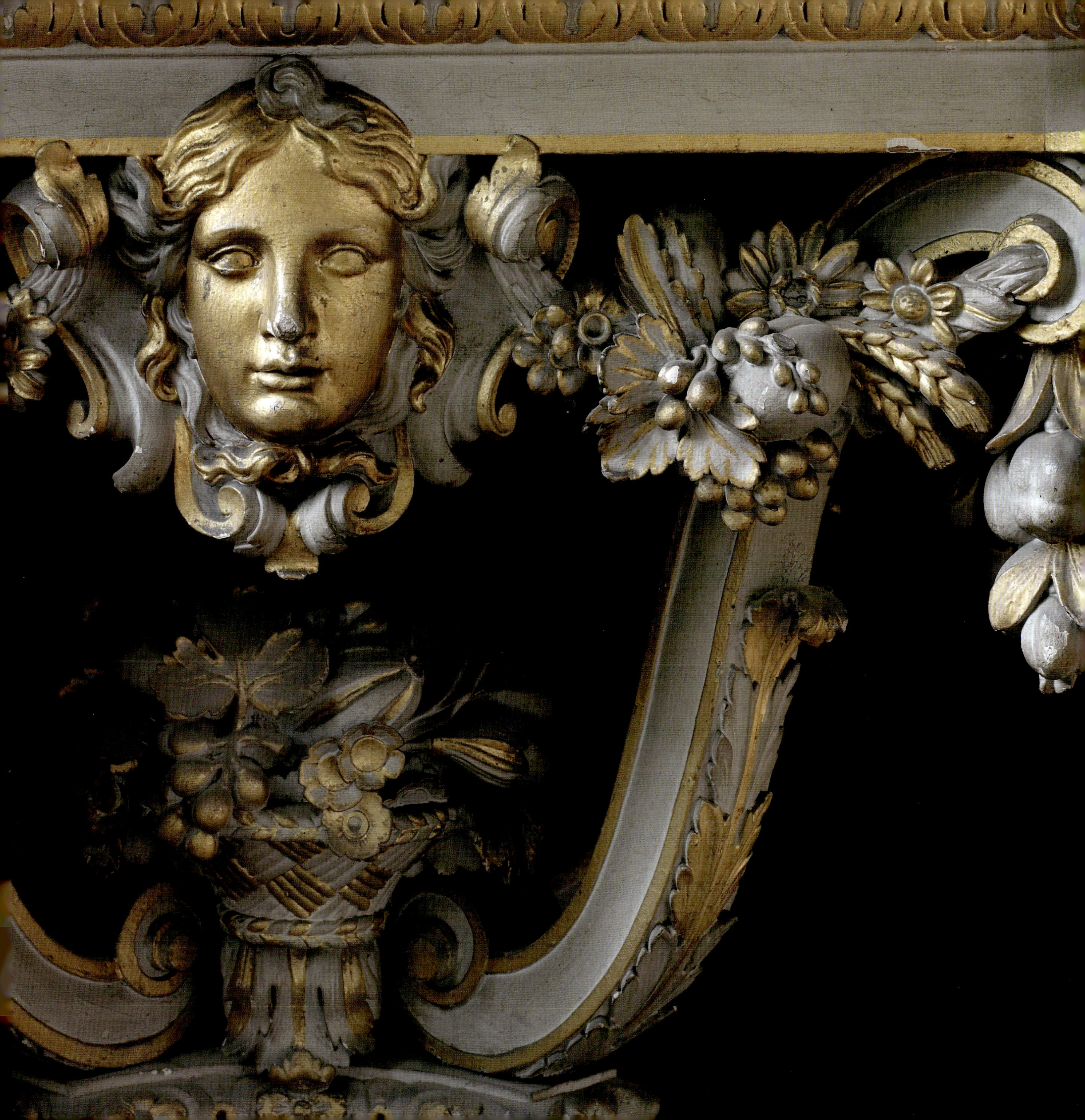

↓ The carved and gilded stand under a japanned cabinet contrasts beautifully with the mellow dark oak panelling.

→ Family portraits of three centuries on one wall: the full-length painting is a copy after Gainsborough's portrait of a member of the family, Elizabeth Lowndes-Stone.

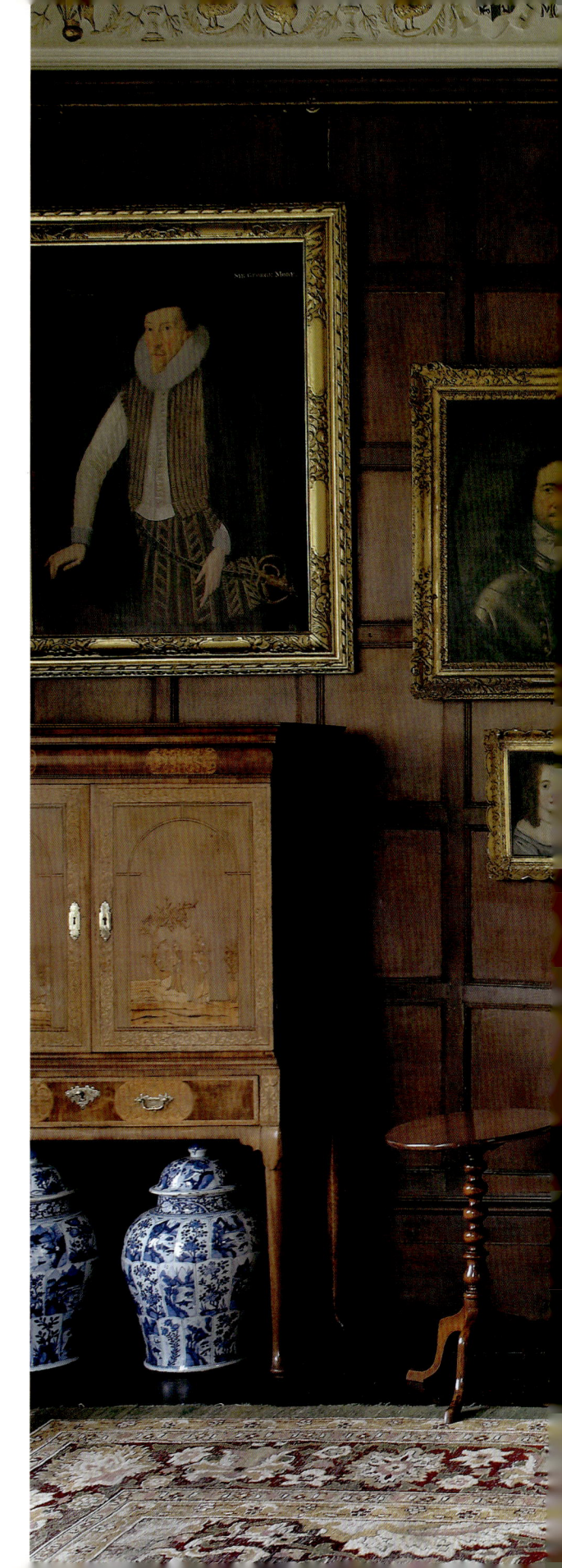

30 | LOSELEY PARK

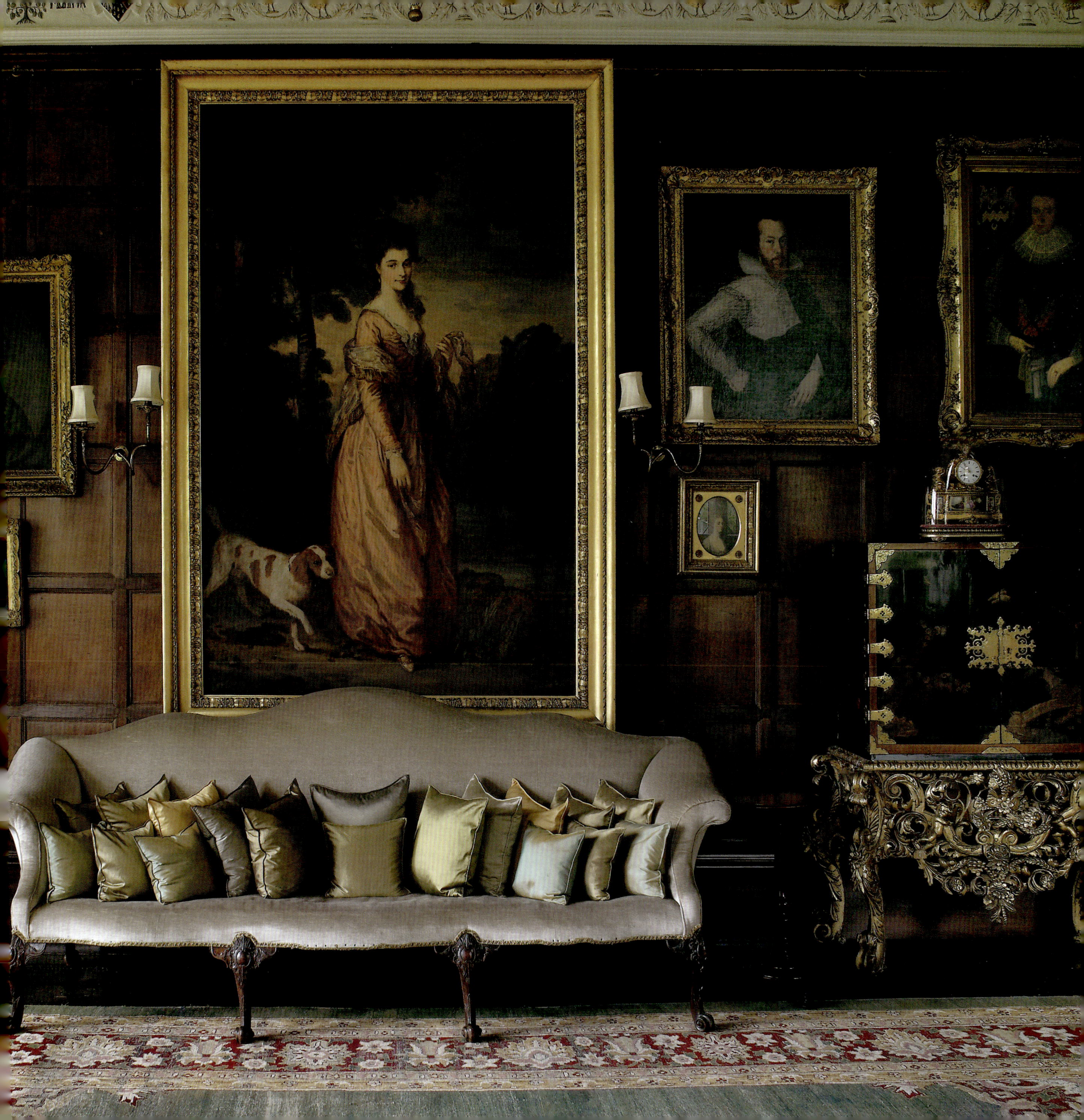

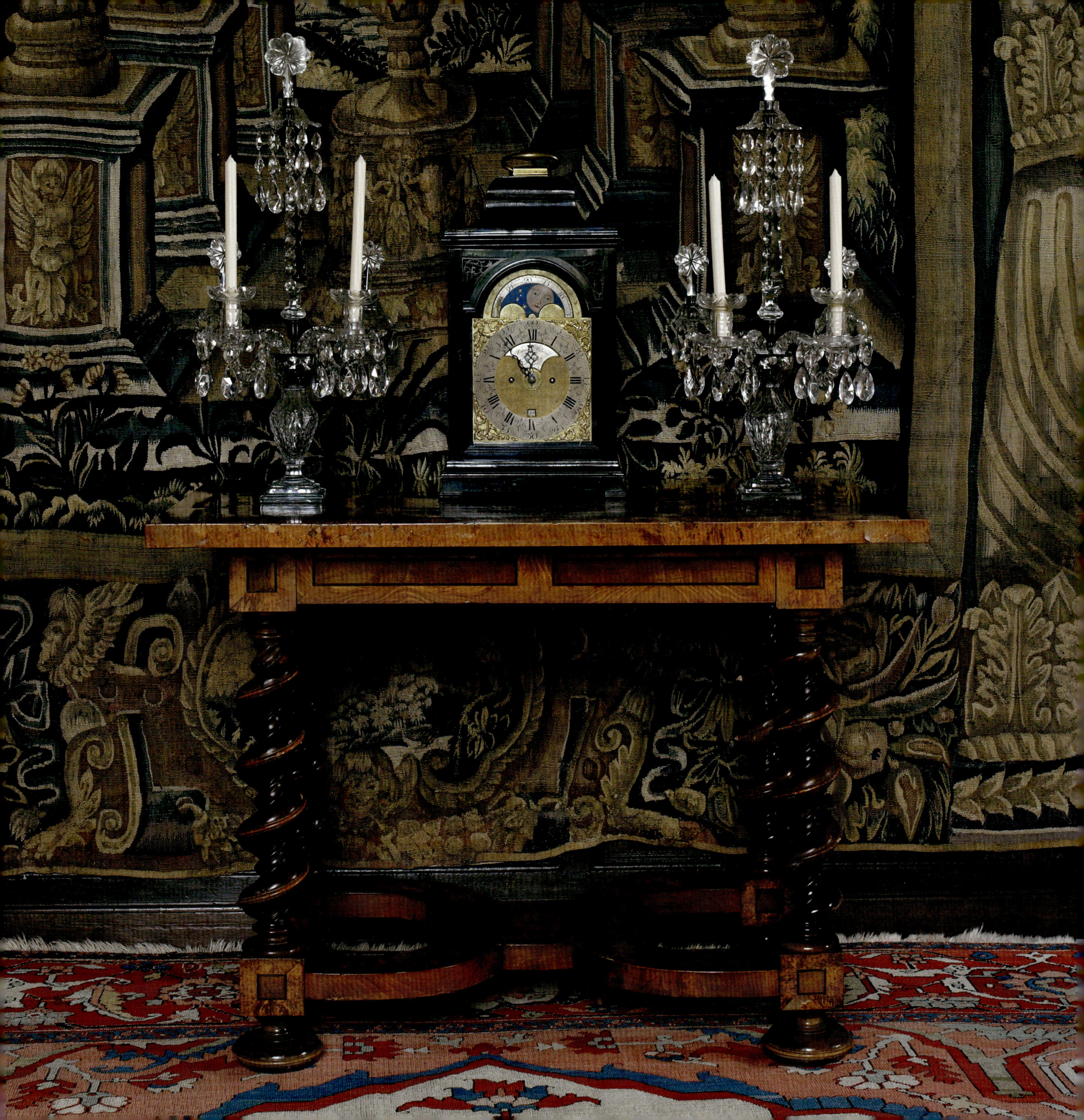

I · EVOLUTION · THE SIXTEENTH TO EIGHTEENTH CENTURIES

South Wraxall Manor

Renaissance vivacity: the drawing room at this Wiltshire manor house was remodelled in the early 1600s.

South Wraxall Manor is a mellow, stone West-country manor house that wraps around a courtyard, approached through a finely detailed gatehouse. Yet to even the most casual observer, the jaunty composition of the fifteenth-century great hall, with its porch and extravagantly carved gargoyles, is dominated by the huge mullioned windows of the drawing room, which, originally a Great Chamber, was extended in the early 1600s, as a Great Parlour or high dining room.[1]

In the 1670s John Aubrey called it "a dining room, a very noble one ... with a stately chimneypiece in freestone."[2] It had become known as the drawing room by the early nineteenth century. In the third volume of *Examples of Gothic Architecture* (1838), which T. L. Walker published with A. W. N. Pugin, Walker used the expressions "drawing room" and "withdrawing room" to describe it.[3] Certainly, from around 1600 this impressive, characterful room with its barrel-vaulted ceiling of vivid, lively plasterwork decoration (moons and suns, faces and fruits) has been the principal room of state and reception in South Wraxall Manor. A signature recently discovered in the ceiling with the date of 1611 might give us the date of completion.[4]

The house was probably begun around 1410 by one Robert Long, who made his money as a lawyer in the service of the Hungerford family. His high-ceilinged hall remains in its original form, with a distinctive pair of oriel windows. The drawing room was part of the improvements to the house added by Sir Walter Long (d. 1610), during a major rebuilding of what was originally the fifteenth-century Great Chamber on the first floor at the north end of the Great Hall. The date 1598 appears on the contemporary chimneypiece in the Great Hall. The old Great Chamber was made much larger at this time and is flooded with light from a pair of fine eight-light bay windows, one of which faces west into the courtyard and to the north into the garden (glass was an expensive commodity in the early 1600s).

A most unusual feature in this room (Pevsner called it "unexplained") is the semi-hexagonal projection on the north side, opposite the fireplace, with five stone recesses with shell canopies and wood panelling above.[5] It seems that this was there mostly to provide support for the original fifteenth-century roof by leaving part of the north wall in situ. Nonetheless the finely detailed alcoves were clearly intended to be seats and were perhaps the places from which the family or honoured guests watched entertainments.

The rippling effect of the decorative plasterwork is reflected in the most impressive stone-carved chimneypiece. This dominates the room and has an elaborate decorative iconography, reflecting both Renaissance classical ideas and the Gothic tradition of rich ornament. Dan Cruickshank wrote recently that it is "the greatest, most satisfying and most intriguing fireplaces of Elizabethan England."[6] The historian Anthony Wells-Cole has also described this chimneypiece as "a veritable thesaurus of Flemish mannerist ornament," referring to the several printed sources from which the decorative details were drawn.[7] Mr. Wells-Cole indeed saw possible links in the use of these sources to the work of mason William Griffin, who was employed at Hardwick Hall in the 1570s and may well have worked at Longleat, the local great noble house, and the home of the family of Walter Long's formidable second wife, Catherine, daughter of Sir John Thynne.

The "term" figures supporting the entablature are taken from a plate in Vredeman de Vries's *Caryatidum* (1565), and the cartouches on the lintel were copied from Benedetto Battini's *Vigilate quia Nescitis Diem Neque Horam* (1553), both published

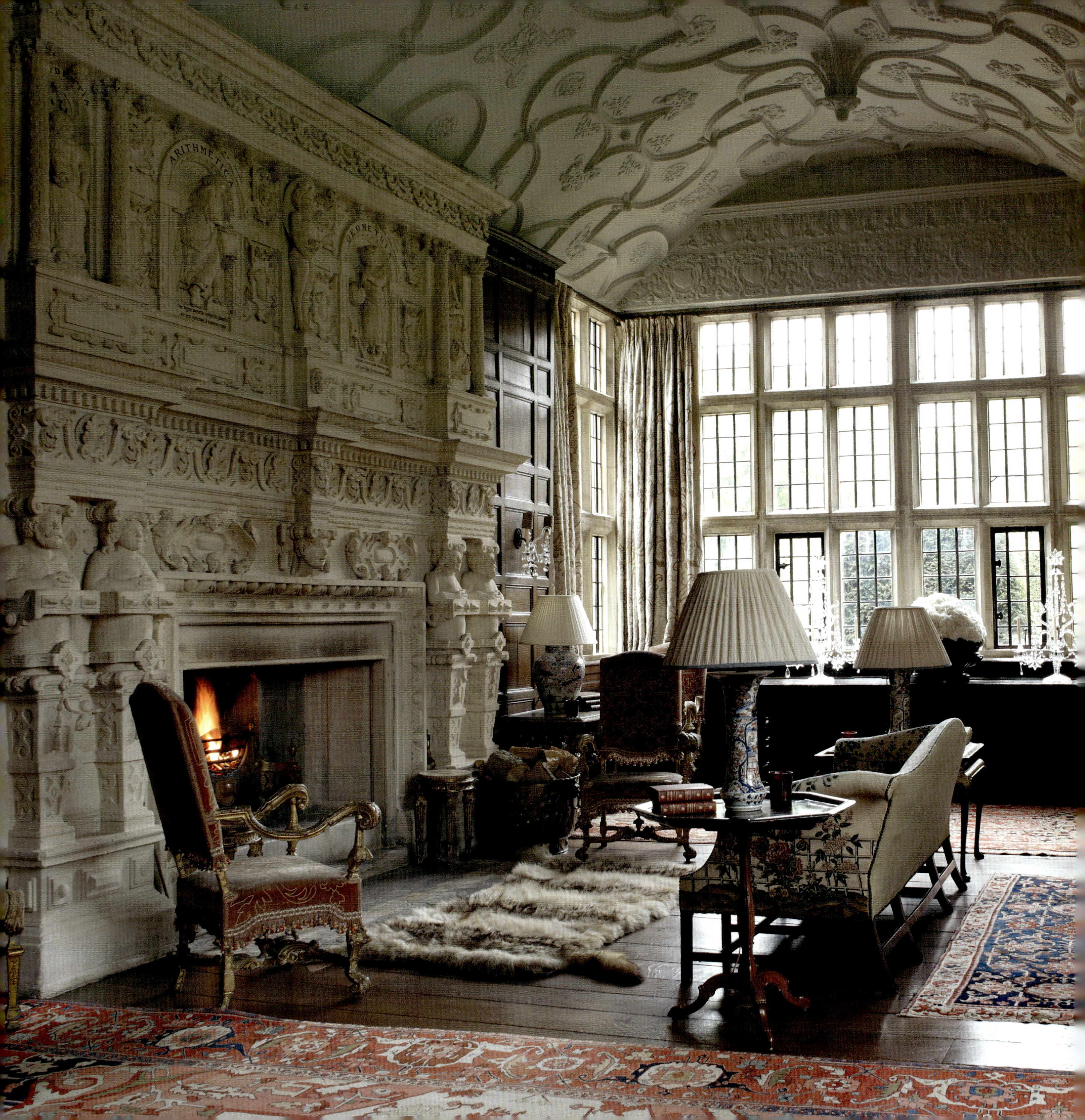
ARITHMETICA

← The drawing room at South Wraxall Manor, originally the fifteenth-century Great Chamber, was much extended in around 1600, when it was flooded with light from two huge new windows. The room seems to have become known as the Parlour by the 1620s. The recent restoration for John Taylor and Gela Nash-Taylor has brought out the soaring elegance of the room, with advice from Robert Kime and Patrick Kinmonth.

↓ The enigmatic carved caryatid figures on the huge chimneypiece are drawn from published Flemish mannerist sources.

The extraordinary sculpted niches opposite the great chimneypiece: the decorative stonework concealed the substantial structural element, which supported the extended roof of the huge room.

in Antwerp. The figures of *Prudentia*, *Justicia*, *Arithmetica*, and *Geometria* are presumably emblematic of Sir Walter's sound judgement as a local magistrate and representative of government. The figures were copied from engravings after Maarten de Vos, while the small cartouches were taken from another book of engravings by Vredeman de Vries, *Das Erst Buch* (1565).[8] There are several fine stone-carved chimneypieces of this date in the house.

Sir Walter Long was also a friend of Sir Walter Raleigh. According to John Aubrey, it was through this friendship that tobacco smoking was introduced into north Wiltshire, and one bedchamber at South Wraxall is still named in his honour.[9] South Wraxall Manor remained in the Long family ownership until the 1960s, but from the early 1800s, they lived principally at their Rood Ashton House estate (the house there was rebuilt in 1808 by Jeffry Wyatville but was since largely demolished). Thus South Wraxall Manor, as was so often the case with ancient manor houses that survive today, was tenanted. In fact, it appears that the house was empty for long periods, except for a resident caretaker (although it was also a school for a time).

The house had long been regarded as an antiquarian delight before Walter Hume Long, later 1st Viscount Long, restored it.[10] However, it did not become his permanent home, and he lived at Rood Ashton for most of his life. He was elected MP for North Wiltshire in 1880, shortly after his marriage to Lady Dorothy Boyle, daughter of the 9th Earl of Cork. In around 1900 the house was leased by a Major Richardson-Cox, who carried out an extensive restoration with architect A. C. Martin, who also designed the gardens (this restoration was celebrated in *Country Life* in 1905).

In 2005 South Wraxall Manor was bought by its current owners, John Taylor (bass player with the band Duran Duran) and his wife, Gela Nash (founder of the fashion house Juicy Couture). The couple has restored the house and refurnished it with great elegance, advised by interior decorator Robert Kime, opera designer Patrick Kinmonth, and architect Mary-Lou Arscott, of Knox Bhavan Architects. (A friend, Hamish Bowles of *Vogue*, introduced the Taylors to both Kime and Kinmonth who had not worked together before.)[11]

The furnishing of the drawing room has been celebrated in *Vogue* and *World of Interiors*, and the interior is deliberately romantic and timeless. John Taylor refers to the feeling of history and "the good bones" of the house, Gela Nash-Taylor has referred to how "everything is layered" in these interiors and to the importance of patina.[12] The drawing room is hung with tapestry and portraits, and Persian carpets add colour, warmth, and pattern. There are also well-chosen antique furnishings, including late-seventeenth-century Florentine giltwood chairs and an early-eighteenth-century gilt wood saloon, known as the "Napoleon Suite." There is also a three-seater settee with chinoiserie floral trellis needlepoint, which beautifully reflects the plasterwork of the ceiling. A portrait of George III by Gainsborough Dupont and a marquetry table in the room were both acquired from the recent sale of part of the collection of the royal house of Hanover. The ensemble is as satisfactory and complete as a seventeenth-century Dutch Old Master painting.

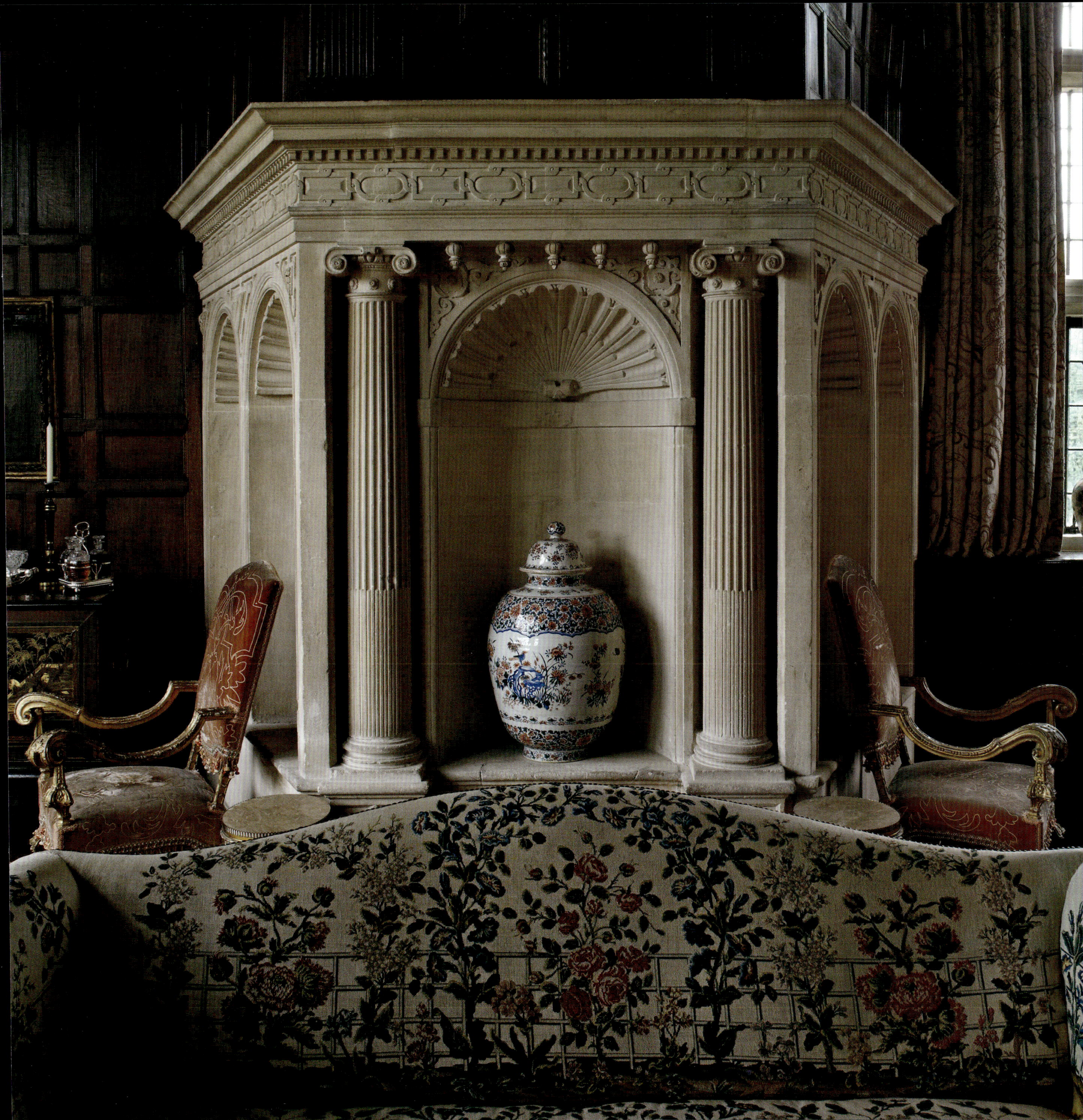

↓ A crystal candle-stand captures the light of the tall window.

→ A detail of the original 1600 plasterwork ceiling with its elegant interlaced ribs and decorated pendants.

SOUTH WRAXALL MANOR

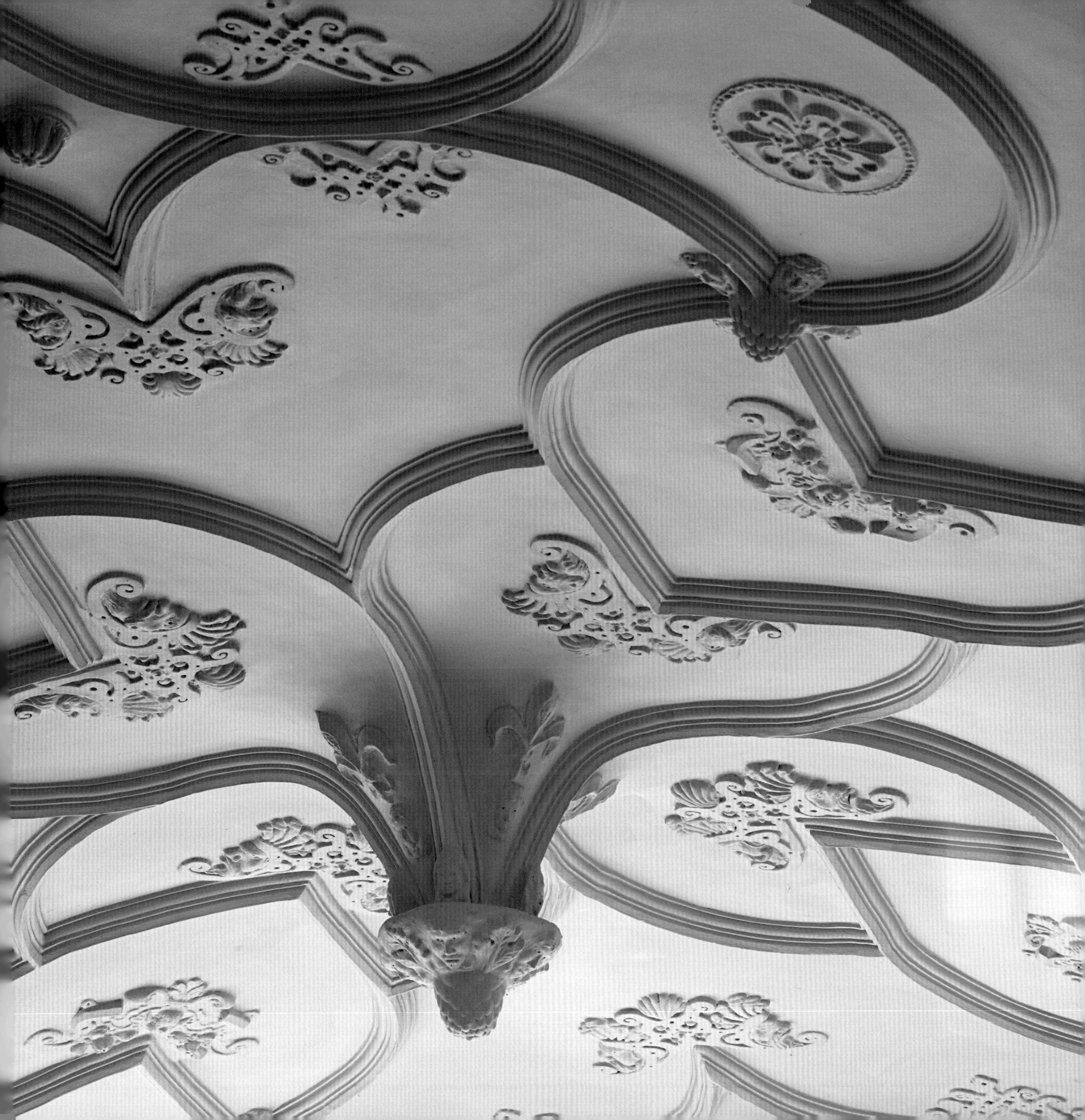

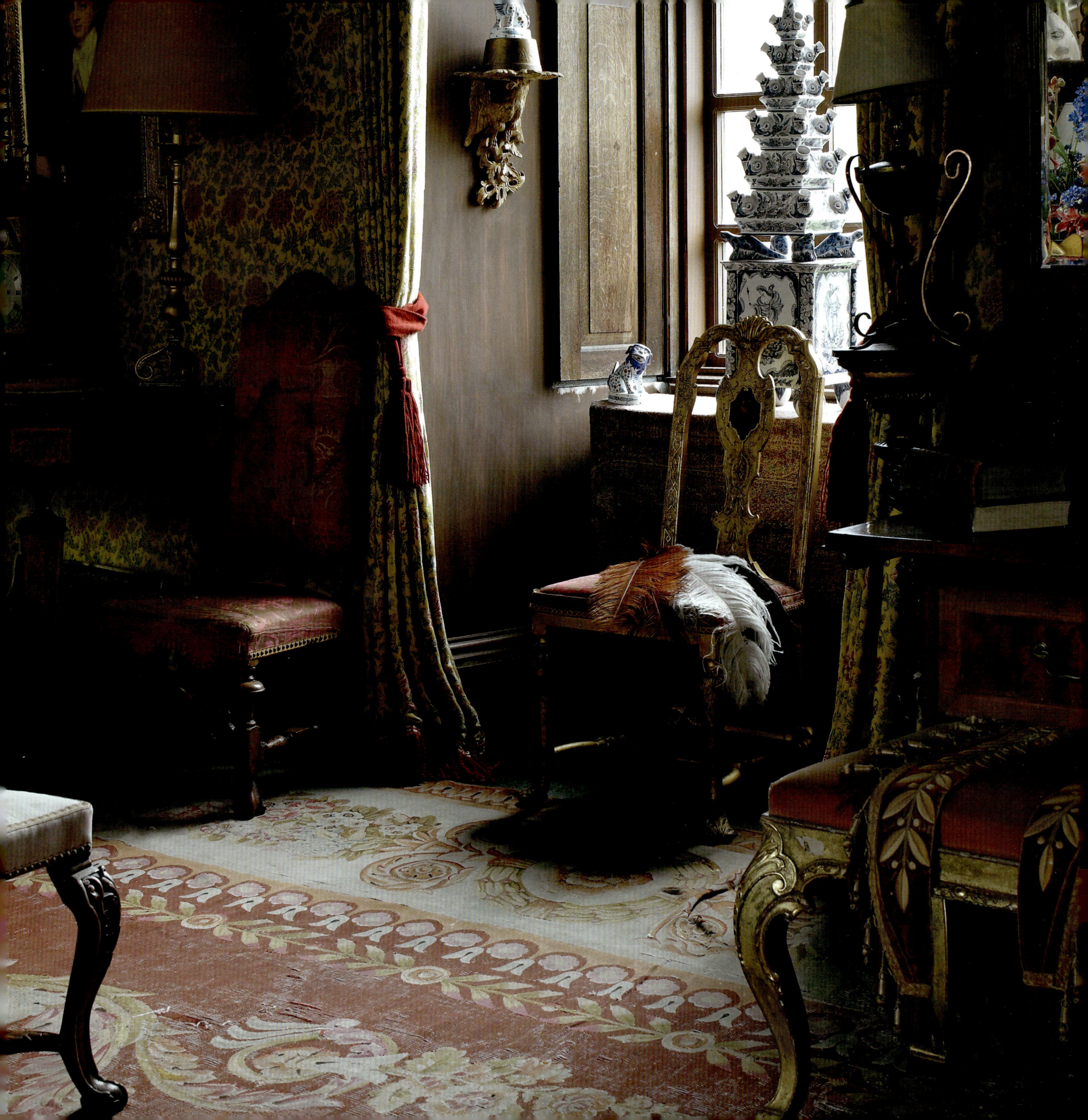

I · EVOLUTION · THE SIXTEENTH TO EIGHTEENTH CENTURIES

Chillingham Castle

Chillingham's great chamber of the 1590s restored in the 1980s as the drawing room

Chillingham Castle is a remarkable house and has been a romantic border stronghold since the thirteenth century at least. The castle structure dates mostly to the fourteenth century, but in the intervening centuries the ranges in between have been remodelled and reworked to create a large and many-layered country house. Some of this was done by Sir Jeffry Wyatville in the early nineteenth century as only a small part of a huge plan to extend the castle that was never executed. The house had become expensive to manage in the early twentieth century, and in the 1930s its contents were sold and the house shut up. Parts of the house became seriously decayed; it was in short "a roofless, floorless wreck of a castle with jungle having taken over the garden and the grounds."[1]

Chillingham was heroically restored in the 1980s and 1990s by Sir Humphry Wakefield, Bt., whose wife, the Hon. Lady Wakefield, is a descendant of the Grey family, who owned Chillingham since 1246 (her mother was born Lady Mary Grey and inherited the nearby Howick Hall estate, once part of the Chillingham estates). The Greys have been an illustrious aristocratic line that included the remarkable Earl of Tankerville, who commanded the cavalry for the Duke of Monmouth's rebellion yet survived with his head (he also built Uppark in Sussex).[2] The restoration of Chillingham Castle was carried out under Sir Humphry's personal direction and has been imaginative and inspired.

The drawing room is perhaps one of the finest surviving historic interiors in the house, and was the original great chamber of the castle at the dawn of the seventeenth century. Situated above the Great Hall, it is known as the James 1st Room, after that king's recorded visits to Chillingham in 1603 and 1617, and is part of a suite of three rooms thought to have been prepared especially to receive the future king in the 1590s.[3] It has an elegant plasterwork ceiling with the interconnecting gilded ribs and finely moulded detail (the ceiling was in a poor state in 1981 but was expertly restored with the help of Stevensons of Norwich).

Sir Humphry relates: "The room was built in the late sixteenth century in anticipation of the new king James, the then Earl Grey, a godson of both Queen Elizabeth I and secretary Cecil, and there is an immense correspondence relating to the Scottish succession. Grey built the range between two fourteenth-century towers to create three rooms for a state apartment: a great chamber or receiving room, a state bedroom, and a more private room beyond (the panelling was removed from this room in the eighteenth century and is now in an officer's mess in Aldershot in Hampshire).

"I opened up original windows in the north side and restored their stone mullions. In the 1840s the frieze level immediately below was covered over with fish-pin brackets to strengthen the ceiling; and two columns were also inserted. But all of that 1840s work had decayed and fallen apart, so we took the decision to restore the window and put the chimneypiece on the east wall; we also removed the later work to the ceilings, to reveal the full glory of the 1590s ceiling to be fully appreciated. I also inserted new windows in the late-seventeenth-century style in the manner of windows which survived the fire at Uppark."

This room is furnished with pieces brought together by Sir Humphry, including inherited family items; some antiques, including a pair of fine Irish Georgian tables; carved and gilded Italian chairs from the Mentmore Towers sale; as well as some elegant copies of antique originals made by Baker Furniture for a company he founded. After a period as an officer, in the 10th Hussars, Sir Humphry pursued a career in the world of antique

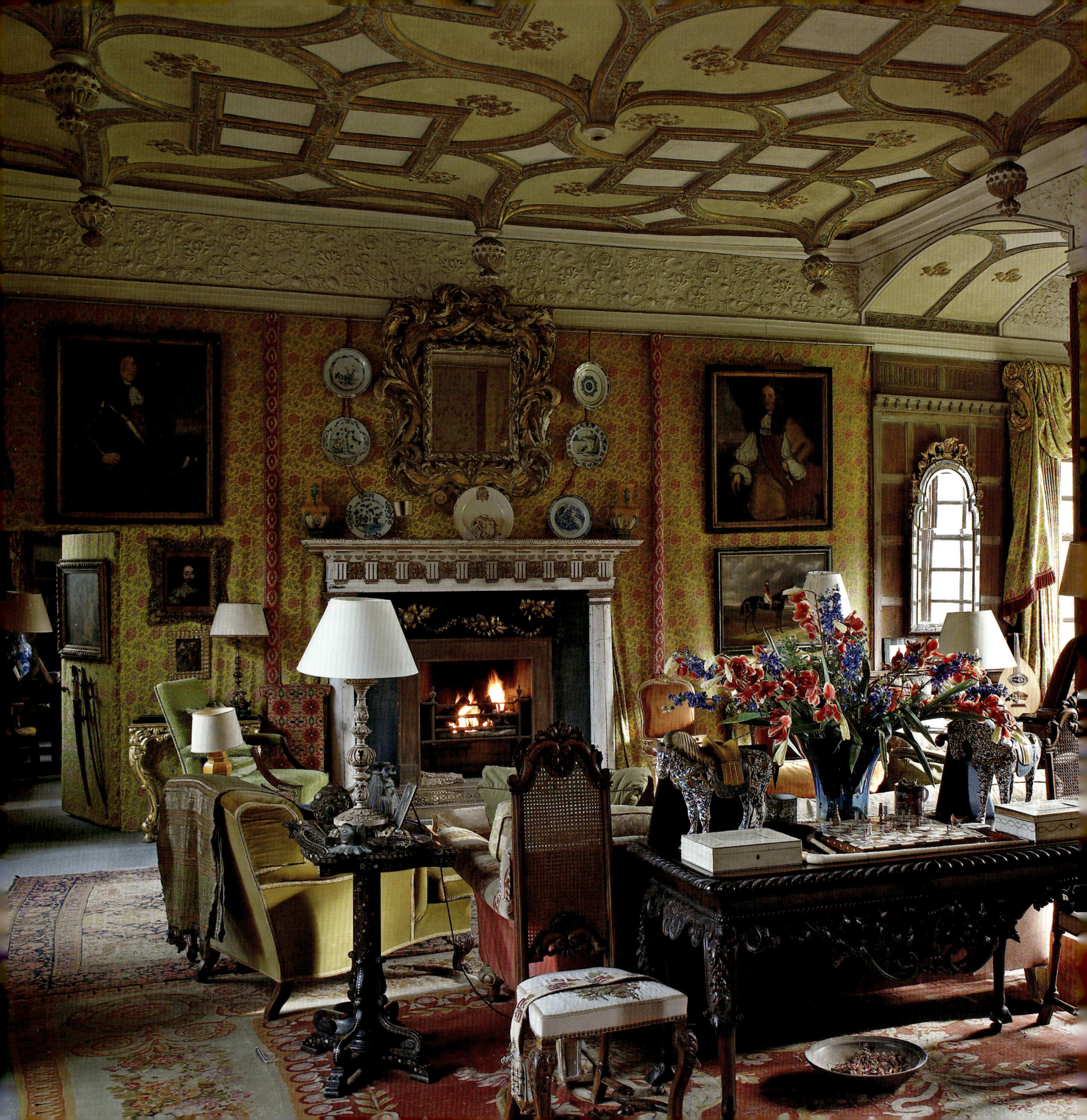

← The King James I Room at Chillingham Castle was created in the late 1590s above the Great Hall. The house was restored by Sir Humphry and Lady Wakefield in the 1980s. Lady Wakefield is a descendant of the Grey family, who built the castle in the 1300s.

↓ The silk hangings were woven on the royal looms at Caserta, near Naples, and "toned" by the Glyndebourne set designer.

EVOLUTION | 43

↓ Sir Humphry Wakefield has taken an imaginative approach to mixing family heirlooms, antiques, and modern furniture.

→ Pieces of fine furniture from different periods stand on a vast Aubusson carpet, the result of a wager with Geoffrey Bennison.

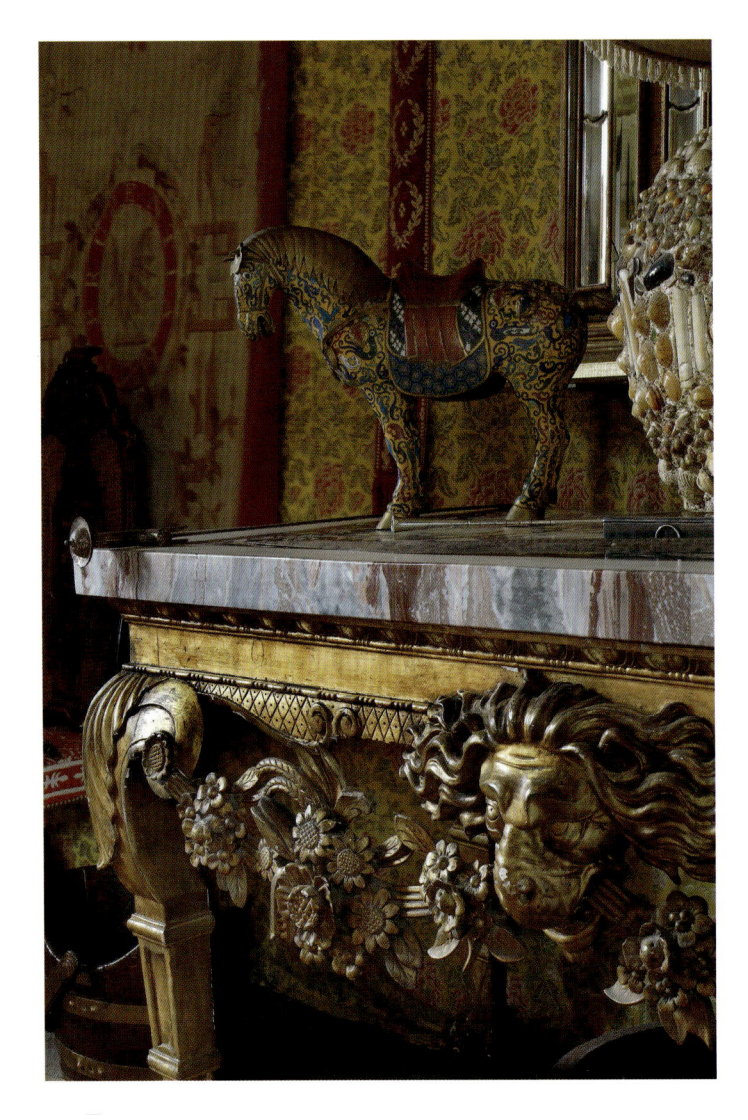

furniture and historic restoration. Having worked as a specialist for Christie's of London and a director of Mallets, he was able to pour his knowledge and skill into his work at Chillingham, though he is more widely known today as an antiquarian, aesthete, courageous horseman, and explorer. He is a member of the prestigious Society of the Dilettanti and the only living person included in John Jolliffe's book *Eccentrics*.

The drawing room is lined with an elegant yellow silk of a 1780s pattern woven in modern times for Chatsworth on the original looms at Caserta in Italy. The first two hundred yards ordered for Chatsworth contained a fault, so Sir Humphry acquired them all and, on the recommendation of George Christie, employed Alex Corey, the brilliant "finisher" of the Glyndebourne opera sets, to give them just the tone he required as a backdrop to this carefully imagined interior.[4]

Some elements came by luck rather than design, including the large Aubusson carpet, which he won as the result of a wager with the London interior decorator and dealer Geoffrey Bennison. The paintings in the room are mostly of the Wakefield family and include a portrait of Edward Wakefield by Romney and a portrait of another Edward Wakefield on horseback by Joseph Herring Junior. There is also a portrait of the Countess Grey, wife of the prime minister Earl Grey. Everything has been put together with a cultured elegance that is highly suitable to a house of the historic character of Chillingham with a deft touch of theatre. Sir Humphry recalls: "I went to Knole to study the effect of paint and plasterwork in the James I room and the palette worked out very happily indeed."

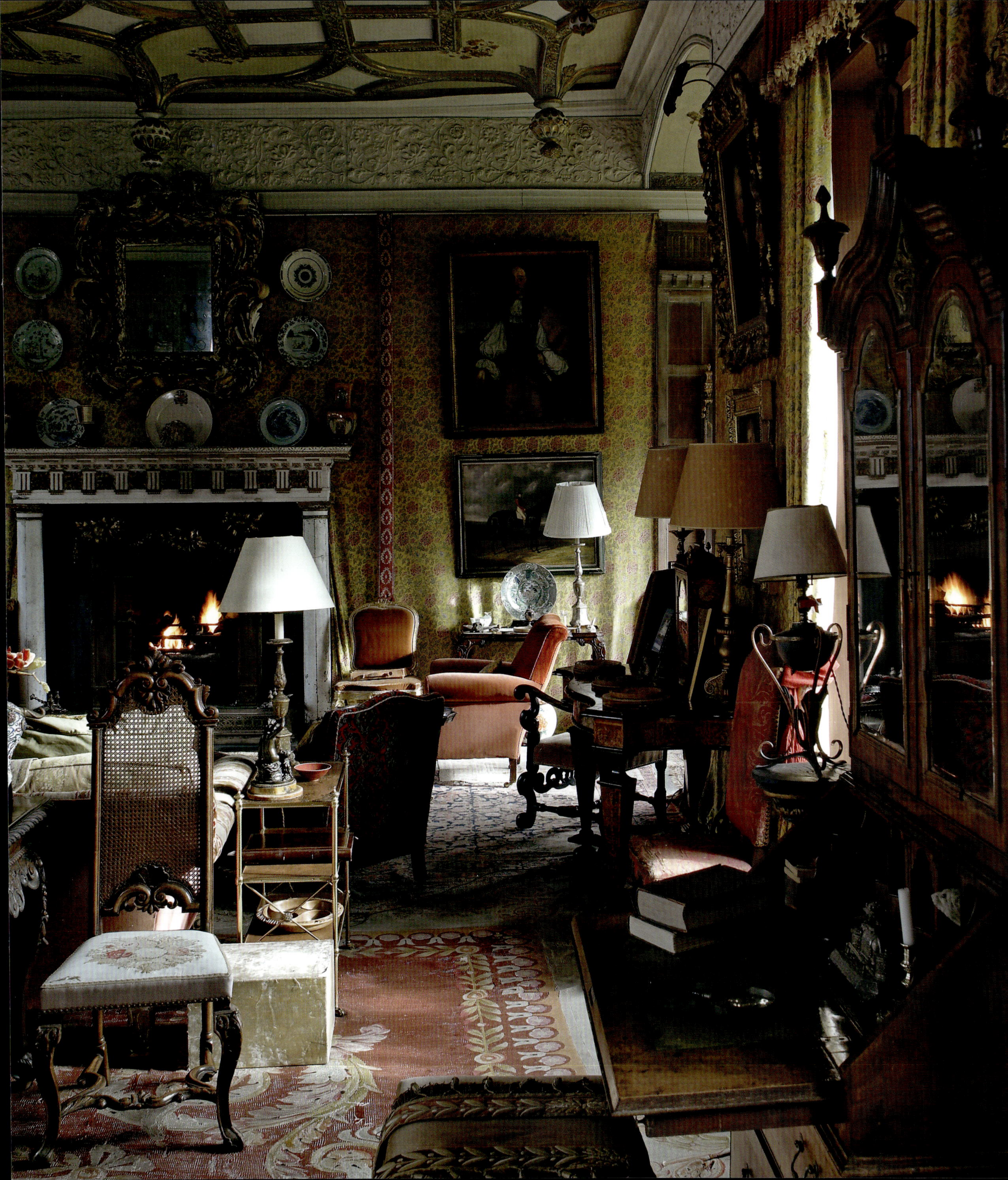

↓ The bay window is arranged like a Dutch still-life painting, including a cleverly contrived drinks table.

→ Wakefield family portraits and tapestries line the walls. The plasterwork ceiling was expertly restored in the 1980s.

46 | CHILLINGHAM CASTLE

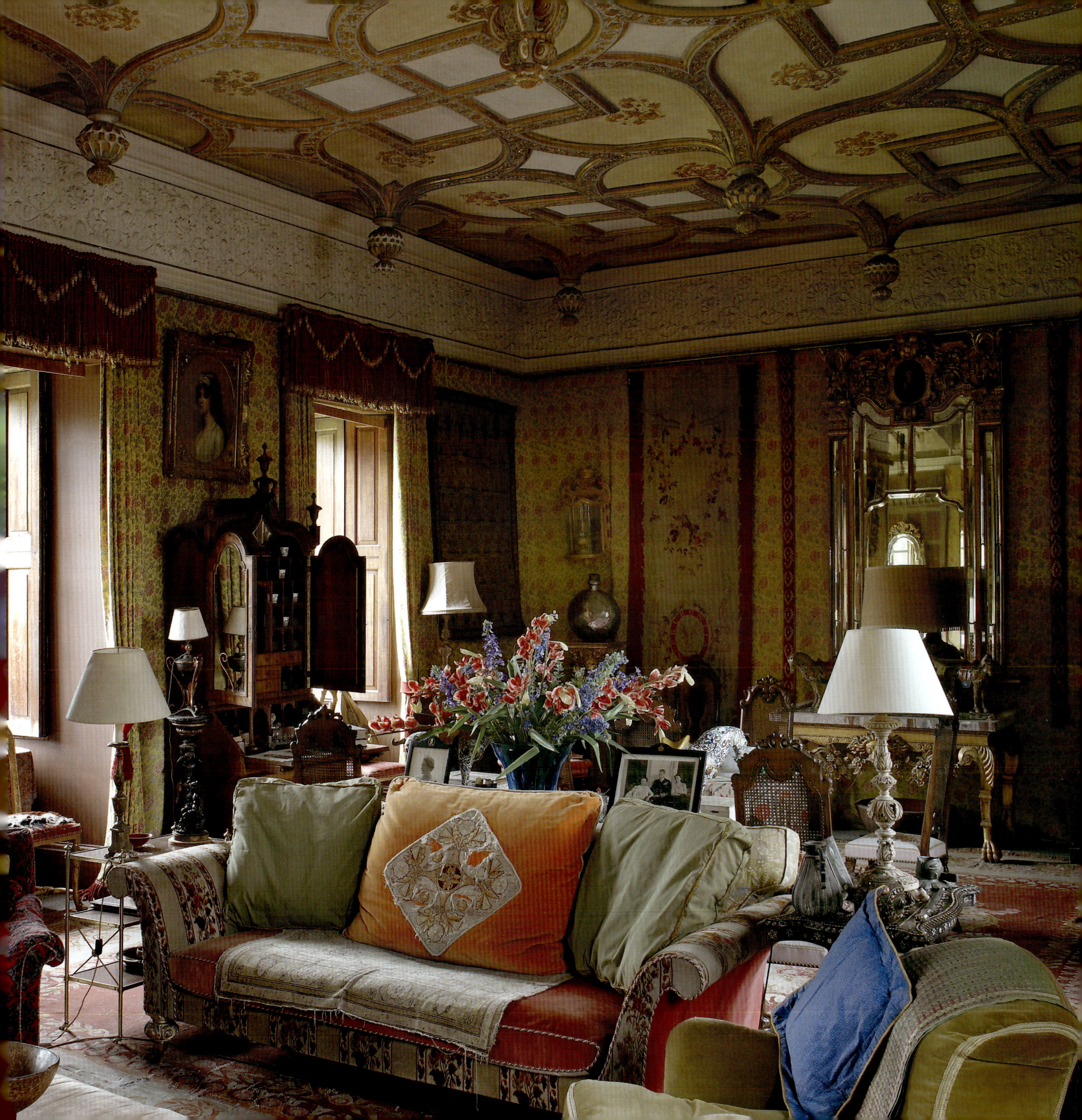

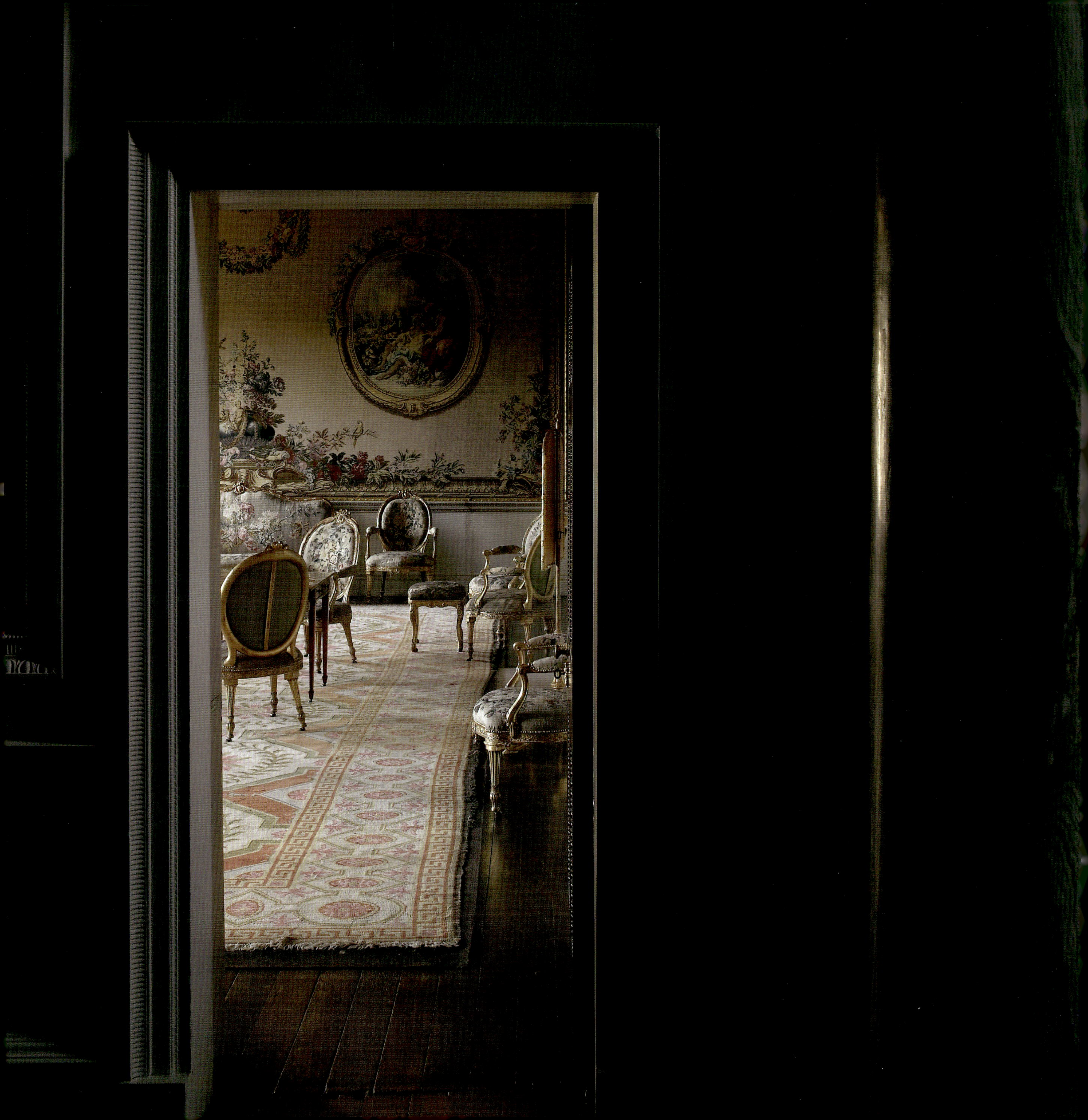

I · EVOLUTION · THE SIXTEENTH TO EIGHTEENTH CENTURIES

Newby Hall

A private paradise: Gobelins tapestries in a room designed by Robert Adam for the civilised William Weddell.

Newby Hall in Yorkshire was remodelled in the 1760s for William Weddell, a young Yorkshire landowner who had recently inherited the estate. Weddell was a man of considerable education and culture, and his friend the Reverend William Palgrave called him, "that storehouse and repository of ancient and modern taste."[1] There is a splendid portrait by Sir Nathaniel Dance-Holland depicting both men seated in the Campagna, which hangs now at Upton House in Warwickshire.[2]

Weddell sought designs from the leading York architect John Carr and also consulted the Rome-trained court architects William Chamber and Robert Adam. The latter contrived for him a magnificent "pantheonic" sculpture gallery for his important collection of antiquities in a south wing, on axis to the new dining room. Weddell went on his Grand Tour in 1765 and was described as having "[bought] such a quantity of pictures, marbles, etc. as will astonish the West Riding of Yorkshire."[3] Adam is renowned as a great architect but showed his greatest talents in the invention of his own classically sourced vision of interior design, based on intensive study during his own Grand Tour.

The sculpture gallery, of two square rooms with a central rotunda, was designed on the pattern of an ancient Roman house. Adam's concept for this room was rooted in his study of Roman ruins at Tivoli and the influence of Piranesi and Clerisseau. Adam also designed the library and the entrance hall, the latter with a bold Doric frieze and panels of martial trophies in stucco. To walk through these rooms at Newby Hall today is to journey through a re-creation of the Roman classical world. He also designed the drawing room beyond—one of the most memorable eighteenth-century interiors to survive intact in England.[4]

Both the hall and sculpture gallery coolly prepare the palette before the opulent warmth of the drawing room, which is hung with tapestry *à la Français* and upholstered en suite. The tapestry was acquired direct from the Gobelins Manufactory, and the oval medallions of these tapestries are after paintings by the artist Boucher, depicting the elements personified by deities: *Venus and Vulcan* (fire), *Vertumnus and Pomona* (earth), *Aurora and Cephalus* (air), and the *Birth of Venus* (water). The latter was from a new Boucher painting dated 1766. Known as *Tentures de Boucher*, the tapestries beautifully evoke the Roman themes of lyric poetry.

The tapestries belong to the last phase of expensive tapestry commissions in the world of the English country house. It was the second of six Gobelins tapestry drawing rooms to be so furnished in the 1760s and early 1770s in England; the first was that commissioned by the Earl of Coventry for Croome Court (and now in the Metropolitan Museum of Art, in New York), which did not benefit from the 1766 painting by Boucher. Weddell may have been to the Gobelins Manufactory on one of his two visits to Paris, in 1763 or 1765. The tapestries were delivered in two sets, one in 1767; the other was made in 1768 and delivered later, probably in 1769.

Adam was often at his most ingenious and inventive when working within an older house, as can be seen by his work at Syon and elsewhere.[5] There is no surviving overall design by Adam for the Tapestry Drawing Room at Newby, but the very unity and echo of the detail and motif suggest that Adam was designing the room for these tapestries. The furnishings include the tall neoclassical pier glasses and the low side tables, all made in Paris. The twelve chairs and two settees, provided by Thomas Chippendale, have Roman medallion backs to harmonise with the Roman medallioned wall hangings. This

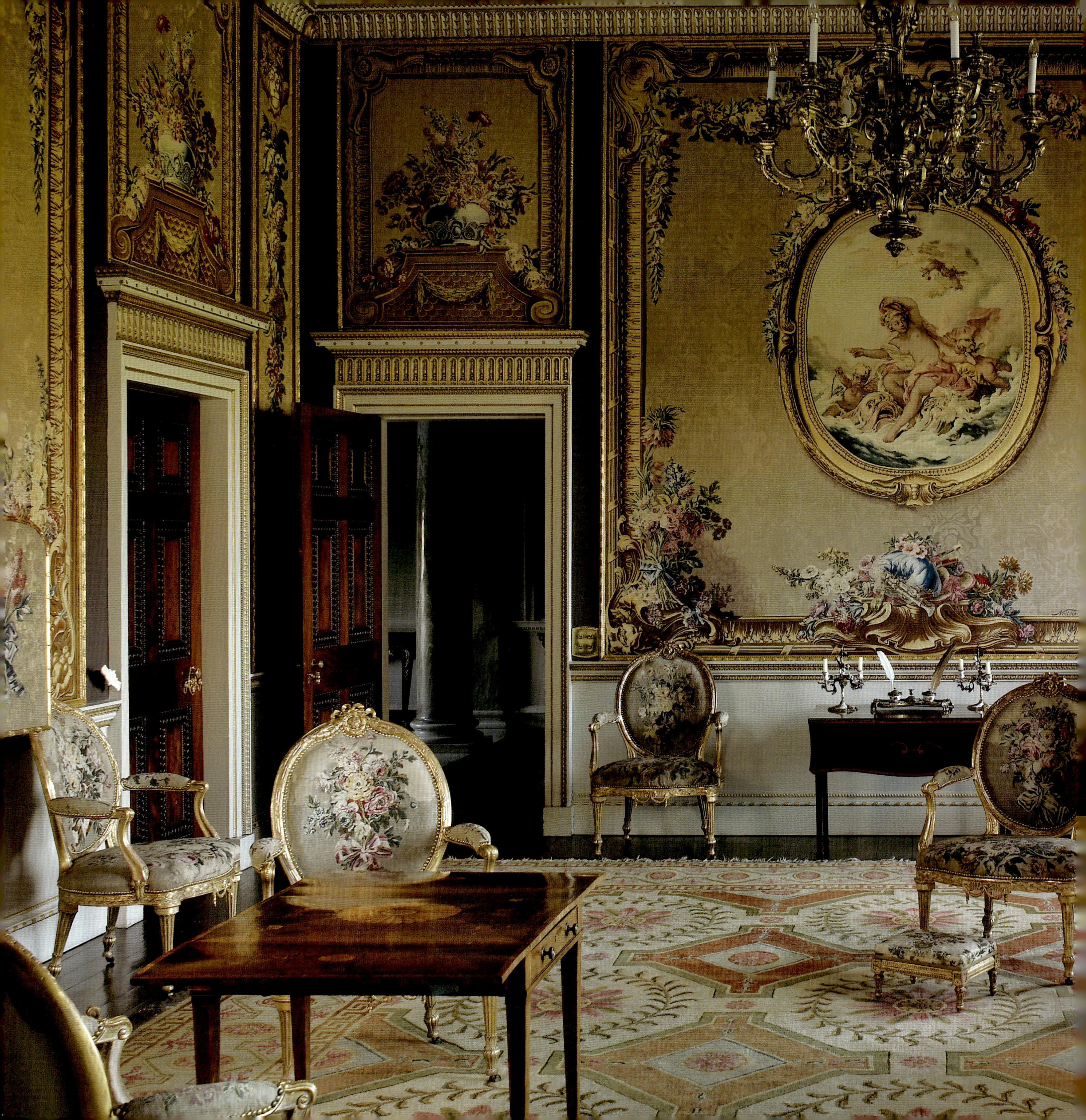

The Tapestry Drawing Room, Newby Hall, Yorkshire, designed by Robert Adam and hung in the late 1760s with "tenture du Boucher" Gobelins tapestry ordered especially for the room.

EVOLUTION | 51

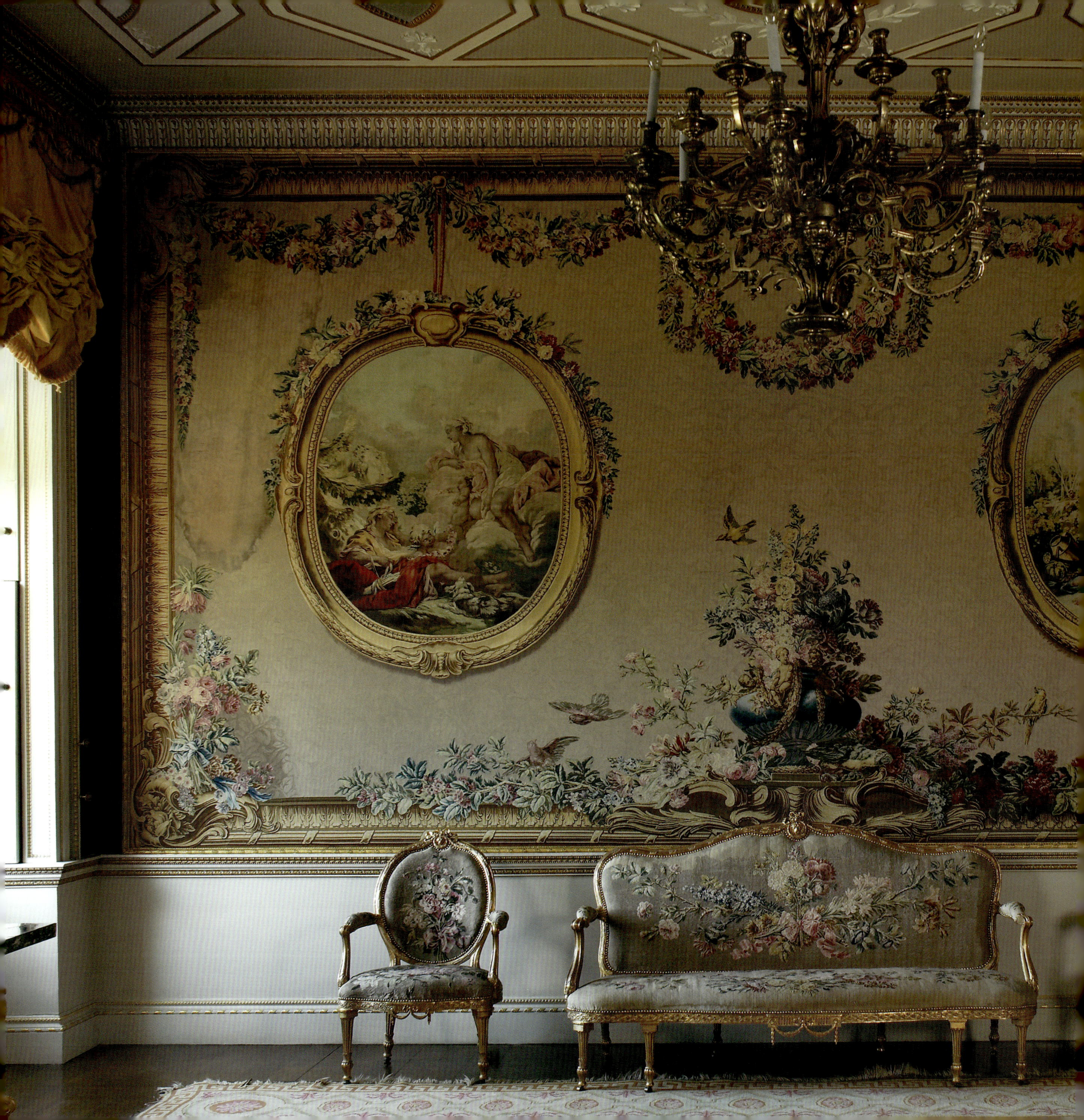

← The Gobelins tapestries still transmit a strong sense of feminine delicacy and French glamour.

↓ Robert Adam's delicate classical ornament provides the perfect foil to the floral abundance of the tapestry hangings. The paint colours were adjusted in the 1970s.

EVOLUTION | 53

The tapestry-upholstered chairs come from the original set provided by Thomas Chippendale in the 1760s.

precious suite of furnishings preserves its original upholstery and is unique as a complete surviving scheme of upholstered furniture made by Chippendale to remain within its original interior.

Adam designed the drawing room ceiling with a strong geometric pattern: originally of a pink and pale green, with eleven paintings by Antonio Zucchi.[6] The ceiling's ground colours were repainted in 1978 to mute the contrast of the bright Adam colour schemes with the now part-faded tapestry. The borders and medallions of the tapestry are in wool and have faded very little and are still vibrant. The background of the tapestry is a mixture of silk and wool intended to give the effect of a damask hanging, and this has faded over time. The tapestry has recently been removed and refixed allowing for an inspection of its reverse. It is now thought that the original colour may have been a pale rose-pink (other examples of tentures de Boucher woven by Gobelins are a deep rose-crimson).[7] Adam also designed the strongly compartmented pattern of the specially woven carpet. Throughout the room, the unity of detail is breathtaking, with the detail of the gilt fillet used to secure the tapestries echoed in the backs of the chairs, in the frame of the fire screen, and in the cornice decoration.

These tapestry drawing rooms were all the rage in the 1760s and clearly appealed especially to the well-travelled English aristocratic and landowner who often knew France as well as Italy. They seem exceptionally formal to modern eyes, but what is important to remember is the feminine identity of the drawing room: the visual richness, warmth, and delicacy of this room is in deliberate contrast to the sober and chaste classical interior of the hall and Adam's dining room (which later became the library). Such rooms would have seemed intensely cheerful and feminine in the eighteenth century. Weddell would have been planning an appropriate alliance then and was indeed married in 1771 to Elizabeth Ramsden, half-sister to Lady Rockingham. All fashionable ladies of this period wanted their drawing rooms to be in the French style, as stages for their entertaining. The profusion of flowers, garlands, and flying birds seems to suggest almost a billowing tented pavilion in an idealized garden — even the carved girandoles are depicted as baskets of flowers. The birds of paradise are depicted so vividly they almost seem to move as the viewer walks through the room. This is a space within a dream landscape in which all the protection of the loving deities is invoked. As John Cornforth observed in *Country Life* in 1979, "the more one looks, the more one becomes aware of what a brilliant piece of orchestration is achieved in the room."[8]

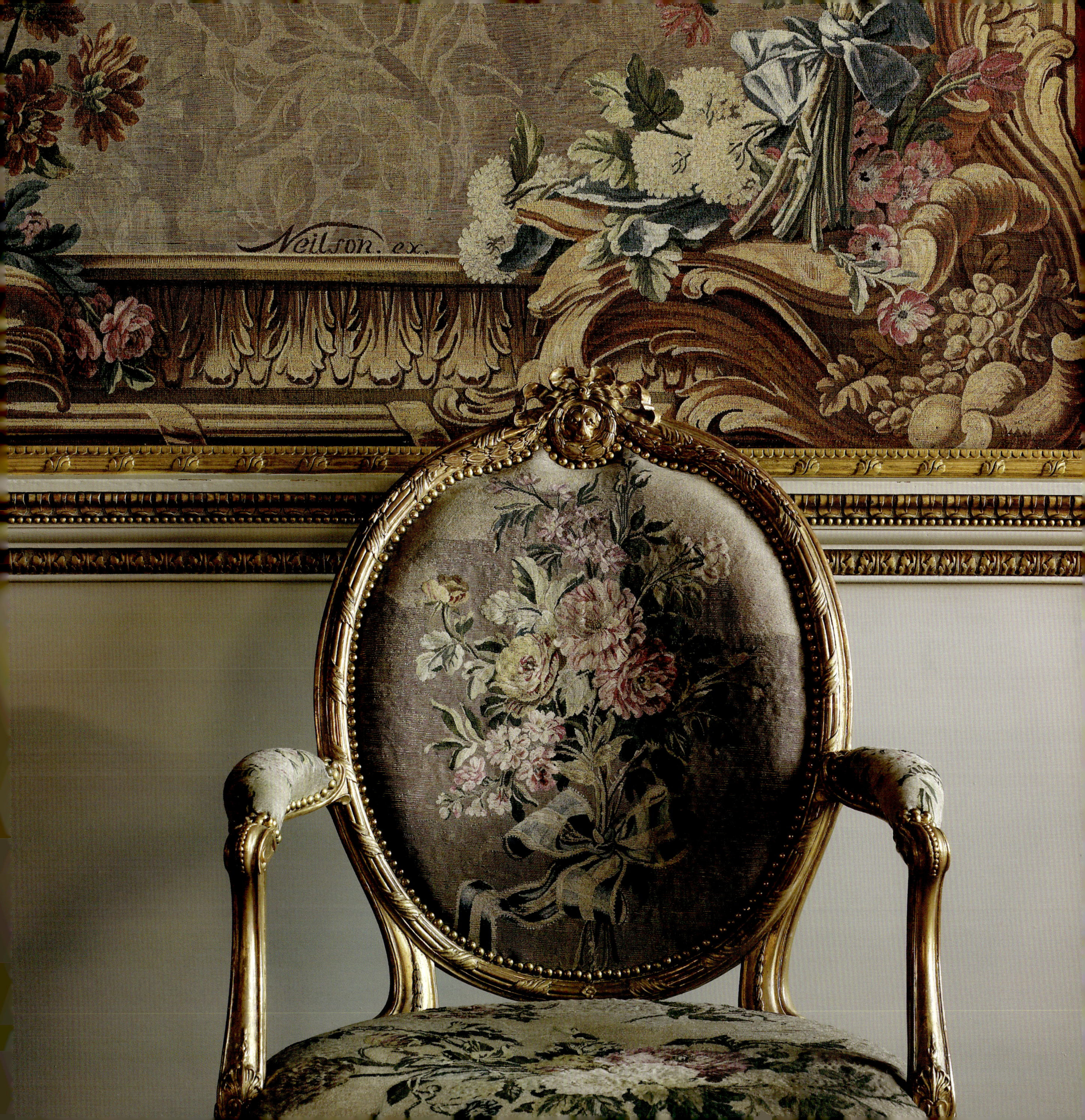
Neilson. ex.

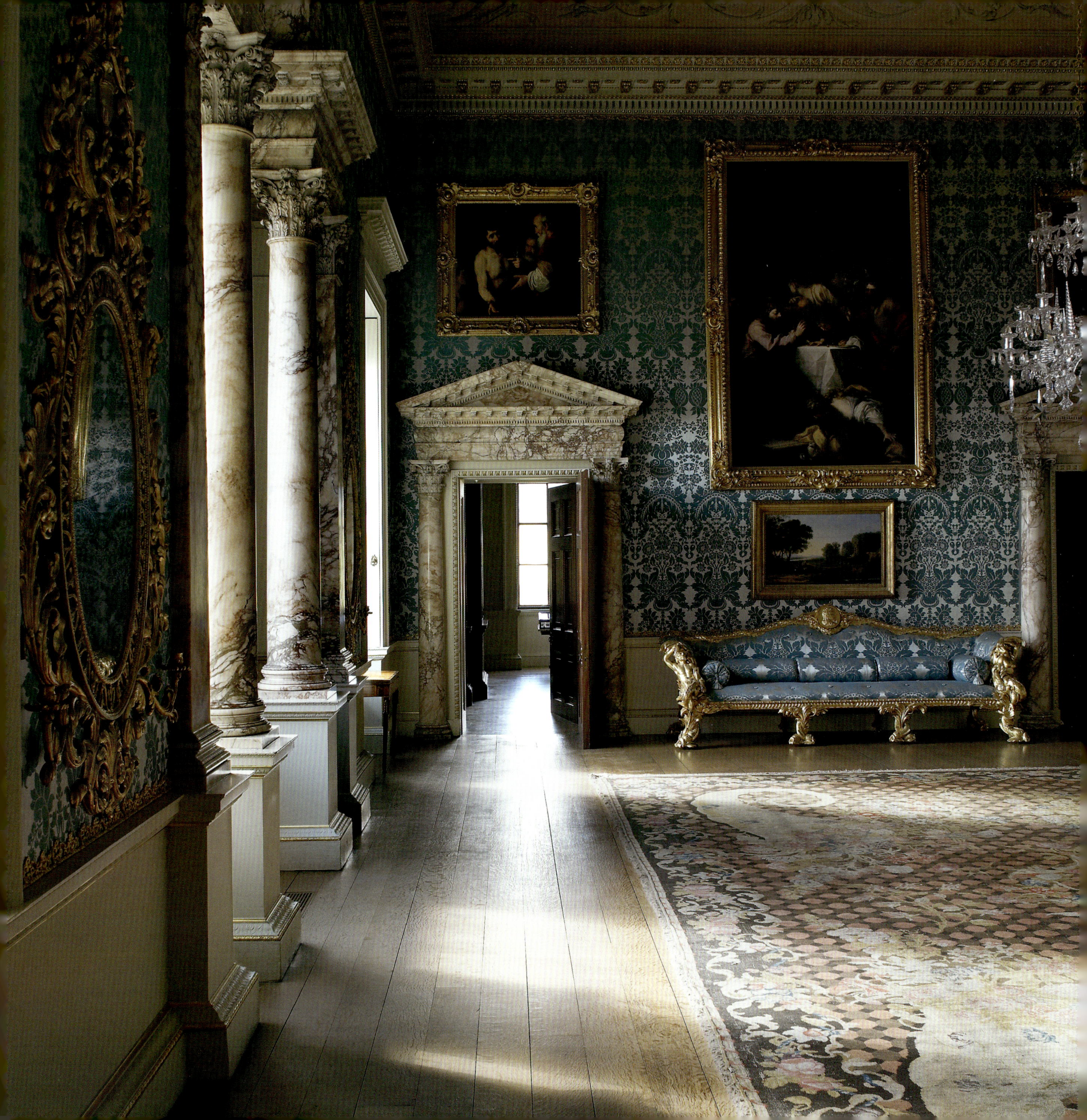

I · EVOLUTION · THE SIXTEENTH TO EIGHTEENTH CENTURIES

Kedleston Hall

Palatial visions: this Adam-designed drawing room has an exuberant set of seat furniture by Linnell.

The State Drawing Room at Kedleston Hall in Derbyshire is one of the most magnificent of the formal drawing rooms created in the 1760s, a period still in transition between Palladian and neoclassical styles.[1] It was created for Sir Nathaniel Curzon (1726–1804), 5th Baronet (raised to the peerage as Baron Scarsdale in 1761), as part of a suite of great rooms grand enough to display his refinement in general and his art collection in particular. Following the lead of his older friend and mentor, the 1st Earl of Leicester, famous as the builder of Holkham Hall in Norfolk, his purpose may well have been to create a Tory "power house" in Derbyshire, which would rival the "Whig" Chatsworth.

In his magnificent drawing room, a private room of assembly for the discussion of governance, the patriotic Scarsdale also explicitly celebrates the nation's nautical heroes. The theme of cultivation is also clearly evident in the finish and detail of the interiors. The three staterooms of the east front were each dedicated to a different art—music, painting, and literature—and each honoured with a different architectural order: Corinthian for the drawing room, Ionic for the music room, and Doric for the library. On embarking on his project, Scarsdale famously composed a poetic prayer: "Grant me, ye Gods, a pleasant seat, in attick elegance made neat."[2]

The music room, hung with magnificent pictures and provided with an organ, was a mere prelude to the great drawing room itself, where the best of the picture collection was hung originally on a pale blue silk damask, which has been re-created and rehung in recent times. The layered magnificence of the silvery-blue silk damask with its pomegranate pattern, hung with richly framed pictures, is dazzling. The gilded frames of the pictures were especially noted as "immensely expensive" by the observant Duchess of Northumberland, who visited in 1766 and described the room as "hung with very fine pictures on blue damask" (which reference confirms its early use in this room, as it is known that Curzon had first considered a red velvet, the blue perhaps chosen in deference to the marine theme).[3] Indeed the lavishness of the whole project at Kedleston caught the eye of the ubiquitous Horace Walpole when he visited while the work was still in progress: "magnificently furnished and finished; all designed by Adam in the best taste, but too expensive."[4]

In creating his magnificent house, Curzon passed through a number of designers. Scarsdale's original architect, Matthew Brettingham, derived the original plan inspired by Palladio's Villa Mocenigo, with quadrant wings. James Paine was then brought in, and he may be responsible for some of the interior detail of the drawing room: the pedimented pink-vined Derbyshire alabaster door cases and the huge Venetian window that dominates the east wall of the drawing room, as these are more traditionally Palladian in character. By 1761 Robert Adam had taken over the whole project, and while he revolutionized much of the design and interior decoration of the house, it appears that he had resolved to follow the essential layout of this central room as his predecessors had imagined it.[5]

Adam did design the characteristic ornament of the coved ceiling and the boldly sculptural chimneypiece supported by two carved caryatids. An earlier ceiling design had been provided by the artist Spang, but on the flat ceiling Adam used a motif of an interlaced trefoil taken from Bartoli's engravings in *Pictorae Antiquae*. On the cove Adam used a nautical theme of merfolk and seahorses, which was a deliberate allusion to the great naval triumphs of the time, especially against the French in Canada, which contributed to the growth of what came to be called the British Empire.

↓ The Adam-designed ornament of the coved ceiling of the State Drawing Room at Kedleston Hall in Derbyshire: the merfolk refer to the great naval triumphs of the late eighteenth century.

→ The State Drawing Room, at Kedleston Hall, Derbyshire, completed by Robert Adam in the 1760s: the blue silk hangings were rewoven to match the original, allowing the exuberant Linnell furniture to be fully appreciated.

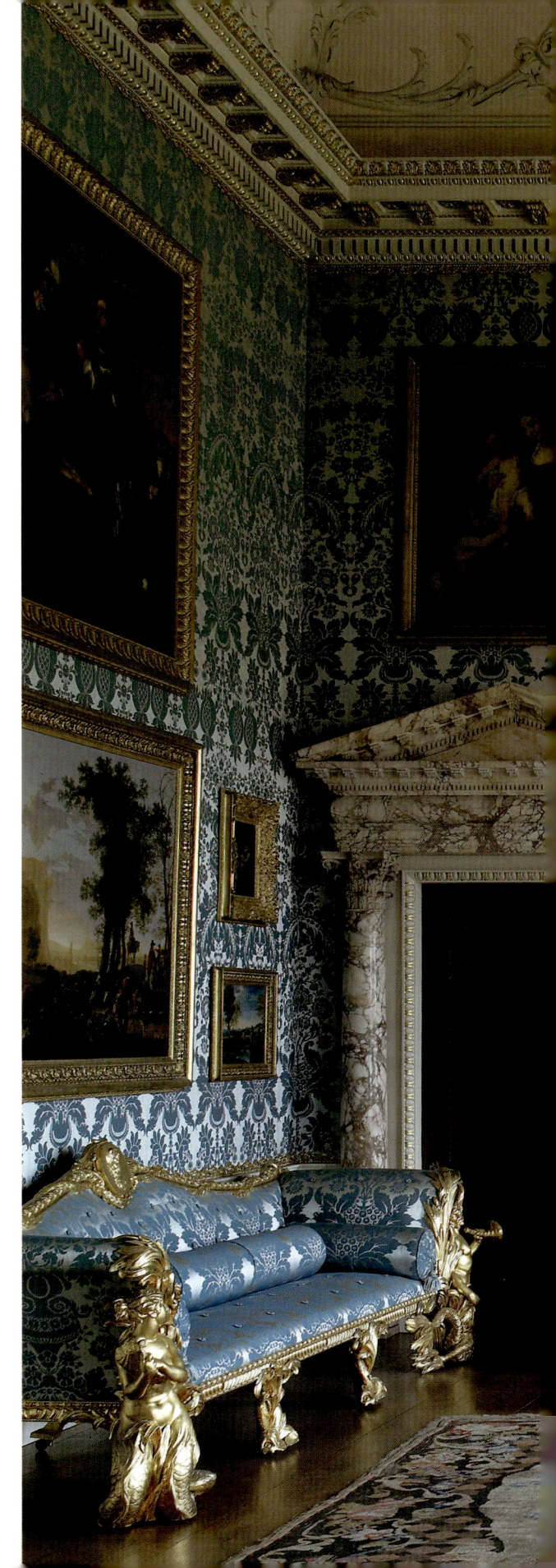

58 | KEDLESTON HALL

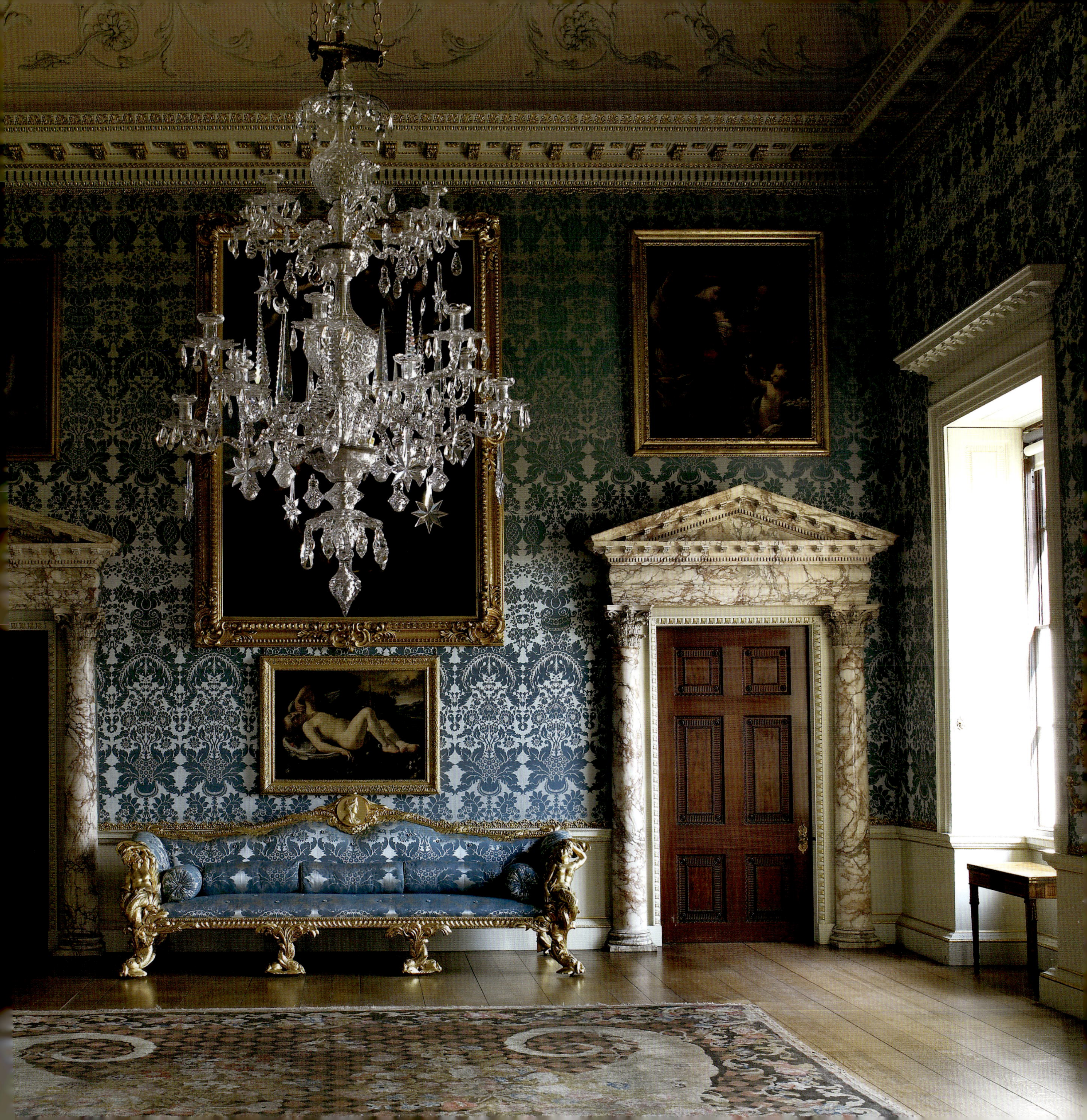

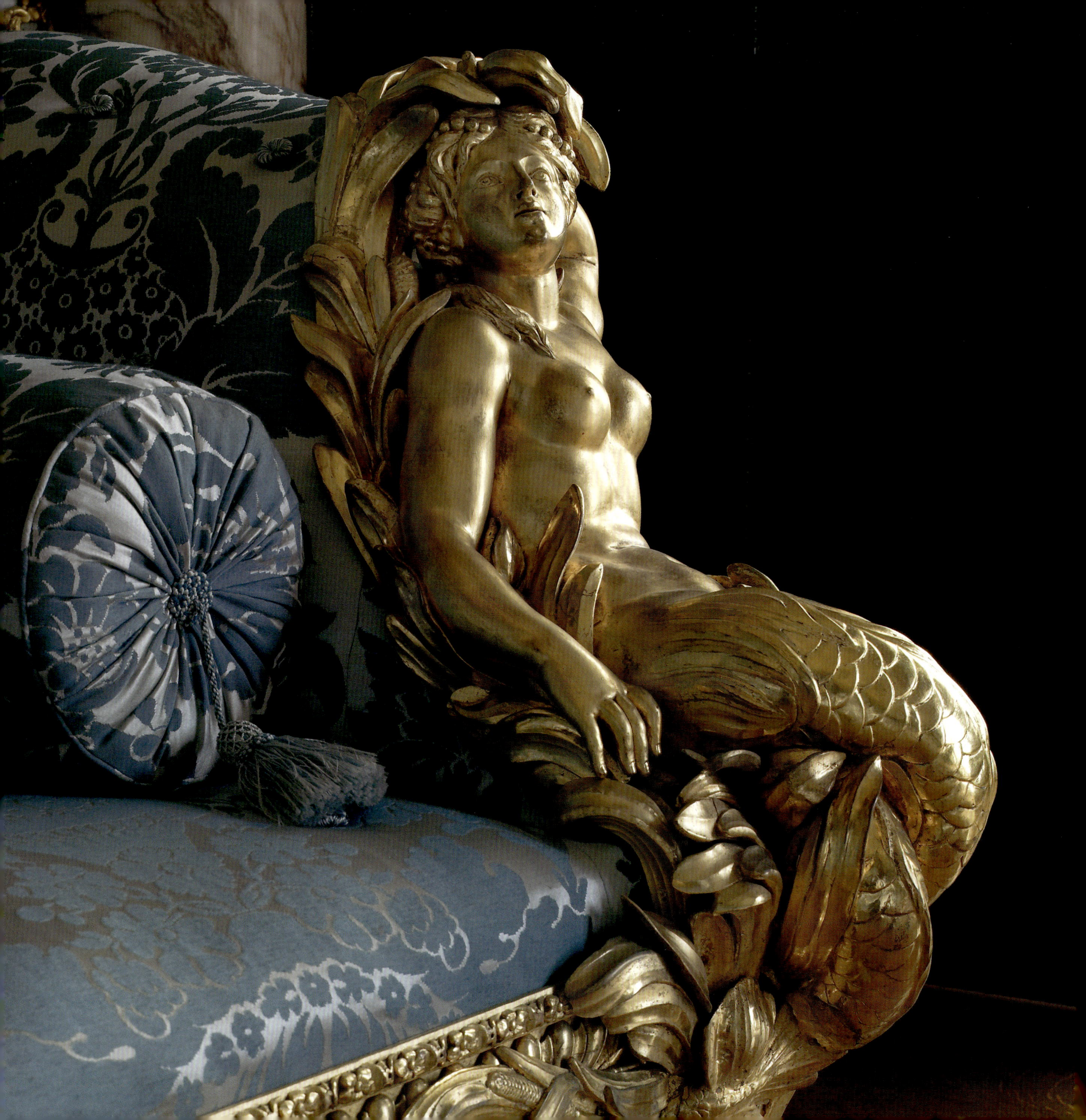

The sinuous carved and gilded mermaid figure at the end of the Linnell sofa. The carved and gilded figures on these sofas create a startling baroque effect.

This theme was followed in the exuberant seat furniture by cabinetmaker John Linnell (a drawing exists for the sofas by Adam but this is now thought to be a record of Linnell's design for the room), which was also upholstered in the same blue damask and delivered to the house in 1762. There is a clever visual link between the sinuous sea nymphs entwined with dolphins of the sofa end and the *Sleeping Cupid* in the painting hanging above it. Indeed, there is a lively link between the merfolk and the caryatids, giving the room a curiously baroque undertone that suits the drama of the great paintings in this room. Linnell also supplied the two card tables that stand under the oval wall mirrors placed on either side of the Venetian window. Adam had advised Scarsdale: "I should think that marble tables are not so proper for a withdrawing room as card tables or tables for tea china".[6]

These oval glasses were designed by Adam, framed with acanthus scrolls and anthemia, and fitted with candle-branches. These were carved by James Gravenor, who also carved the Corinthian capitals of the window and door cases. Adam prepared designs for a pair of girandoles that would have hung on either side of the chimneypiece. After the drawing room, the library is decidedly and deliberately sober and masculine. These rooms all connected with the magnificent marble hall, which is one of Adam's great triumphs, and the great dining room on the southwest corner of the house. Horace Walpole particularly admired the dining room, which he called the Great Parlour.

The blue damask of the great drawing room was removed in around 1870, and the walls painted.[7] Such a scheme never quite caught the glory of the original conception and the walls were rehung in a pale blue silk and cotton mix woven in the 1970s based on fragments in the house. The house passed to the National Trust in 1984. In the early 2000s research was carried out by Simon Murray and Tim Knox to establish the correct colour balance for new silk. A new set of hangings was woven by Richard Humphreys, closer to the blue wool-silk originally used in this room. The sofas were also recovered and the original water gilding revealed. Fittingly, the next new weaving of silk for the state apartment at Kedleston was part funded by the John Cornforth Memorial Fund, in memory of one of the great scholars of English interiors who advised the National Trust over many decades, who had taken a special interest in Kedleston and died in 2004.

The rehung drawing room is a spectacular interior and plunges the visitor back into the glorious visual feast intended in the later eighteenth century. This unforgettable room does indeed now feel, as Tim Knox wrote in 2006, "like the *gran salone* of some magnificent palace in Rome or Genoa" and fittingly recalls the palatial ambitions of Sir Nathaniel Curzon.[8]

EVOLUTION | 61

↓ A detail of a stately carved marble caryatid supporting the chimneypiece designed by Robert Adam.

→ The ensemble of the seat furniture, great paintings, and dazzling blue silk damask would have framed Lady Scarsdale, who would have received visitors seated on the sofa to the left of the picture.

62 | KEDLESTON HALL

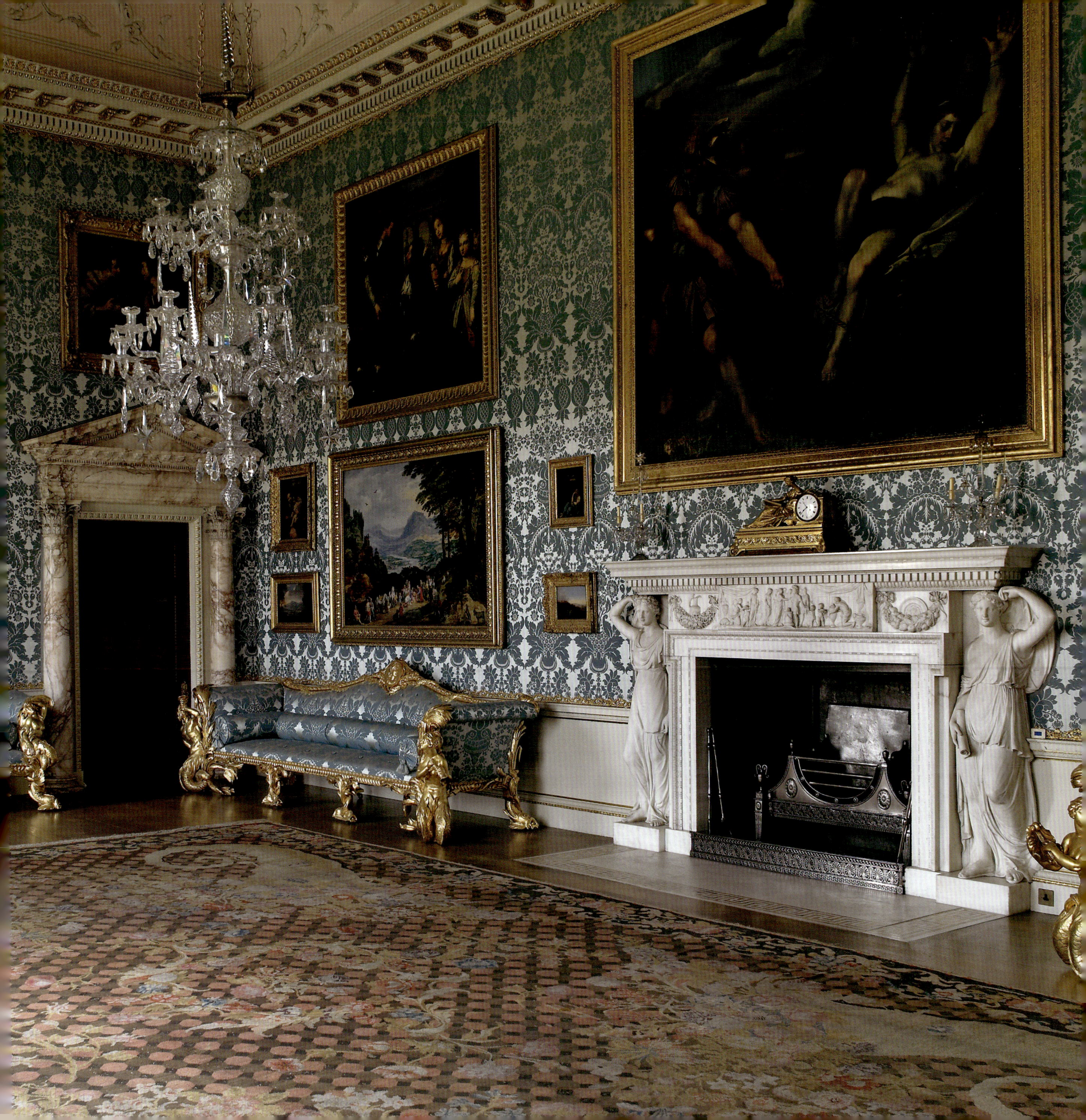

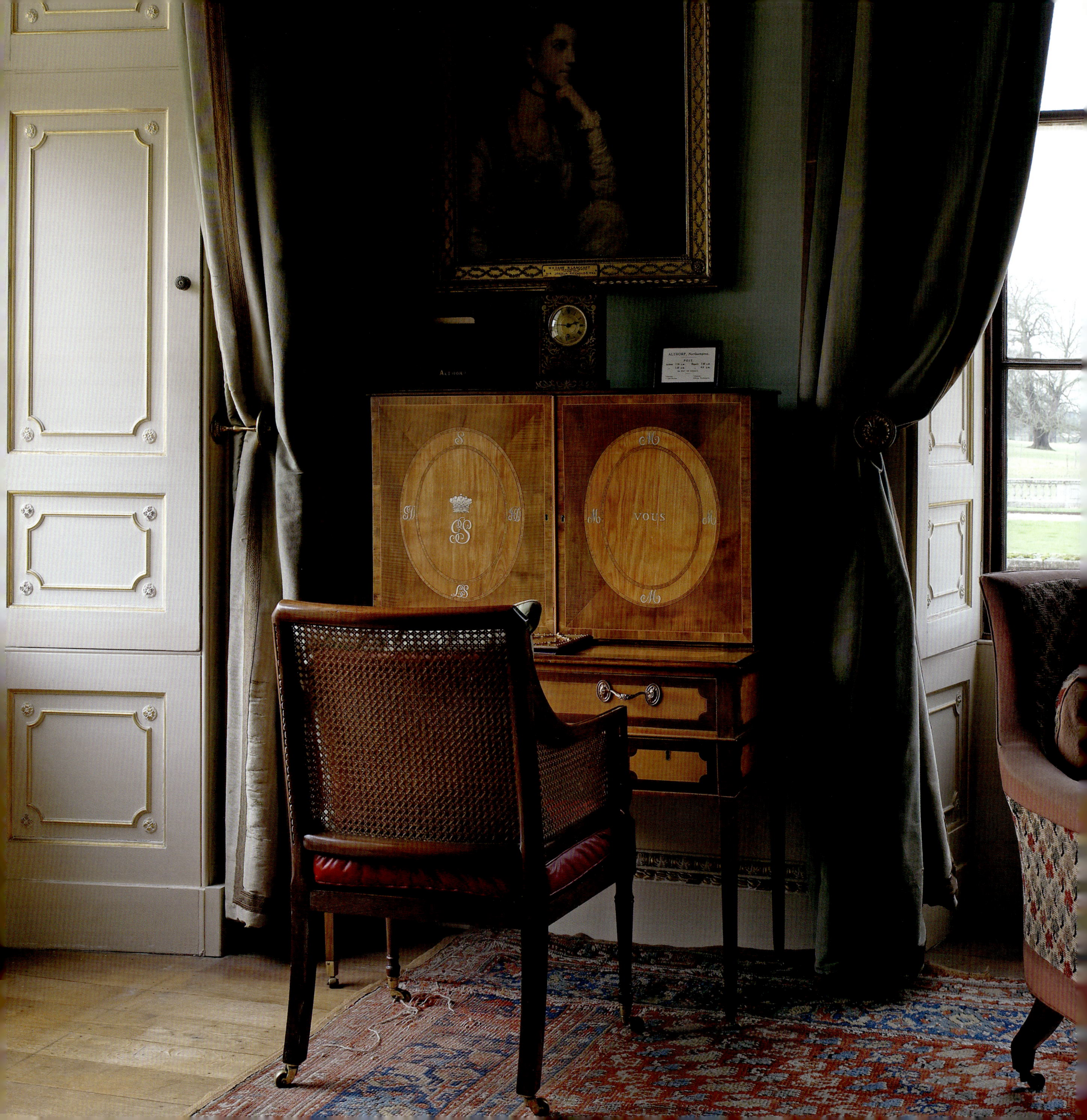
VOUS

I · EVOLUTION · THE SIXTEENTH TO EIGHTEENTH CENTURIES

Althorp

Portraits of women seen against duck egg blue walls define Earl Spencer's late-eighteenth-century drawing room.

The South Drawing Room at Althorp is a room of refined neoclassical elegance facing south and east. It has a superlative collection of Georgian portraits and is one of the high points of the suite of rooms remodelled by architect Henry Holland for the 2nd Earl Spencer, who succeeded in 1783. The originally Elizabethan house had already been remodelled in the late seventeenth century. The elegant Palladian stable block was built and the huge hunting and racing paintings by Wootton were installed in the hall in the 1730s, but otherwise the house was not greatly changed during the eighteenth century, until Holland's work.[1]

The 2nd Earl Spencer was a sharp-witted, erudite politician and bibliophile; he founded the famous Roxburghe Club and served as Home Secretary in the early 1800s. After inheriting his family seat in the 1780s, he wrote that he intended to make "the apartments we live in weatherproof" and that he was "saving the house from tumbling down."[2] He engaged the architect Henry Holland, already renowned for his own French-inspired neoclassical style. Holland was partner and son-in-law of the famous landscapist Capability Brown and was much admired for his skill in planning, as demonstrated by his work at Carlton House and Woburn. He made a great study of French architectural treatises and employed a French assistant, J. P. Trecourt, and a number of French craftsmen to deliver the style with confidence.[3]

Holland refaced the whole house with white mathematical tiles — then highly fashionable — and formed new ground floor rooms along the south range to provide the principal rooms of reception in place of the first-floor staterooms. The 2nd Earl was immensely pleased with his achievement: "the image of comfort, convenient, so cheerful, so neat, so roomy yet so compact." Horace Walpole thought the house had lost some of its "old simplicity," but as Christopher Hussey wrote in the 1950s, "we may consider he beautifully substituted a new simplicity."[4]

Althorp is the home of Charles, 9th Earl Spencer, brother to the late Diana, Princess of Wales. Author, journalist, and broadcaster, Lord Spencer has done much to restore the house, since inheriting, with advice from interior designer Edward Bulmer, with whom he reviewed the presentation of the whole house, making improvements and amendments over a number of years.[5] Lord Spencer has introduced several new colour schemes in different rooms and rehung the paintings throughout. He has carefully redecorated all the adjoining rooms on the south front, some of which had been remodelled in the 1950s by his father the 8th Earl to accommodate high-quality fittings brought from the family's London house, Spencer House. The library on the southwest corner of the house was returned to the original white scheme associated with Holland's work. The Holland rooms are all on enfilade, with openings tactfully widened in 1877 by John MacVicar Anderson for an even more fluid circulation between the rooms for social events.[6] In the most recent programme of redecoration, many pieces — from furniture to fabrics, paintings and portraits — were brought out of store.

The South Drawing Room belongs to the late 1780s work for the 2nd Earl. The low marble chimneypiece, installed in 1802, was carved by Lancelot Wood in a characteristic French style. There are later touches too, as the plaster ceiling was executed in 1865 by Broadbent of Leicester.[7] On Holland's plan this room is shown as a dining room although it is some distance from the kitchen and probably for that reason it was changed to a drawing room in the 1870s, when a large new

THE DRAWING ROOM | 65

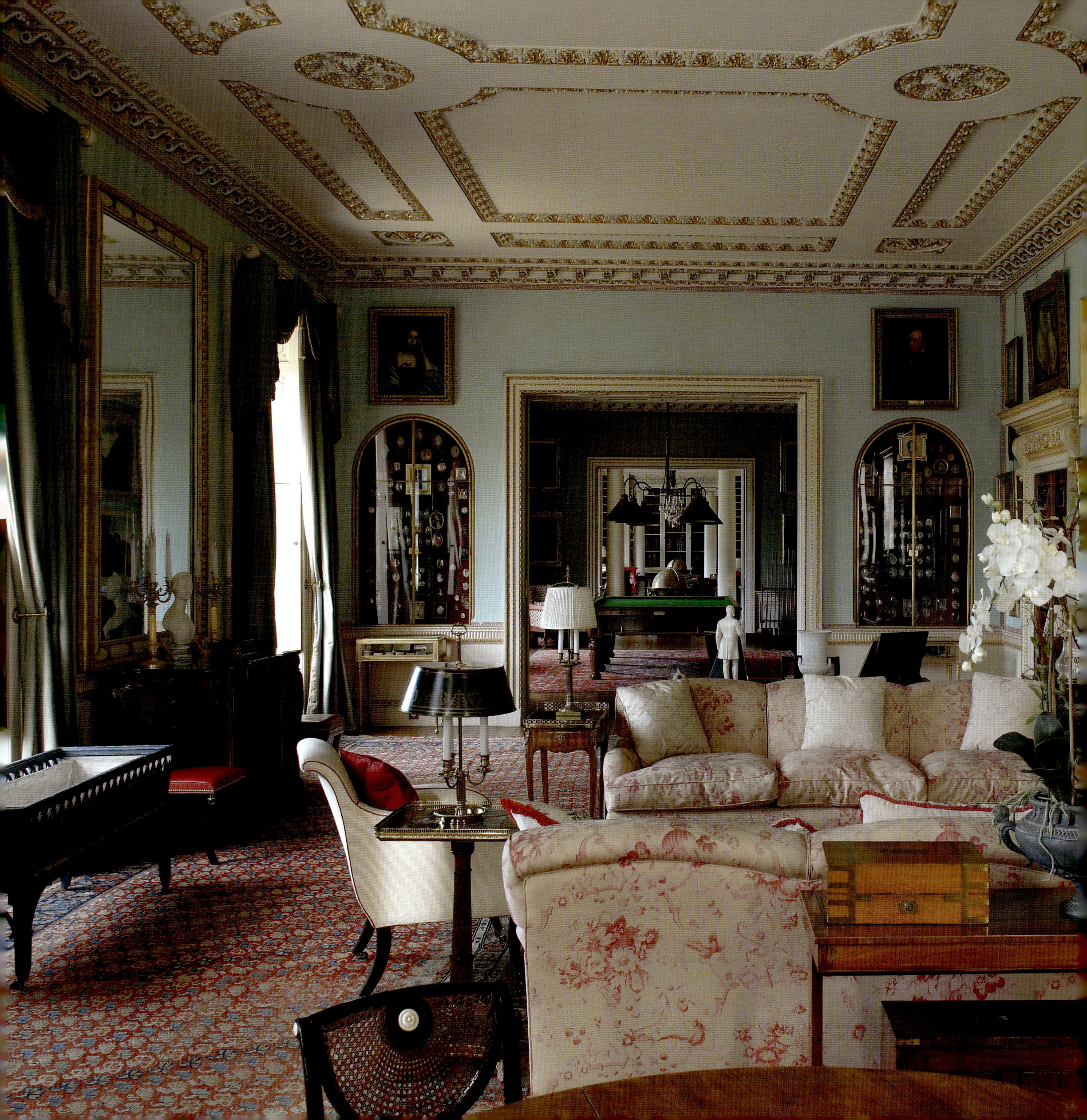

← The South Drawing Room at Althorp belongs to the 1790s remodelling of the house by architect Henry Holland. Originally the dining room, it became the drawing room in the late nineteenth century, when the axial doors were widened. The Palladian door case to the right-hand side of the picture was brought here in the 1950s from Spencer House in London.

↓ A detail of the delicate, French-inspired chimneypiece designed by Henry Holland and installed in 1802.

EVOLUTION | 67

↓ *The small needlework armchair was introduced in the recent restoration by Lord Spencer, which brought many items from the attics back into use.*

→ *The alcoves have been filled with a memorable display of a large number of delicate miniature portraits.*

dining room, nearer the kitchen, was added to designs by MacVicar Anderson. In the 1950s the South Drawing Room was rather more sparsely furnished and hung with green figured damask chosen as a fitting background for Italian paintings of the sixteenth and seventeenth centuries.

Under the present Lord Spencer, the character of the South Drawing Room has softened; the room is now hung almost entirely with the best of the eighteenth-century Spencer family portraits of women—which is partly a restoration to their historic location. These portraits are principally by Reynolds, a close friend of the Spencers, and their concentration within this one space makes it one of the unforgettable rooms in an English country house today. The most recent colour scheme was a carefully chosen duck egg blue, with a small pink paper border, which complements the dress fabrics of the eighteenth-century portraits. The aim with both the colours and the paintings in this room was to create a feminine and comfortable space. The curtains were brought out of the house's own store and reused. Two alcoves on either side of the opening to the billiard room contain a dense hang of the family collection of miniature portraits, which reinforces the sense of intimacy and interest in this room.

The furniture is comfortably arranged for modern use but makes the best of the historic context—"so neat, so roomy, yet so compact," to quote the 2nd Earl. There are some exceptional pieces, including a pair of large Saunnier lacquer commodes acquired by Henry Holland in Paris, complemented by Regency chairs, tables, and comfortable sofas. The magnificent pier glass was originally supplied for Spencer House. Several chairs are covered in gross point worked by the 7th Earl himself, while others are covered in appropriate modern fabrics. The elegant cabinet against the south wall given to Georgiana, wife of the 1st Earl Spencer and mother of the 2nd Earl who created these rooms, was affectionately inlaid with initials of her husband and their children (including the famous Georgiana, Duchess of Devonshire). The present Lord Spencer describes this in his recent book *Impressions of Althorp* (2012) as "one of the loveliest pieces at Althorp."[8] Her portrait by Reynolds hangs over the chimneypiece; it is in itself one of the great images of familial affection in any country house in England.

BY MARGARET, COUNTESS OF LUCAN
1740 — 1814

The stately South Drawing Room is lit from two sides and hung with some of the finest late-eighteenth-century portraits of women from the Spencer family, by Reynolds. The early-eighteenth-century pier glass is the focal point of a long axis through the main reception rooms.

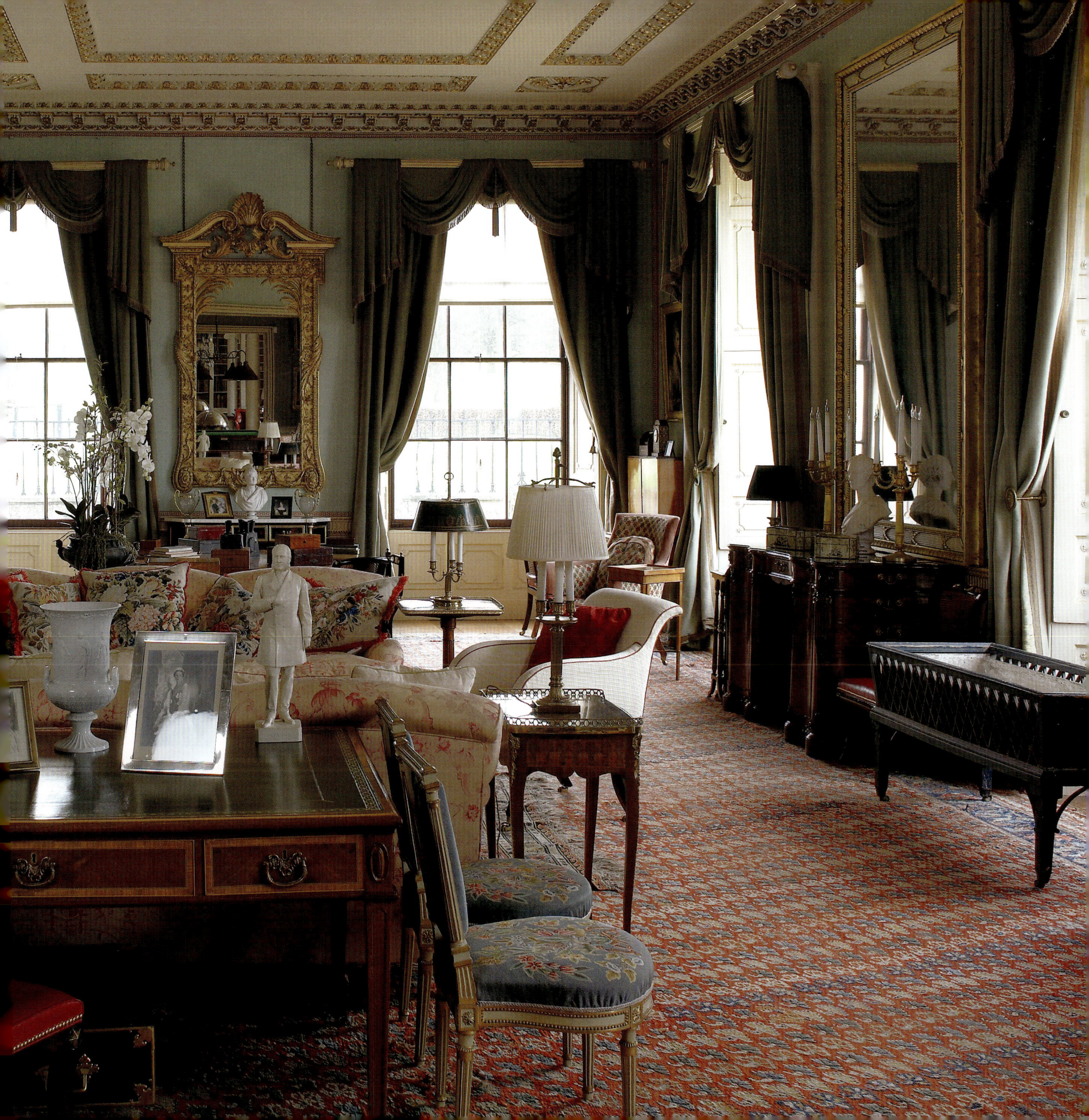

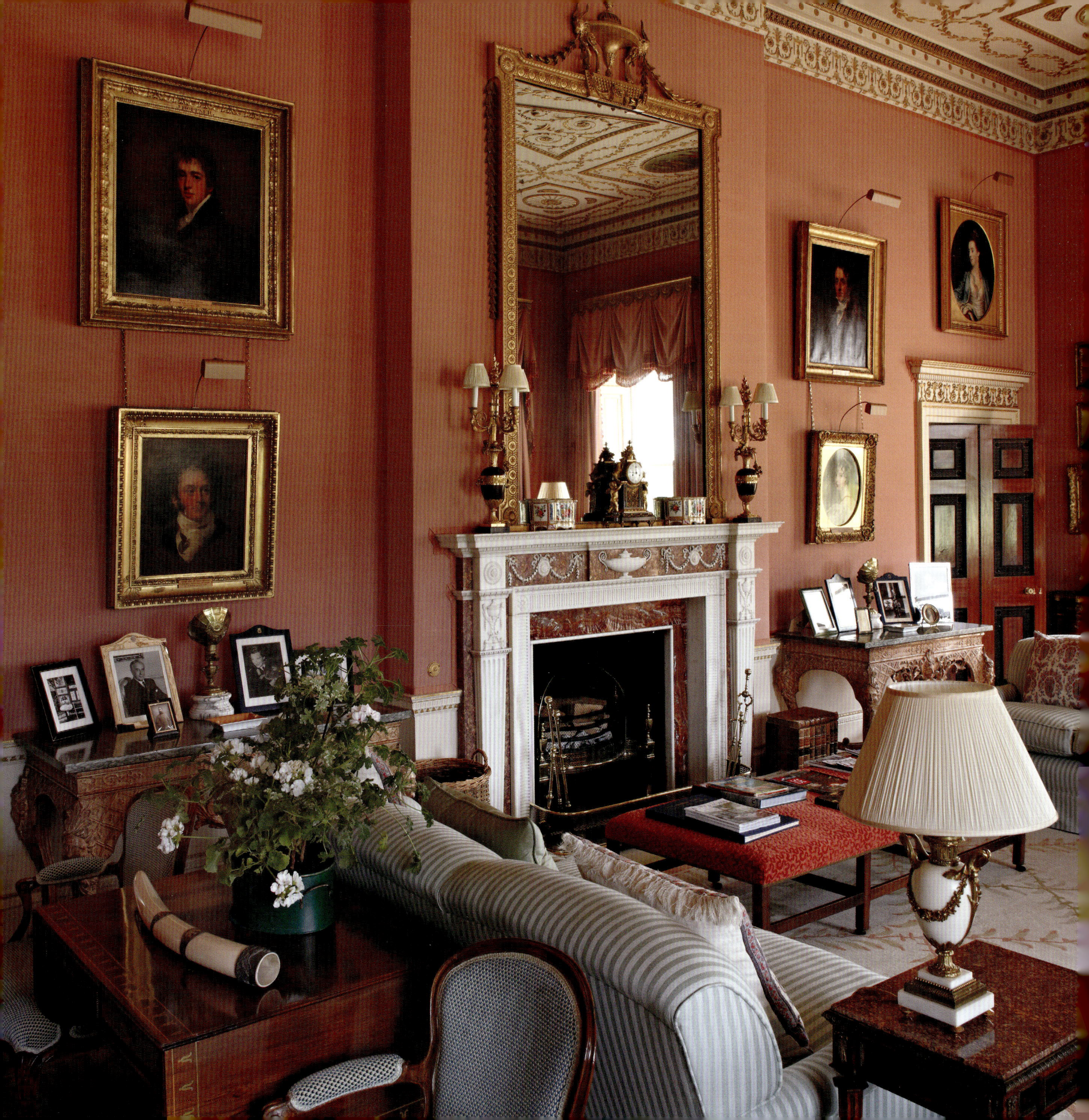

I · EVOLUTION · THE SIXTEENTH TO EIGHTEENTH CENTURIES

Broadlands

The elegant late eighteenth-century drawing room was recently redecorated with advice from David Mlinaric.

Although it appears in every way an essentially late-Georgian house, with walls of white brickwork in Flemish bond with Portland stone dressings, Broadlands in Hampshire in fact has as its core a U-shaped Elizabethan house (in the late seventeenth-century, diarist Celia Fiennes described it as a "halfe a Roman H").[1] This house was refaced and remodelled for Henry Temple, the 2nd Lord Palmerston, into a classical design of a square plan, in two main stages. The first stage was carried out in 1768–71 by the great landscapist and architect, Capability Brown, and the second in 1788 by Brown's son-in-law, Henry Holland.

Palmerston was a landowner, politician, art collector, and member of the Dilettanti and the Literary Club. Mrs. Sheridan, wife of the playwright and orator, described him as "a good natured poetical, stuttering viscount."[2] But he had taste, and in 1763–64 he went on a Grand Tour, staying with Voltaire at Ferney and travelling to Rome and Paestum. He bought antiquities from Gavin Hamilton and Piranesi, and sculptures from Nollekens.

Sadly Lady Palmerston died young in 1769, but they had a son, the 3rd Viscount, who married Emily Lamb, sister of Lord Melbourne, the prime minister to Queen Victoria. Following her marriage she wrote, "nothing can be more comfortable than this house. It is magnificent when we have company and when alone it seems to be only a cottage with a beautiful garden."[3] The 3rd Viscount's stepson inherited Broadlands and was made Lord Mount Temple in 1880. The house and estate then passed by descent to his great-nephew (also made Lord Mount Temple) and then to his eldest daughter, Edwina Ashley, and her husband, Earl Mountbatten of Burma.

The two stages of the later eighteenth-century work can be clearly seen in a comparison of the two main fronts, which nonetheless make a perfectly harmonious composition. The west front of 1771 is a refacing of the original building with an Ionic stone portico with pediment, approached by a flight of steps flanked by walls. James "Athenian" Stuart may have worked here in the 1760s on the furnishing of the reception rooms. The first volume of his *Antiquities of Athens* was published in 1762, which was sponsored by the Society of Dilettanti—of which Lord Palmerston was a leading member.[4]

The east front is the work of Henry Holland as part of the 1788 alterations, during which the ends of the Elizabethan wings were widened, and the former forecourt was filled with a recessed portico. Behind this Holland created an octagonal top-lit vestibule, which formed, with Brown's inner hall, a gallery for Lord Palmerston's collection of classical and neoclassical sculptures. The stone portico has four slender Ionic columns with pilasters at each side. T. L. Donaldson raised the wall to the attic in 1859, creating a taller elevation.

The drawing room is one of the principal rooms on the west front, part of a circuit of rooms of reception, around a central saloon. A new dining room was created on the south front by Holland in 1788.[5] The drawing room is a comfortably proportioned space, lit from the south and the east, with doors to the morning room, hall, and saloon (the latter probably widened in the nineteenth century). Thus it is a room which could always be enjoyed in its own right or as part of a suite of rooms of entertaining.

Lady Brabourne has recently overseen a refurbishment of six of the major rooms of the house and a rehang of the pictures throughout, with advice from interior designer David Mlinaric.[6] The prompt for the redecoration was, prosaically enough, the need to replace all the heating and electricity of

THE DRAWING ROOM | 73

↓ The old rose pink colour rep has been hung as part of the recent redecoration of the drawing room.

→ The late-eighteenth-century drawing room at Broadlands. The room has been redecorated by Lady Brabourne, with advice from David Mlinaric. The rep was supplied by Jean Roze of Tours, who also supplied the curtain fabric. The hand-knotted carpet was designed by Hugh Henry and supplied by Veedon Fleece.

74 | BROADLANDS

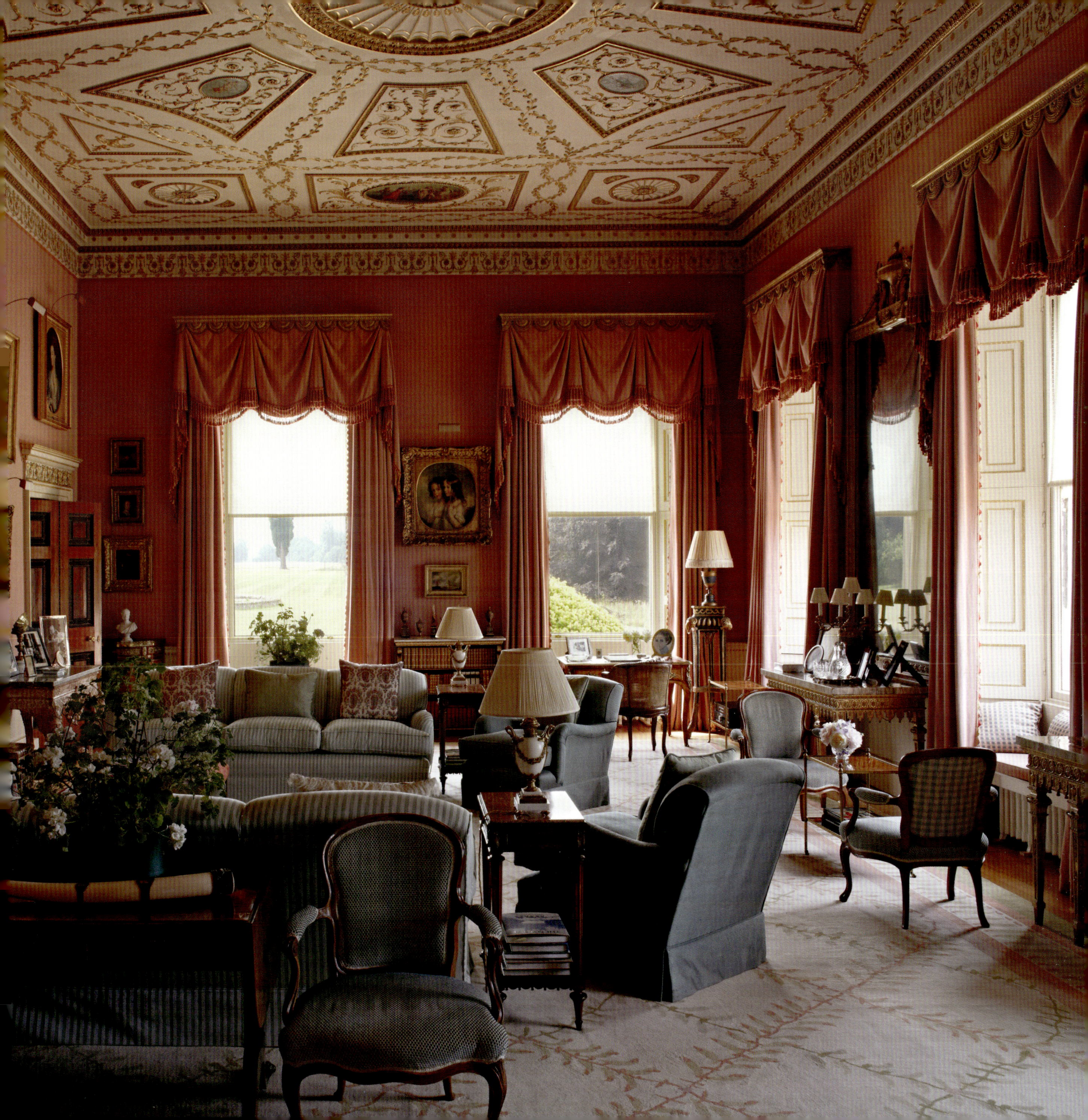

A detail of the marble chimneypiece and overmantel mirror with its closely related detail.

the house for the first time in many decades; the result was a rethinking of several of the most important rooms. The sculpture gallery was repainted. The two staircases, which lie north and south of the hall, were also redecorated and then rehung with portraits of many of the German, Russian, and English family members: Lord Mountbatten's ancestors on the north staircase and those of Lady Mountbatten on the south staircase.

The drawing room was probably changed most and yet retains virtually all of its original furnishings (including pier glasses and tables), so it is as it must always have been intended to be: a room to be enjoyed after dinner with company around a good fire, or a place to enjoy the beguiling views down to the river during the day. The scheme devised by Mlinaric was, typically for him, a careful balancing of historical understanding and evidence, with some new choices to enhance those original elements and help the room work for modern family use.

The gilding of the plasterwork ceiling, and the inset oval paintings by Angelica Kauffman, were lightly cleaned. New upholstered furniture was introduced around the chimneypiece, and grouped comfortably on a new hand-knotted carpet by Veedon Fleece. This carpet was designed by Hugh Henry and lightens the room but at the same time picks up on the interweaving leaves and colours of the plasterwork ceiling. The carpet previously in this room was reused in the dining room.

The drawing room was for a long time always hung with a textile, so the walls have been rehung in an old rose pink rep, giving an attractive warmth to the room, although the colour is subtle enough to change with the different light of the day and evening. The rep is produced by Jean Roze of Tours; curtains and wall coverings were made up by English specialists. The walls under the chair rail were repainted in the original stone colour by Hare and Humphreys, as was the woodwork and its gilding.

The drawing room also has many of the best eighteenth- and early-nineteenth-century portraits in the house, works by Lawrence, Hoppner, and Zoffany.[7] The essence of the recent work has been to reduce clutter, to simplify and make comfortable. In Lady Brabourne's words, the room now works "with the winter and summer aspects of the room. It creates a tranquil feeling which enhances the fine furniture and objects which have always been here. Above all, it has a harmony, representative of the whole house."

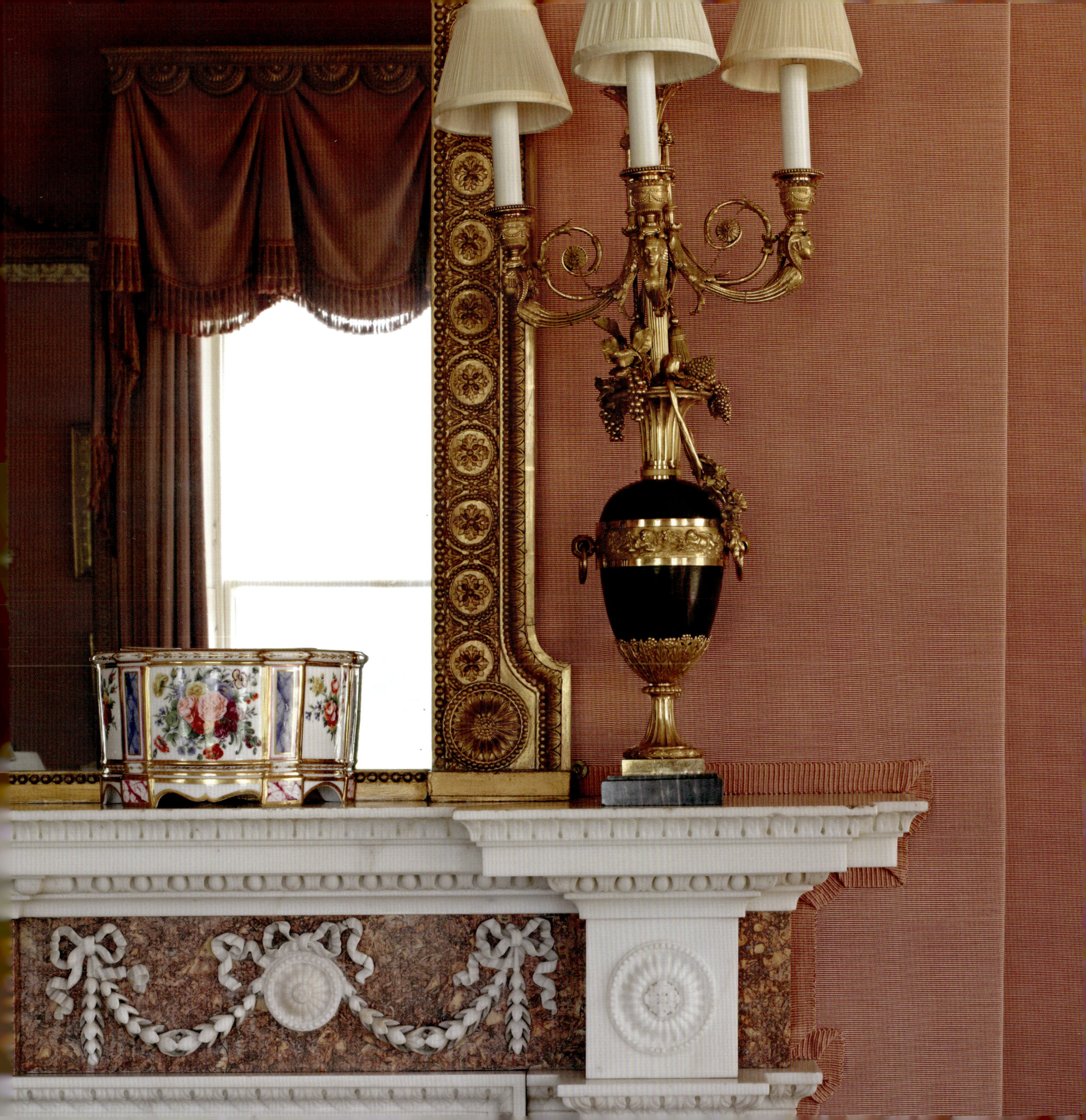

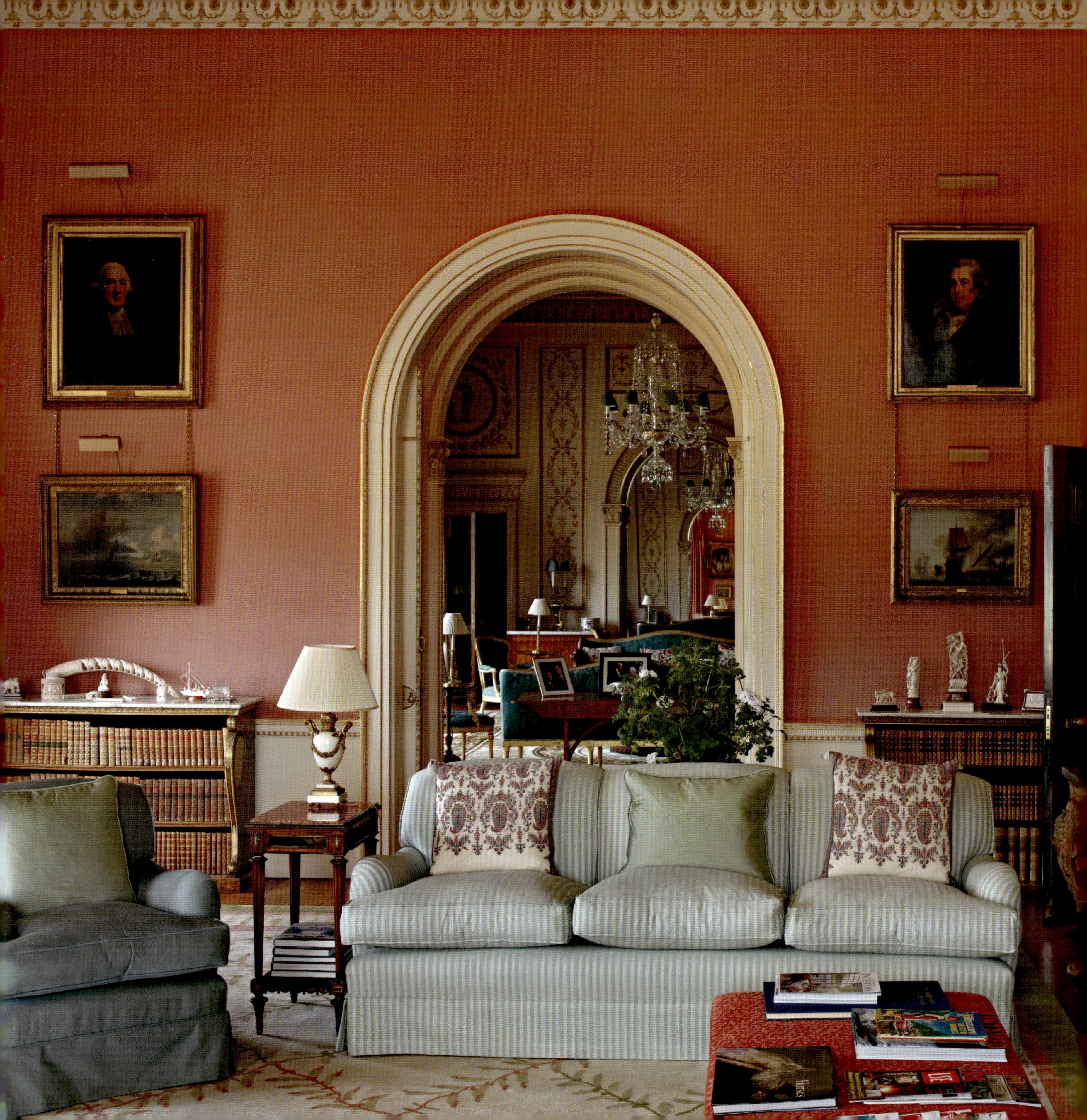

← The drawing room looking through to the saloon. Some of the best eighteenth- and early-nineteenth-century portraits of the house are hung in this room.

↓ The curtains were made up by English specialists.

EVOLUTION | 79

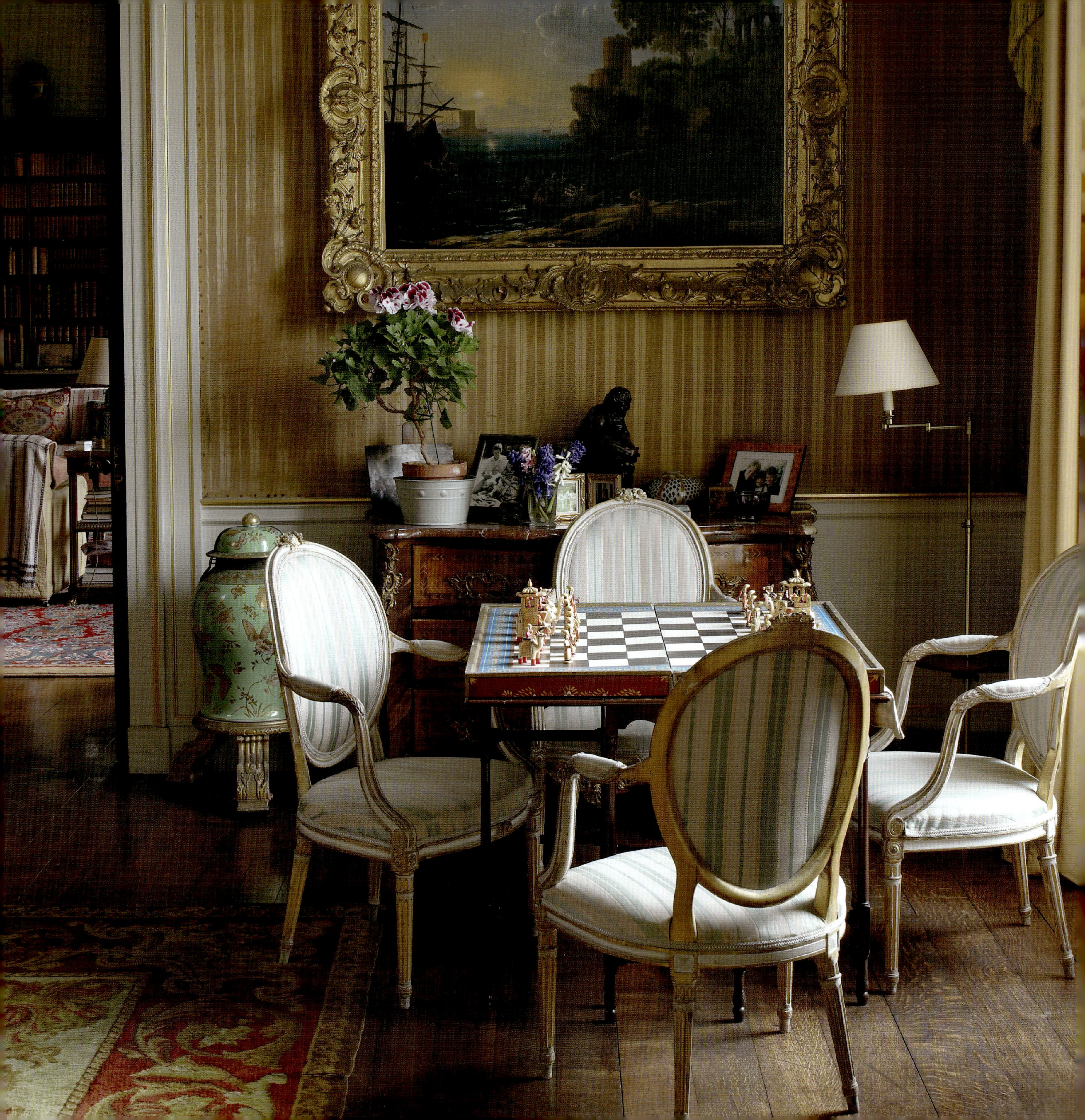

II · ELEGANCE · THE EARLY NINETEENTH CENTURY

Oakly Park

Stately and simple: an elegant Regency drawing room and library combination, designed by C.R. Cockerell.

The beauty of the drawing room at Oakly Park is the sense of well-proportioned elegance and comfort combined. It has been the drawing room since 1819, when neoclassical architect C. R. Cockerell was engaged to remodel the house for the Hon. Robert Clive, grandson of the great British general "Clive of India." R. H. Clive had just married Lady Harriet Hickman, a daughter of Lord Plymouth and later Baroness Windsor in her own right. The resulting house is considered an excellent example of what Philip Webb called the "imagination with graceful simplicity" of Cockerell.[1]

This drawing room was, in fact, originally the dining room, designed as part of the 1780s house built for the Clive family to designs by Shrewsbury architect John Haycock. The plasterer Joseph Bromfield created the delicate and naturalistic wreaths of vines and wheat — typical decorative motifs for a dining room. The drawing room has a mid-eighteenth-century chimneypiece, thought to have come from Clive of India's town house on Berkeley Square in London.[2]

The elegant proportions of the room were clearly carefully studied by Cockerell, who added a completely new library of identical size but in the more restrained Greek revival style, adjoining it through tall double doors. As in many Regency houses, the rooms could almost be treated as one, but the library also played the role of a more intimate family sitting room. Cockerell also remodelled the great top-lit staircase hall, which connected the rooms to the entrance hall, and created a new dining room, which he extended again in the 1830s.

Having met on the committee of the Travellers' Club, Robert Henry Clive and Cockerell were clearly friends as well as client and patron. Cockerell had made an extensive tour of Italy and Greece, drawing on this experience in his designs — especially in his use of the Doric order from the Temple of Apollo at Delos.[3] He also included in the hall a cast of the bas relief of the Temple of Apollo at Bassae, which he had helped to excavate himself. The library chimneypiece was given a distinctly Indian character presumably as an homage to Clive of India.

Cockerell was proud of their "joint labours" over ten years at Oakly Park and referred to the solid proportions "shewing a refinement that would escape vulgar eyes" and considered the work "a very picture" of his patron. He liked his patron and described him as "of the modern school … Bred in diplomacy in the midst of all the exertions made in the late wars, companions of Wellington and Castlereagh … [with] no corrupting leisure of Italy or India."[4]

A young American visitor, Anna Maria Fay, described a dinner party at Oakly in 1852 in a letter home, and her account gives a vivid picture of how the rooms of the house, as redesigned by Cockerell, were used, decorated, and enjoyed.[5] On arrival guests were greeted by "two footmen in red plush breeches and blue coats and silver buttons, and the groom of the chambers in black," who led them through the staircase hall and into a "large and beautiful library … an elegant circle of ladies and gentlemen rose to meet us." The party made a little procession into the dining room, also designed and indeed later also extended by Cockerell. The magnificence and many-coursed meal is described minutely, as is the seating plan, with all its nuances of social precedence and hospitality. At a signal from Lady Harriet, the ladies withdrew to the drawing room, "coffee was brought in and some of the ladies sat down to their beautiful worsted work, while others disposed themselves around the room."

Anna Maria notes the paintings in the room, including the two Claude landscapes acquired by Benjamin West for

THE DRAWING ROOM | 81

↓ The curtains and gold striped silk hangings were introduced to Oakly Park, Shropshire, by John Fowler in the 1950s.

→ The drawing room was designed originally as the dining room of the house in the 1780s by John Haycock. The plaster ceiling was by Joseph Bromfield. It became the drawing room in 1819 during works by C. R. Cockerell, which added a larger dining room and also the adjoining library.

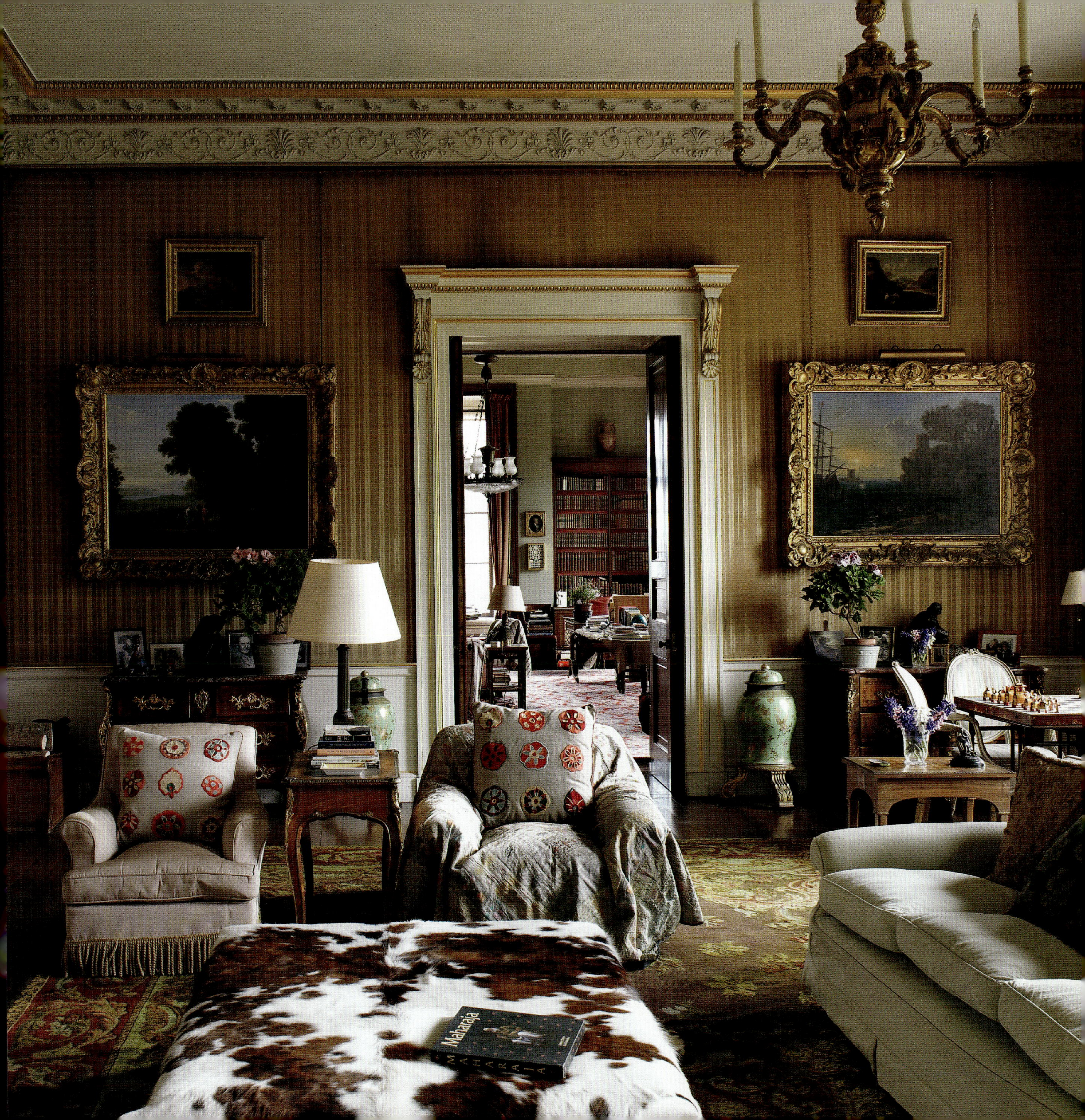
Maharaja

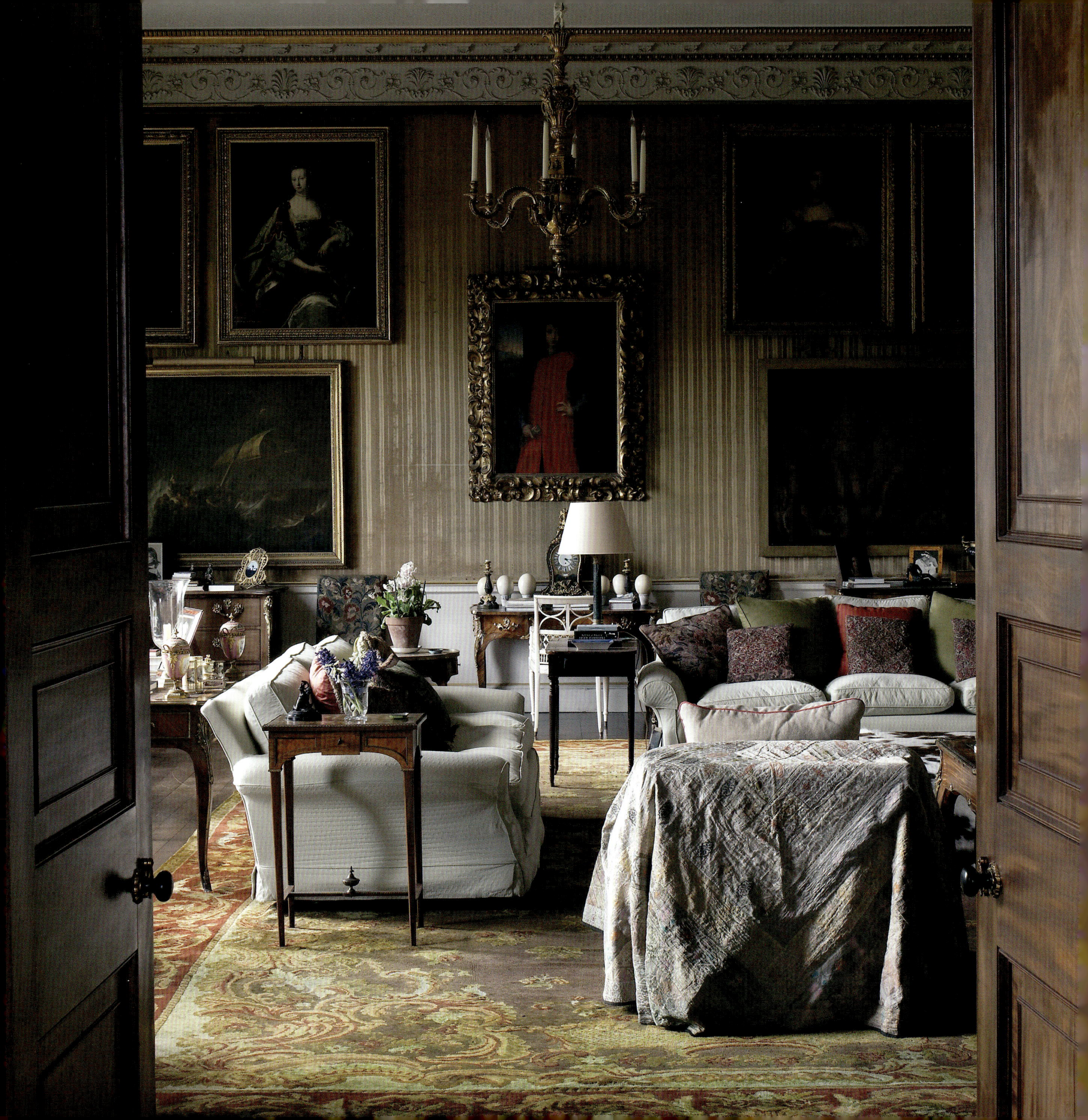

Looking from the library through the double doors to the drawing room, which is hung with some of the finest pictures in the house

the Clives—which still hang in this room today, as does Thomas Lawrence's portrait of Lady Harriet. Anna Maria asks Miss Clive to show them her watercolours of Italy, which she does, and lithographs of Mr. Clive's Middle Eastern subjects are also discussed. When the gentlemen join the ladies, Lady Harriet entertains them with pieces on the piano, composed by Blumenthal. Songs are performed by the family before the American guests are called upon to sing "Negro Melodies," such as the "Blue Tail Fish," which they do to applause.

R. H. Clive died in 1854, so this delightful vignette of the formal dinner party and the associated use of the drawing room capture the house as it was intended to function after his long period of improvement with his architect Cockerell. The house was once again in effect a dower house and then let to cousins, so that when it was photographed by Bedford Lemere in 1892, we see the drawing room and library much as they were in the 1850s, with the addition of more comfortable seating and plants. At that time the Windsor-Clive family's principal seats were St. Fagan's Castle in Wales, and the newly built Hewell Grange in Worcestershire. By the middle of the twentieth century, both of these great houses had been sold, and Oakly Park in its magnificent landscape setting became the family's principal house, but only after being used for military purposes during the Second World War and a sale of furniture and works of art to settle death duties.

The present Earl of Plymouth spent four decades repairing the house and bringing the interiors back to a worthy condition, supplementing the picture hang with works of art from other family houses. Lord Plymouth now lives in another house on the estate and his son, Viscount Windsor, and his family live at Oakly. John Fowler advised Lord and Lady Plymouth in the 1950s, and suggested the striped gold silk on the walls in the drawing room that gives an appropriate Regency elegance to the room. Viscount Windsor and his wife, the Viscountess Windsor, have continued to enhance these rooms over the past twenty years, and a comparison of articles in *Country Life* in 1990 and 2012 admirably show this continuing process of stylish but historically sensitive treatment.[6]

Lord Windsor acknowledges the example of his father, and the advice and encouragement of the late John Napper, a distinguished artist and family friend. The overall Fowler colour scheme has been preserved, and the picture hang and furnishing in both the drawing room and the library follow in spirit those shown in the Bedford Lemere photographs. The unfinished sketch portrait of Robert Henry Clive by Lawrence hangs in the drawing room close to that of his wife, and the end wall is focused on a striking Italian Mannerist portrait of a young nobleman. There are also modern and individual touches, especially in the soft furnishings and textiles, from India, that make this a comfortable room for today's use while retaining the spirit of the Regency original.

The library at Oakly Park, Shropshire, designed by C.R.Cockerell, with the drawing room seen through the double doors. As in many Regency houses, these rooms would have been used together.

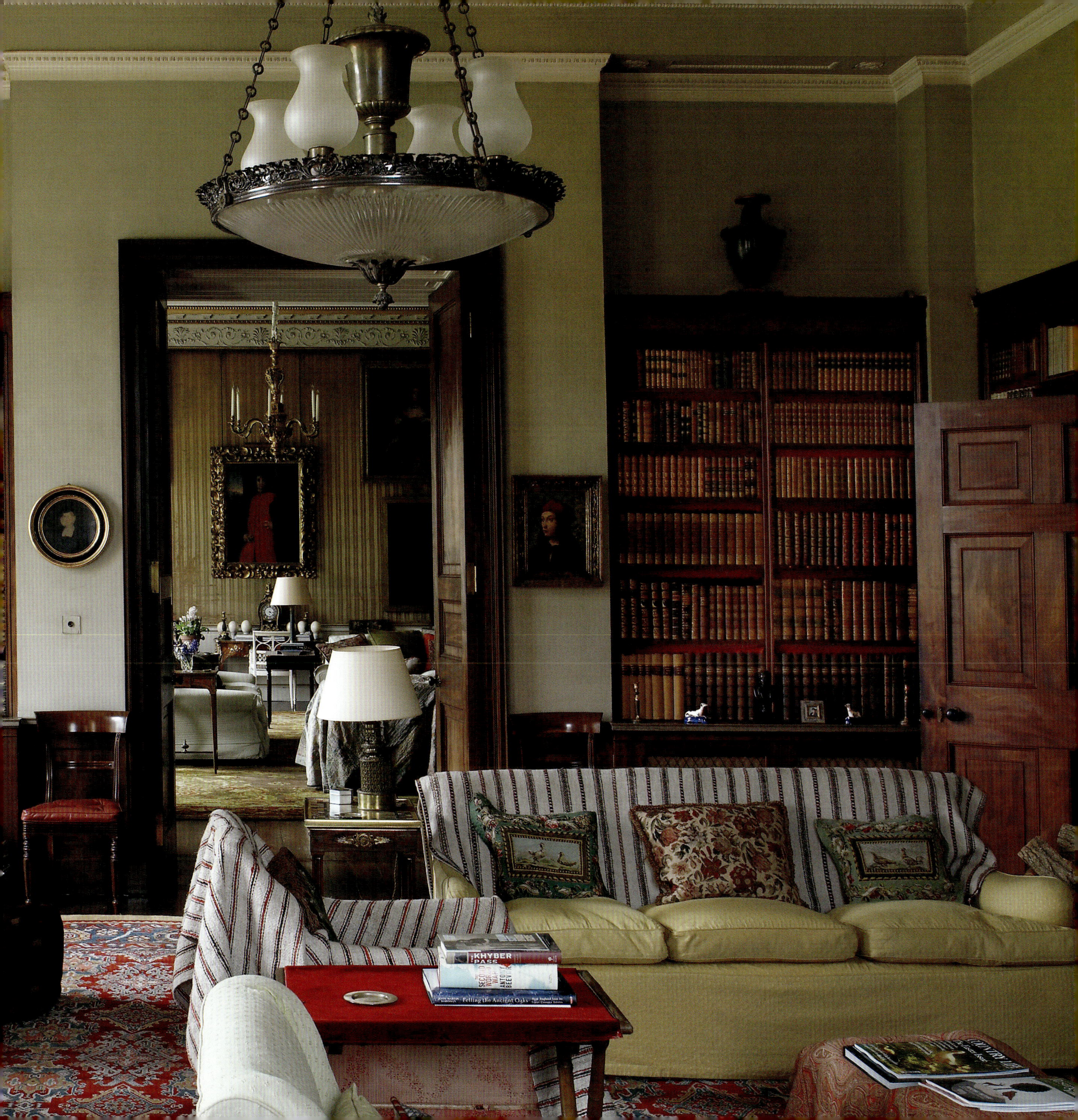
KHYBER
PASS
Felling the Ancient Oaks

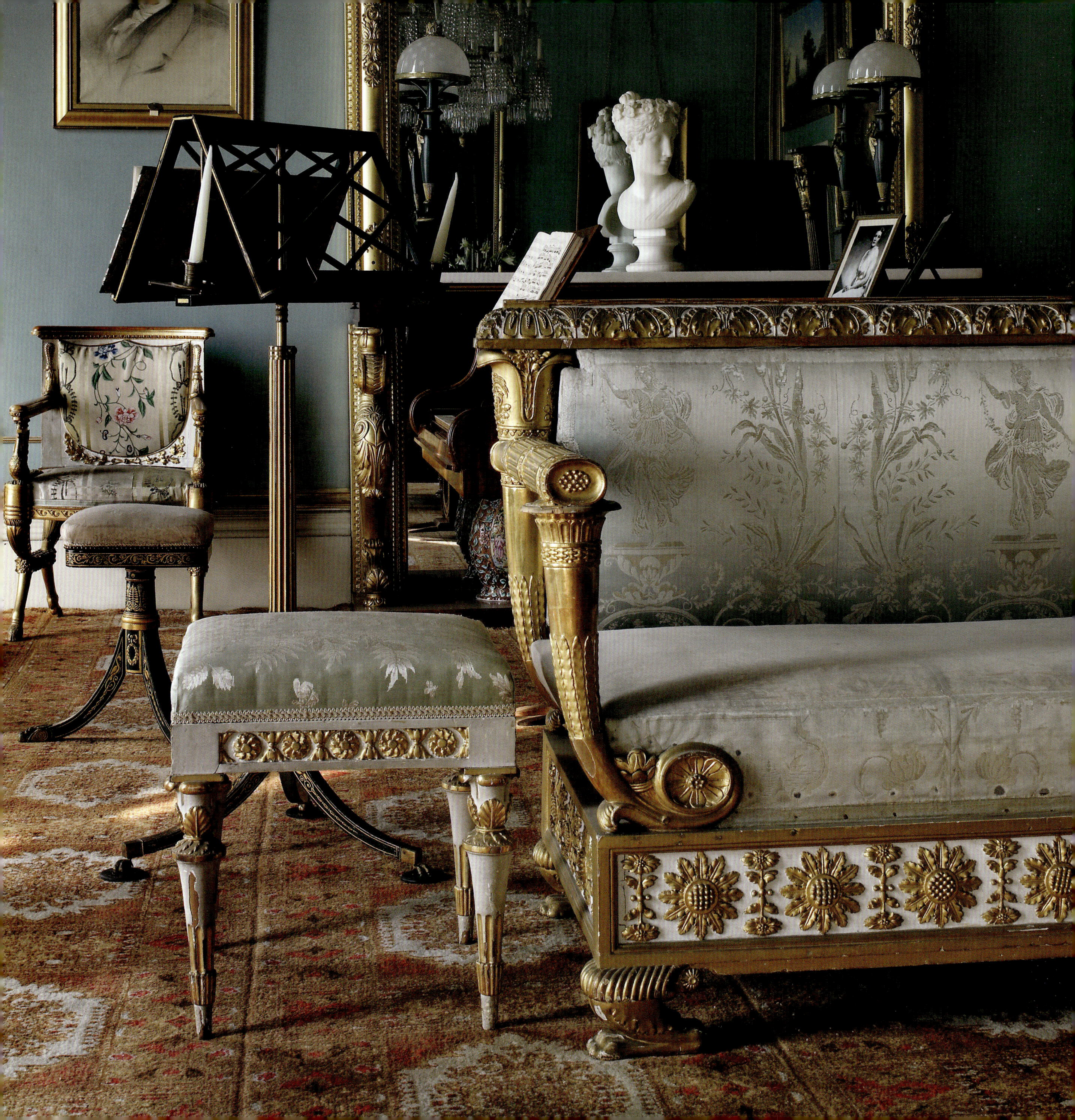

II · ELEGANCE · THE EARLY NINETEENTH CENTURY

Attingham Park

Mediterranean muses: A classical room with furniture from the palace of Caroline Murat, Queen of Naples.

Attingham is one of the great houses of Shropshire, and the drawing room illustrates the evolving currents of classical taste of the eighteenth and early nineteenth centuries—with an attractive Italianate twist of early-twentieth-century artistic taste. The dining room and drawing room lie on either side of an elegant hall with grey marbled walls and scagliola columns. The dining room is a cavernous red room, while the drawing room is a pale sky blue. The furniture, art, and decoration inspired architectural writer Gervase Jackson-Stops to describe this room, in his book *The English Country House: A Grand Tour*, with accuracy, as "a breath of the Mediterranean in rural Shropshire."[1]

The drawing room is one of the major rooms of reception on the south front of the 1780s house built for Noel Hill, the 1st Lord Berwick, by George Steuart around an older house (known as Tern Hall). A sequence of smaller rooms, including a boudoir, extend back from the drawing room, and two libraries behind the dining room, reflecting a division of these suites into the accepted masculine and feminine zones. Steuart's design included the delicate plaster ceiling decoration. The portrait by Angelica Kauffman of the 2nd Lord Berwick on his Grand Tour still presides over the room today.[2]

The centre of the house is taken up with a huge picture gallery designed and built in 1805–07 by John Nash for Thomas, the 2nd Lord Berwick, who carried out an almost ten-year programme of redecoration of the house from around 1805. This Lord Berwick was an irrepressible collector and patron who collected the Kauffmans and Hackerts that hang in the drawing room to this day.

The unique quality of the drawing room's furniture, however, also owes much to the 2nd Lord Berwick's younger brother, William, later the 3rd Lord Berwick.[3] William was a successful diplomat who leased the house from his brother, saving it from being sold or denuded of its contents altogether when the latter became bankrupt, and also managed to buy back some of the paintings and furniture being sold in 1827. He also brought to Attingham the results of his own two decades of living and collecting in Italy. This included the highly unusual suite of gold and white neoclassical furniture, some upholstered in blue silk, some in a flowered pattern. This came originally from the Palazzo Belvedere, the home of Napoleon's sister, Caroline Murat, Queen of Naples, which Lord Berwick had leased as a residence—he presumably acquired the furniture at the end of his occupation.

The drawing room is mentioned in bills and accounts from the 1790s as the "Great Drawing Room," and a George Burnett was paid for hanging pictures and putting up curtains. The chimneypiece was installed in 1799. In 1806 the room was painted in "wet lake," a crimson red colour; one visitor in 1808 described the room as "hung with crimson," but this could refer to the damask curtains (or the walls could have been lined with fabric).[4] A considerable amount of gilding was carried out in 1812–13, perhaps to please Thomas's new wife, a young woman of great beauty but no great reputation, called Sophia Dubochet. Much of the gilding of this date survives, although recent research in the accounts by James Finlay suggests that the room was also hung with paper by Gillow & Co.

In his 1816 book *The Stranger in Shrewsbury*, Thomas Howell described the "house ... built originally from a design by Mr. Stewart, but it has lately undergone a very expensive alteration, under the superintendence of Mr. Nash; the rich and costly carvings and ornamental furniture were executed by Mr. Donaldson, of Shrewsbury, whose correct taste in that fine art

THE DRAWING ROOM | 89

↓ Attingham Park, Shropshire. The 8th Lord Berwick introduced the Canova figure of Venus in the 1920s to complement the furniture he had inherited.

→ The stately classical drawing room at Attingham Park in Shropshire is part of the 1780s house designed for 1st Lord Berwick by George Steuart; 2nd Lord Berwick, who can be seen in the portrait over the chimneypiece, carried out a ten-year programme of redecoration and had a picture gallery created by Nash.

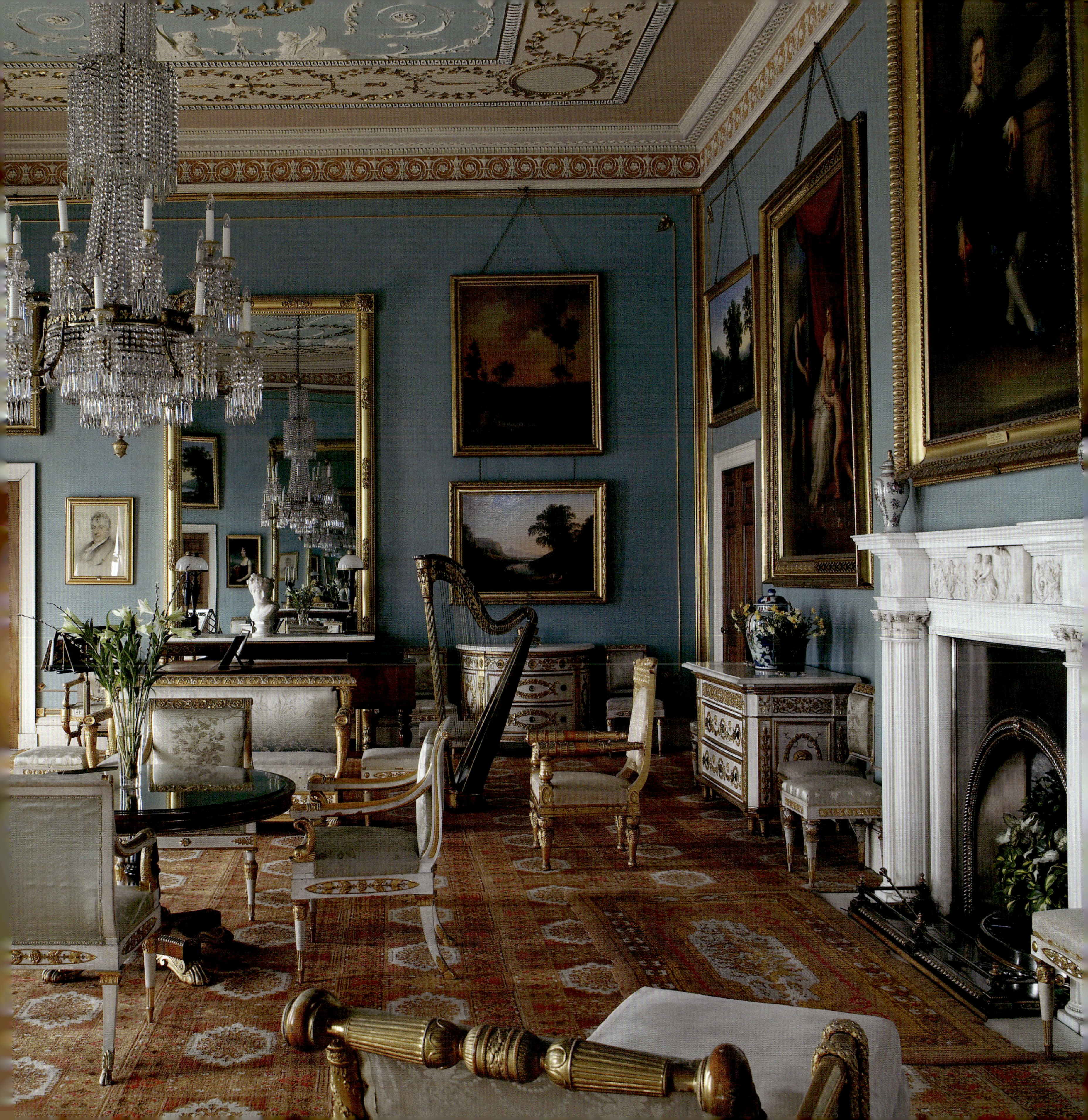

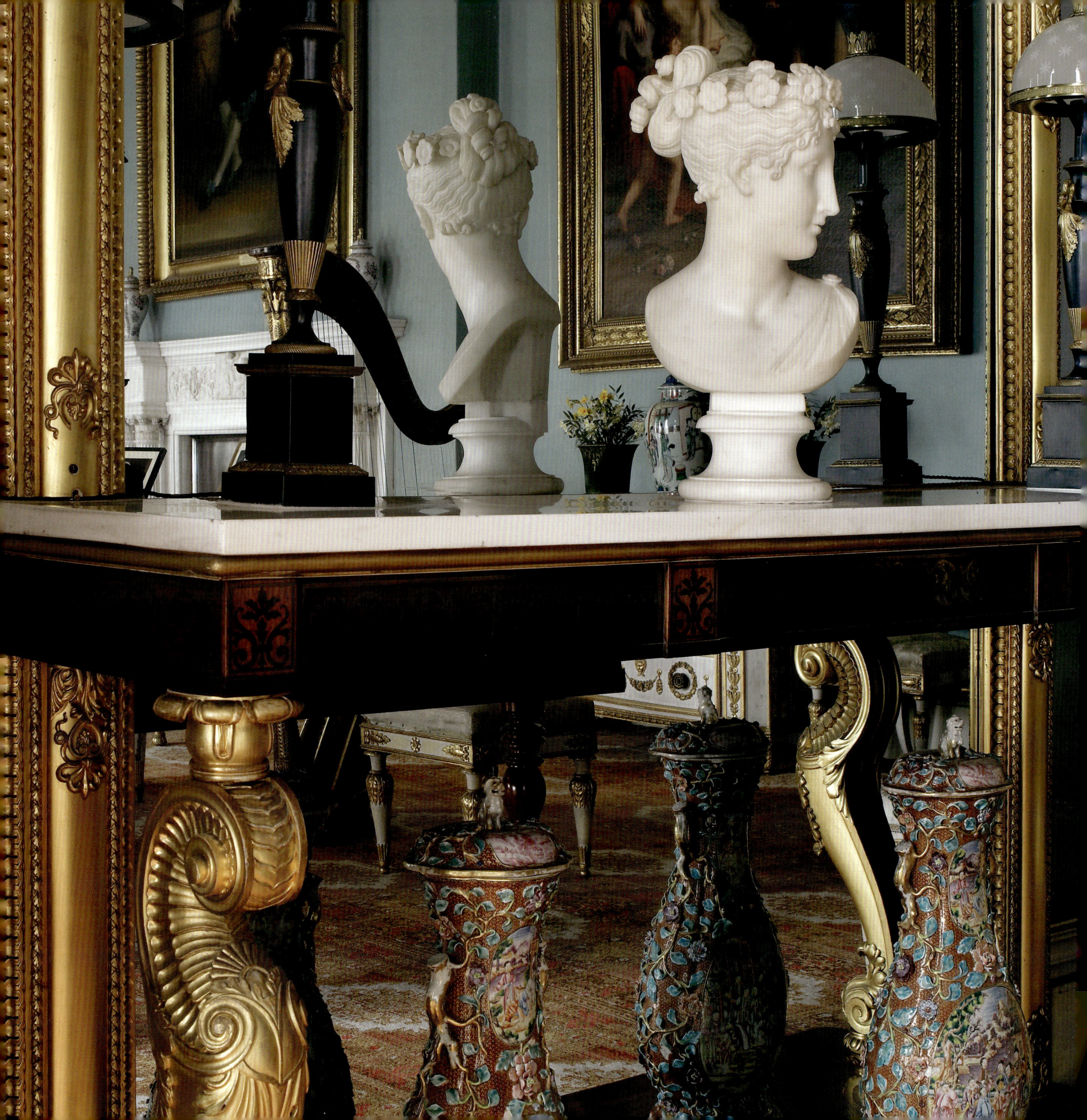

The pier table, gilt-framed mirror, and vases show the rich contrasts of texture and reflection in the drawing room.

is too well appreciated to need any eulogium here. The suite of drawing rooms is superbly furnished with immense plate glasses and burnished gold furniture, and the ceilings are richly gilt."[5]

Despite the upheavals of the 1820s, the drawing room was richly refurnished during the 1830s and maintained as a really magnificent room. Its later nineteenth-century appearance was described in detail in *The County Seats of Shropshire*, 1891: "The East Drawing Room is a spacious apartment, furnished in the most luxurious fashion. The ceiling is picked out in delicate tones of salmon colour and blue, relieved with gold; it has floral decorations, and a border of snow-white marble. The suite is almost fabulous in value and unequalled in beauty. The frameworks of the chairs are mounted in gilt, while the seats are covered in satin, worked with figures and flowers.... The greater part of this magnificent furniture was brought from Italy during the time of the French war. Several large mirrors add to the brilliancy of the effect."[6] The author also mentions work by Velázquez, Italian landscapes by Hackert, and mythological subjects by Angelica Kauffman.

The only notable period of change for the drawing room after the 1830s was in the early twentieth century, although it is, in its way, a significant one. Thomas, the 8th Lord Berwick, who inherited in 1897, took his responsibility seriously. He bought French art and furniture for the house, especially in Paris, where he was in the diplomatic service. He was married in 1919 to Teresa Hulton, an accomplished musician who had been raised in Venice and Florence as the daughter of a distinguished English artist resident in Italy, William Hulton—a friend of Sargent and Sickert—and famous for painting interior views of palaces and their courtyards.

The Berwicks had intended to live at Cronkhill, the more manageably sized Italianate house designed for the 2nd Lord Berwick's agent by John Nash. But unable to find a tenant for the main house, they were obliged to move into it and began a period of restoration and redecoration that included introducing blue silk curtains, commissioned from the factory that had supplied the silk for the furniture to the 8th Lord Berwick in 1911, before his marriage. The walls were painted in a pale blue to complement these new curtains. The original colour scheme of crimson must have been superseded in the late nineteenth century, as photographs suggest a pale wall colour in the early 1900s.

The Berwicks both brought considerable artistic sensitivity to their redecoration of the house, and were advised on the picture hang and colours by one Reggie Temple. Lady Berwick wrote to her mother on July 27, 1920: "We had some people to tea at Att on Sunday—took all the covers off drawing room and gallery—the house looked lovely. We have rehung the drawing room pictures with Reggie (Temple) ... also brought more white and gold furniture in there. Reggie was quite delightful ... He has taught me how to gild and next year will paint the blank panel in the Boudoir for us."[7]

The Berwicks also acquired the Canova sculptures for the room, including the *Venus Italica*, which stands between the windows, reflected rather effectively in the pier glass. The portrait of Caroline Murat by Louis Ducis was bought by Lord Berwick in 1927 (from the sale of the collection of the former Empress Eugenie of France). This hangs now in the drawing room on the east wall, where a portrait of Lady Berwick also hangs. Photographs taken for *Country Life* in 1956 show the room's slightly spare but elegant arrangement that could well have been devised for a painting by Sargent or William Hulton.[8] The house and estate were left to the National Trust in 1947, and great efforts continue to be made to preserve the artistic ensemble of this memorable room.

ELEGANCE | 93

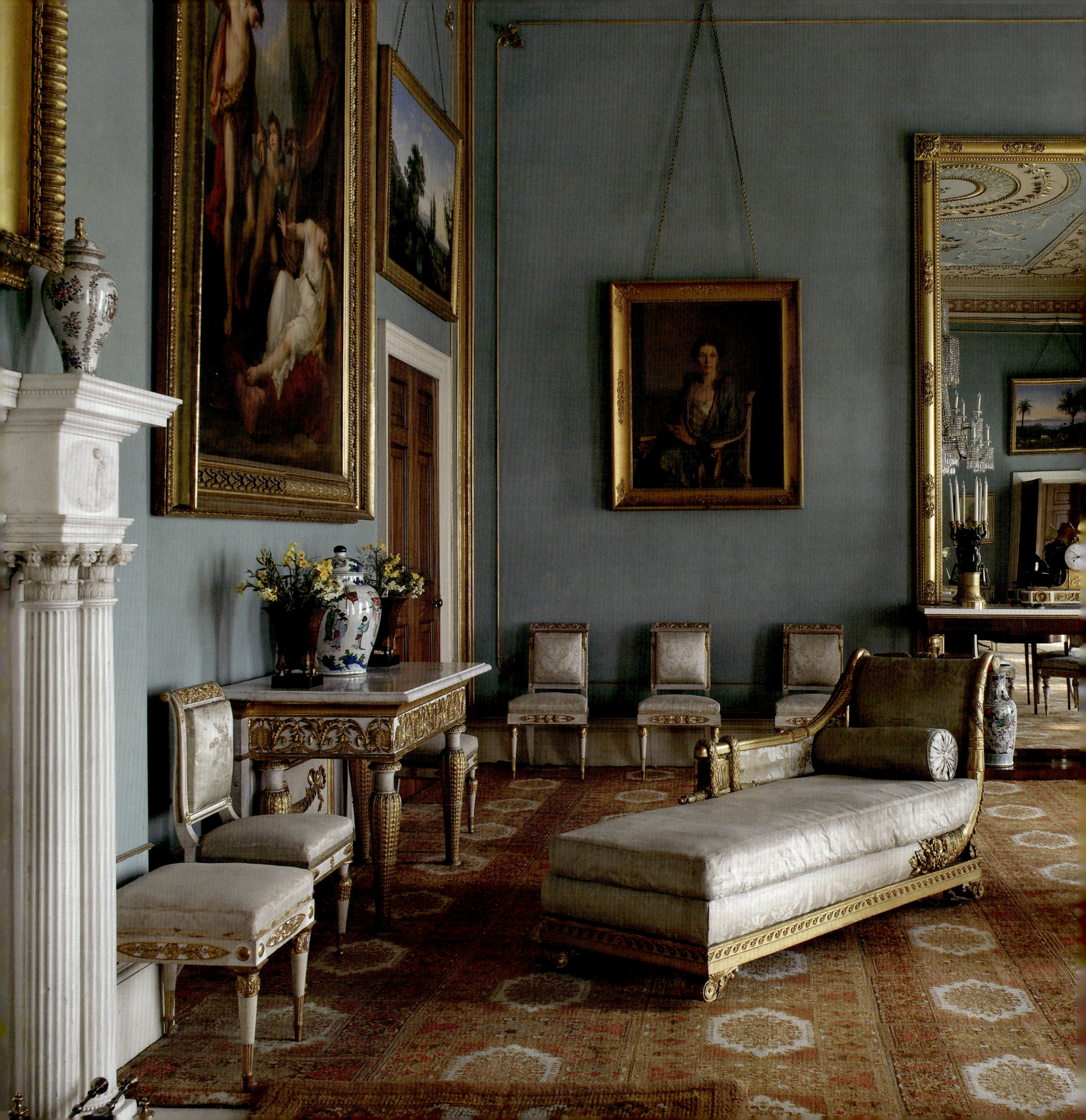

← Some of the white-painted neoclassical furniture came from the home of Napoleon's sister, Caroline Murat, one-time Queen of Naples, and was acquired by the 3rd Lord Berwick. A portrait of Caroline Murat can be seen to the right of the mirror. The room was described in 1891 as "furnished in the most luxurious manner."

↓ The blue silk for the curtains was commissioned by the 8th Lord Berwick in 1911–12 and put up in the 1920s.

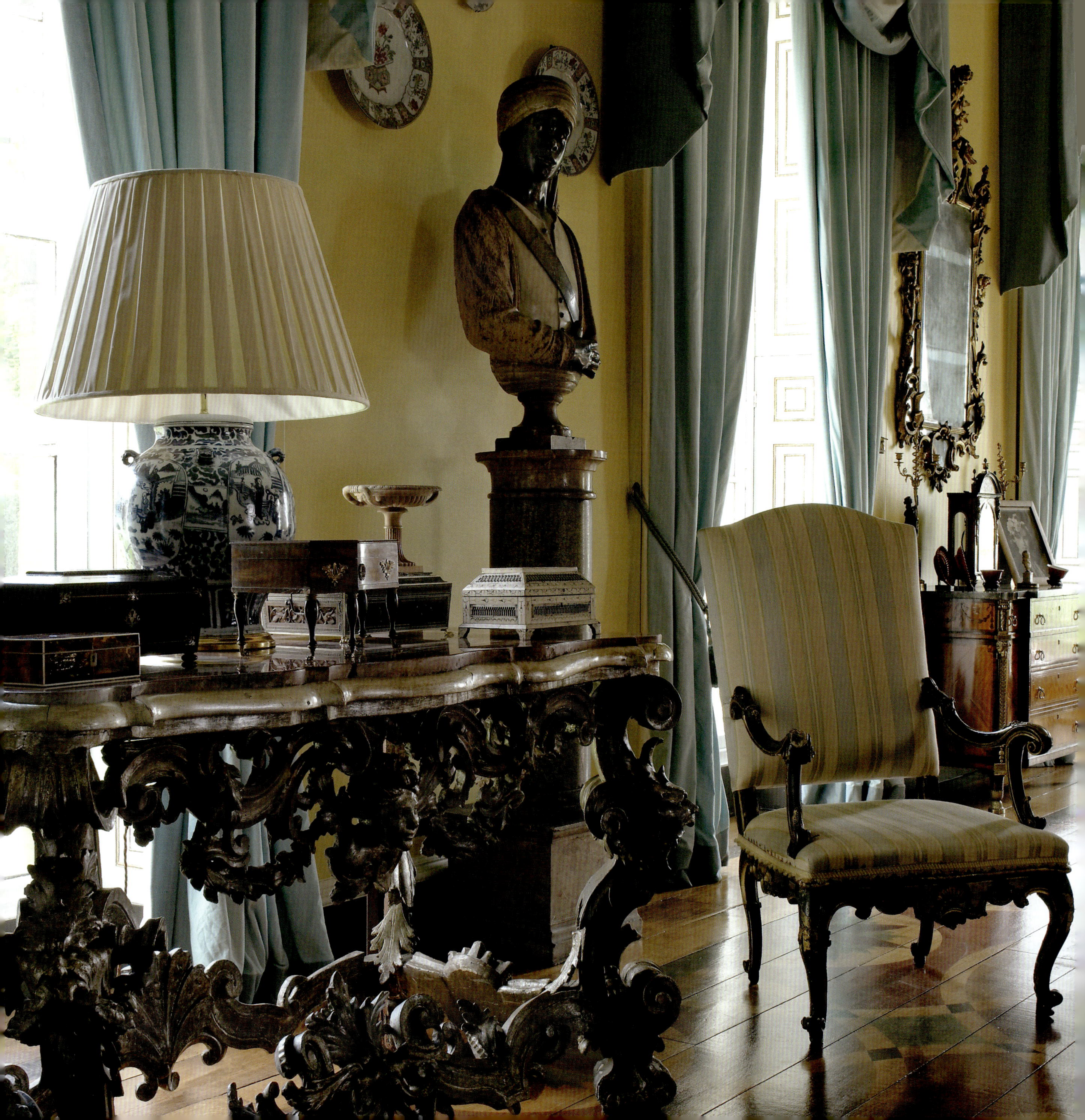

II · ELEGANCE · THE EARLY NINETEENTH CENTURY

Renishaw Hall

Fun and poetry: the Sitwells' drawing room is the model of a room designed for modern country house hospitality.

Renishaw Hall in Derbyshire is at heart a Jacobean house but was considerably enlarged between 1793 and 1808 for Sir Sitwell Sitwell. He had inherited the estate in 1793 and began to extend the house immediately, adding a huge new dining room with an apsidal recess for the buffet designed by the Sheffield architect Joseph Badger, completed by 1795.[1] Sitwell clearly got a taste for building, and Badger was almost immediately called upon to design a large new drawing room, completed by 1803. Badger then began on a huge ballroom, which was completed in 1808 just in time for a visit from the Prince Regent and his daughter Princess Charlotte (the prince's *fleur de lys* crest appears on the plasterwork decoration of the ceiling). These high-ceilinged Regency rooms are approached through the low-ceilinged rooms of the Jacobean core of the house, with the result that the late Sir Reresby Sitwell used to say that the house "opened up well."[2] Indeed, Sitwell Sitwell was rewarded for his ambitious building and hospitality with a baronetcy in 1808.

Sir Sitwell is said to have furnished the house throughout with notable extravagance, but only a few objects survived a major contents sale in 1847. Amongst the finest pieces to remain in the house is the Chippendale commode, which still stands today on the west wall of the drawing room between the two doors. The commode may well have come from Melbourne House (now Albany) in London as it is closely identified with one supplied for that house in the 1770s and sold in 1802 (the sale is almost certainly the source for the marble chimneypiece in the dining room at Renishaw).[3] Sir George Sitwell's memoirs recalled his step-grandmother saying the commode, which he thought was French, had been in the house in 1798. Above this fine piece of furniture hangs the other great masterpiece in the house, the huge John Singer Sargent group portrait of Sir George, Lady Ida Sitwell, and their children, commissioned in the spring of 1900, the sitting for which was recorded in vivid detail in Osbert Sitwell's memoirs *Left Hand! Right Hand!*[4]

After exhibition at the Royal Academy, where it was admired by Sergei Diaghilev, among others, the painting was intended to be hung at Renishaw Hall as a companion to the Copley portrait now hanging in the dining room. Osbert Sitwell relished pointing out its innate absurdities: Sir George (who seldom rode) wears polished riding boots, while his charming but wayward mother Lady Ida was the picture of the dutiful wife, elegantly arranging flowers in a silver bowl—something she would have never done at home. Sir George remarked to the painter that his plain daughter's nose was crooked, which Sargent thought cruel so he painted her nose straight and Sir George's crooked. It is nonetheless one of the great group portraits of an English landed family, posed against carefully chosen heirlooms brought down from Renishaw Hall to the artist's studio in Chelsea for the purpose.

A watercolour by Sewell records the room as it was in around 1820, with a panel of the tapestry by De Vos—one of a set of three still in the room today—just visible. Osbert's younger brother recalled how the De Vos tapestries, which dominate the drawing room, inspired his enthusiasm for the European Baroque on which he became a leading authority, publishing the bestselling *Baroque and Rococo*.[5]

Sir George consulted the cabinetmaker Temple Smith about taking the De Vos tapestries to Montegufoni, his castle in Italy, shortly before the First World War, and discussed the gaps they would leave. Sir George remarked, "it doesn't much matter ... because when I have people here I always take them straight through into the ballroom, so they never see this part of the drawing room."[6] In 1906 he had sought the advice of

THE DRAWING ROOM | 97

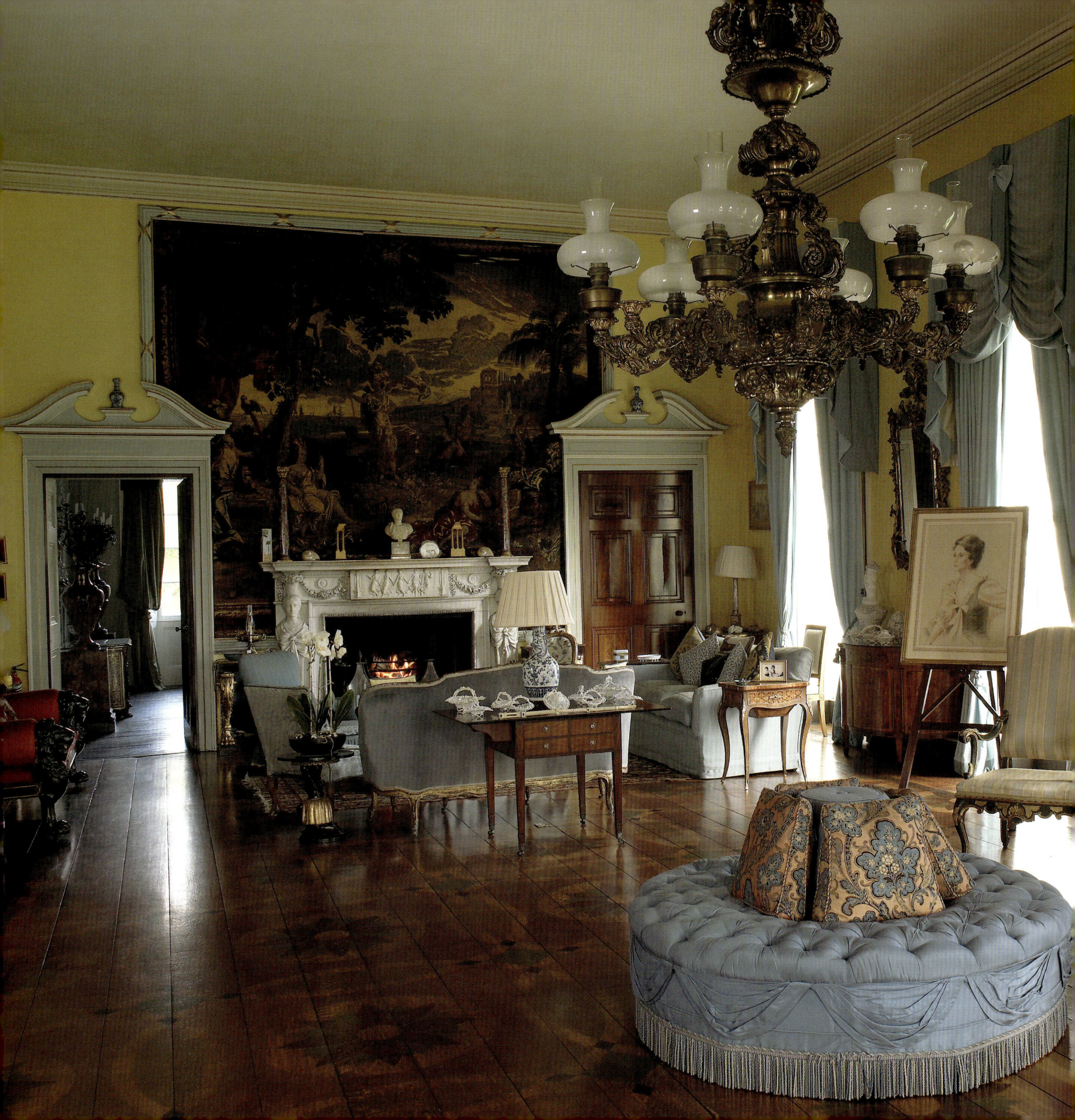

← The spacious drawing room at Renishaw Hall, Derbyshire, designed by Joseph Badger for Sitwell Sitwell and completed in 1803. The floor was painted in the 1980s to resemble the painted floor at Pavlosk Palace.

↓ The tall windows frame views to the Italian-inspired garden laid out by Sir George Sitwell. The curtains belong to a period of modern revival in the 1980s and were introduced by Lady Sitwell.

ELEGANCE | 99

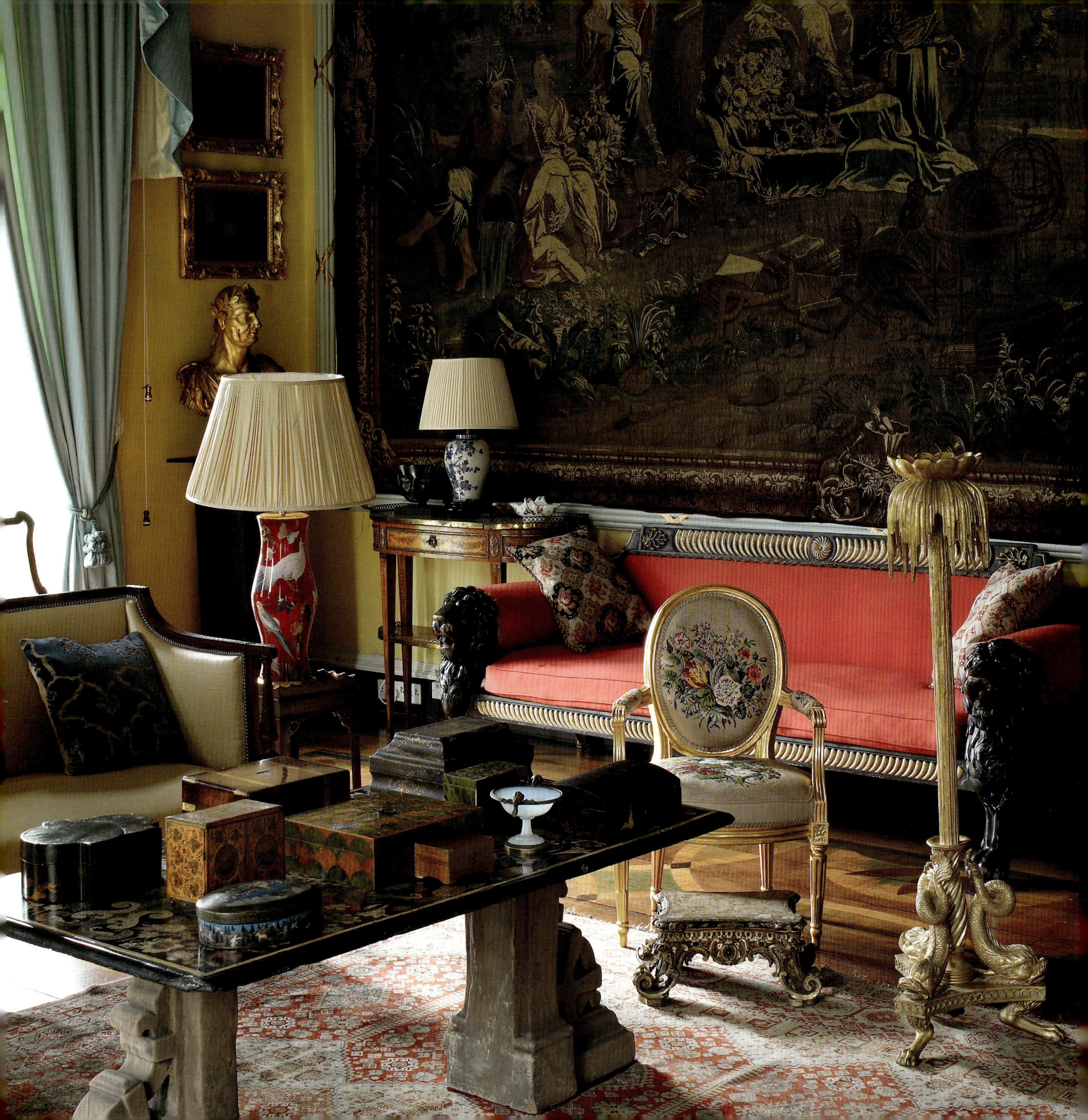

← The De Vos tapestry has been in this room since the early nineteenth century and is recorded as one of the inspirations for Sacheverell Sitwell to study the European Baroque.

↓ The Sargent group portrait of Sir George and Lady Ida Sitwell and their three talented children, Edith, Osbert, and Sacheverell; it depicts the Chippendale commode which was taken down from Renishaw to Sargent's studio in London, to serve as a prop.

J. L. Davenport of Watts & Co., who had advised him to concentrate his Italian furniture in the ballroom, and it appears in that year that Sir George rearranged the lofty ballroom as "a sitting room." It seems Lutyens was also consulted on reordering the Regency rooms but only worked on the anteroom in the end.

In the Sewell watercolour—published in John Cornforth's *Quest for Comfort*—a settee can also be glimpsed that is one of a pair supplied to the house by Thomas Oxenham of Oxford Street in 1808.[7] The colza oil chandelier is also original to the early 1800s refitting and remains in the room today. This watercolour shows an elegant and comfortable room literally crammed with upholstered armchairs and sofas, a piano and a harp, and tall pier glasses on the walls (there seems barely any space to move but many places to drop into a comfortable seat and talk). Afternoon tea was a feature of life, as we know from the memoirs of Mrs. Campbell Swinton, who recorded that it was "not until about 1849 or 1850, when I was about twenty-six or twenty-seven, that five o'clock tea in the drawing room was made an institution, and then only in a few fashionable houses where the dinner was as late as half-past seven or eight o'clock."[8]

A similar feeling of hospitable comfort and aesthetic elegance is still evident in the drawing room at Renishaw Hall today, although a different character was introduced by Sir George Sitwell, who was responsible for some of the Italian furniture in the room. It was redecorated in the 1980s by Sir Reresby and Lady Sitwell, whose daughter Alexandra and husband Rick Hayward live there now. The walls are a rich yellow and the curtains a pale blue, while the floor has been stained in a decorative pattern inspired by the early-nineteenth-century treatment of the floors at Pavlosk Palace in Russia by Janet and Paul Czianski.[9] It is an ingenious touch, adding a suitably idiosyncratic and theatrical twist to the Sitwellian stamp of this elegant interior.

ELEGANCE | 101

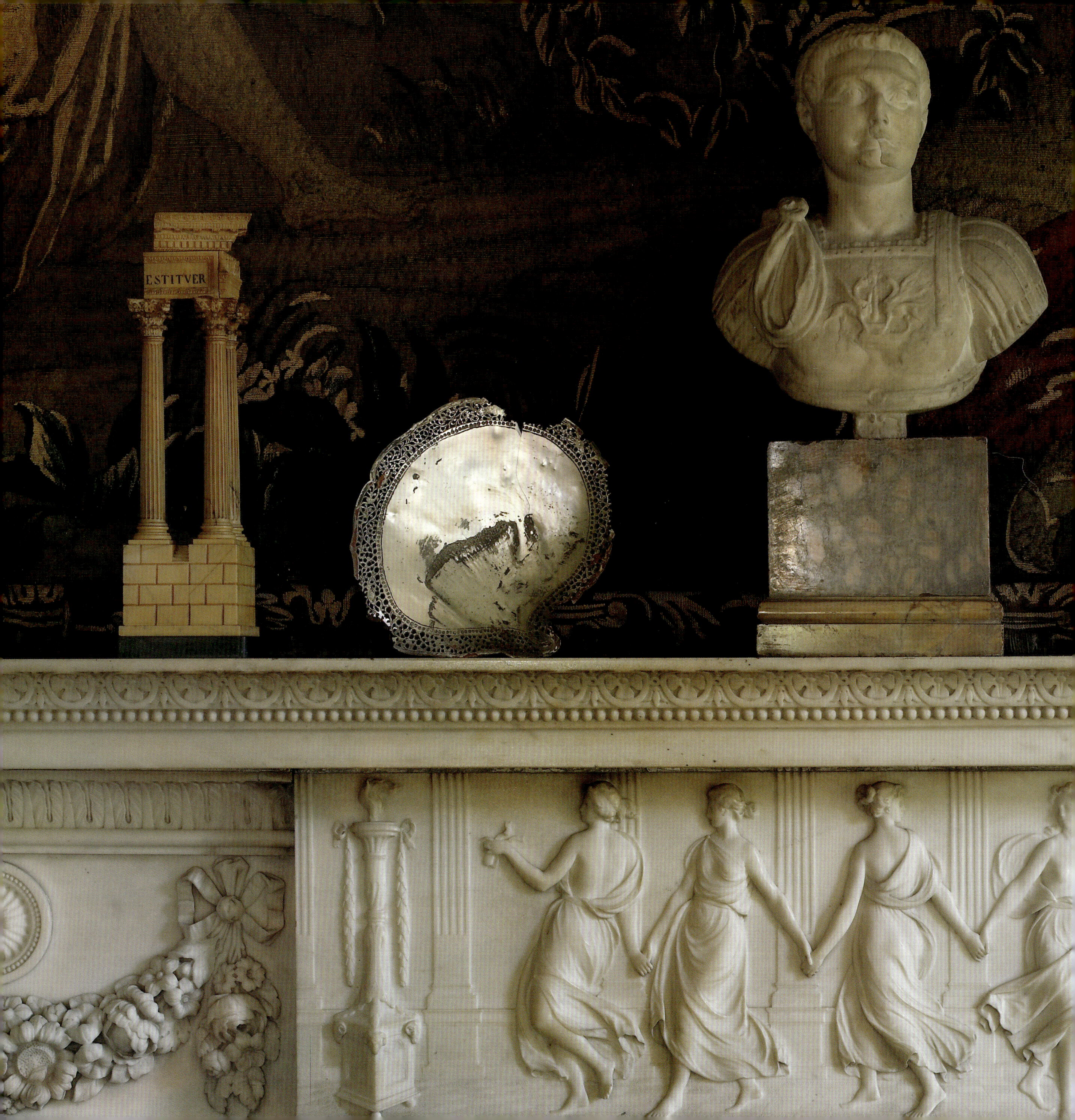
ESTITVER

The chimneypiece in the drawing room at Renishaw is thought to come from Melbourne House in Piccadilly (now Albany) designed by Sir William Chambers and acquired for Renishaw in 1802. The carved frieze, Grand Tour souvenirs, and shells strike a festive note.

ELEGANCE | 103

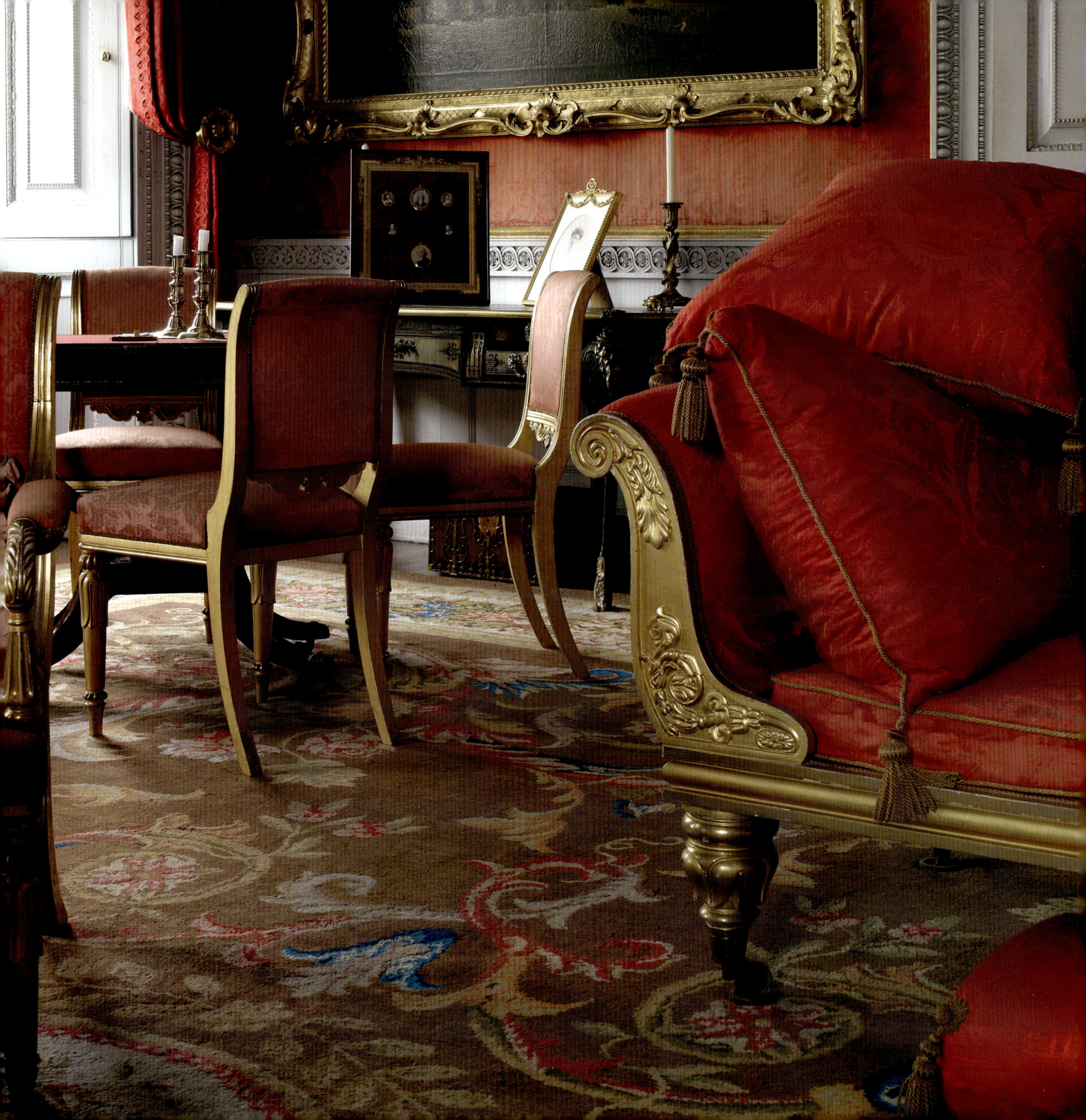

II · ELEGANCE · THE EARLY NINETEENTH CENTURY

Felbrigg Hall

A drawing room refurnished in the 1830s that has largely survived with its period character into the present day.

Felbrigg in Norfolk is a house of many layers and delightful contrasts, not least the division of the main house into two ranges: one Jacobean and the other Restoration. These ranges stand at right angles to each other, both stately in their way, the 1680s range defiantly modern, making no concessions to the other portion of the house, while early-nineteenth-century additions are in a neo-Tudor style.[1]

The main drawing room lies at the heart of the 1680s house, as designed by William Samwell for William Windham I. In that period this room was known as the Great Parlour, effectively combining a room of more public reception and a dining room. This is reflected in the 1680s plasterwork of the ceiling — by Edward Goudge, who had worked at Belton — which shows both game, fruit, and flowers. At that time the walls were panelled, or wainscoted, in oak and hung with paintings. A small section of the original parquetry floor is still in situ.

The room was remodelled in the 1750s by the architect James Paine for William Windham II, who had returned in 1742 from an extensive Grand Tour with a huge collection of pictures and books.[2] He remodelled many of the principal rooms of the house at this time, creating the dining room (formerly the staircase hall) and the adjoining Cabinet (formerly the drawing room to which the family withdrew from meals in the Great Parlour). In the latter he hung many of the views of Classical ruins by Giovanni-Battista Busiri (there are six large oils by this artist and twenty-six small gouaches). Many of the finest marine and topographical paintings collected by William Windham II, however, were displayed in the drawing room and hang there still.

The Siena marble chimneypiece was designed for the Cabinet but later installed in the drawing room. Paine removed the wainscot panelling, introduced the new cornice, added the dado rail, and introduced new doors and door-frames — these doors could be thrown open so that the three main rooms on this front could be enjoyed together. The drawing room was described as being hung with a red flowered paper, but it may have been damask to match the Cabinet room.

William Windham II was the Grand Tourist par excellence. He combined a love of boxing and an "apparent dissipation" with being excessively well read in ancient and modern languages, "and from these various sources, his amazing parts, equally quick and retentive, had drawn and amassed treasures of science and amusement."[3] Of his hospitality at Felbrigg one friend wrote, "I could cram you with compliments upon your House, Park, &c, the Elegance and convenience, the Utile Dulci; the freedom and Ease; just enough Civility without Ceremony."

His son and heir, William Windham III, was a successful politician, a diarist, and a friend of Samuel Johnson. His portrait, a copy by John Jackson of a painting by Thomas Lawrence, hangs over the chimneypiece in the drawing room. He had no children, so his heir was a nephew, Admiral William Lukin, who adopted the name Windham. He did not take over the house until the death of Celia Windham, his uncle's widow, in 1824.

He had ambitious plans for the house but had to measure his dreams against the need to provide for a large family. Nonetheless, in around 1830 he introduced a new gilt and damask suite of decoration and furnishing into the drawing room (the name of Great Parlour seems to have survived right up until this time). New curtains were also introduced, which survive today, as described in the accounts as "3 pr of splendid window curtains, crimson damask furniture with gilt cornices, pins, drapery and Holland covers." The sofa, suite of gilt chairs, and fire screens were all upholstered to match.[4]

THE DRAWING ROOM | 105

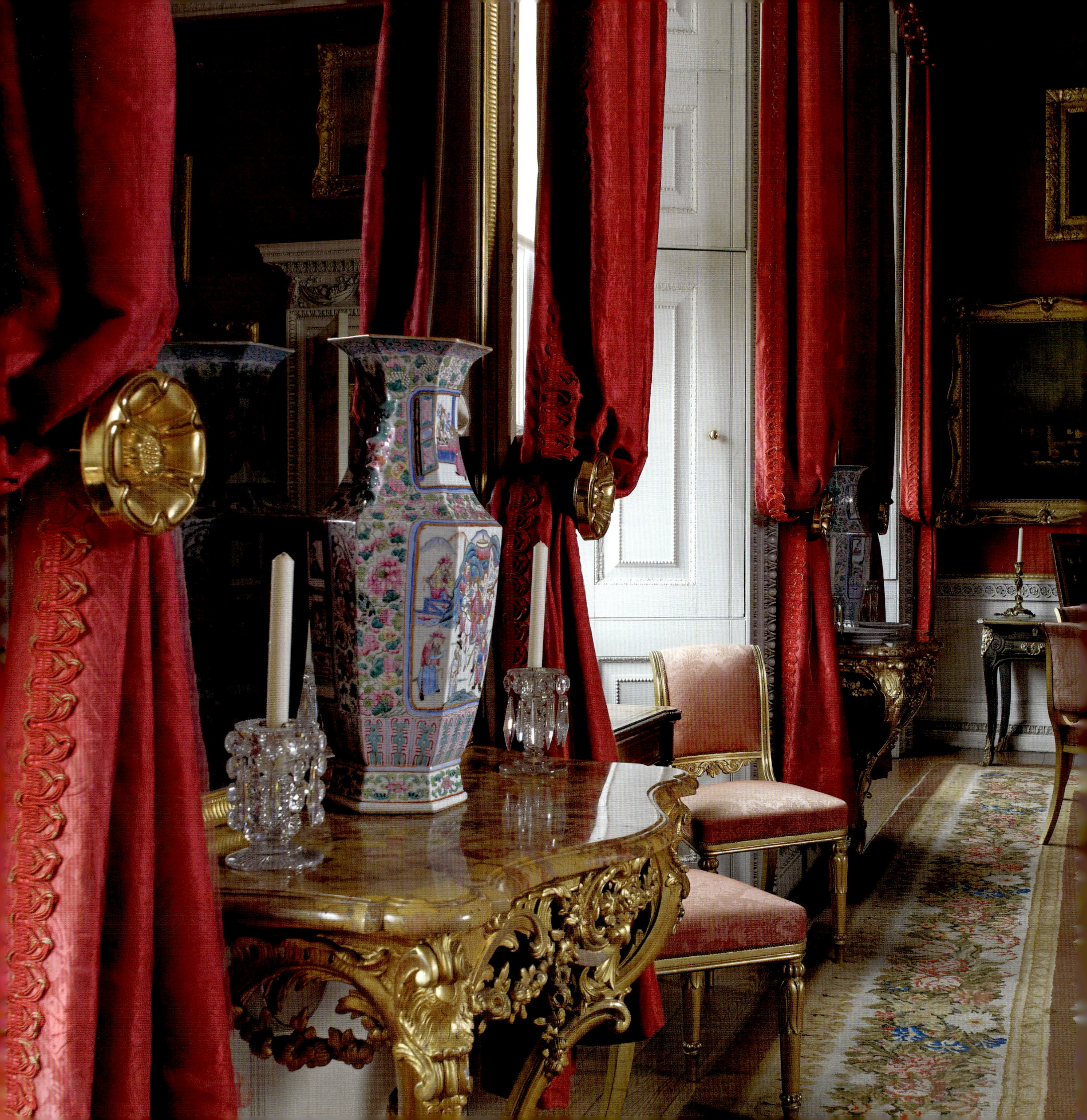

← Felbrigg's drawing room began as the Great Parlour of the 1680s house and was used as more of a dining room. It was remodelled in the 1750s to become the main drawing room. Admiral William Windham, who took over the house in 1824, introduced the crimson damask in around 1830.

↓ The fine French boulle furniture was collected by Admiral William Windham.

ELEGANCE | 107

Richness in detail: layers and layers of decorative ornament, in the door frame, dado rail, picture frame, bureau and curtain fringes, all contribute to the stately richness of effect.

The rosewood tables and the French boulle furniture, including the elegant *bureau de Mazarin* in the drawing room, were also acquired by the admiral, following the early-nineteenth-century fashion for all things French, which had been cultivated by the Prince Regent and others. The rococo gilt candle-brackets in the form of mermen were in fact first made for the Cabinet Room in the 1750s but transferred into this room. The carpet is an "English Savonnerie" design of around 1851 but complements the rich colours of the room and the vivid relief of the ceiling plasterwork well.[5]

The survival of so much of the historic contents of the drawing room, which give us such a vision of mid-eighteenth- and mid-nineteenth-century taste combined, is surprising. In the later twentieth century this has been the responsibility of the National Trust: the house and estate were left to the trust in 1969 by Robert Wyndham Ketton-Cremer. His family had acquired the house in 1863 from the admiral's deeply eccentric and naïve grandson "Mad Windham," who liked dressing up as a policeman and got into debt. It was a most unusual acquisition in which the Wyndhams' entire collections, library, and portraits throughout the house were bought outright by a Norwich merchant, John Ketton, who had made his fortune in oil cake and cattle feed. There were modest sales in the 1890s, but the house passed to a grandson of Ketton's who was actually descended from the original Wyndhams, and it was his son, Robert Wyndham Ketton-Cremer, who left it to the trust.[6]

Robert Ketton-Cremer was the last and most learned of the squires of Felbrigg—he was the author of biographies of Horace Walpole and Thomas Gray, as well as a study of his home, *Felbrigg: The Story of a House*. He lived principally in the Great Hall, then furnished comfortably as a living room. The other rooms were kept carefully shuttered and opened up on special occasions, for monthly dinner parties and for visits from Queen Mary.[7] A shy, scholarly bachelor, Ketton-Cremer nonetheless fulfilled his obligations to the house and landscape with a long campaign of restoration and study, and was devastated by the death of his younger brother and heir during the Second World War. His gift of the house and estate to the National Trust meant that these wonderful interiors have been preserved for posterity. Few rooms in England capture so well the cultivated layers of a gentry family's taste and travels expressed in the comfort of their own drawing room.

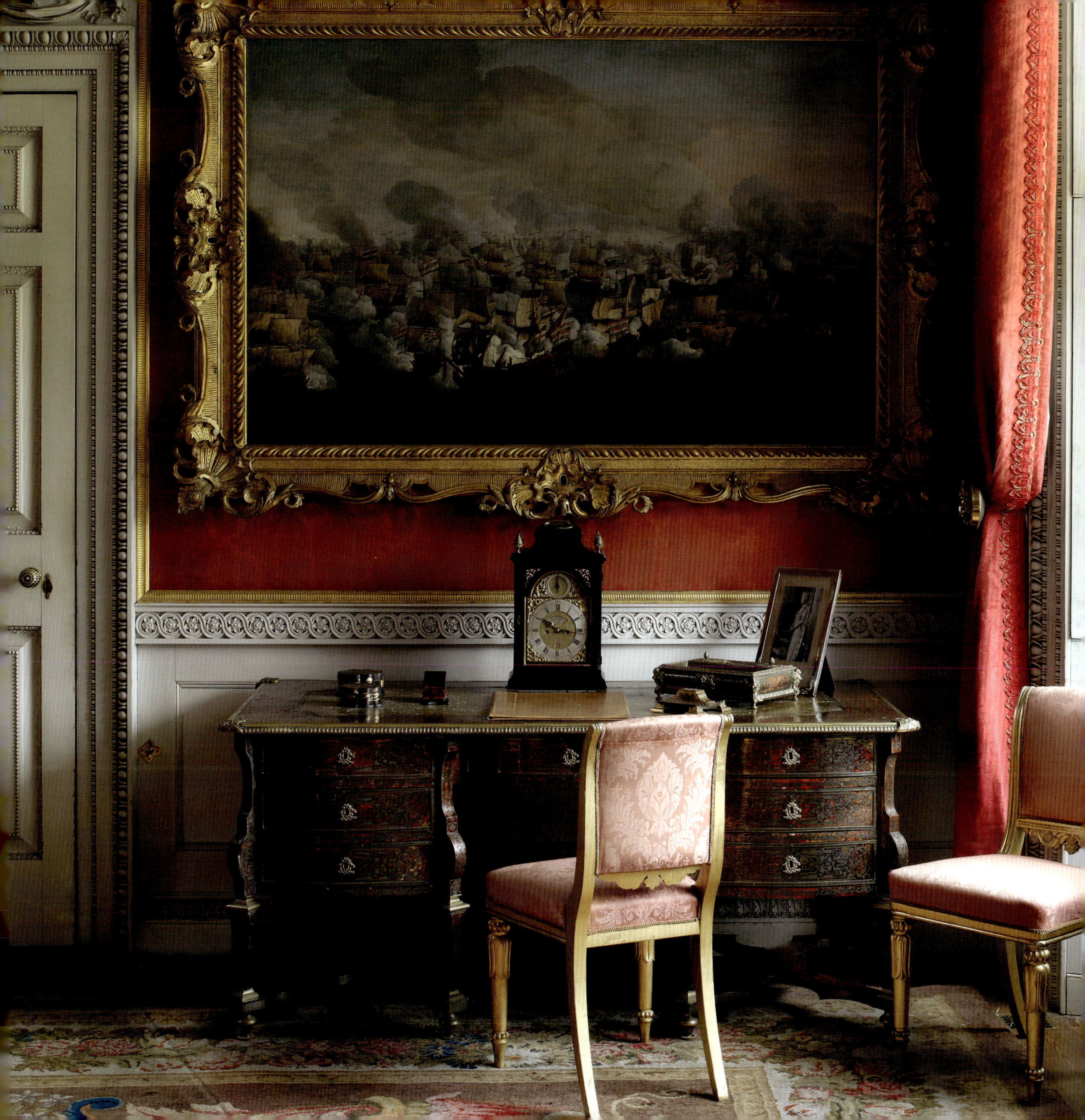

↓ Elegant contrasts: a detail of the corner of the carved marble chimneypiece with sienna marble inset.

→ The main carpet, dating to around 1852, is an English "Savonnerie" design and complements the rich colours of the room. The ceiling plasterwork by Goudge survives from the 1680s house.

110 | FELBRIGG HALL

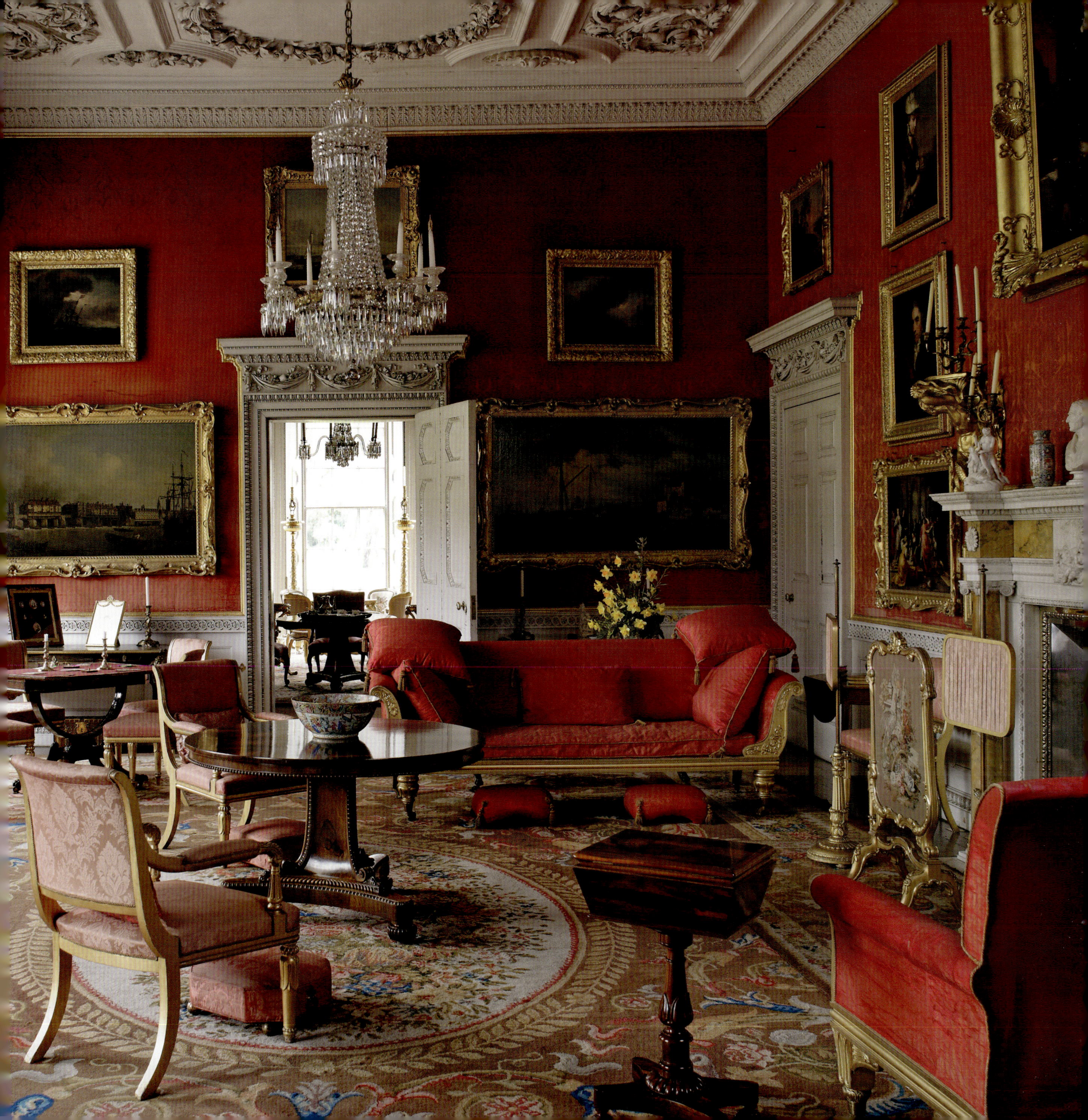

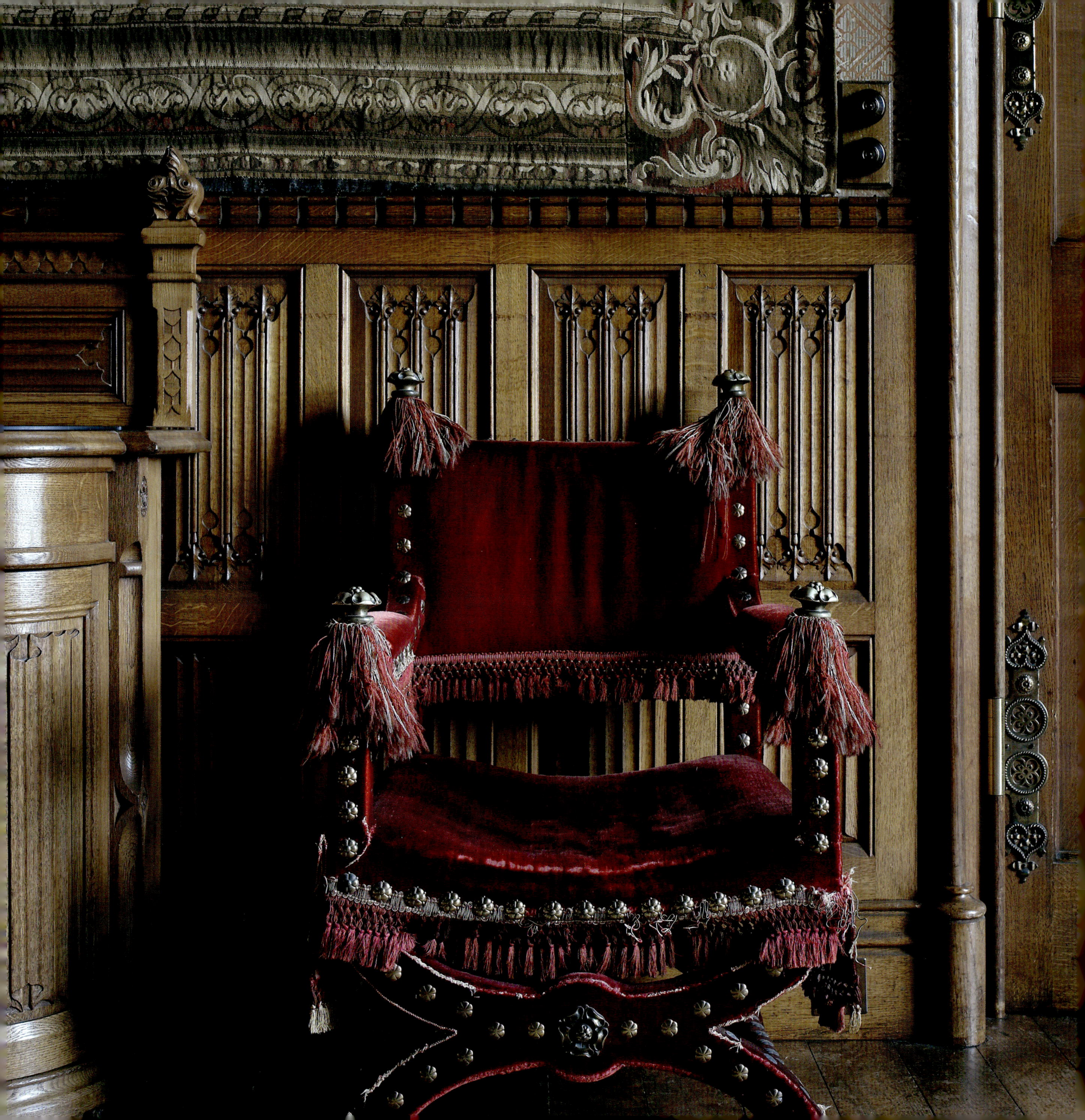

III · OPULENCE · THE LATER NINETEENTH CENTURY

Eastnor Castle

In honour of the medieval: Eastnor is one of the best surviving masterpieces of John Crace working with Pugin.

So powerful was the inspiration of the past in the mid-nineteenth century that the drawing room was often cast as something like a neo-medieval stage set — which seems almost ecclesiastical to modern eyes. One of the best surviving examples of this is found at Eastnor Castle in Herefordshire, at the heart of an early-nineteenth-century castle. Eastnor Castle, begun in 1812 and completed in 1821, was designed in the Norman castellar style by the young Robert Smirke for the 2nd Lord Somers (who later became Earl Somers).[1] It was intended to give the impression of an ancient baronial fortress guarding the Welsh Borders, and although the symmetry of the design emphasised authority, such is the nature of the landscape that the castle is often seen in more Picturesque character.

Gothic tastes changed during the late nineteenth century. According to the Victorian critic Charles Eastlake, Smirke ranked third in importance amongst the Gothic revival architects of his generation, after John Nash and James Wyatt. Eastlake thought Eastnor had a degree of theatrical impracticability and "might have made a tolerable fort before the invention of gunpowder, but as a residence it was a picturesque mistake."[2] But today, it is impossible not to admire the theatrical imagination of the project and the Picturesque success of its setting in the landscape. Its ambitious scale was widely noted even before the building was completed in 1821, coinciding with Lord Somers's elevation to an Earldom. The 2nd and 3rd Earls were left with the job of completing the interior decoration of the sparsely decorated rooms.

In 1849 the 2nd Earl engaged the foremost Gothic revival designer of the succeeding generation, Augustus Pugin, to create an appropriately resonant scheme of decoration. He had just completed his work for the Palace of Westminster.[3] Pugin was considered by G. G. Scott as "the great reformer of architecture," but his influence on interior decoration and furniture was just as great. Pugin's scheme added considerable vitality to the fan-vaulted and compartmented plaster ceilings of Smirke's drawing room, which had been executed by the plasterer Francis Bernasconi before 1820.

The vividly coloured, jewel-box-like decoration in Eastnor's drawing room, its panelling and doorcases, was designed by Pugin and executed by John Gregory Crace, with Hardman providing the metalwork, the lock plates, the door handles, and the heraldic fire dogs. The chandelier is based on an example in the Lorenzkirche, Nuremberg.[4] So complete is the room that it is considered one of the most important survivals of a Pugin interior outside the House of Lords.

The work at Eastnor Castle is a late example of the collaboration between the Crace family of decorators and Pugin. J. G. Crace felt he had begun to understand Pugin's ideas well, and allowed himself to depart from Pugin's design detail if he thought he could improve. Pugin was not usually enthusiastic about such departures and wrote tetchily to Crace in 1850: "I think the chimney piece quite ruined by the way the gilding is done, I assure you I never saw so fine a job so completely ruined and cut to Fritters."[5] It is difficult to agree with Pugin's harsh judgement today; rather, a visitor is immediately impressed by the painted celebration of the ancient lineage of the family over the chimneypiece, evoking the religious feudalism of the Middle Ages from which Pugin took inspiration (the Earl and the Countess are depicted in medieval dress). Pugin had not visited the house when Crace involved him in the design, and his fine chimneypiece arrived too deep for the opening. Pugin had not realized it was a modern castle: "I thought it was a very old place with tremendous thick walls."[6]

↓ The plasterwork ceiling was executed by Francesco Bernasconi before 1820; the decoration was executed in 1849–50. The new carpet, woven in Turkey by Asad Carpets takes its inspiration from the Pugin and Crace decoration and the family's heraldry. It was masterminded by James Hervey-Bathurst's wife, Lucy, and installed in 2011.

→ The richly Gothic drawing room at Eastnor Castle in Herefordshire is lined with carved panelling and tapestry. The whole ensemble is a magnificent example of Gothic revival vitality: the chimneypiece designed by Pugin and the overmantel decoration giving Lord Somers's genealogy in painted form.

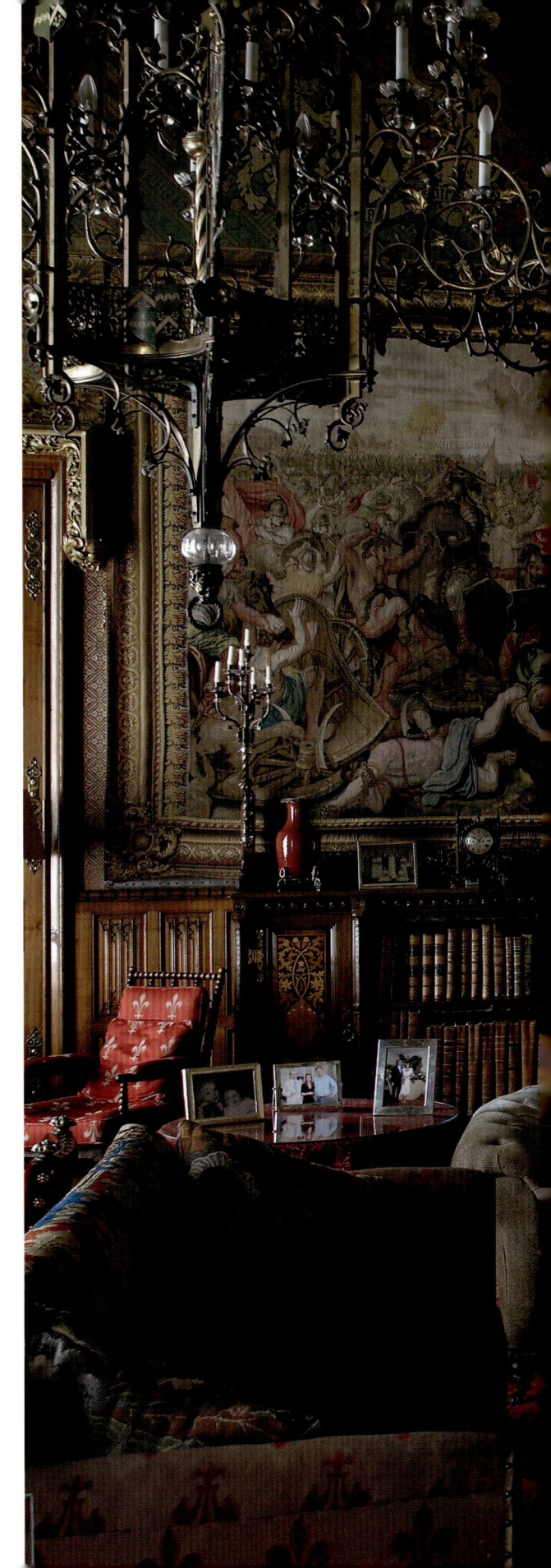

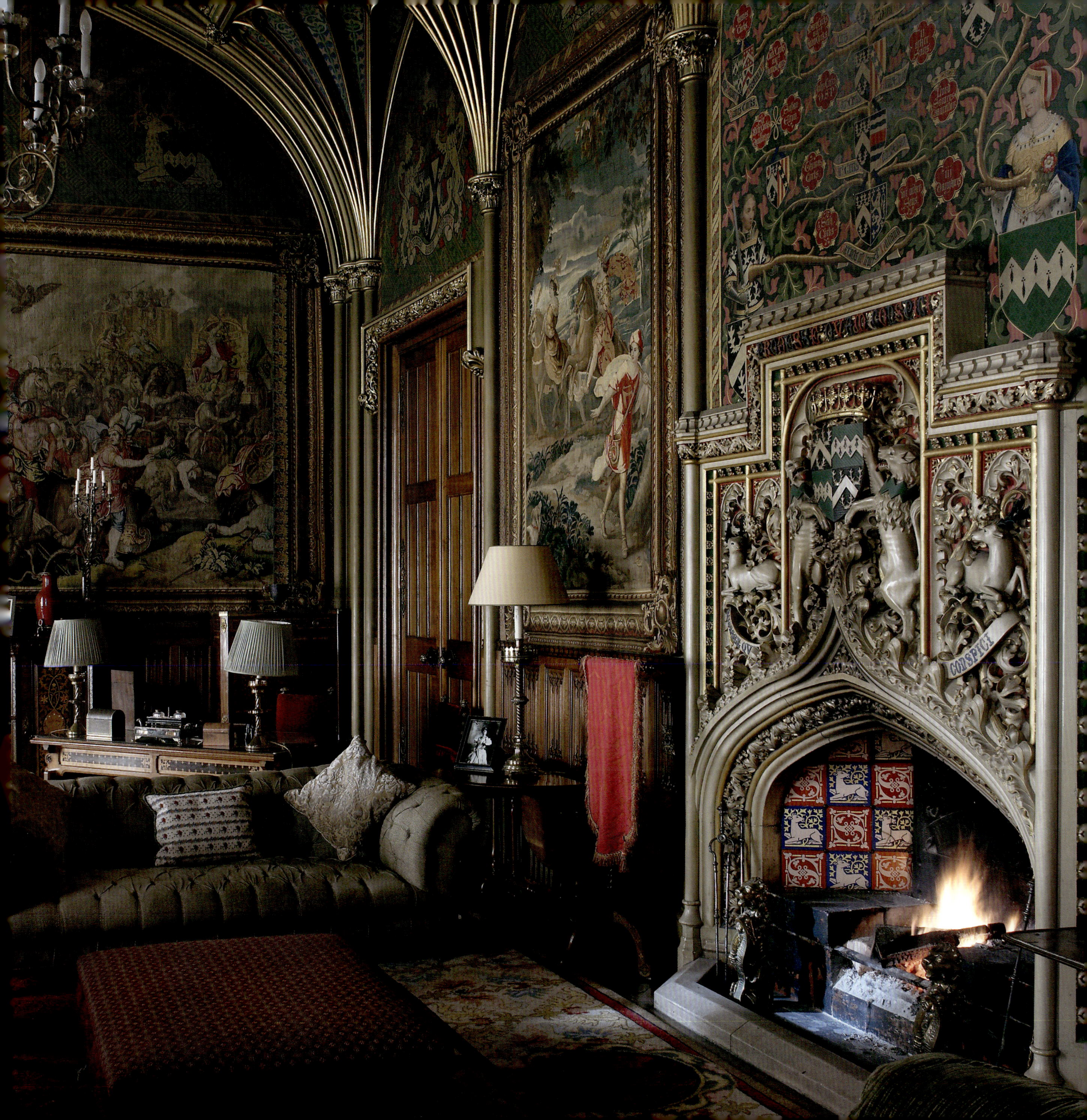

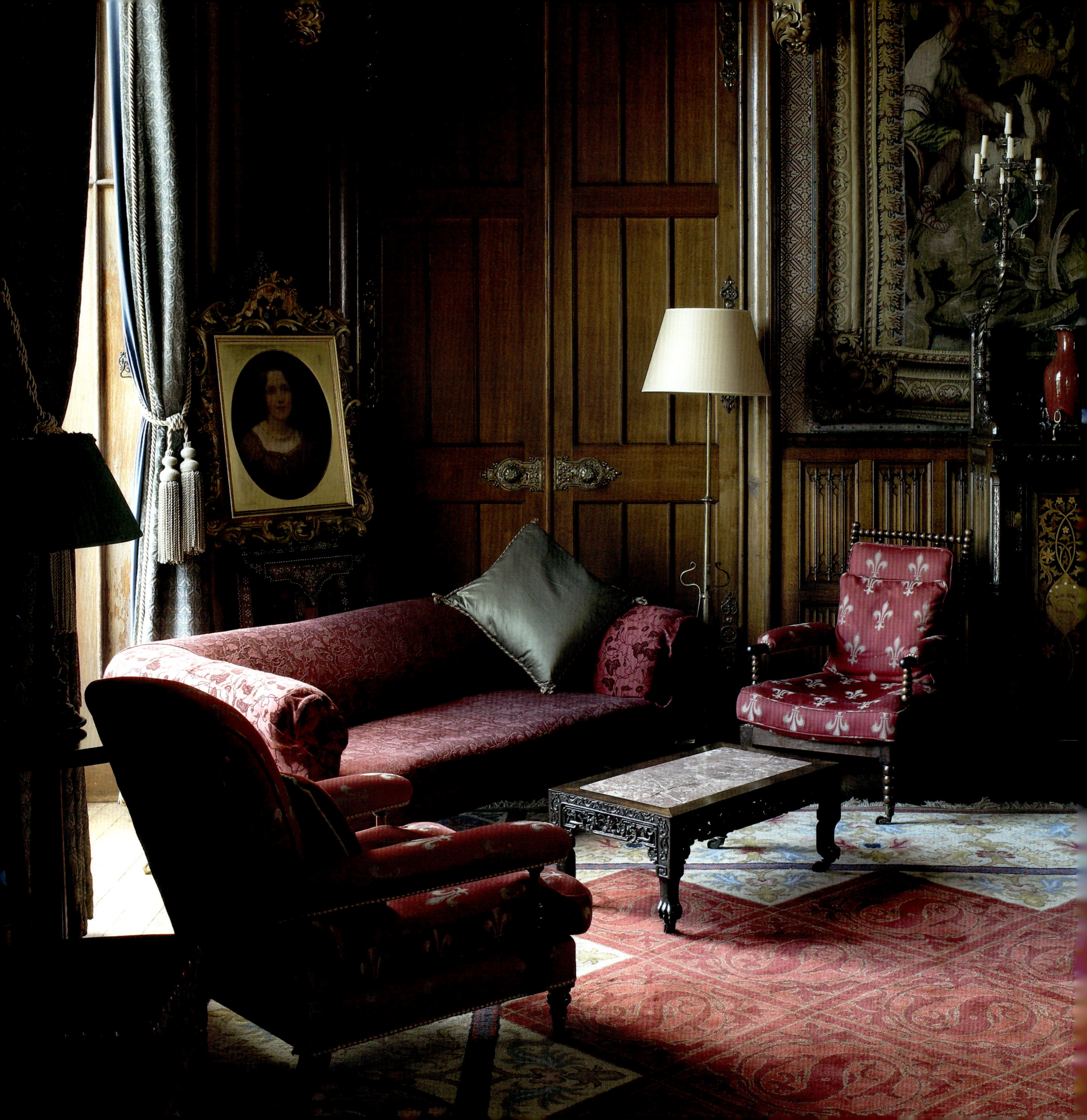

← *Few Gothic revival rooms in England manage to be as comfortable and inviting as the drawing room at Eastnor.*

↓ *Every detail is decorated, down to the bell to summon a servant.*

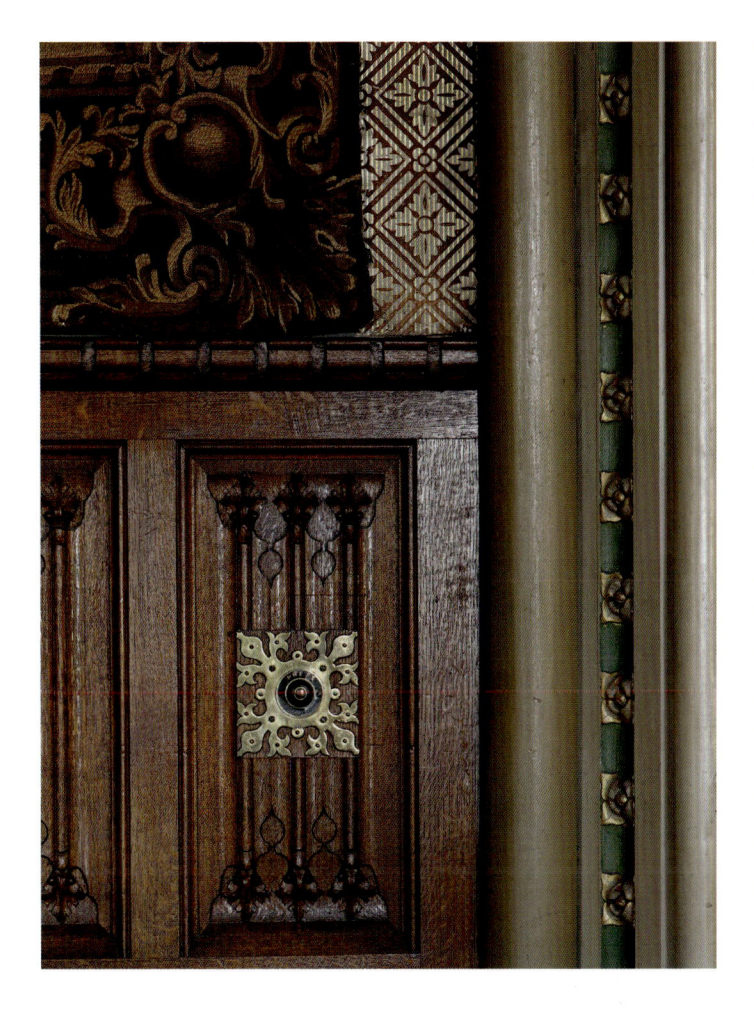

The Metropolitan Museum of Art in New York has a drawing by Crace for the decoration of the room, which illustrates the ceiling, an upholstered settee, and an oak buffet. And preserved in the Victoria and Albert Museum are a number of designs by Pugin for furniture that was made by the firm and remains in the house today, including the inlaid walnut writing table (which was exhibited in the *Treasure Houses of Britain*).[7] Despite his genius, or perhaps because of it, Pugin was often driven to distraction by his domestic commissions, remarking to Crace of one of his other jobs: "I could make a church as easy as a grate … Such a job as Chirk [Castle] is enough to drive any man mad. All little things and as difficult to get properly done as the greatest. It is worse than the House of Lords."[8] Nonetheless, for all Pugin's creative self-doubt, the results speak for themselves. In *England's Thousand Best Houses*, 2004, Simon Jenkins observed: "The room is as good as anything Pugin did in the House of Lords, a blaze of Gothic fantasy."[9] The 3rd Earl undertook more lavish embellishments in the 1860s and 1870s, notably in the Long Library and the State Bedroom.

The fortunes of the family declined by the beginning of the next century, and the house was packed up during the Second World War for government use, but it in fact lay unused. The widowed Lady Somers moved back into the servants' wing in the late 1940s, but the revival of Eastnor was started by her daughter, Hon. Elizabeth Somers Cocks, and her husband, Benjamin Hervey-Bathurst, the parents of the present owner. They moved into the castle in 1949, when the slow process of reinhabiting the rooms began, laying the groundwork for the full restoration carried out in the 1990s by their son, James Hervey-Bathurst, and his wife, who moved in with their family in 1988. The large new carpet was handmade and hand-dyed by Asad Carpets. Designed by Hazel Fox — and inspired by Crace and Pugin's decorative work, with the family's coat of arms in the centre — it was woven in Konya in Turkey and installed in 2011.[10] There are few places that preserve the rich aesthetic of the nineteenth century and are also as comfortable as the drawing room at Eastnor Castle, which is used by the family and also enjoyed by thousands of visitors every year.

OPULENCE | 117

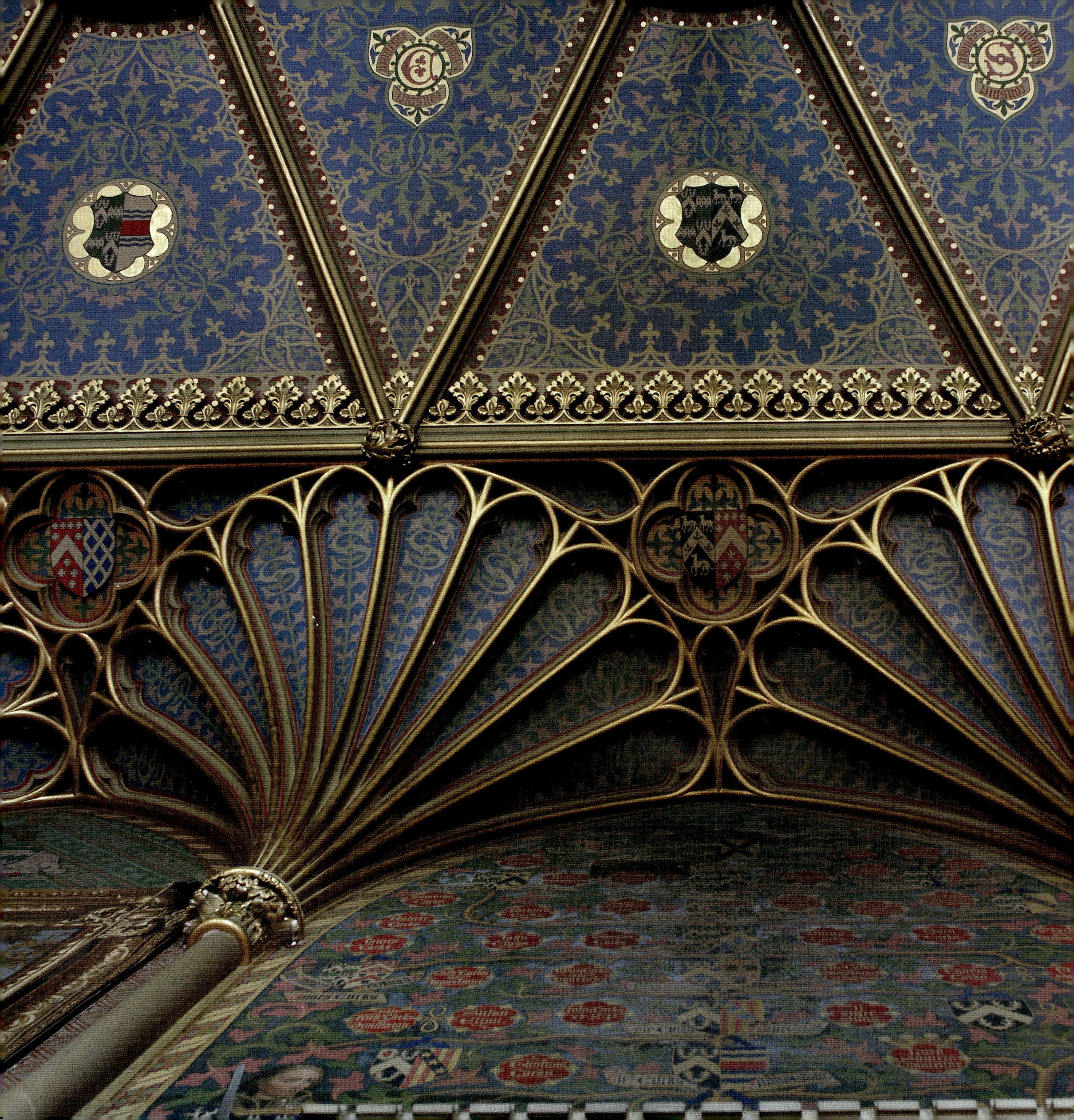

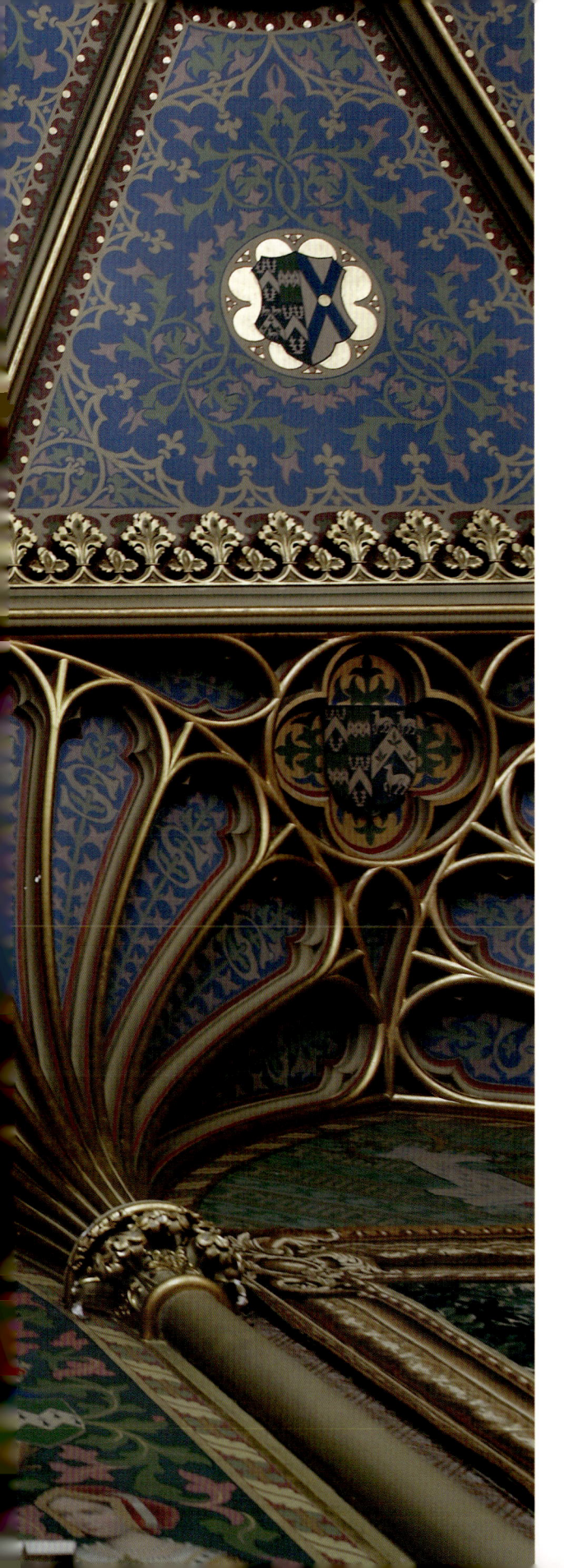

← *The painted ceiling of the drawing room is an outstanding example of the collaboration between the Crace family of decorators and Pugin.*

↓ *Typically for a high Victorian Gothic interior, every opportunity was taken to incorporate the families' initials and heraldic achievements.*

OPULENCE | 119

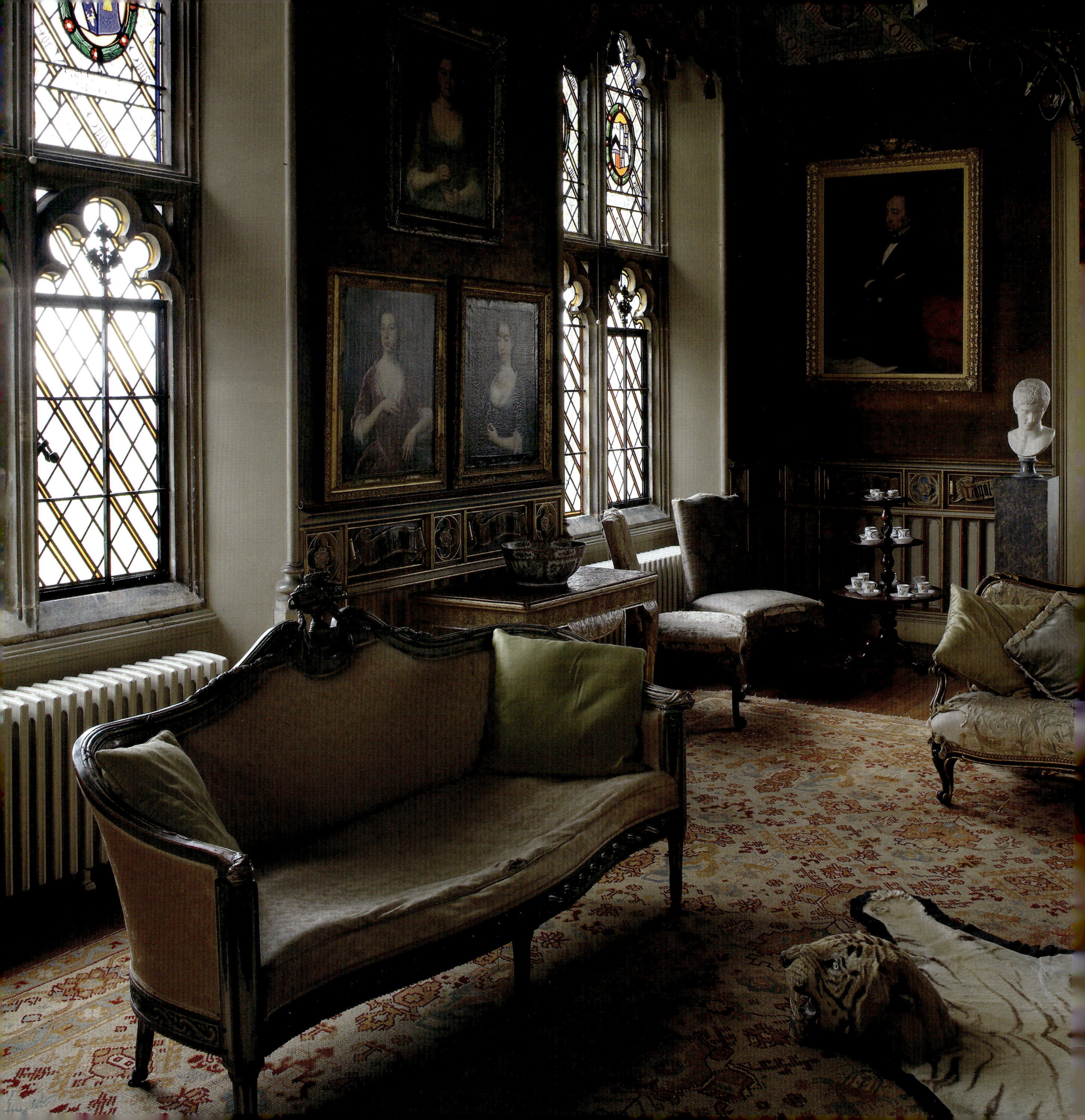

III · OPULENCE · THE LATER NINETEENTH CENTURY

Knebworth

Lord Lytton's State Drawing Room provides no better example of the Gothic Revival imagination at play.

Knebworth is one of the most full-blooded of the Gothic revival country houses of the early- to mid-nineteenth century. A house of venerable age, it was remodelled in three phases, first in around 1811 by Elizabeth Bulwer Lytton, widow of General William Bulwer, and second by their son, the remarkable Edward Bulwer-Lytton, novelist, politician, friend of Disraeli.[1] He effectively rebuilt the house as a Tudor-Gothic fantasy and embellished it throughout with decorative heraldry celebrating his own ancestry and the history of his home. (His son also made alterations in the 1880s.)

Edward Bulwer Lytton was a radical MP in his early days, leaving Parliament in 1841, and a decade later being returned for Hertford in the conservative interest. In 1866 he was raised to the peerage as Baron Lytton of Knebworth.[2] His literary career began in the 1820s. In 1828 his novel *Pelham* brought him to the attention of a wide public and established his reputation as a wit and dandy. He was a prolific novelist and has been considered the inventor of the ghost story as it is now understood. He was a friend of Dickens, who came to Knebworth to indulge his passion for amateur dramatics, in performances intended to raise money for impoverished writers and their dependents.

Despite Bulwer-Lytton being a rather modern figure in so many ways, it was the romance of the past that stimulated his imagination, and interiors of Knebworth were crammed with heraldic banners and portraits of English kings. He lived here in exotic isolation after the desperate failure of his marriage. The translator Edward Fitzgerald described his impressions of Edward Lytton, like an "Eastern potentate sitting on a luxurious cushion, with dreamy eyes and reposeful manner."[3] Fittingly for this image, son and grandson (the 1st and 2nd Earls of Lytton) were both to be Viceroys of India, although the 2nd Earl was only acting Viceroy while he was Governor of Bengal).

The state drawing room was decorated and furnished in 1844 by John Gregory Crace, who also decorated the two anterooms, one of which was Bulwer-Lytton's own study, the library, and a bedroom.[4] The State Drawing Room is also the only one to survive intact through the twentieth century. This was partly because other rooms received the attention of Sir Edwin Lutyens, who married a daughter of the 2nd Earl, working for the 3rd Earl and his Countess. The house is still in family hands: the 3rd Earl's daughter, Lady Hermione, married 1st Baron Cobbold. Their son, Lord Cobbold, lives nearby, having handed over the running of the place to his son, Henry, and his wife, Martha.

Henry Lytton Cobbold still relishes the Gothic imagination of Lord Lytton and faithfully preserves this extraordinary room. Every inch of the State Drawing Room is encrusted in painted Gothic and heraldic decoration, and the stacked portraits of the Bulwer Lytton family look down on this Gothic dream. The preserved bills refer to "Emblazoning the woodwork in Color and Gilding the Moldings" and painting "heraldic shields" and "names on scrolls."[5] It is a profoundly historicist and genealogical space, an embodiment of romantic ancestor worship projected into decorative form. The designer was a master of his art. J. G. Crace was the eldest son of Frederick Crace, and was around the same time working on Chatsworth for the Duke of Devonshire, and Taymouth Castle for Lord Breadalbane.

In 1843 Crace also travelled to Italy and modern Bavaria, where he was hugely impressed by the fresco decoration being carried out for Ludwig I. In the same year, he also met Pugin for the first time. According to historian Dr. Megan Aldrich, in *The Craces* (1990), Crace was deeply impressed by "the way that Bavarian artists used colour to emphasise the architectural composition of a building and to set off figurative paintings on

THE DRAWING ROOM | 121

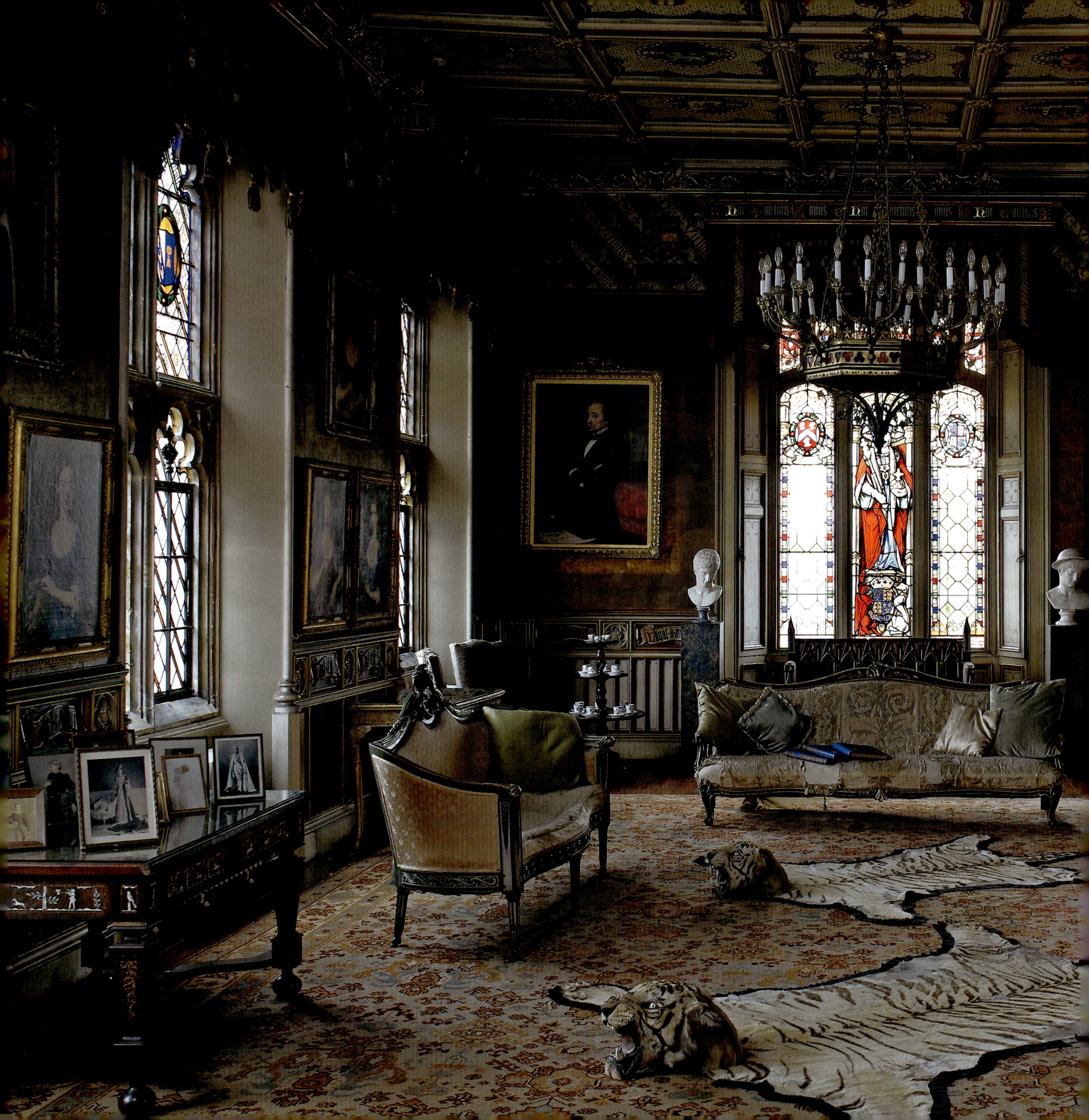

The State Drawing Room of Knebworth House in Hertfordshire is one of the most explicit examples of the way the Gothic revival style was used to express a family's illustrious lineage, down to the stained glass depicting Henry VII. The room was decorated and furnished by John Crace in 1844. Even the incorporation of a vast Georgian group family portrait does not alter the overwhelmingly Victorian feeling of the room.

OPULENCE | 123

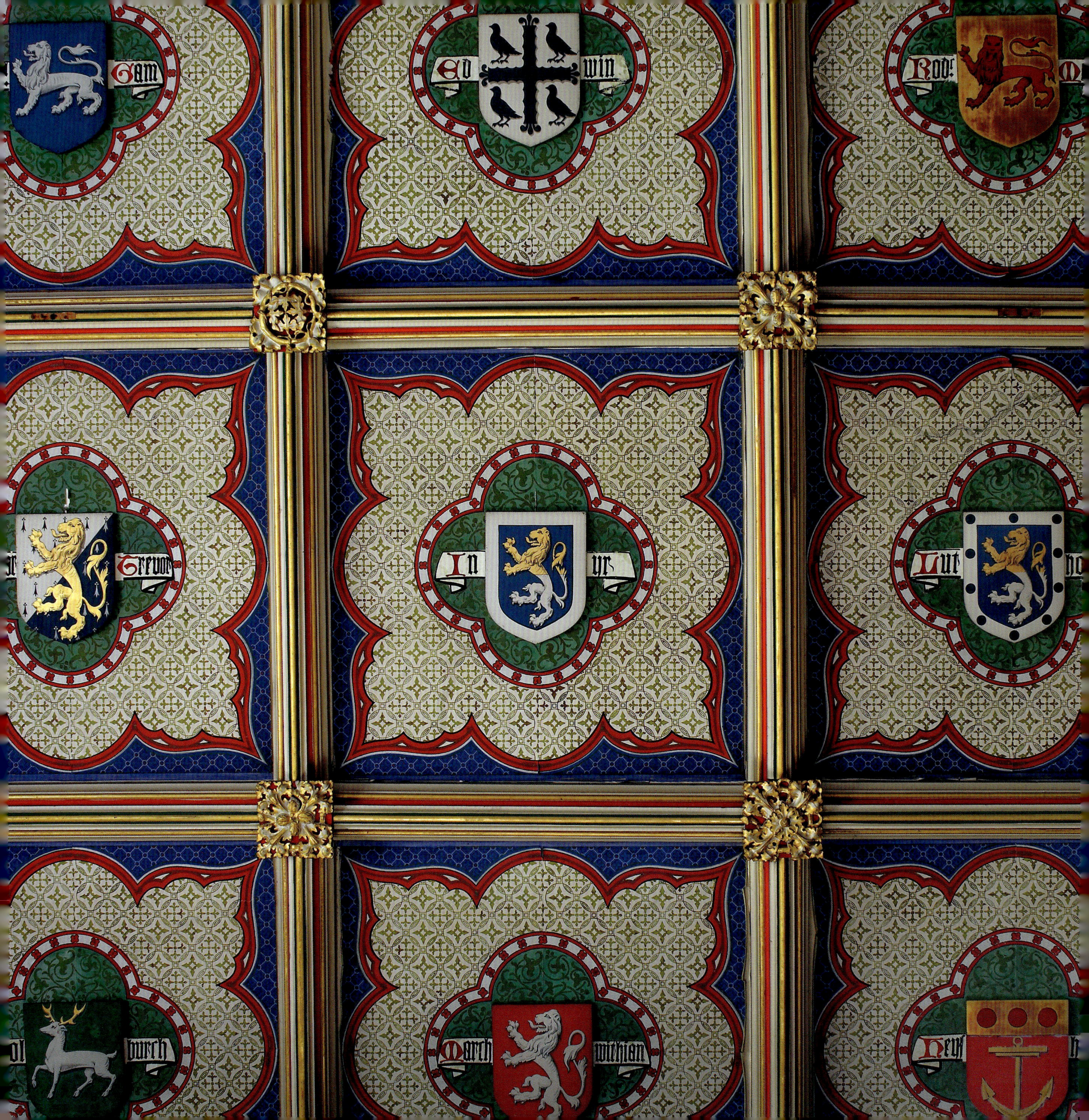
Ed
win
In
yr

The ceiling decoration by John Crace uses strong colour and intricate pattern to great effect, and includes the forty-four quarterings of Lord Lytton's illustrious ancestry.

the wall surfaces."[6] Knebworth was his first major commission after returning and clearly inspired his new full-blooded use of bold colour contrasts.

Bulwer Lytton was presumably introduced to Crace and his work through friend and fellow MP Charles Tennyson d'Eyncourt, for whom Crace had decorated a Gothic pile at Bayons Manor in Lincolnshire in 1841. Heraldic detail and genealogical celebration were so important that Crace was obliged to wait for the Lyttons' family tree to be fully researched by genealogist and herald William Courthope before he could commence work. The ceiling represents forty-four armourial quarterings, and the frieze displays arms of the many distinguished families that claimed descent through Bulwer Lytton's mother.

There are strong parallels in Crace's work here to that he did at Taymouth Castle, but the more abstracted quality of the ceiling and frieze illustrate the inspiration of his Bavarian travels. His colour choice alone, of strong reds, blues, and greens as the principal colours, marked a departure from the pastels of his work at Taymouth and elsewhere, and can be compared to the contrast of red and blue in the Royal Library at Munich, which he openly admired in a lecture to the RIBA.

J. G. Crace himself described the overall impact of this room as "very Gothic."[7] The Crace firm also supplied the stained glass, curtains, and some of the furniture, including a pair of Gothic side tables with carved legs and marble tops (although the latter tables are surprisingly not mentioned in the surviving bills for 1844). The legs are like a faceted jewel, with lozenges picked out in strong colours and gilding.

The stained glass included an impressive full-length figure of Henry VII, whom Bulwer Lytton claimed as an ancestor. J. G. Crace also designed the Gothic overmantel mirror, with carved figures under canopied niches. Knebworth was not only a high artistic achievement in itself but also a demonstration of Crace's new and deeper feeling for Gothic, at a time when he had just been in contact with A. W. N. Pugin, the great champion of the Gothic revival, with whom he was to work closely and indeed continue his vision beyond Pugin's early death. The painting by Daniel Maclise represents *Caxton's Printing Press*, and in 1850, Maclise wrote to Lord Lytton saying, "I have derived every idea I required as to my personages from *The Last of the Barons*."[8] Lord Lytton appears as the figure of Lord Rivers in armour.

Despite its self-conscious Gothic character, a surprising exoticism is often invoked by writers. In the late nineteenth century, the novelist and poet William Hurrell Mallock recalled playing cards in the State Drawing Room at Knebworth, after the ladies had gone to bed, and Bulwer Lytton's son, the 1st Earl of Lytton, reciting to the assembled company a poem he had once dreamt in India: "Presently he spoke as though his mind were coming back from a distance. 'I,' he said, 'dreamed a poem in India. It has never been written down, but I still can remember every line of it. Listen.' The poem, which was full of vague Oriental imagery, was perfectly intelligible, and throbbed with a certain sonority like that of distant gongs; but no sane man would have written it in his waking moments. In that fact lay its charm. The author's voice, naturally low and musical, acquired new tones as he recited it, giving to it the qualities of an incantation; and round us, as though fashioned out of shadows, was the large, dimly lighted drawing-room, which the old novelist had incrusted with impossible heraldries, culminating in escutcheons of pre-Christian Welsh kings."[9]

OPULENCE | 125

↓ The canopied overmantel mirror and carved stone chimneypiece in the Gothic spirit.

→ One of the painted Gothic side tables supplied for the room in the 1840s, on which stand family miniatures, shells, and small caskets.

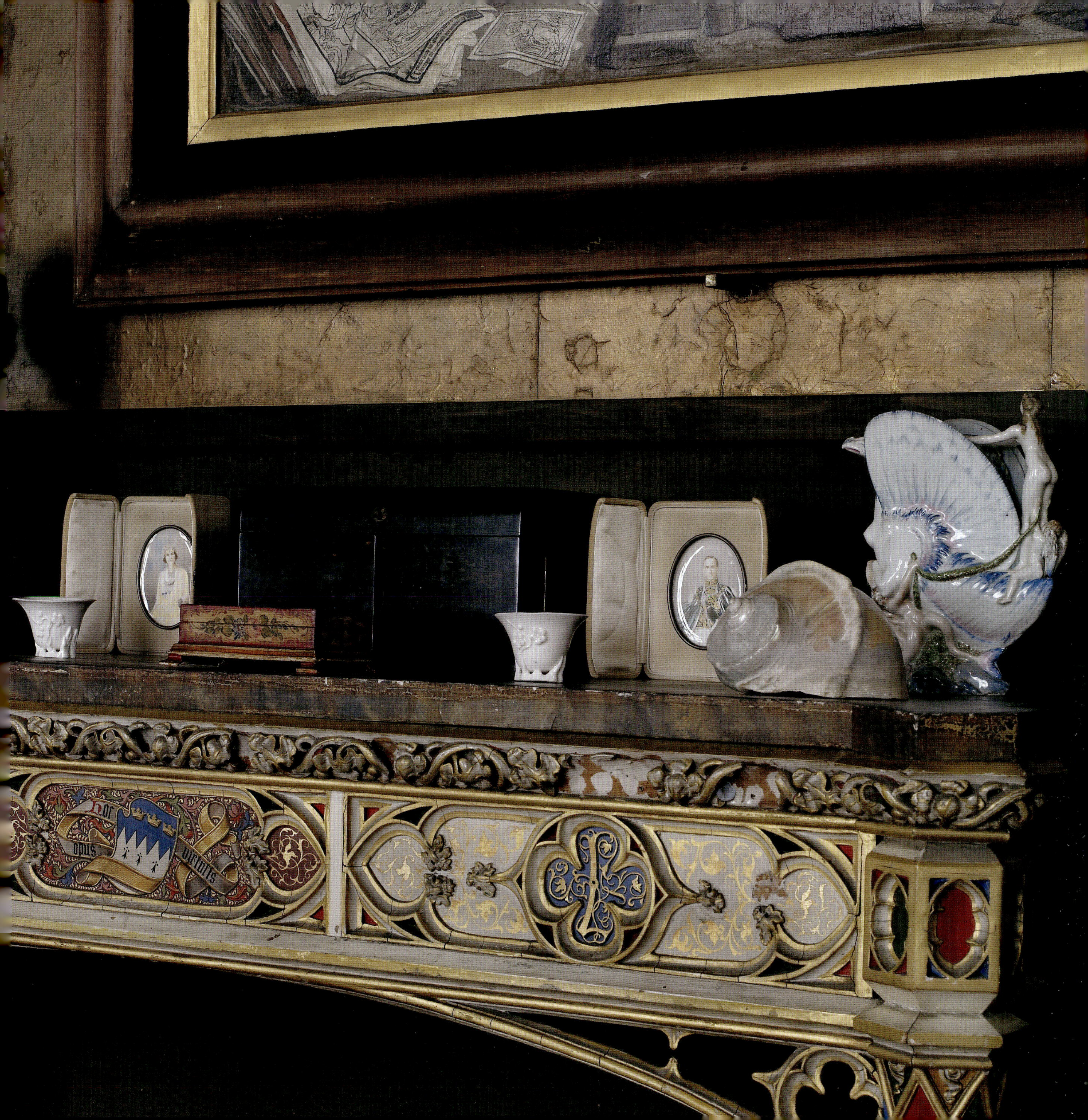
hoc
opus
virtutis

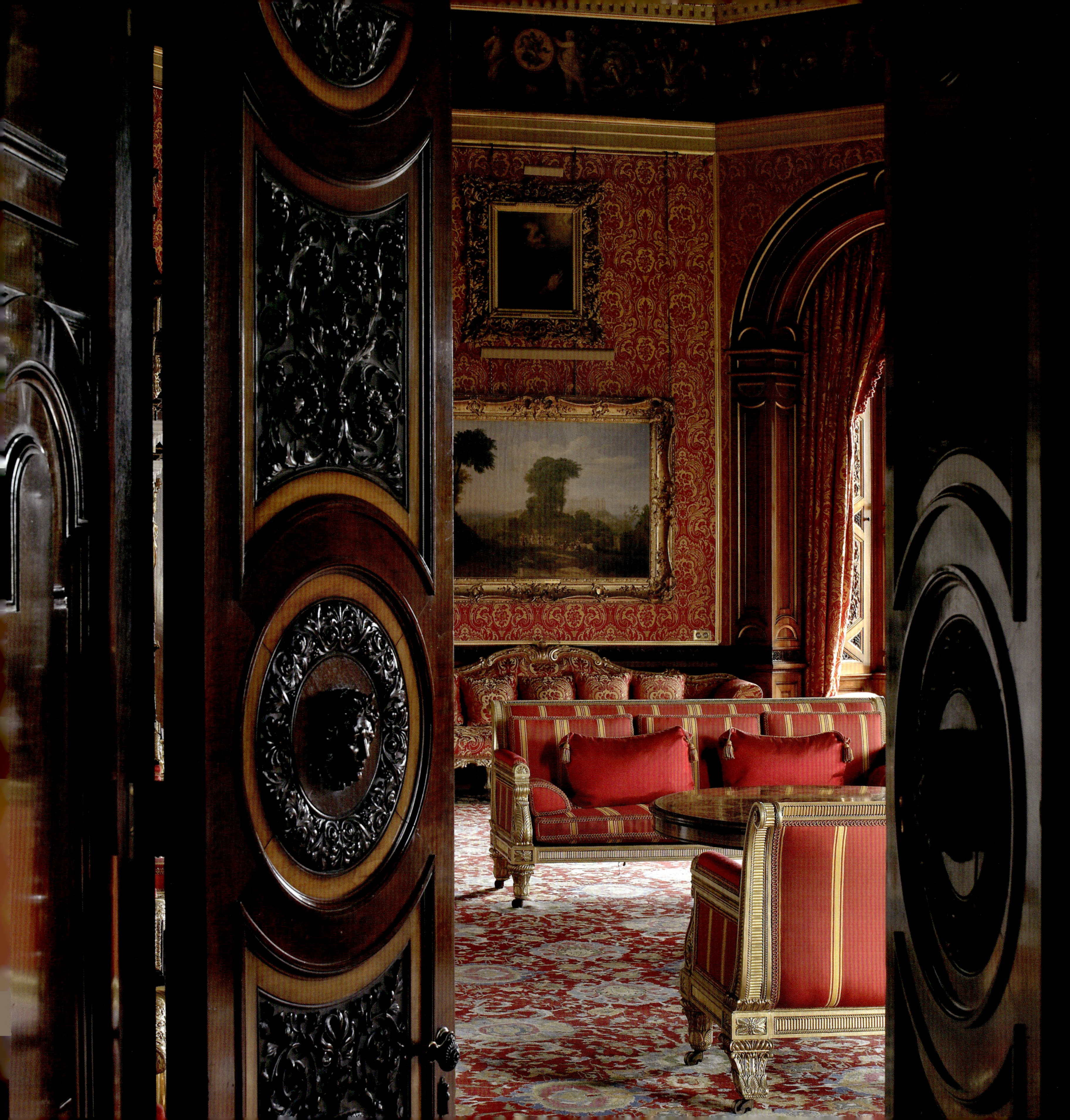

III · OPULENCE · THE LATER NINETEENTH CENTURY

Alnwick Castle

The 4th Duke of Northumberland created magnificent princely interiors within a Gothic revival castle.

There are few more glorious sequences of interiors than the principal "state" rooms of Alnwick Castle in Northumberland, the result of one of the most ambitious mid-nineteenth-century remodellings of a major historic ducal seat.[1] The drawing room at Alnwick belongs to this richly decorated sequence of rooms created in the 1850s. On his inheritance, the 4th Duke, and his wife, the Duchess Eleanor, "found a great absence of domestic comfort and a deficiency in those modern conveniences requisite in the residence of a nobleman of his Grace's rank."[2] According to Professor T. L. Donaldson writing in 1856, they felt that eighteenth-century alterations "had caused it to lose many striking features, important parts having been reduced in size and consequence, depriving it of much of that original dignity and variety of effect, which it had doubtless possessed in ancient times." This was the inspiration for a radical transformation in which the castle was remodelled into one of the most dazzling and princely interiors in England.

The 4th Duke (who died in 1865) called in Gothic revival architect Anthony Salvin, who redesigned the eighteenth-century parts of the castle into an architectural form that they both felt was more fitting for the history of this ancient castle. In essence, the 4th Duke asked Salvin to restore Alnwick to its original character of an early-fourteenth-century castle and also wanted, at the same time, to render it a "comfortable modern residence."[3] For his interiors, the Duke chose the Italian Renaissance style, as during the course of his extensive travels in Italy he had conceived "a great admiration for Italian art and decoration of the fifteenth and sixteenth centuries."

The Duke's principal adviser on the interiors was an Italian, the Commendatore Canina, director of Capitoline Museum in Rome, who was assisted by Signor Montiroli and Signor Montovani. A highly respected figure, Canina was surprisingly on good terms with Anthony Salvin, who clearly would have rather designed the interiors himself in Gothic style, as well as leading figures of the Royal Institute of British Architects, C. R. Cockerell and T. L. Donaldson, who both travelled to Alnwick with Canina. Canina prepared a full schedule of works, although he died on his journey back to Italy. The schedule was published in 1857, along with the paper on Canina's life and career, read to the Royal Institute of British Architects in November 1856. Canina also offered his designs for discussion "to promote a more extensive application in England of that kind of noble decoration, which was the result of the studies made by our masters at the revival of the fine arts, in Italy especially, upon the most ancient monuments of Rome, from which circumstances this style became at once noble, and adapted to modern uses."[4]

Montiroli took over the work after Canina's death in 1856, designing and completing various key elements. The principal woodcarving was carried out by Signor Bulletti of Florence. The designers and artists had all been recommended by Cardinal Antonelli, secretary to the Vatican and a friend of the Duke's. Mr. John Brown became foreman of the carving school, and the castle became something of a school of art, with twenty-one carvers and six apprentices.[5] The carving school continued until 1861. There were as many as 786 men working on the restoration—all invited to an annual dinner.[6]

Canina's detailed specification for the drawing room described the room thus: "of a polygonal form, composed of the three sides, half octagonal and one rectangular."[7] The ceiling was described as follows: "a well-studied combination of the polygonal form produces the decoration of the ceiling. All the ceiling is executed in wood, and at present ornaments are being

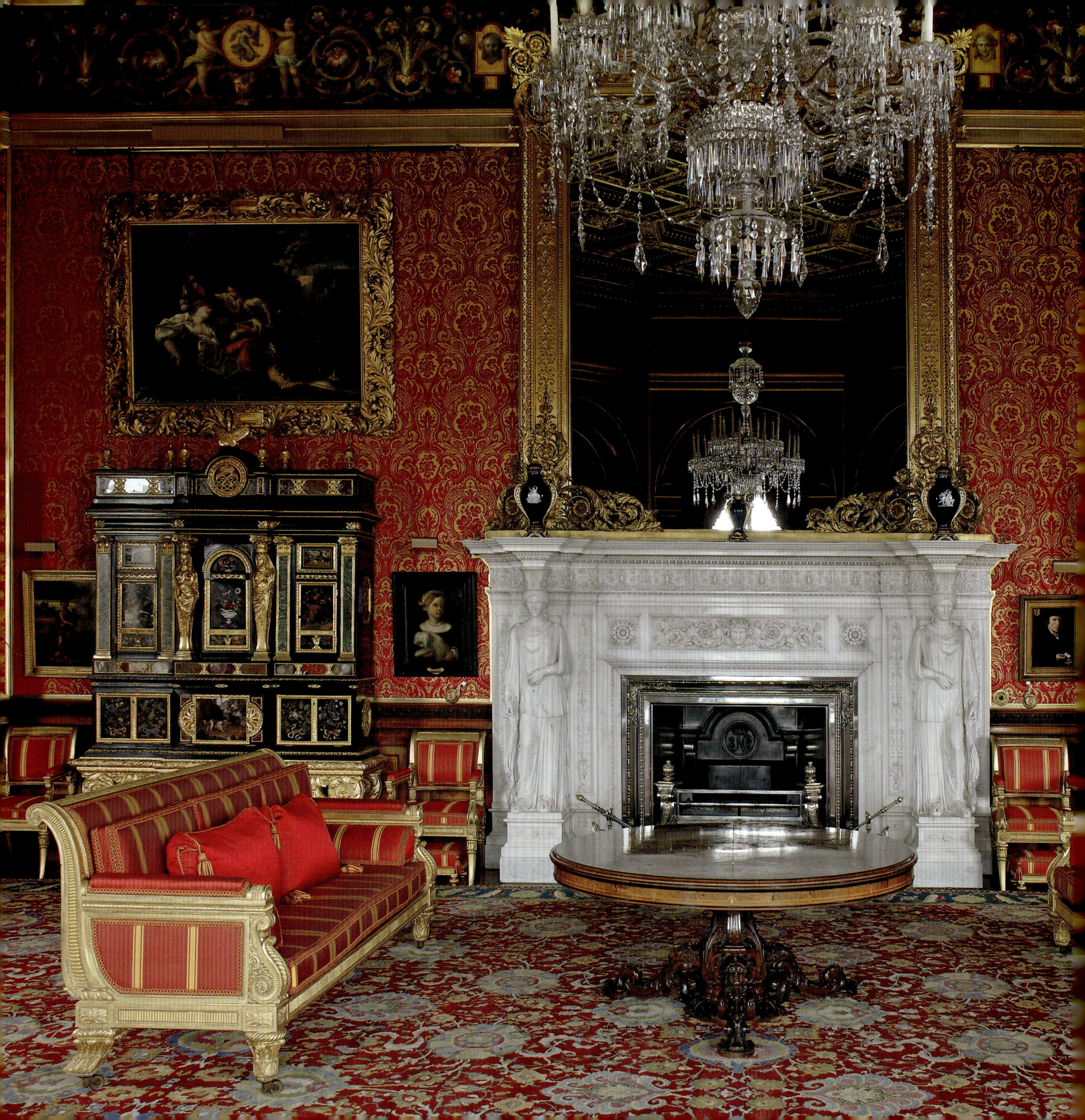

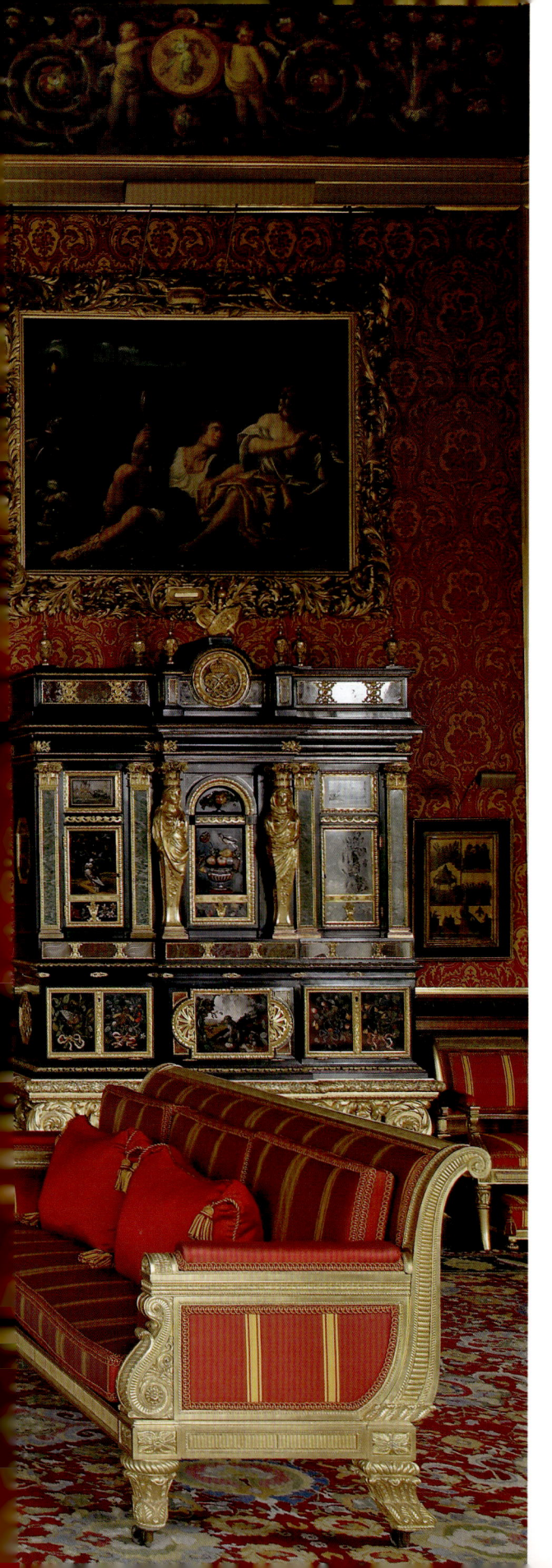

← The superb State Drawing Room at Alnwick Castle was decorated in the 1850s for the 4th Duke of Northumberland, on the advice of the Italian Commendatore Canina, director of the Capitoline Museum in Rome, to provide a home for his new collection of paintings, bought from the estate of the Italian history painter Vincenzo Camuccini, which included many Renaissance works.

↓ Commendatore Canina helped the Duke realise his ambition to have a princely interior reminiscent of fifteenth-century Italian palaces.

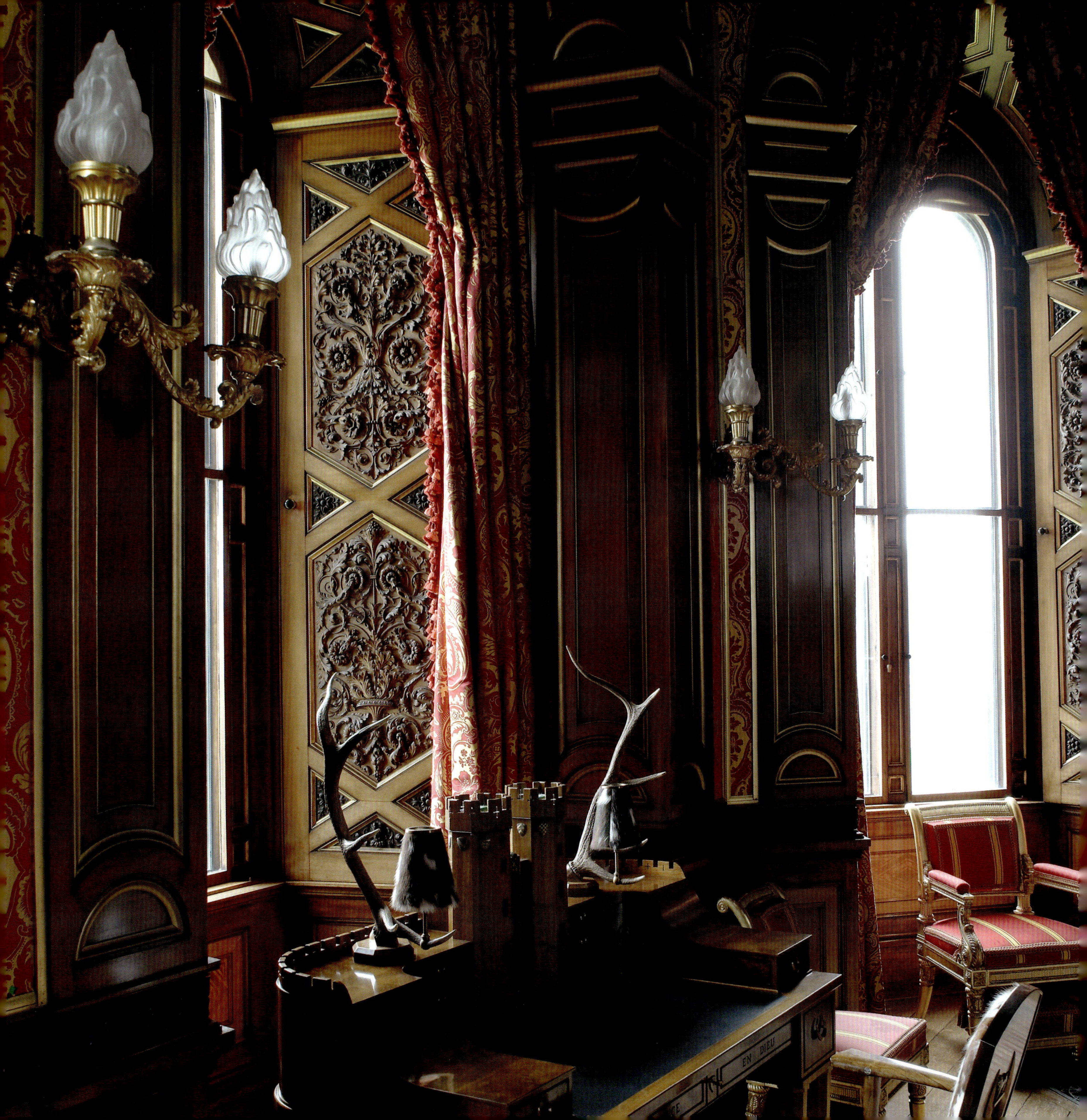
EN DIEU

Every surface was adorned with carved work, executed both by Italian carvers and local craftsmen trained by the Italians.

executed in wood; these will serve as a model, both for the carving and the decoration in colour." The frieze was "composed of ornaments with boys, on a blue ground, already painted in Rome by Sig. Montavani." The chimneypiece (carved in Rome by Signor Taccalozzi) had two caryatid figures carved by the sculptor Signor Nucci. The dado was "of dark Italian walnut."

With its richly coffered Cinquecento-style ceiling — the walls hung with crimson silk damask (Canina had originally specified "a red satin drapery, of Bolognese manufacture, from a drawing for the purpose") — this room was to be a fitting setting for part of the Duke's magnificent art collection of Old Masters, acquired in Rome, in 1856, from the estate of the famous history painter Vincenzo Camuccini.[8] The Duke's collection of Renaissance art was one of the most important to be formed by an English aristocrat. Amongst the paintings still hanging in the drawing room are a portrait of a young man by Andrea del Sarto, *Crucifixion* by Guido Reni, and *The Holy Family* by Giorgio Vasari. In 1865 there were also paintings by Bellini, Raphael, and Domenichino.

The room is also today dominated by two great cabinets made around 1683 for Louis XIV's Versailles, by Domenico Cucci, from ebony, marble, and bronze gilt, and covered with semiprecious stones, amethyst, and lapis lazuli. It has been suggested that the cabinets were made for the apartments of Madame de Montespan. In his 1931 account of the house, the 8th Duke recorded the family legend that the cabinets were "looted from the Tuileries during the French Revolution and were found in a cellar in Paris in 1800, when they were purchased by the 2nd Duke."[9] There does not seem to be any further documentary evidence of this enjoyable story. The cabinets were in fact acquired in 1822 by the 3rd Duke for Northumberland House in London; the stately gilt sofa and chairs by London cabinetmakers Morel and Hughes were also made for Northumberland House but brought to Alnwick in the 1920s. The London house of the Percy family, Northumberland House was sold and demolished to make way for a road (Northumberland Avenue) in 1874.[10]

The choice of style made by the Duke was criticised by some, such as the Gothic revivalist architect George Gilbert Scott, who observed rather ungenerously in *Remarks on Secular Domestic Architecture, Present and Future* (1857): "Whether the princely Lord of Alnwick thought he had no alternative between the debased Gothic of Windsor and (what I hope I shall be pardoned for calling) the mimic feudalism of Peckferten, I know not; but the result was this — that happening at the time to winter in Rome, his Grace became enamoured of the interiors of the Renaissance palaces, and fostered the infelicitous idea of making his ancestral residence a feudal castle without and a Roman palazzo within."[11] Even Salvin (also the architect of Peckforton Castle) in 1857, admitted the Italian interiors would not have been his first choice but he also said publicly he did not think as some did "that because the doors, the windows and ceilings are Medieval, therefore the floors must be covered with rushes, and the furniture benches.[12]

Others leapt to the Duke's defence. In the November 1856 debate at the RIBA, M. D. Wyatt, who had been Secretary of the Great Exhibition, felt the interior decoration had been well chosen for the picture collection he housed. T. L. Donaldson responded to those who objected that the interiors were not neo-medieval with the Duke's own reported view, namely that the Duke chose Italian Renaissance because he thought most modern medievalised interiors had been failures (including Windsor Castle).[13] The magnificent drawing room at Alnwick was restored in 2008–09 by the present Duke and Duchess of Northumberland and it remains one of the finest neo-Renaissance interiors in the country — although the family prefers the undoubted charms of the library as their usual sitting room.

↓ One of the great cabinets in ebony, marble, and bronze-gilt, made by Domenico Cucci for Versailles in around 1683, acquired for Northumberland House and moved to Alnwick by 1930.

→ The ensemble of the drawing room at Alnwick Castle is one of remarkable richness in ornament and texture, in the spirit of a Renaissance palace interior.

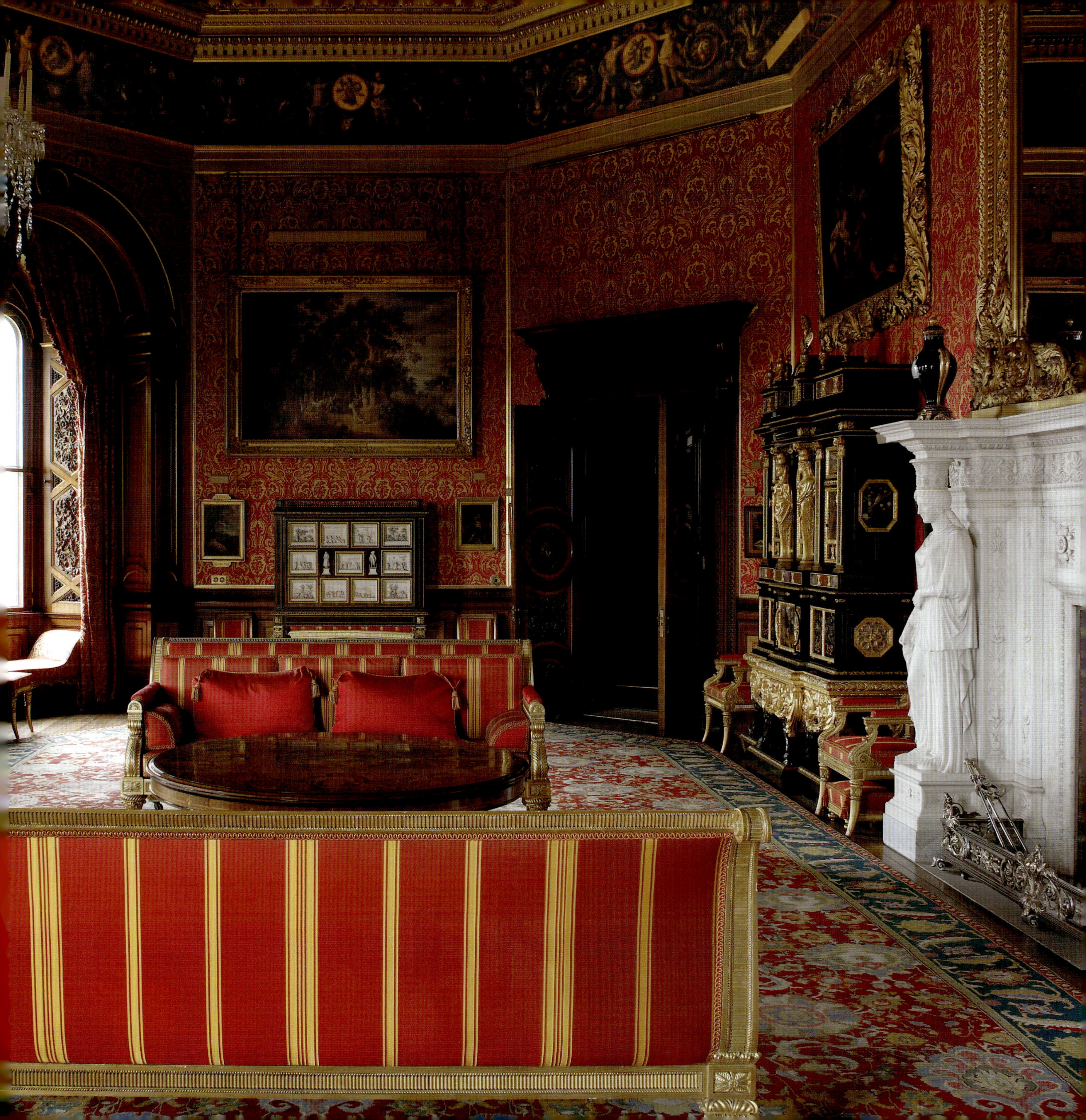

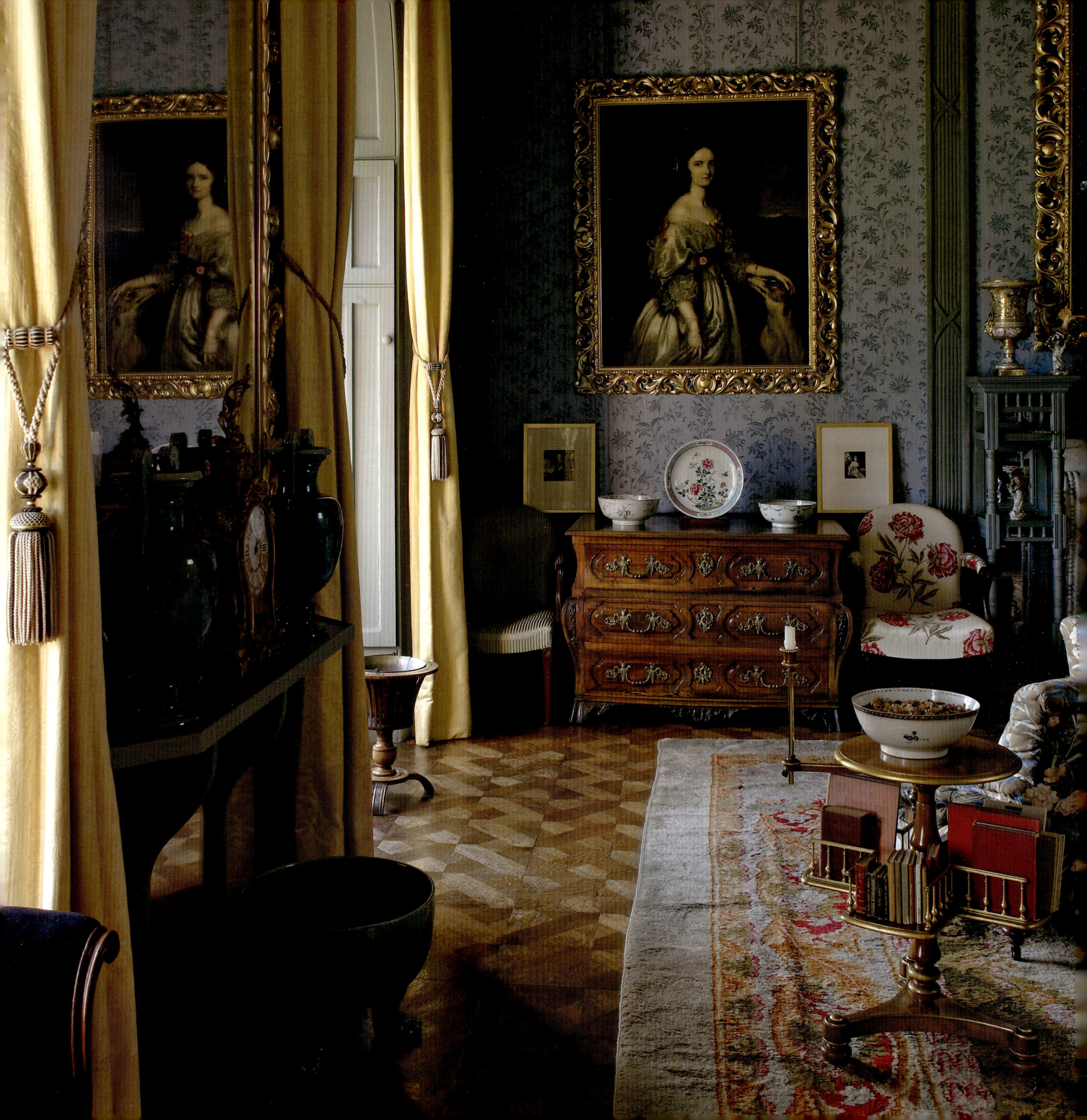

III · OPULENCE · THE LATER NINETEENTH CENTURY

Hutton in the Forest

The aesthetic moment: Morris & Co. wallpaper at Hutton in the Forest captures the artistic taste of the 1870s.

Hutton in the Forest, the home of Lord Inglewood, is a layered house of many periods, built mostly between the mid-fourteenth and the mid-nineteenth centuries. In brief, Hutton in the Forest is a fortified tower with an early-seventeenth-century gallery by Alexander Pogmire for Henry Fletcher, with further 1680s changes to the facade by Edward Addison, probably working to designs by William Talman for Sir George Fletcher. There are some Georgian interiors designed possibly by Daniel Garrett, with decorative ceiling plasterwork by Thomas Perritt and Joseph Rose Senior.[1] Like many ancient houses, Hutton was reinvented with alterations and remodelling in Picturesque Gothic revival spirit in the nineteenth century. There were substantial alterations in the late 1820s to designs by George Webster. It is somewhat difficult to disentangle the different contributions made by Webster and those by Anthony Salvin for the Fletcher Vane family in the succeeding four decades—these included the Romantic crenellation of the house's south front. Salvin was a family friend who advised and provided designs for various projects.

Salvin's later work was done for Sir Henry Vane, the 4th Bt., who had inherited the estate at the age of twelve in 1842, after the early death of his father, Sir Francis. In 1870 Sir Henry married the somewhat highbrow and artistic Margaret Gladstone, a cousin of the famous Liberal Prime Minister. She took an interest in the interior decoration of the house and was a competent artist and architect herself, as well as an Arts and Crafts enthusiast and promoter of handicraft.[2]

Lady Vane seems to have played a decisive role in helping to resolve the alterations that had been made over the previous decades into an attractive and grand interior. According to notes made by Lady Vane herself, the room over the hall was originally the drawing room, which Sir Henry turned into a library for which Salvin designed the doors. In 1872 the gallery was restored, and in 1877 a way was cut through to an 1820s room within the tower, which then became the drawing room situated above the dining room on the ground floor. As John Cornforth wrote in 1965, "the final result of these changes was a spectacular progress through the house on formal occasions from drawing room to dining room and back."[3]

Through Lady Vane's interest in the work of William Morris, she visited Morris & Co. in London to choose papers for the drawing room and other rooms; there are still some six rooms decorated in various Morris & Co. papers, including the dining room. The drawing room paper is an unusually well-preserved example of a rare design called Spray, first produced in about 1871. Interestingly, Spray was not designed by Morris but is a copy of a historic paper from a house in Co Cork: Palace Anne, near Brandon. Morris knew of the original design through a sample he was given by the architect Charles C. Townsend in 1866.[4] The combination of the soft distemper-blue background and the darker blue details feels very fresh today; the green-painted woodwork and the painted chimneypiece with its shelves for the display of china are all of a piece.

Lady Vane's portrait by Karl Wilhelm Friedrich Bauerle dominates the drawing room, which she had decorated with such aesthetic spirit. Lady Vane clearly cared deeply about her husband's family home, and in the 1880s she commissioned a Romantic castellated tower, known in her honour as the Gladstone Tower, which she once described as "my gift to the old house."[5] Sir Henry died in 1909, and his widow died in 1916, after which the drawing room seems to have been little used. Much of the furniture in this room therefore has been here since the late nineteenth century, certainly since 1916.

This room at Hutton in the Forest in Cumbria became the principal drawing room in the late 1870s. The Morris & Co. paper, known as Spray and first produced in 1871, was copied from an eighteenth-century paper found in Ireland.

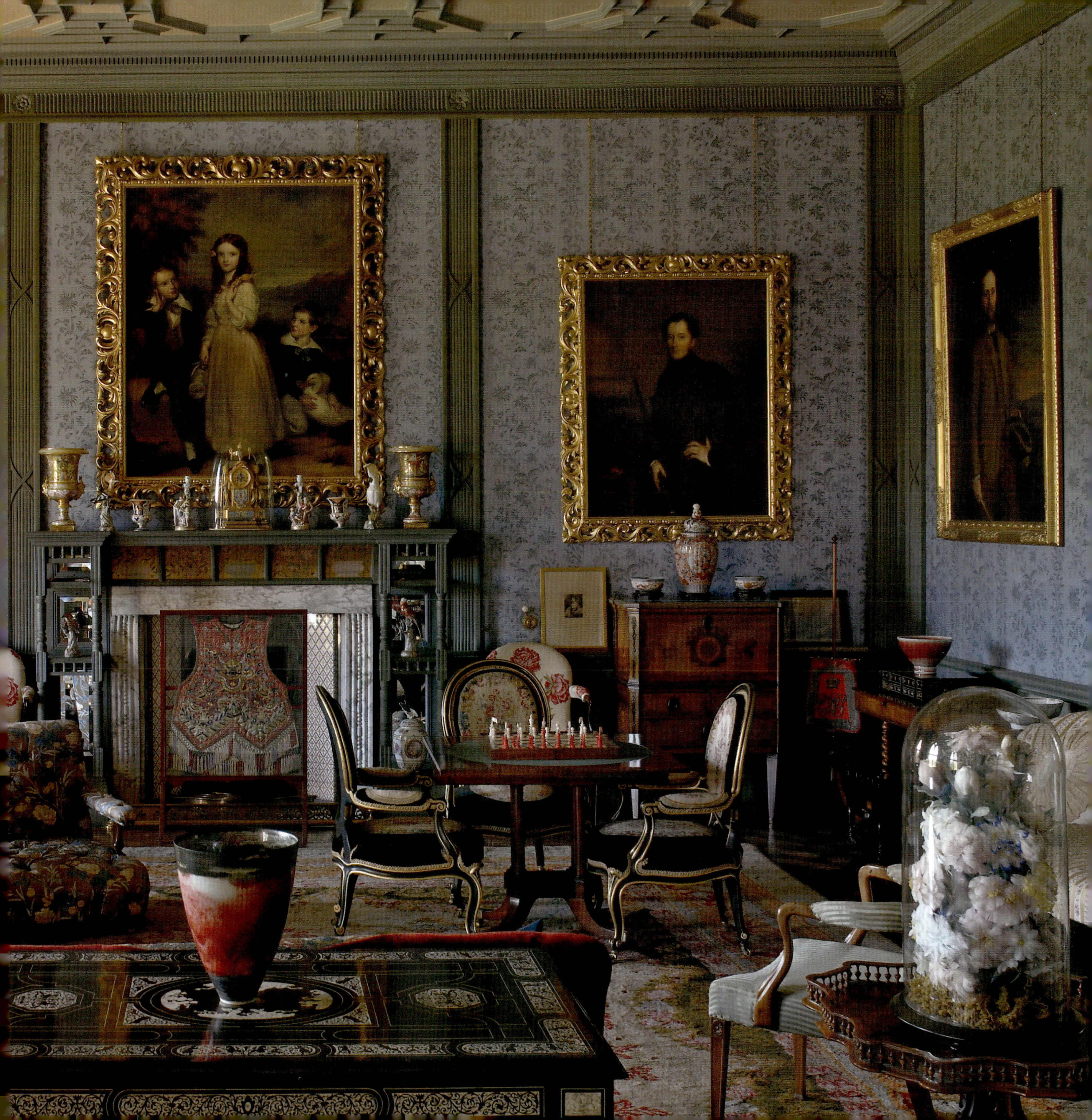

↓ The soft distemper blue and green painted dado rail creates a fine backdrop to the furniture in the drawing room.

→ Lord and Lady Inglewood have preserved the essentially late Victorian character of the room. A typically nineteenth-century feel of layered decoration is immediately apparent.

As well as the upholstered seat furniture, there is an unusual suite of Gillows furniture in the Hepplewhite style, as well as a Broadwood piano. Certain foreign pieces are also found in this room, including an Italian inlaid ebony table thought to have belonged to Charles Beauclerk, who had lived in Pisa for a time; a late-eighteenth-century Swedish bureau; and a Beidermeyer cabinet inherited from Viscountess Gough, Lord Inglewood's great aunt. There are numerous family portraits by Romney, Reynolds, and Trevisani (the latter of 1st Lord Barnard); a group portrait over the chimneypiece by Frederick Hurlstone shows Sir Henry and his siblings as children; two others are of his parents, Sir Francis and Diana Olivia (née Beauclerk). A recent portrait of the present Lord and Lady Inglewood and their eldest daughter, by Anthony Eyton, RA, brings the story up to date.

The survival of this atmospheric late-nineteenth-century drawing room owes much to the present Lord and Lady Inglewood, who have preserved it as an important survival of the late Victorian "house beautiful" taste associated with Morris & Co. Lord Inglewood comments: "The room has been little altered after 1916, partly because my father who inherited in 1933 when he was leaving Cambridge, worked in London and then went to War in 1939. He became an MP in 1945, only marrying in 1949. Hutton was also requisitioned during the war, but an aunt of mine kept an eye on things and I suspect the drawing room was shut up. Later on, my parents prefered to use the sitting rooms in the southwest corner of the house, as do we, as they are also more convenient for contemporary living and the garden. This drawing room was used only on rare occasions."[6] Lord and Lady Inglewood have replaced the faded yellow silk curtains with yellow cotton from Cummersdale outside Carlisle but otherwise have kept the room in the spirit in which they found it.

140 | HUTTON IN THE FOREST

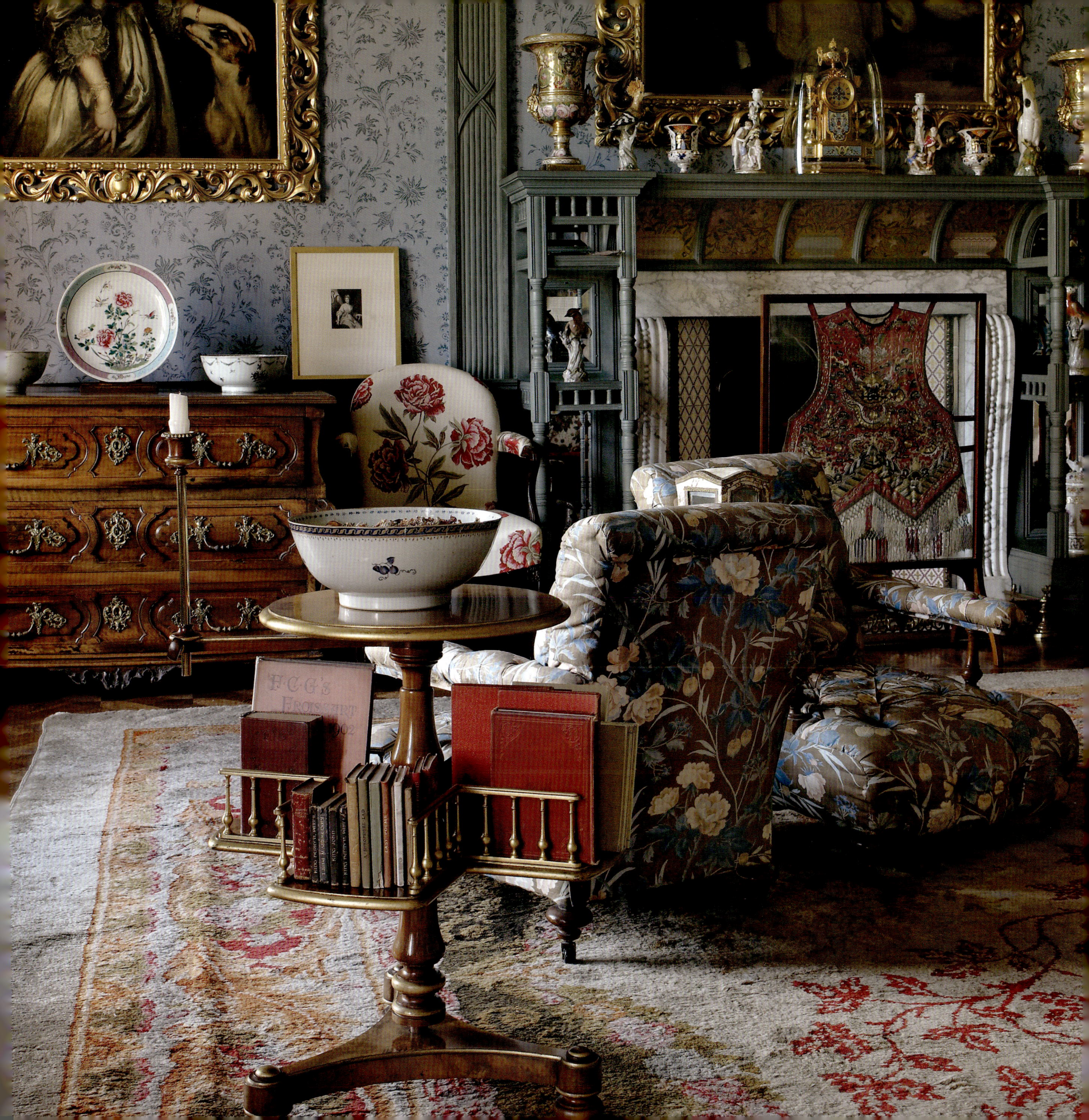
F.C.G's

↓ The Gothic windows date from the early nineteenth century remodellings by George Webster. A portrait of Lady Vane, who masterminded the redecoration in the late 1870s, can be glimpsed reflected in the mirror.

→ The furnishings of this room have mostly been in situ since 1916 and include furniture supplied by Gillows of Lancaster and a Broadwood piano.

142 | HUTTON IN THE FOREST

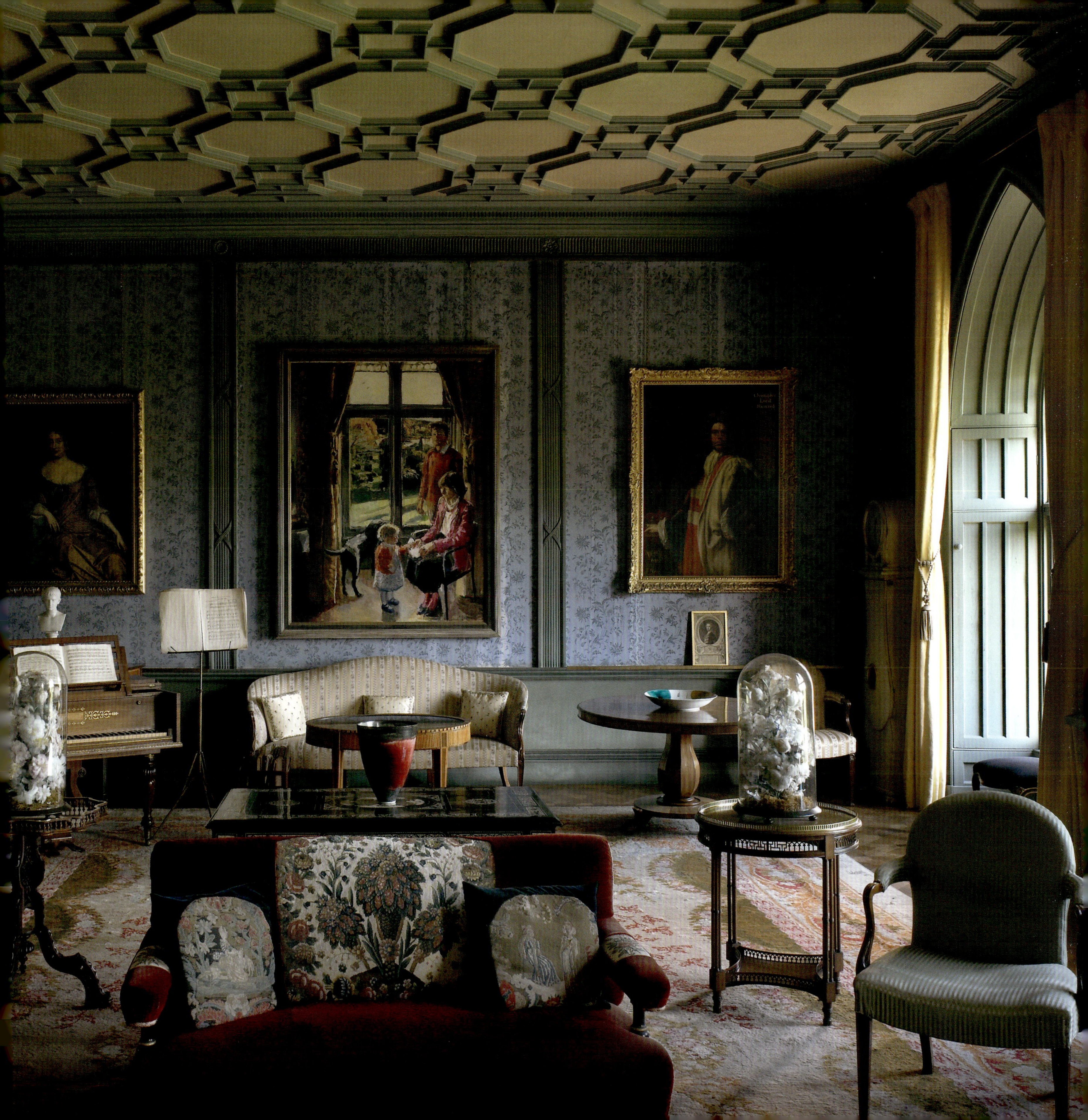

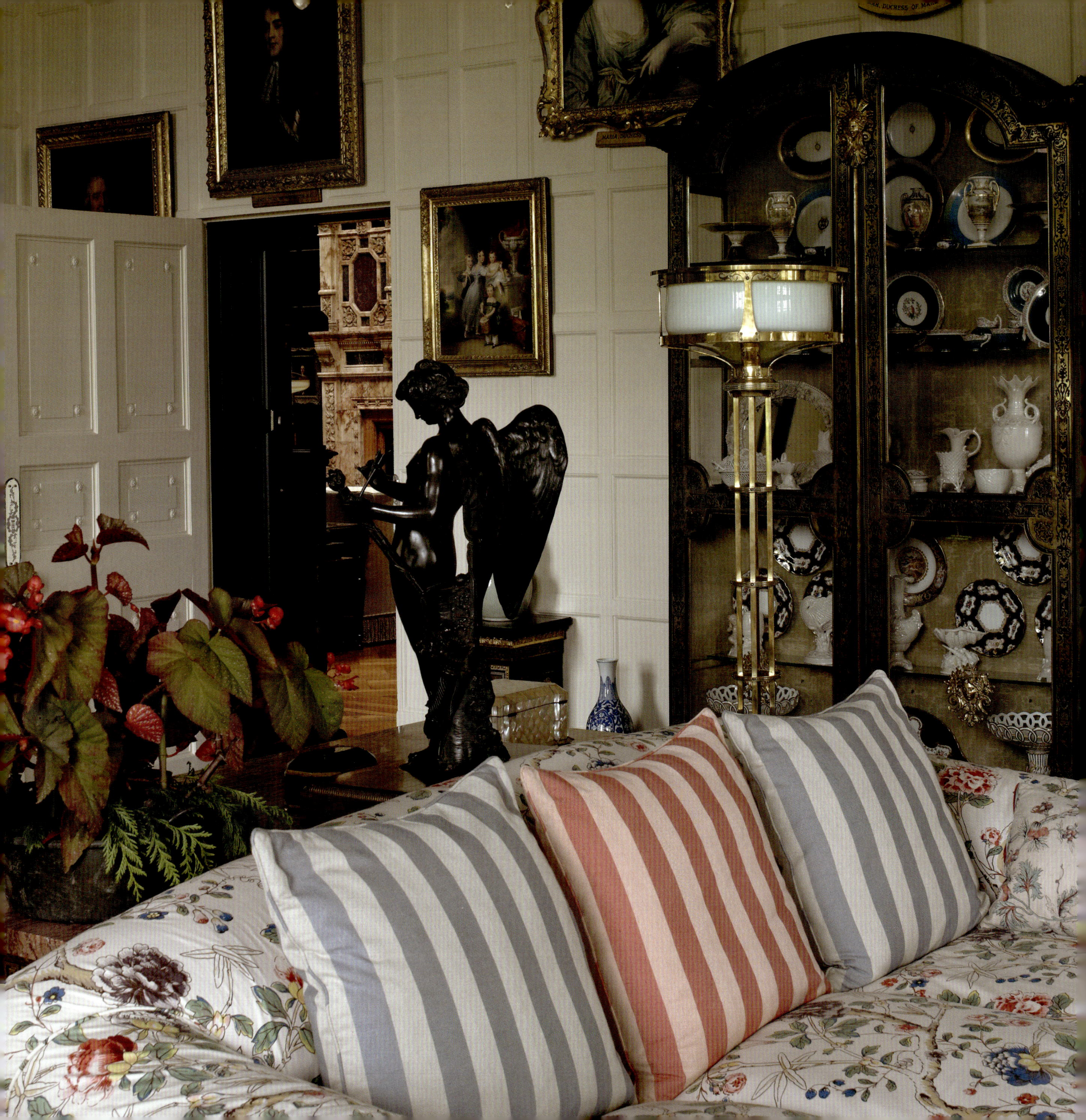

III · OPULENCE · THE LATER NINETEENTH CENTURY

Madresfield Court

Eclectic interiors reflect the long residence of one family in pursuit of modern comfort.

The stately drawing room at Madresfield Court is a surprising mixture of periods and inspirations. It is a huge room in part of the understated "Jacobethan" style of the house as remodelled by High Victorian architect P. C. Hardwick from 1864 for the 6th Earl of Beauchamp.[1] This work was intended to recapture the age and antiquity of the house and its remarkable moated site. Hardwick retained the medieval core while removing eighteenth-century additions, and the physical restrictions of the moated site seem to have inspired him to an unusually imaginative and picturesque result—although little of the older house is visible today.

Madresfield Court is remarkable too in that it has never been bought or sold "since records began." The Chenevix-Trench family living here today are descendants through the Lygons of William de Bracy, who first lived here in around 1260. The Lygons became Earls of Beauchamp in 1815, and the last Earl died in 1979, after which the house was lived in by his niece, Lady Morrison. Her daughter and her husband, Lucy and John Chenevix-Trench, have recently taken over.

It was at Madresfield that Evelyn Waugh, a friend at Oxford of Lord Hugh Lygon, one of the many children of the house, came to stay for house parties in the 1930s. Waugh used these experiences as the basis of his novel *Brideshead Revisited*. The 7th Earl by then lived abroad in exile, but according to his instructions the house was still run by a full liveried staff, so his young adult children were served by nineteen indoor servants and only vaguely chaperoned by the children's former governess.[2]

It was not just the ritual of the house party that caught Waugh's imagination but the architecture too. In *A Handful of Dust* he describes a fictional country house, Hetton Abbey, with something of the spirit of Madresfield, speaking of "The general aspect and atmosphere of the place; the line of its battlements against the sky; the central clock tower where quarterly chimes disturb all but the heaviest sleepers; the ecclesiastical gloom of the great hall, its ceiling groined and painted in diapers of red and gold." The narrator of *Brideshead*, Charles Ryder, also describes how "More even than the work of great architects, I loved buildings that grew silently with the centuries," capturing the effect Hardwick was trying to achieve here.[3]

Waugh protested that the house in *Brideshead* was not a portrait of the Lygons's family home—indeed the Flytes were not the Lygons: "I am writing a very beautiful book, to bring tears, about very rich, beautiful, high-born people who live in palaces and have no troubles except what they make themselves and those are mainly the demons sex and drink which after all are easy to bear as troubles go nowadays." The book is "all about a family whose father lives abroad, as it might be Boom [Lord Beauchamp]—but it's not Boom … and a younger son: people will say he's like Hughie, but you'll see he's not really Hughie—and there's a house as it might be Mad, but it isn't really Mad."[4]

Even without its remarkable role in literature, Madresfield is many layered, and is otherwise best known for its library designed in the Arts and Crafts spirit by C. R. Ashbee, and the unforgettable decoration of its High Church chapel, designed by Hardwick but decorated in 1902 (as a wedding present for the 7th Earl's new bride) by the Birmingham Group. Henry Payne painted the key frescoes. The great staircase hall was the result of a transformation by the Earl Beauchamp in the 1890s, as he opened up three rooms and ran a gallery with a crystal balustrade around the first floor level.

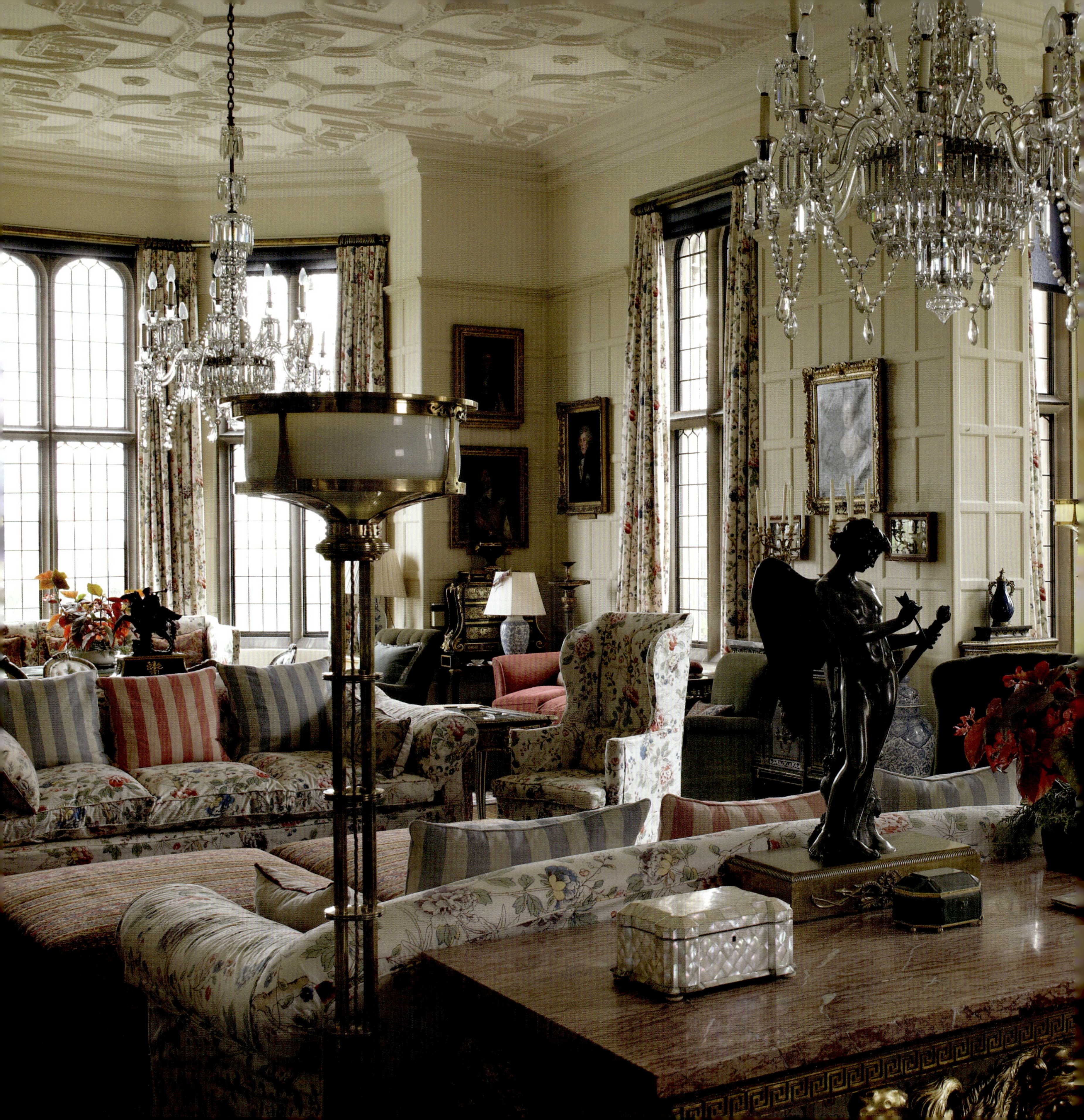

The vast drawing room at Madresfield Court in Worcestershire was created in the 1860s Jacobethan style by P. C. Hardwick for the 6th Earl Beauchamp. Much of the fine French furniture in this room was acquired by the Countess of Beauchamp (wife of the 1st Earl), who travelled to Paris in 1815.

OPULENCE | 147

Looking through to the drawing room from the saloon, the latter retains the moss-green colour scheme introduced a hundred years before by the 7th Earl.

The drawing room is perhaps the most conventionally stately of all the principal rooms at Madresfield and provides the climax for a progression through atmospheric but unusual rooms. It is a very large room—sixty feet long, forty feet wide, with surprisingly high ceilings—well lit with southern and western aspects through two huge bay windows, one looking out over the moat towards the Park and the Bredon Hills. The plasterwork ceiling is of a sober geometric Jacobean style, and the room is panelled in seventeenth-century style. But there are some very unusual elements: the chimneypiece is in a distinctive variegated green marble, and the tall, brass standard "electroliers," provided as part of the 7th Earl's work to the interior, are chastely art nouveau in character.

The great gilt table that cuts the room in two is attributed to William Kent and was made around 1740. But what predominates in the room is the *ancient regime* French boulle furniture mostly acquired by Catherine Denne, the Countess of Beauchamp—wife of the 1st Earl—when travelling to Paris in 1815 to visit her sons, who were serving in the army of occupation after Waterloo.[5] Lucy Chenevix-Trench refers to her ancestor's "great shopping spree": Lady Beauchamp certainly brought back with her an impressive range of commodes and cabinets from the former collections of the French nobility. One boulle cupboard in the saloon was reputedly from Louis XVI's private rooms at Versailles.

This Lady Beauchamp was also considered a great beauty—Lord Raglan recalled her "dark hair and blue eyes"—and there are two memorable portraits of her in the drawing room, one painted by Sir Joshua Reynolds and the other by Hoppner. Over the chimneypiece is a portrait of the esteemed historian Edward Gibbon, whose features were possibly less memorable than his mind. Cabinets contain items of family interest, including strands of hair from both the Duke of Wellington and William Pitt the Younger, as well as a bullet taken from the neck of the 4th Earl when he was injured in the Peninsular war.

There are later touches in the room too: amongst the portraits is one by G. F. Watts of the 6th Earl of Beauchamp. In the 7th Earl's time the room was painted in a deep mossy green, which survives in the saloon next door. This muted colour was popular with art collectors in the late nineteenth and early twentieth centuries (it was associated with early-eighteenth-century-styled interiors created by Lenygon and Morant of London).[6] The adjoining saloon's French-inspired interior detail was created for the wife of the 6th Earl in the 1870s, although this was toned down by the 7th Earl to bring the room into closer uniformity to the drawing room. In the 1980s, on the advice of Piers von Westenholz, Lucy Chenevix-Trench's mother Lady Morrison introduced a new colour scheme for the main drawing room: the panelling was repainted in a much lighter pale stone colour, and strong patterned fabrics were introduced for the sofa, chairs, and soft furnishings.[7] It remains a room with a gracious, comfortable feeling, one devoted to hospitality and full of interest, but cheerfully refreshed by new textiles and colours.

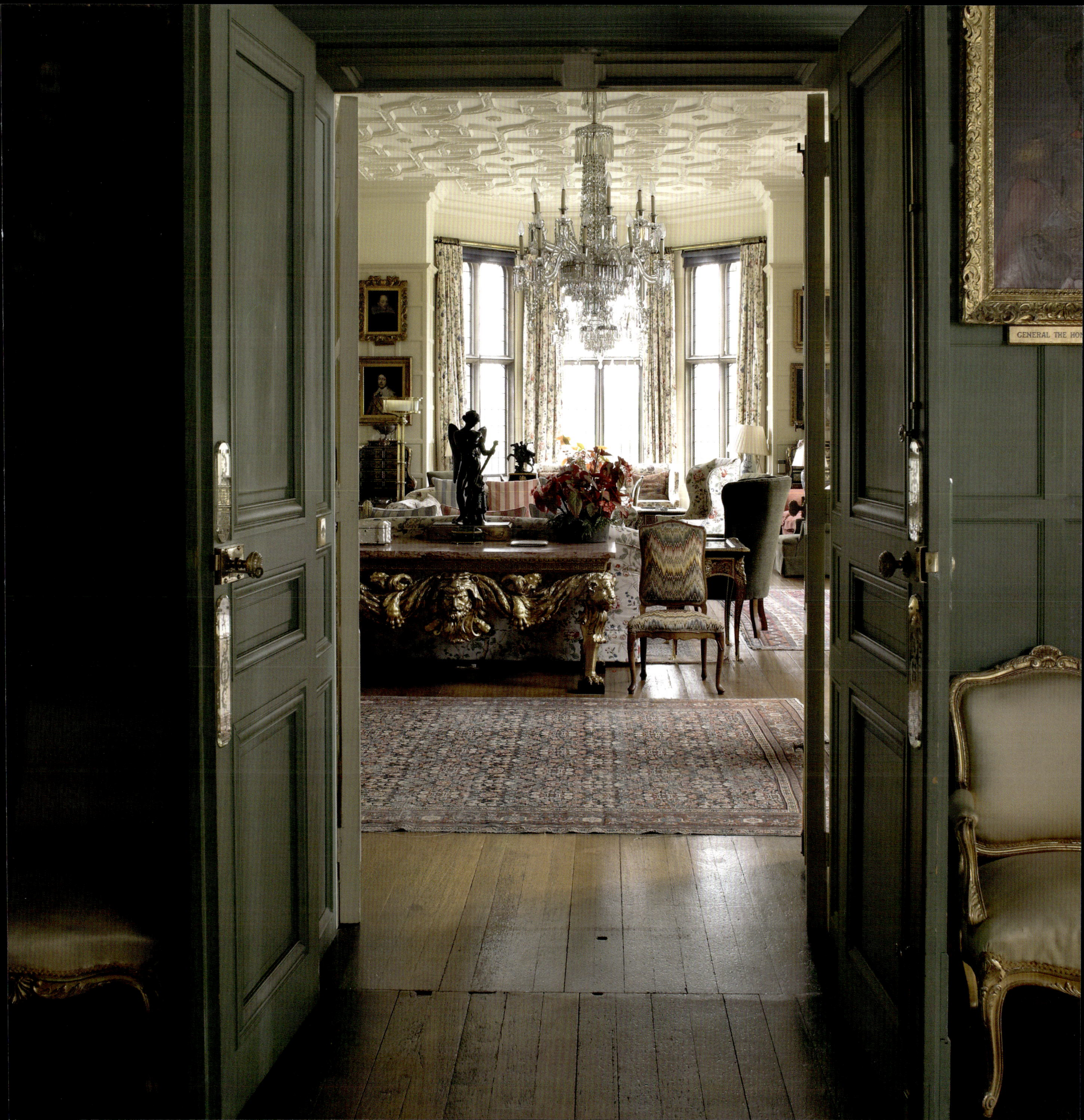
GENERAL THE HON

↓ Two large cabinets in the drawing room of Madresfield display china.

→ In the 1980s, Lady Morrison, on the advice of Piers von Westenholz, painted the drawing room a warm stone colour, much paler than the Edwardian scheme. There are several portraits of the Countess of Beauchamp, Catherine Denne, and the portrait over the chimneypiece is of Edward Gibbon, the author of The Decline and Fall of the Roman Empire.

150 | MADRESFIELD COURT

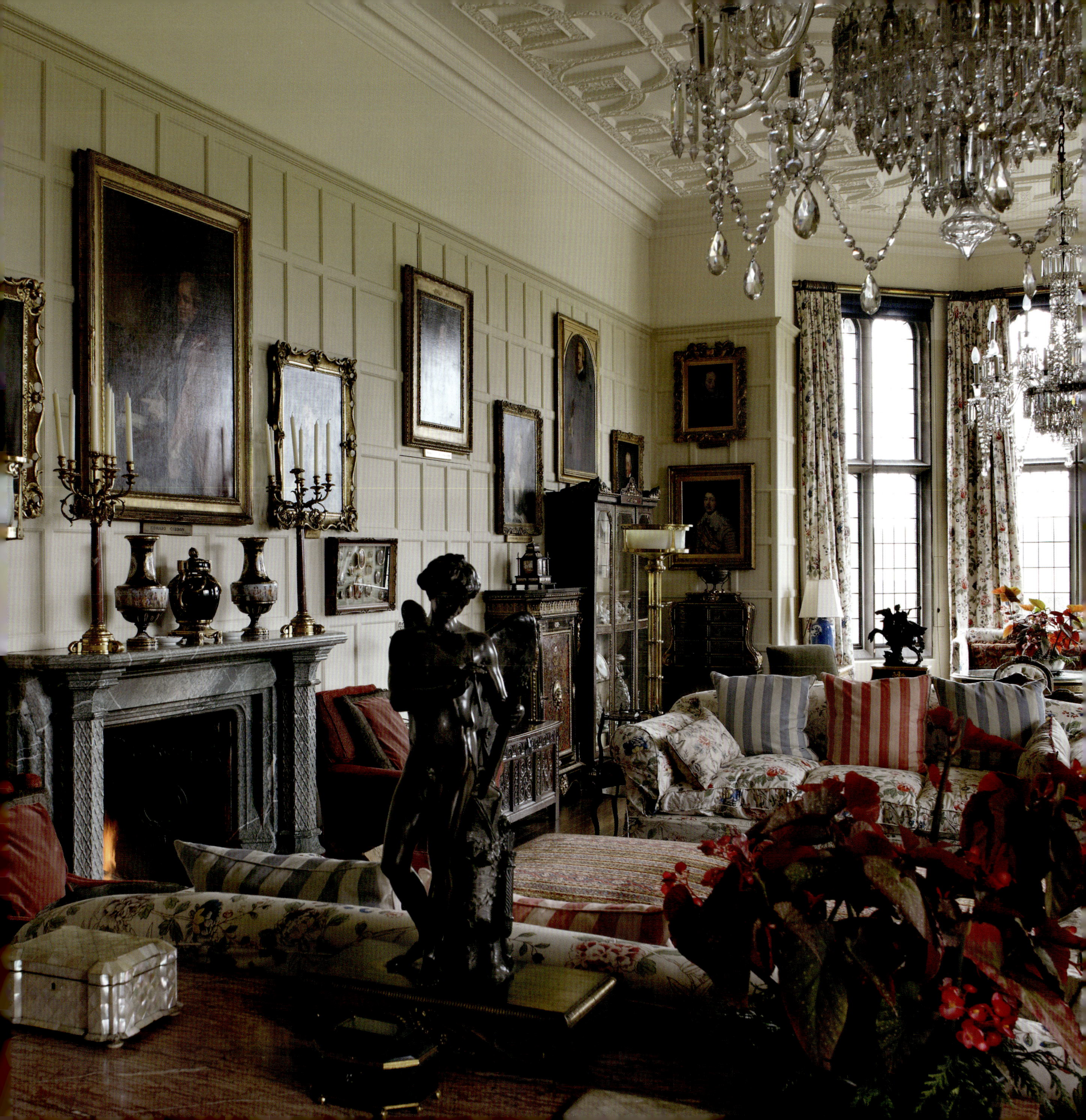

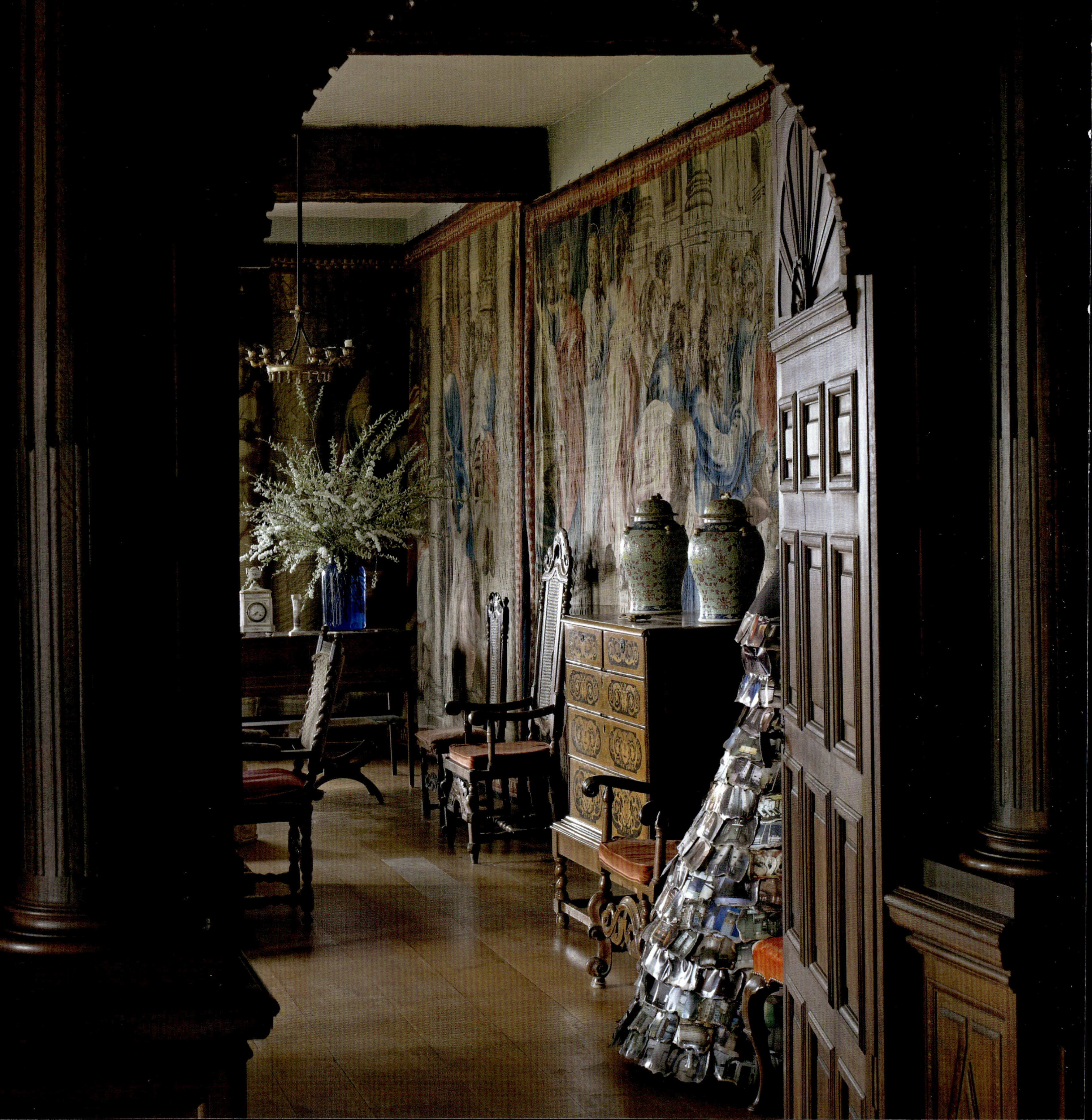

IV · TASTEMAKERS · THE TWENTIETH CENTURY

Hilles House

Arts and Crafts ideals: The Long Room was created by Detmar Blow as part of his Cotswolds dream home.

Hilles is a remarkable house, and the drawing room, known traditionally as the Long Room, expresses much of the aesthetic idealism of its creator, Arts and Crafts architect Detmar Blow (1867–1939), tempered by contributions from his family since, and by the continuing use of the room for family life, performance, and creativity. Hilles, as a house, was recently described by Clive Aslet as "a witness to an ideal, steadily maintained whatever the circumstances" since it was built in 1914–16, "the ideal is that of creative existence, lived amongst the beauties of the English countryside, around a welcoming hearth."[1]

As a young man, Blow met and was befriended by the much older John Ruskin while at Abbeville, in France, on a sketching tour. Ruskin persuaded him to abandon his conventional architectural training and apprentice himself to study the crafts of the traditional builders, which he duly did. He also got to know William Morris, Philip Webb, and William Holman Hunt. He worked as a foreman for Webb's restoration of East Knoyle church, where the client was the Hon. Percy Wyndham, who introduced him to the circle of high-minded aristocrats known as "The Souls," for whom he became quickly a favoured architect.[2] Thus he designed some of the most Romantic of English houses, including Wilsford in Wiltshire for Lady Glenconner. He added a wing to Stanway for Lady Elcho and a chapel at Hewell Grange for the Earl of Plymouth.

Blow was a friend and rival of Lutyens and certainly the more idealistic of the two. Blow's own house, Hilles, was built in 1914–16 and 1922–24, informed by his Romantic aesthetic-socialist vision. According to his grandsons, he loved nothing more than to bring together writers, poets, farmers, and his household servants—the family joke is that the back staircase was added at the insistence of the servants themselves. He certainly loved to gather people in the hall and Long Room to play music, sing, and dance, a tradition of openhearted creativity that continues today.

There is something of the idealized manor house about Hilles. In the early 1900s it was felt that the old manor houses of England almost symbolized an integrated community in which all members were bound in loyalty and each recognised for their contribution. Blow may also have been motivated by a desire to have a house suitable for his wife, who came from a landowning background. In 1910 Blow had married Winifred Tollemache (a granddaughter of Lord Tollemache). Their meeting was suitably romantic, as Blow was on a sketching tour of East Anglia in a gypsy caravan and happened to camp on the grounds of Helmingham Hall, in Suffolk, the family home. At Hilles Blow became a minor landowner himself, with around two thousand acres and sixteen farms. They were a devoted couple, and her love is said to have sustained him through the difficulties of his serious falling out with the Duke of Westminster, who had become his principal client by 1916 (Blow was his private secretary and manager of the Grosvenor London estates).[3]

Architecturally, Hilles is a thoughtful essay on a modestly manorial theme. The kitchen is an integral part of the building, connecting with the dining hall, which is separated from the Long Room by a handsome screen that came originally from Seckford Hall in Suffolk. Built out on a bastion, running into the steep hillside, the house embodies that Morrisian view that traditionally built houses should appear to grow out of the site. But there is a dash of modern vision here, for the effect of this siting is that while the hall is on the ground level, the Long Room feels as if it soars out into the sky. One has to stand in the window bay at the end to look down onto the dazzling Cotswolds patchwork of landscape, villages, and town of

THE DRAWING ROOM | 153

↓ Family portraits hang on sixteenth-century panelling in the Arts and Crafts–inspired drawing room at Hilles, traditionally known as the Long Room.

→ Detmar Blow I created this memorable room by inserting a handsome oak screen from Seckford Hall in Suffolk. Its arches frame beautifully the atmospheric and mellow room beyond.

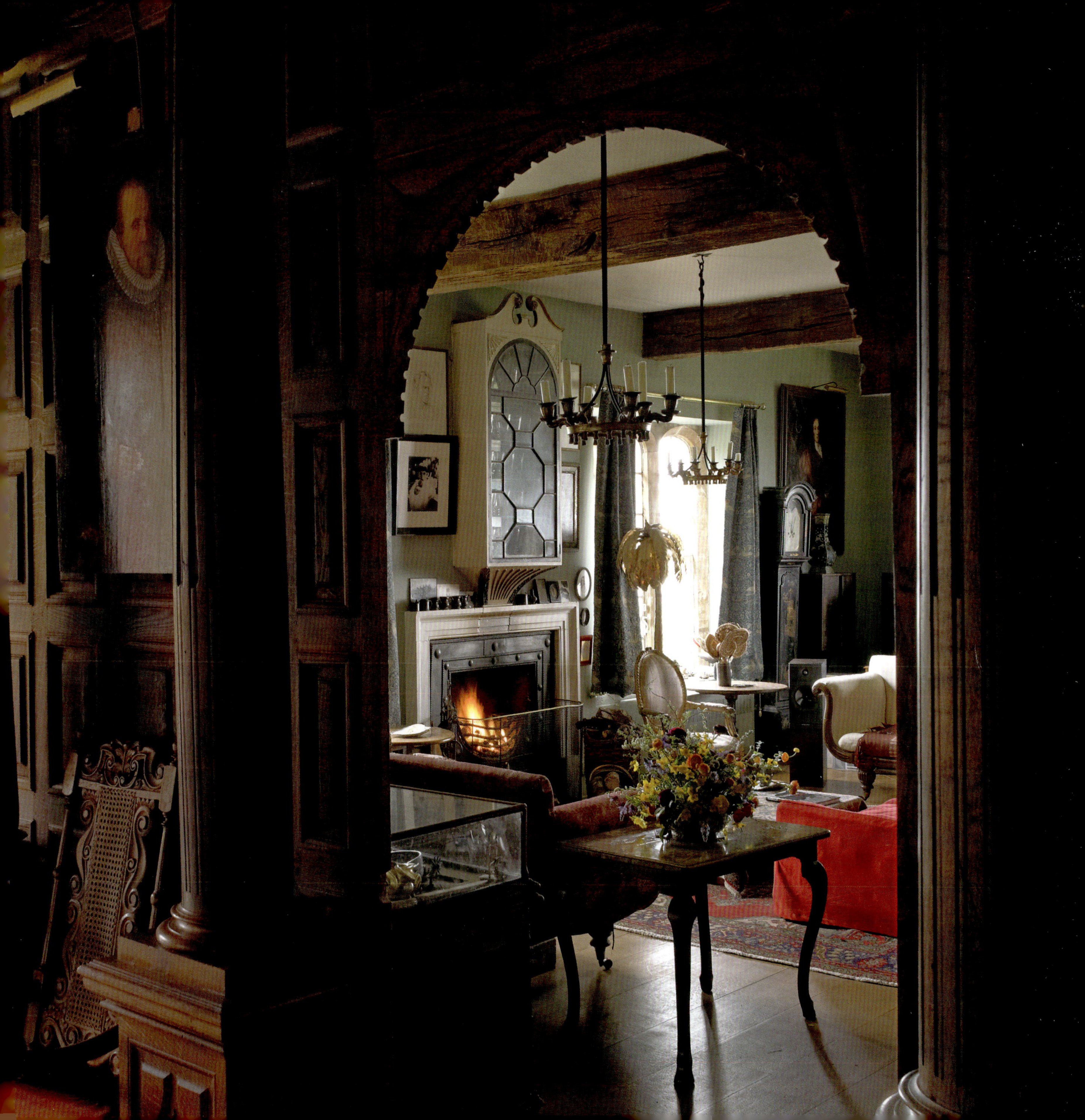

The dress-mannequin sculpture arranged by an artist, Mara Castilho, a former girlfriend of Detmar Blow II, and mother of his young son, Sasha; it stands against the tapestry which covers one wall in the Long Room.

Stroud. Until you move to that part of the room you could be in an airship floating above the clouds.

Blow's friend, the Hon. Neville Lytton wrote, "The rooms are long and full of light … the long drawing room has a floor of raw elm, which cannot be injured by large boots with nails in the soles … There is little furniture — one or two beautiful chests and chests of drawers, three or four tapestries and three or four pictures."[4] Blow was an artist in spirit, and his Long Room is in some ways a distillation of observation and knowledge of the interiors of smaller historic English houses. His original design for this room included windows on three sides, but his unexpected purchase of a set of Mortlake tapestries diverted him from that course, although the outline of where the windows would have been can be seen in the wall behind the tapestries.

Overall there is a strong feeling of the handcrafted house that was Blow's ideal, but tempered with other elements, not least the elegant Regency seat furniture. One would not say there is "little furniture" today, rather the opposite. The subtle red-gold covered sofa, shells, and Asian artifacts are amongst the deft touches added from the 1960s by Sri Lankan Helga de Silva, who married Detmar's son, Jonathan Blow; an additional layer of bohemian theatricality was added by Issie Blow, the fashion editor and late wife of Jonathan's art dealer son, Detmar. The room feels comfortable and loved.[5]

Over the chimneypiece is a cabinet of glasses designed in Murano by Detmar Jellings on a trip to Venice in the 1920s, and to the side hang two sketches of Detmar Blow by Augustus John, which capture a face of considerable sensitivity. There is also a small photograph of the aged Ruskin, Blow's friend and mentor. There is a portrait of Winifred, his wife, who shared his belief in the Arts and Crafts ideals. The gold-painted chandeliers came from the workshop of the Countess of Plymouth at Hewell Grange. Lady Plymouth, a very close friend of Winifred Blow, stayed at Hilles during the Second World War. The remarkable dress-mannequin figure, which stands out headless against the tapestry, is by Mara Castilho, a former partner of Detmar Blow II and mother of his young son, Sasha.

The house was restored after a fire in 1951. Blow's son-in-law, Philip Warre-Cornish, was the architect in charge of the restoration, and while most elements were returned as faithfully as possible to the original, there were a number of simplifications (for instance, the house was not re-thatched but hung with old Cotswold stone slate). Comparison with paintings of the interior in the house and photographs taken in *Country Life* magazine in 1940 shows that the surviving oak screen has been reversed, and the carved, fluted columns appear now on the outside of the screen in the hall.[6] Doors have also been added to close off the room if needed. A second screen dividing the hall into a dining room and entrance hall was not replaced, and that space became known as the Big Hall.

Those family members who live in and around Hilles today still relish the quality of open fire and candlelight, music, conversation, and dancing that takes place in the Long Room and the Hall. This is still a room to live in and a room to dream in — just as it was always meant to be.

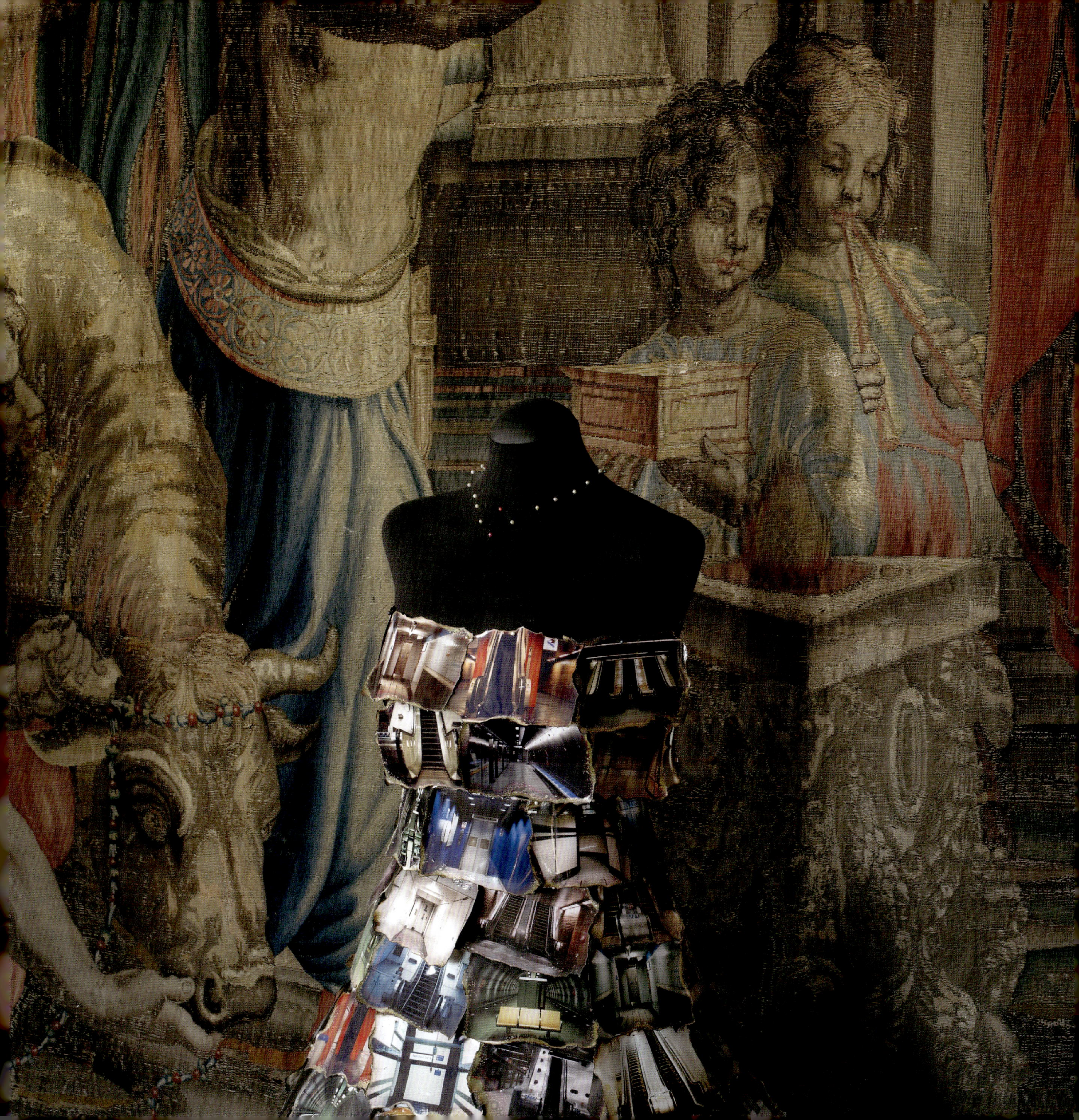

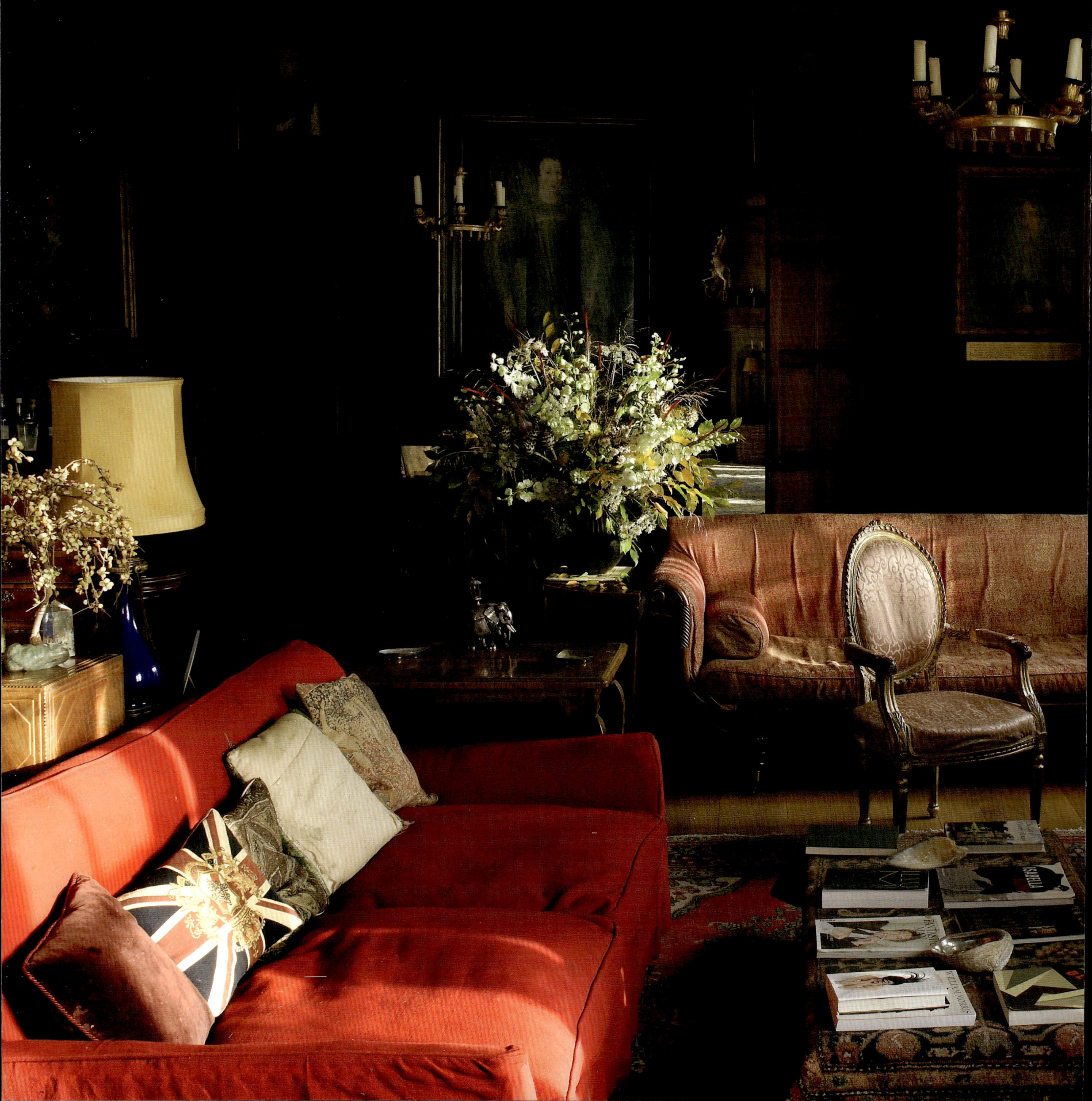
ISABELLA
WILLIAM MORRIS

The stately but human-scale Arts and Crafts character of the Long Room has been enhanced by touches made by later members of the family, including Helga de Silva, mother of Detmar Blow II, and his late wife, Issie Blow.

TASTEMAKERS | 159

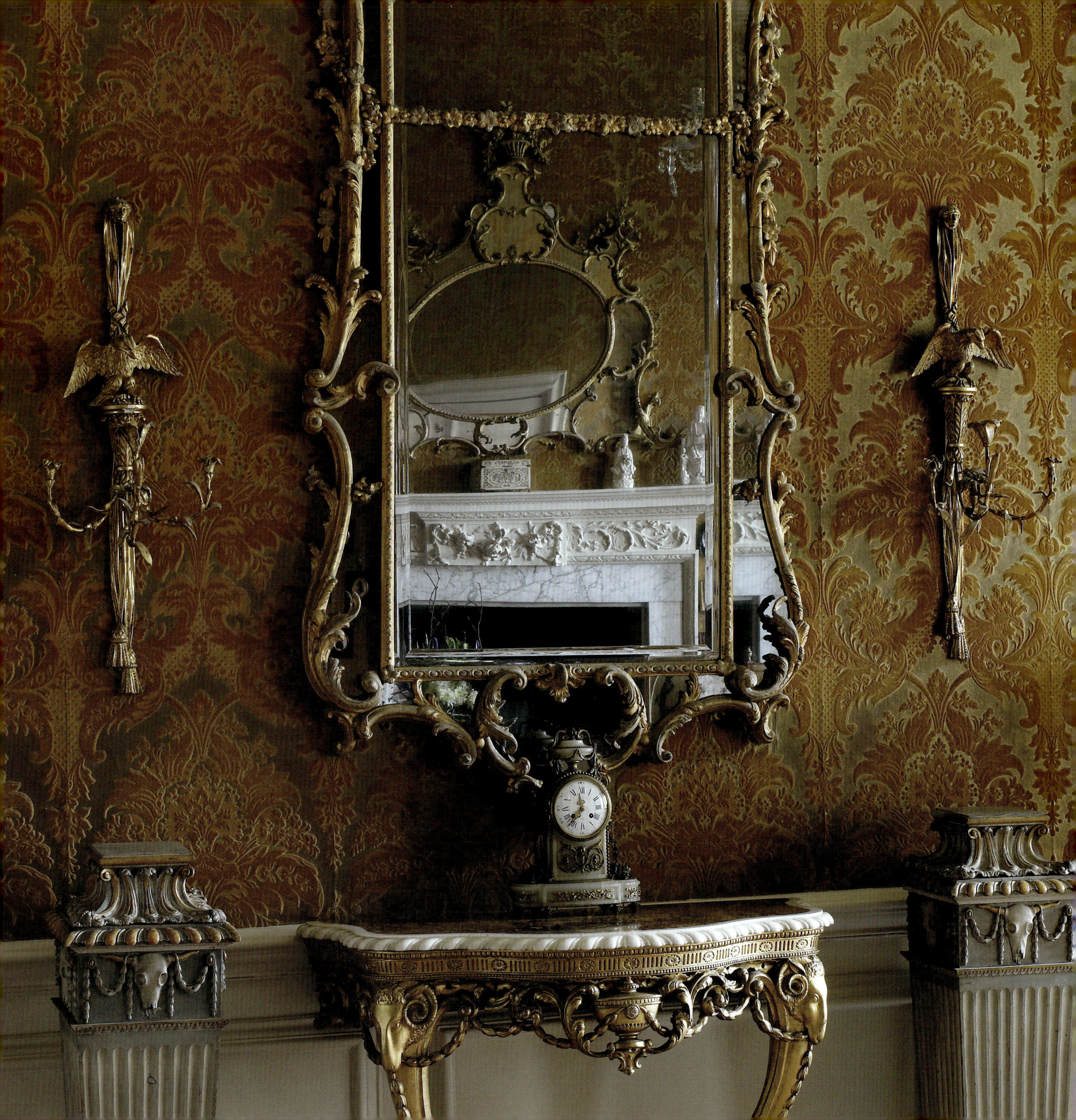

IV · TASTEMAKERS · THE TWENTIETH CENTURY

Dyrham Park

First used as a drawing room by Lady Islington in the 1930s, this room contains some remarkable Gillows furniture.

The drawing room at Dyrham Park has a curious story, and in fact only became the drawing room in the late 1930s, when the house was leased to Anne, Lady Islington, who did her best to cheer up what had become rather gloomy rooms.[1] It is difficult to imagine that time when today you first see Dyrham in its superb setting, a handsome stone house of Tudor origins that took its current romantic form in the late seventeenth and early eighteenth centuries under the influence of William Blathwayt, an able and intelligent Restoration civil servant. Blathwayt was Sir William Temple's secretary at The Hague, secretary at war and clerk to the Privy Council, as well as MP for Bath, who raised himself from relatively humble origins to a position of social prestige and influence and in 1688 married the heiress of Dyrham, Mary Wynter.[2] The west front was then rebuilt by Samuel Hauduroy by 1694 and the east front, by William Talman, was completed in 1703.

The drawing room faces west and is the largest of all the rooms on the ground floor, with the exception of the Great Hall. The room has bolection panelling to dado height and a cornice carved in the 1690s by a "Mr. Vanderlass." It is interesting to note that it was called a drawing room only in 1938; in 1692 the room was known as the Gilt Leather Parlour, when the current dining room was known as the Slop't Parlour. A 1710 inventory lists the many furnishings of the Gilt Leather Parlour, including ten elbow chairs, five Dutch chairs, a couch, and a gilt leather screen.[3]

The Gilt Leather Parlour was then clearly the principal parlour used for dining and entertaining important guests and decorated in prestigious gilt leather hangings. By 1742 the name seems to have become contracted and was known simply as the Great Parlour. In 1839 it became a library and continued in that use until the 1930s.[4] It was adapted as a drawing room by Lady Islington, one of the highly regarded interior decorators of her generation, admired by her contemporaries including Nancy Lancaster, who redecorated Dyrham in the late 1930s.

The 1710 inventory mentions that the panelling of the room was originally grained to imitate walnut, although paint analysis has shown that the doors and all the panelling were grained in a similar style to the dining room, which was grained to appear like cedar. Lady Islington picked everything out in white, and it is presumably during her time that the panelling and chimneypiece of the drawing room were first painted white, as they remain today.

The 1839 inventory described, "A Range of painted Book Cases with Wire Doors 16 ft long / Another Range of 8 feet 3 long / Another d[itt]o in the Angle of the Room 13 feet 6 long / Another d[itt]o 5 feet long / Another d[itt]o including the sham Door 6 feet 3 inches."[5] A photograph shows the library in the late nineteenth century, with these bookcases and the same flock wallpaper used in the Great Hall on the walls above them. In 1845 bills refer to "repairing and New Polishing Old Vein Marble Chimney pieces in the Library and 2 statuary Pier tables same room." A bill of 1845 for "Upholsterers time putting up the leather in the Bedroom laying down carpets in Library" might suggest the gilt leather was removed from this room at this time.

Lady Islington, who leased Dyrham from the Blathwayts on a repairing lease, retained some of the bookshelves when she converted the Great Parlour to a drawing room. She painted the joinery in the room "a pale greenish white colour, with mouldings picked out in pure white."[6] Her taste was hugely admired at that time. She was well born, a child of Dundas Castle, and she was associated with "the Souls," a group of aesthetically

THE DRAWING ROOM | 161

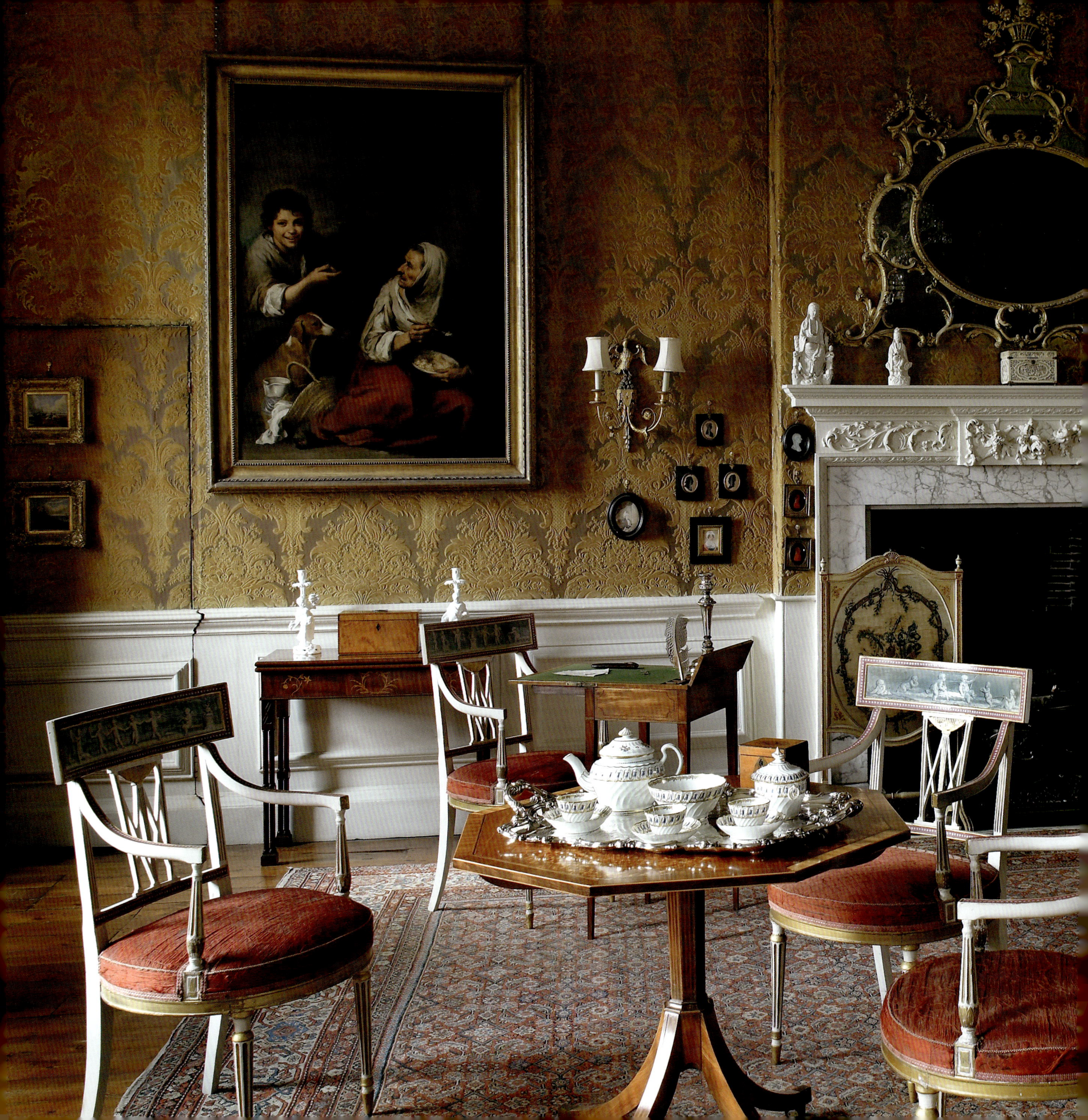

Originally known as the Gilt Leather Parlour, this room at Dyrham Park only became the drawing room in the 1930s, when Lady Islington moved to the house. The gold flock introduced into the drawing room in the 1950s was perhaps intended to evoke the gilt leather which once hung in this room and as an effective backdrop to the Murillo, An Urchin Mocking an Old Woman Eating Migas. Framed miniatures are hung on either side of the chimneypiece. The elegant neoclassical white-painted seat furniture was supplied to the house in the 1790s by Gillows of Lancaster. When the room was rearranged for public display in the 1950s, this suite of furniture set the later Georgian feel of the room.

Looking through to the west staircase hall and beyond into the entrance hall.

minded aristocrats, introduced by the Duchess of Rutland. She married Sir John Dickson-Poynder, later 1st Lord Islington.

They rented Home House in London as their town house and Glynde Place in Sussex for a number of years, and then bought Rushbrooke Hall in Suffolk in 1922, partly to save it from demolition (it was demolished in the 1960s). Nancy Lancaster spoke of her admiration for Lady Islington's eye, saying that she "had the very best taste and the very best colour sense"—high praise indeed from Mrs. Lancaster.[7] Lord Islington died in 1936, so Lady Islington moved back to Wiltshire to be close to her daughter at Todmarton Manor, and leased Dyrham Park from the Blathwayt family, for whom it had been built.

The Blathwayt family had sold their books in 1912, and so the room presumably looked a bit bereft when Lady Islington took the house on. She retained some bookshelves, placing vases along their tops. She painted the chimneypiece white and made the room comfortable: in photographs taken during her occupation the sofa and armchairs are informal, and every table is filled with huge flower arrangements. She painted panelling and chimneypieces white in several rooms, and hung the east hall in white silk—indeed she famously painted the walnut staircase white (this was regarded as vandalism in later years, but it must have cheered up a gloomy house at the time). She painted the dining room in a celadon blue-green.

Lady Islington's tenancy was terminated abruptly in 1948 by the Blathwayts, who moved back into the house but were unable to afford its upkeep, and the house and some of its contents were purchased by the Ministry of Works through the National Land Fund and then transferred to the National Trust in 1956. In 1954, when the Ministry of Works was refurbishing Dyrham Park, it was noted that the "walls lined and distempered need redecorating." The mellow gold flock wallpaper in Italian eighteenth-century pattern was chosen in 1959, perhaps to evoke the long-lost gilt leather—whatever the reason it remains an effective backdrop today to some handsome paintings, including a work by Murillo and a companion piece, a copy of the same picture painted probably when the picture was sold away from the house (it was since bought back). A family legend held it that the copy was made by Gainsborough, which is now thought unlikely.[8]

Mark Girouard noted in *Country Life* in 1962 that the room had "an eighteenth-century atmosphere owing to the Georgian chimneypiece and its mirrors and furniture, which are mostly of this period," which suggests that the room had been consciously re-presented in this character by the National Trust from 1959.[9] A memorable feature of the room is the painted, gilded, and squab-cushioned parlour chairs in white, red, and gilt, which date from around 1795 and were supplied to the Blathwayts by Gillows of Lancaster. In the late eighteenth-century French antique fashion, these chairs have the Etruscan-blue tablets of their Grecian "klismos" rails evoking lyric poetry and depicting Venus's sporting youths of antiquity. The Roman medallioned seats are accompanied by feet and arm supports comprised of antique fluted pillars. These elegant chairs seem to have set the tone for the ensemble of this room and strike an attractive and slightly "posed" note, suggestive of the changing attitude to historic interiors in the twentieth century.

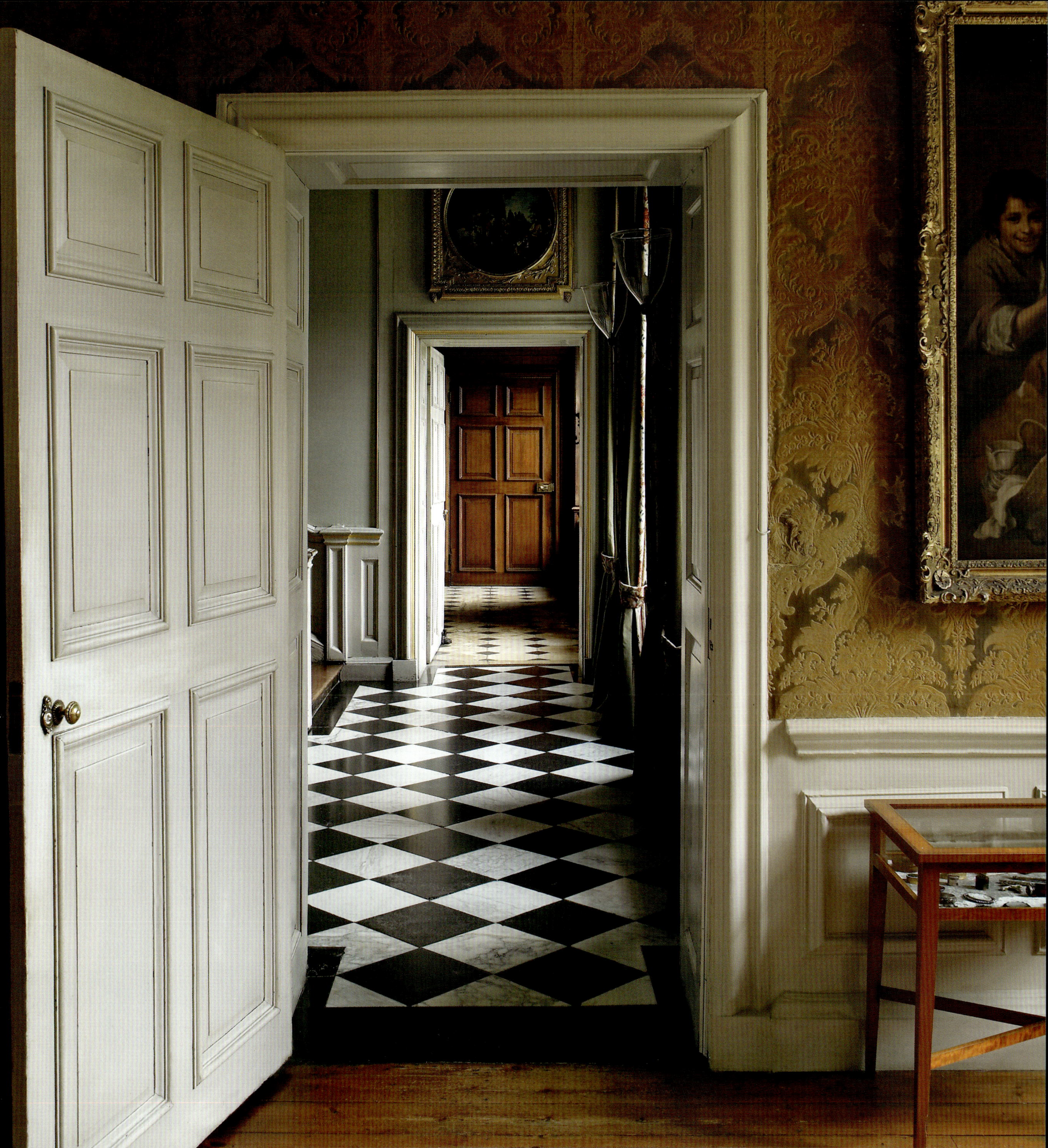

Jack Lenor Larsen
Jack Lenor Larsen Creator and Collector
MERRELL

IV · TASTEMAKERS · THE TWENTIETH CENTURY

The Yellow Room

Nancy Lancaster's own Yellow Room survives as a showroom for Sibyl Colefax and John Fowler in Mayfair.

In a corner of Mayfair lies a handsome late-Georgian room which was for twenty years the drawing room of the London home of one of the most famous interior decorators of the mid-twentieth century, Nancy Lancaster. Mrs. Lancaster influenced the style of countless country house drawing rooms in England and the United States. Although she left the flat in the 1980s, this room remains part of the premises of the interior design firm of Sibyl Colefax and John Fowler, owned by Mrs. Lancaster for many years. Virginian-born Nancy and her second husband, Ronnie Tree, settled in England in the late 1920s, taking the lease on Kelmarsh Hall before buying Ditchley Park in Oxfordshire.[1] Perhaps trying to re-create the comfortable atmosphere of her own Federal-period family home, Mirador in Virginia, Mrs. Lancaster redecorated her houses with a confidence and an originality that gained her many admirers. She in turn acknowledged the influence of Lady Islington and took advice on colour from her uncle, Paul Phipps, the English architect and pupil of Lutyens.

In 1944, after her divorce from Ronnie Tree, Nancy, then soon to be Mrs. Lancaster, bought the decorating company founded by socialite decorator Lady Colefax. This brought Mrs. Lancaster into partnership with the talented decorator and expert on eighteenth-century historic interiors, John Fowler. Between them they evolved a style that drew on many period sources, colours, and contrasts, involving the deft use of antique furniture and well-informed choice of fabrics that came to be thought of as "the English country house look."[2]

Into her own London drawing room she instilled a quality of light and life that gave the feeling of a country house drawing room in town — it looked out, through tall sash windows, to a garden overhung with an old catalpa tree. In fact, Nancy Lancaster famously used it for all purposes: dining, entertaining, giving dances and small concerts. She once said she would have happily had her bed in there as well. The room as it was in Mrs. Lancaster's time, with full-length Elizabethan portraits in silvered frame, is well recorded in photographs.

The Yellow Room was originally built as a gallery in around 1820 (Nancy thought around 1790) for Sir Jeffry Wyatt (later Wyatville), the architect of the remodelling of Windsor Castle. He occupied the house on the corner from 1802, maintaining a drawing office in the old stables, over which he built this spacious room, presumably to entertain clients. It is not known exactly how it was furnished, but it was likely to have had something of the character of Sir John Soane's house or the London home of John Nash, in which he displayed architectural models to amuse and divert his patrons.[3]

The Gallery was already part of the Colefax showrooms when, in 1958, in order to improve the finances of the company, Nancy Lancaster sold her London house on Charles Street, Mayfair, and leased the showrooms facing Avery Row as her private residence. She contrived, with architect R. J. Page, to make an elegant town house or flat using a number of rooms on the ground floor and on the first floor and studio-gallery. She wrote herself how it was "the surprising climax" to the relatively humble entrance hall and stairs. Martin Wood in *Nancy Lancaster* called the room "a wonderful stage set," and Loelia, Duchess of Westminster, once remarked "to call where Mrs. Nancy Lancaster lives in London a 'flat' is like calling the *Queen Mary* a boat."[4]

Mrs. Lancaster recorded her own ideas behind the decorating and furnishing of the Yellow Drawing Room, describing how the anteroom hall had a "pair of tall doors [which] opened into a room 40 ft. long by 16 ft. wide with a high coved ceiling and

THE DRAWING ROOM | 167

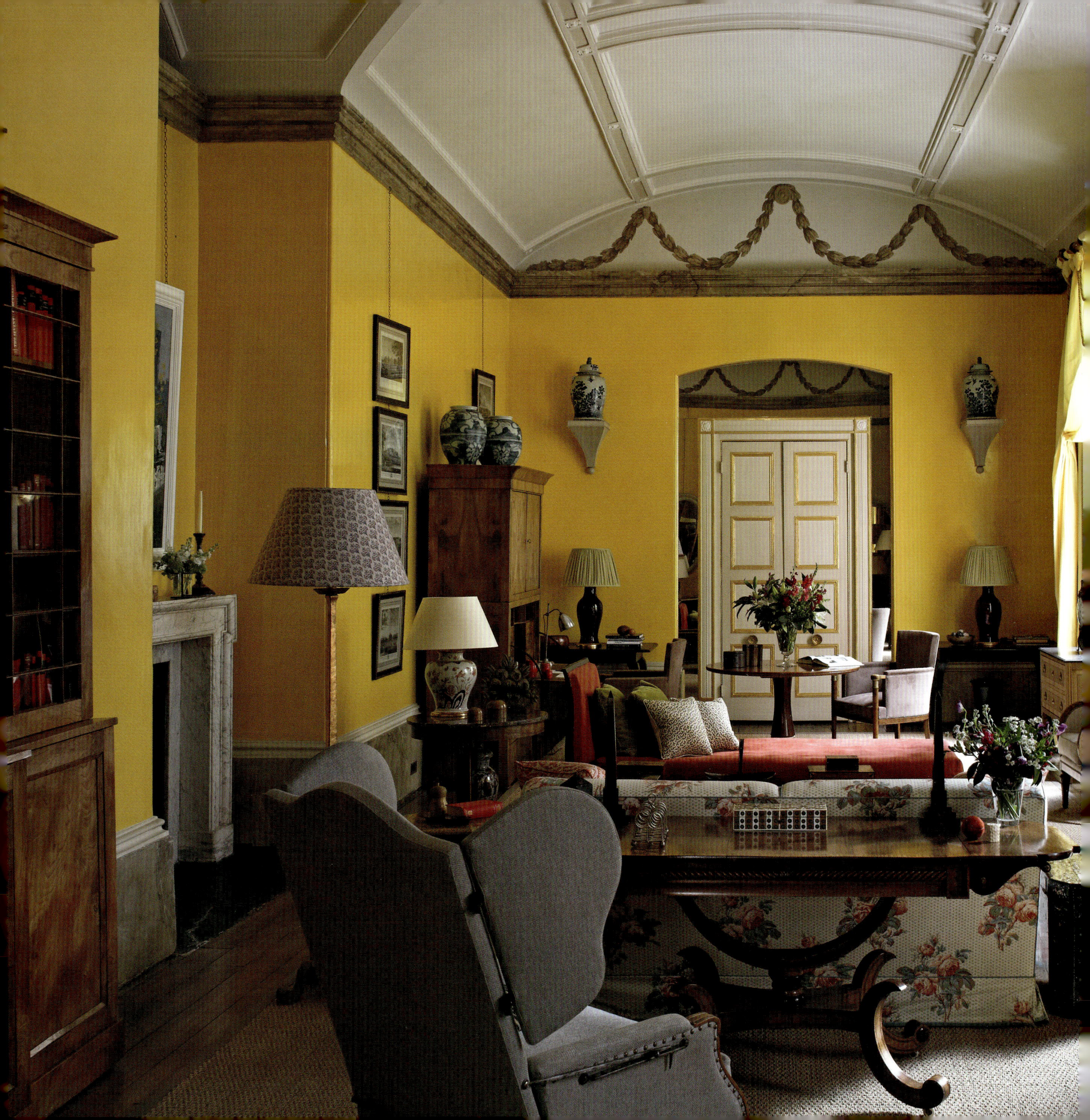

← The Yellow Room was the drawing room for Nancy Lancaster's London house. The huge room was originally the studio gallery for Jeffry Wyatville. Nancy Lancaster installed the marble chimneypiece and her famous decorative colour scheme of "butter yellow," which was restored in the 1980s. The marbled skirting and cornice are original.

↓ The arrangement of the curtain drapes was re-created in the 1980s to preserve the character of Nancy Lancaster's scheme; the tall windows look out onto a courtyard with an old catalpa tree.

TASTEMAKERS | 169

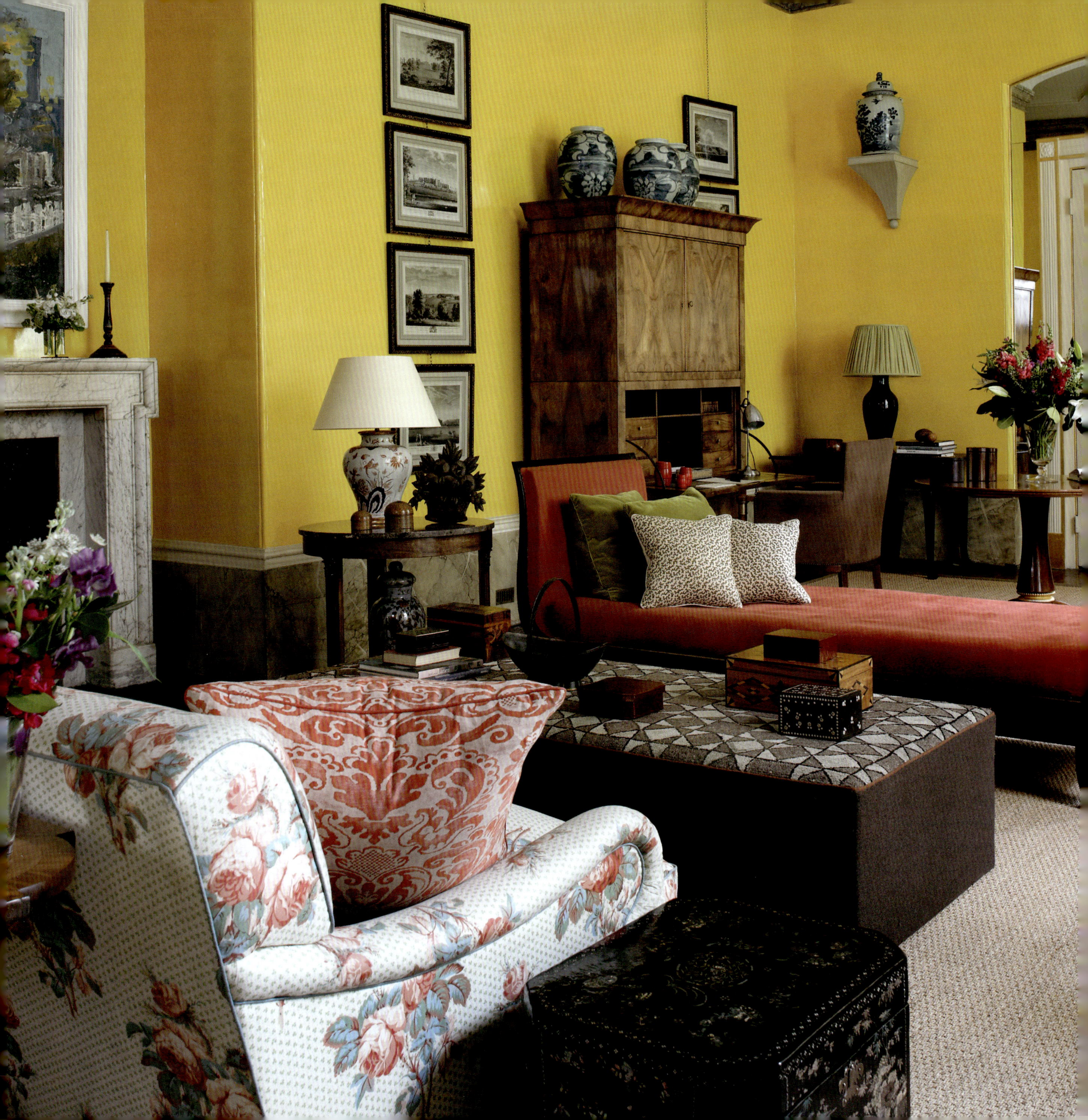

The Yellow Room is now used as a much treasured showroom for Sibyl Colefax and John Fowler, the decorating company which Nancy Lancaster once owned and ran with John Fowler, bringing together two people who had the strongest influence on the English country house.

three tall windows looking into the garden. When the shop used this room it was white picked out in green and I thought it very cold. Remembering Paul Phipps's idea of a butter-yellow room I painted it thusly with a glaze ... The cove ceiling was painted in three tones of sable beige and the woodwork was marbleized in a greyish tone. Between the cornice and the ceiling John Fowler and George Oakes painted grey swags."[5]

Mrs. Lancaster brought items of furniture from her other homes, such as Mirador and Ditchley, and other pieces were acquired at auction, including the portraits from Hartwell in Kentian frames (she also borrowed pieces from the Colefax showrooms); bookcases were made up from one larger breakfront bookcase bought at the great Ashburnham sale. She also introduced the classical chimneypiece to give the room a focus. Over the chimneypiece, she hung a huge carved frame of seashells and beads found by John Fowler and fitted up as a looking glass — it needed a lot of restoration, and Nancy Lancaster insisted that the original gilding be kept and the new wooden carving be left to age naturally, which was a typical Nancy idea.

Furniture was upholstered in various warm shades of yellow or in an "Old Rose" chintz: there was an armchair loose-covered in red and a desk chair with a red leather seat. She recalled on leaving it "an unforgettable room. A stone's throw from Bond Street and Claridges, yet so quiet it could be in the country ... it only needed a bed to live in completely. As I used the far end to dine in.... Lit up it was a perfect room for parties and lovely for music."[6] Her great-niece Melissa Wyndham, who lodged with her there for a time, sums it up in a few words: "it was the glamour of it all that you remember. A party of people arrived from another social gathering and I can remember how they just gasped when they stepped into the room."[7] Many visitors were entertained here, including royalty, the Kennedy family, the Duchess of Devonshire, and many writers and designers inspired by her example.

In 1983 Mrs. Lancaster decided to spend more time at Haseley Court in Oxfordshire, and the Yellow Drawing Room reverted to its earlier use as a showroom for Colefax and Fowler. The furniture and pictures change continually with the flow of stock, but this does mean it is always filled with the choice and the interesting, under the watchful direction of Roger Jones, director of Sibyl Colefax and John Fowler. The decorating wing of the company continues to work in the same traditions but embraces new styles of living, as Mr. Jones observes, "eclecticism, and mixing different periods of furniture have always been part of our decorating style ... we enjoy displaying interesting twentieth-century items with simple, clean lines together with traditional antiques in a less cluttered way than before."[8] The Yellow Drawing Room thus remains an ever-changing stage set for new generations of people seeking inspiration from the old and the new together and retains the overall decorative scheme introduced by Mrs. Lancaster in 1958–59. The vivid yellow walls were repainted a decade ago but the marbled cornices and skirting, and the painted swags, are part of the 1950s scheme. To step into this room today is still to encounter a room of great style and presence.

TASTEMAKERS | 171

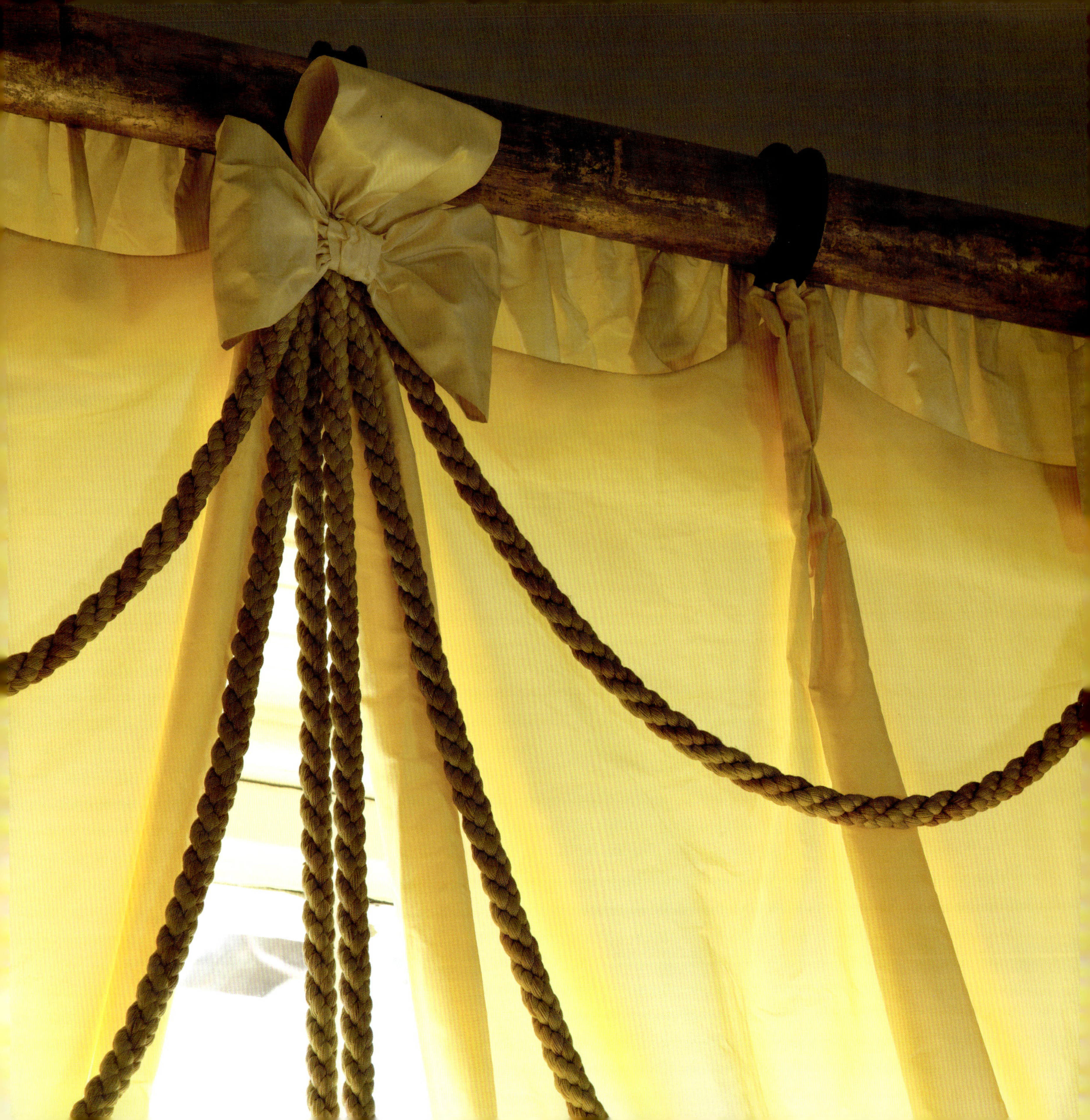

Details of the rope swags of the curtains in the Yellow Room and (below) the cupboards set into the window reveals.

TASTEMAKERS | 173

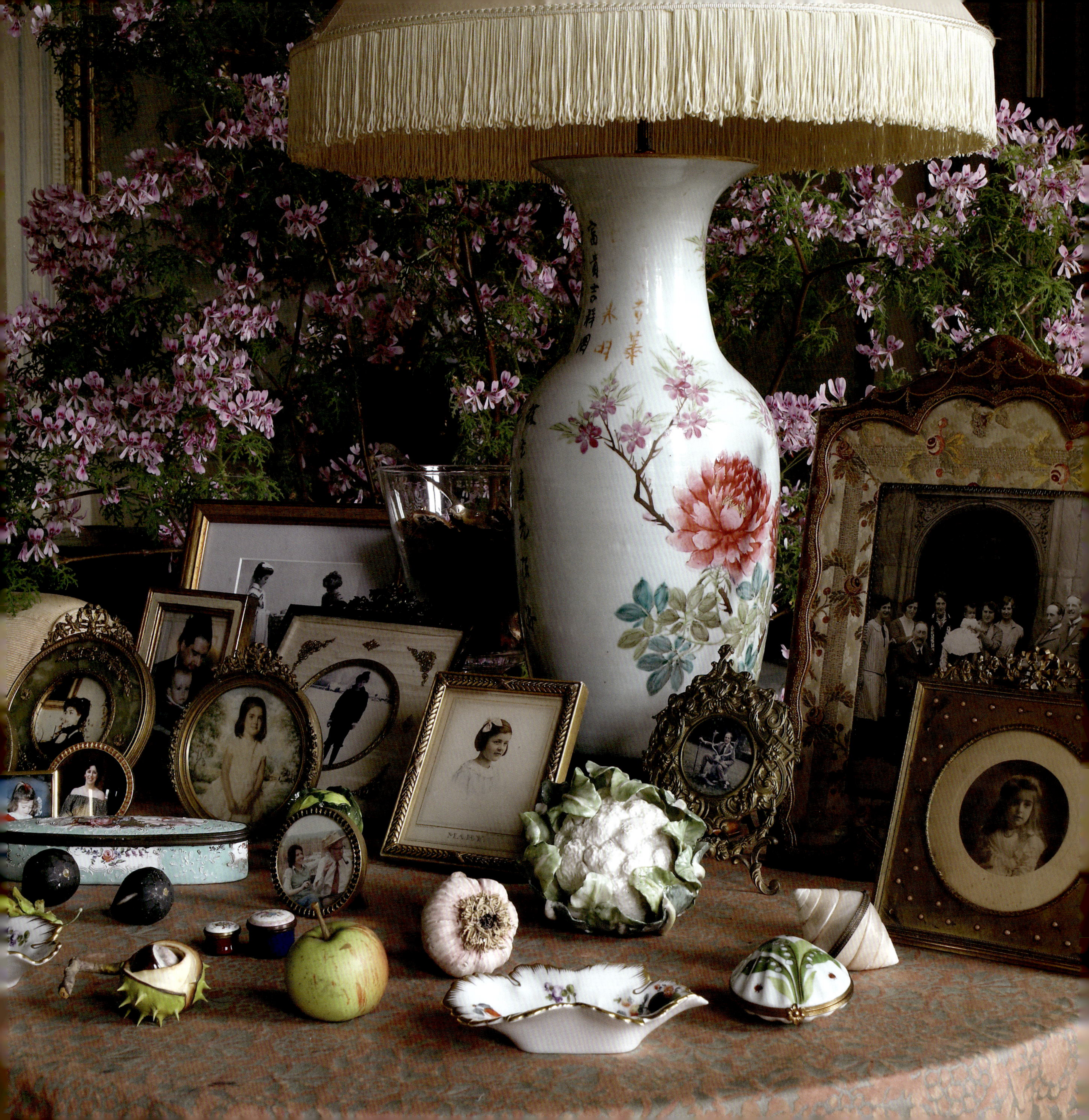
MARY

IV · TASTEMAKERS · THE TWENTIETH CENTURY

Deene Park

The hospitable house: these reception rooms were redecorated and rehung in the 1960s by the Brudenell family.

Deene has been the home of the Brudenell family since 1514. It is an atmospheric, many layered house, both in its architecture and its furnishing and decoration. The overall impression is of a castellated sixteenth-century mansion of fourteenth-century origins—this earlier work can be seen in the billiard room.[1] The heart of the house is still the Great Hall, with its handsome hammer-beam roof of 1571, and the oriel window is enlivened with heraldic stained glass devoted to the Brudenells. Probably the most famous Brudenell was the 7th Earl of Cardigan, who led the Charge of the Light Brigade; relics of the Crimea are displayed in the staircase hall, including the stuffed head of his horse, Ronald. The garden front is part sixteenth century; it was in part remodelled in the late eighteenth and early nineteenth centuries, with a substantial addition including a series of rooms of reception. These restrained classical interiors clothed with Tudor-style elevations were sympathetic to the character of the old house.

Country houses so often have a long history of change and adaptation to new fashions in display, entertaining, and life, and Deene illustrates this as well as any other. There is a sequence of fine early-seventeenth-century interiors, including the Tapestry Room, created for Sir Thomas Brudenell, later the 1st Earl of Cardigan.[2] The main rooms on the south front were begun by the 5th Earl, who inherited in 1790, and completed by the 6th Earl, who succeeded in 1811. Lady Cardigan, wife of the 7th Earl (born Adeline de Horsey), said in her memoirs that her father-in-law, the 6th Earl, was responsible for the dining room, handsomely detailed in the manner of Wyatt, with a frieze of alternating anthemia and wreaths. It is hung in a fine set of equestrian pictures of Lord Cardigan's hunters, brood mares, and foals by John Ferneley, one of the finest sets of his work to be found in a single room in England.

The drawing room alongside is of a slightly different character, and the library or Bow Room beyond is more eighteenth-century in style. John Cornforth observed in *Country Life* in 1972 that although these rooms do have distinctly different characters, they "give the appearance of having been planned as a suite for entertaining on a large scale."[3] The Bow Room is really the most intimate of the three and contains an important library within fitted book presses set into the curved wall. Over the chimneypiece in the Bow Room is Sir Joshua Reynolds's portrait of Lady Mary Montagu, daughter and heiress of the 2nd Duke of Montagu.

The south-facing drawing room, a large room with a view over the garden and lake, lies between the Bow Room and the dining room. The rococo-revival chimneypiece is thought to have been introduced in the 7th Earl's time. The elegant character of the room overall comes from the restoration of the house by Edmund and Marian Brudenell in the 1960s. The late Mrs. Brudenell (who died in 2013) recalled: "The original pale blue silk was in tatters by the end of the last war, when the house was occupied by soldiers; a plain paper had been used before we redecorated the room in 1966."[4] John Cornforth praised the "warmth and a stimulating variety of mood" of the drawing room at Deene and added that in his opinion, "no photographs can capture the gaiety and ease of the drawing room in the evening. Certainly one vital element is that it is not just effective decoration: there is the deeper thread provided by the portraits, which in the first two rooms are almost all earlier than their setting."[5]

In the 1966 scheme, the Brudenells had the cornice and cove cleaned and retained all the old gilding. The lightly coloured American wallpaper—suggested by the decorator Oliver Ford

THE DRAWING ROOM | 175

↓ Deene Park, Northamptonshire: a series of sixteenth-century portraits of women and children, thought to be members of the Tresham family, are hung grouped in pairs under seventeenth-century family portraits.

→ This grand drawing room of the old school was redecorated in the 1960s for Marian and Edmund Brudenell, part of a sequence of rooms, including the dining room, seen through the doors, and the Bow Room (a library), created between 1790 and 1811.

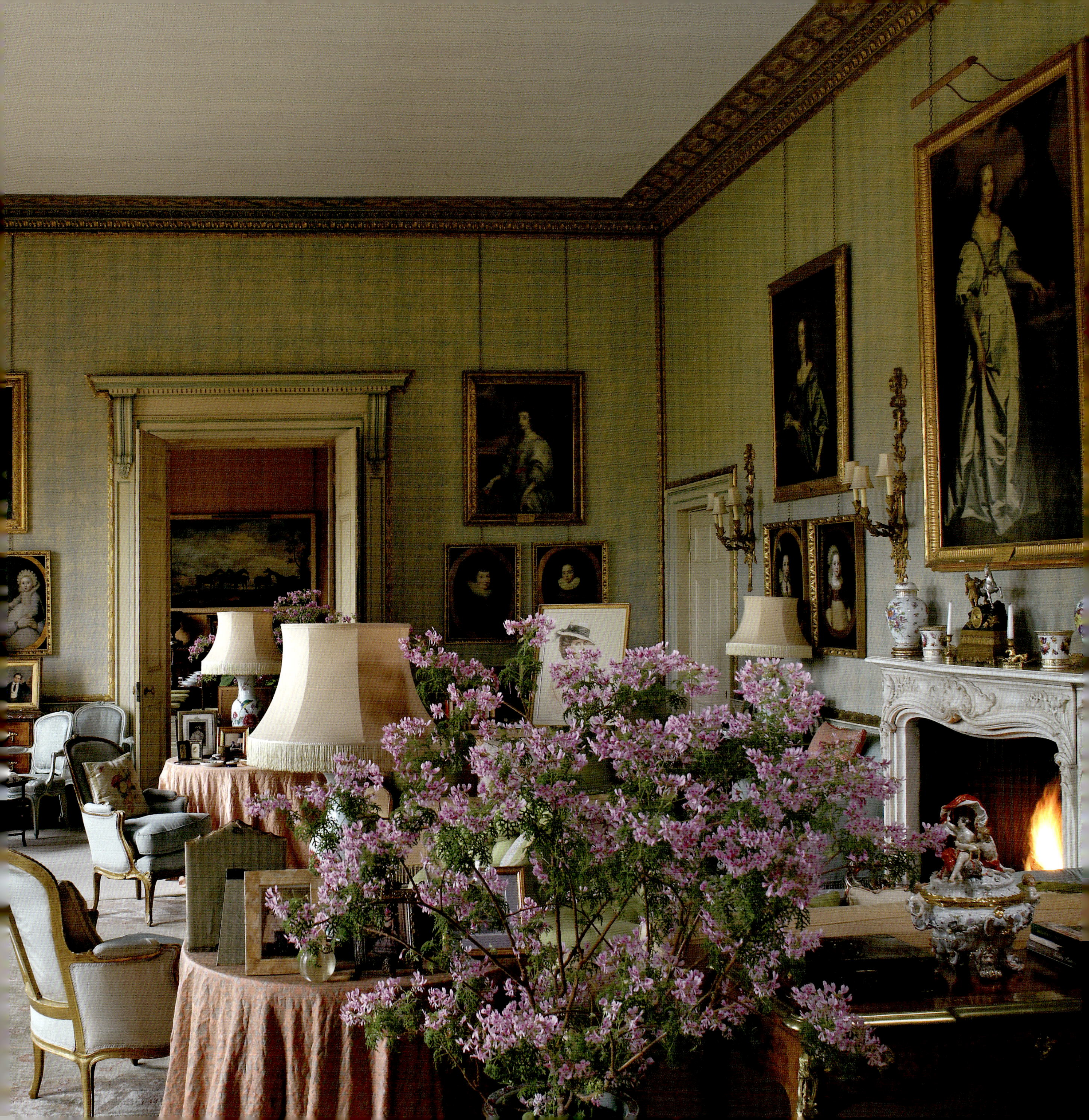

The drawing room connects with the Bow Room, or library, and the two rooms are often used together for house parties.

178 | DEENE PARK

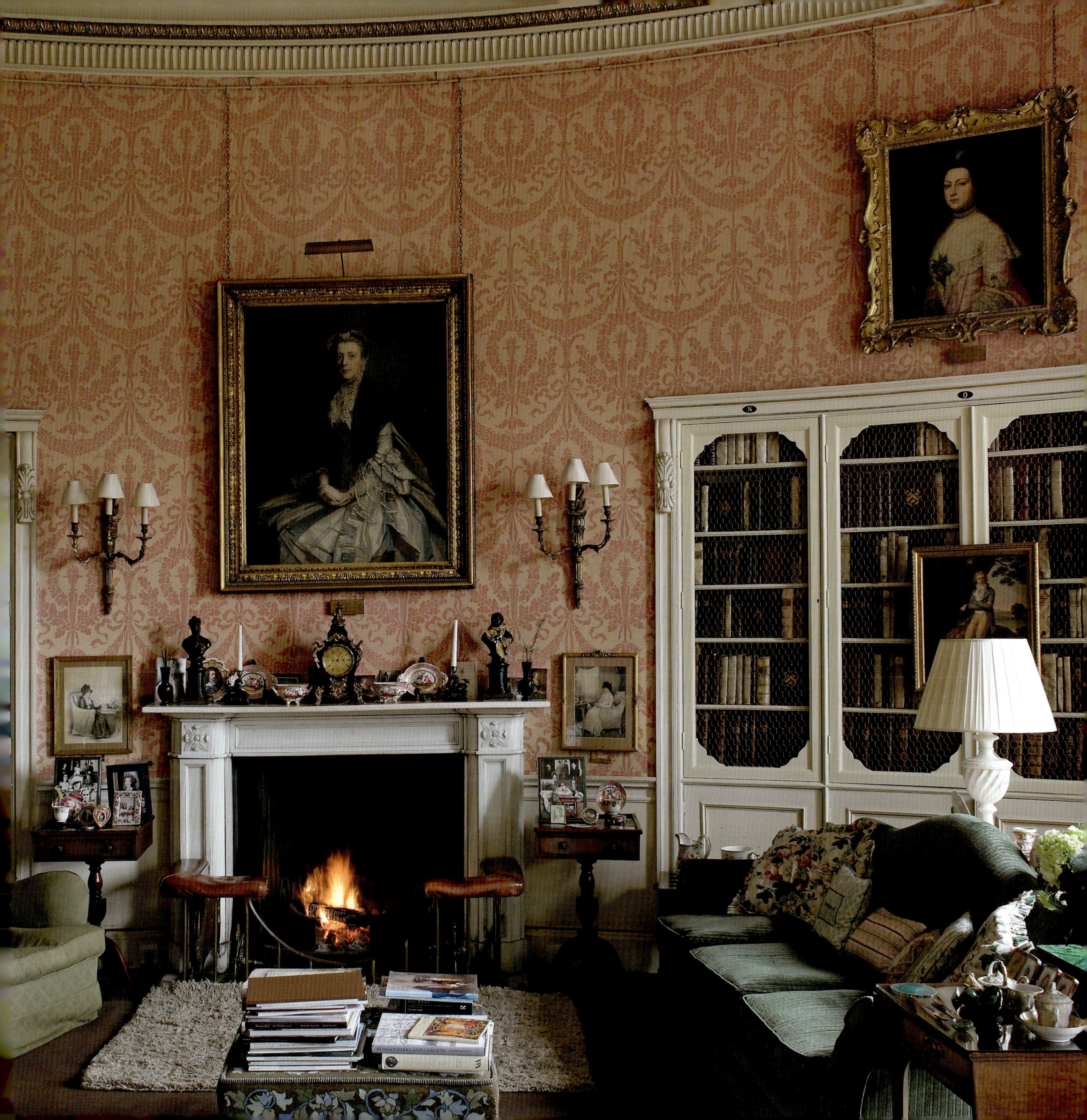
RUSSIAN PARKS AND GARDENS

Comfort and elegance: the drawing room at Deene Park is carefully arranged with chairs and tables, so that different groups can sit and converse after dinner. The colours of the drawing room were carefully chosen to make the room light and comfortable. The tall windows look out over the garden while cut-leaf potted geraniums fill the room with colour and scent.

and patterned to resemble damask—was chosen as a suitable backdrop to portraits and the original pale blue silk hangings. The gilt fillet—which had once held the original silk in place—was retained, repaired, and extended around the door cases. The paintings all come from family collections, and the picture over the chimneypiece is of the Countess of Cardigan, wife of the 1st Earl, by Van Dyck and studio.

The rare set of twelve small oil portraits, painted around 1615 by a Flemish artist, is of unknown women and children but could be members of the Tresham family, which intermarried with the Brudenells. The furniture of the room includes comfortable armchairs, sofas, and a suite of French *bergère* chairs in blues and coral pinks. A handsome pair of Gerrit Jensen tables may have come from Boughton, which the 4th Earl of Cardigan also owned, his wife being the heiress of the 2nd Duke of Montagu. The Dukedom of Montagu was recreated for him by George III, but as his son had predeceased him, his daughter's family inherited Boughton while his brother inherited Deene.

The overall effect of this room is of one designed for enjoyable entertaining in the traditional manner. The upholstered chairs are arranged to make a series of small groups for parties of up to twenty to sit and talk comfortably after dinner. The use of a central rug bordered at each end with white carpets was described by Marian Brudenell as "a direct crib from Nancy Lancaster's drawing room." Instead of cut flowers, generously scaled potted geraniums provide both colour and scent. It is easy to forget how much has been done in modern times to make this ancestral home as elegant and comfortable as it is. Joan Wake recorded the house at the end of the Second World War: "By 1945 the already dilapidated house was virtually derelict, exceedingly uncomfortable and the roof leaked. The kitchen was so distant that Mrs. George Brudenell used to ride there on a bicycle."[6] So, as James Miller rightly observed in *Hidden Treasure Houses* (2006), "Edmund and Marian's achievements are all the more remarkable when seen against this background. They have brought back the warmth and character of the house, and have made it an oasis of fun for family and friends."[7]

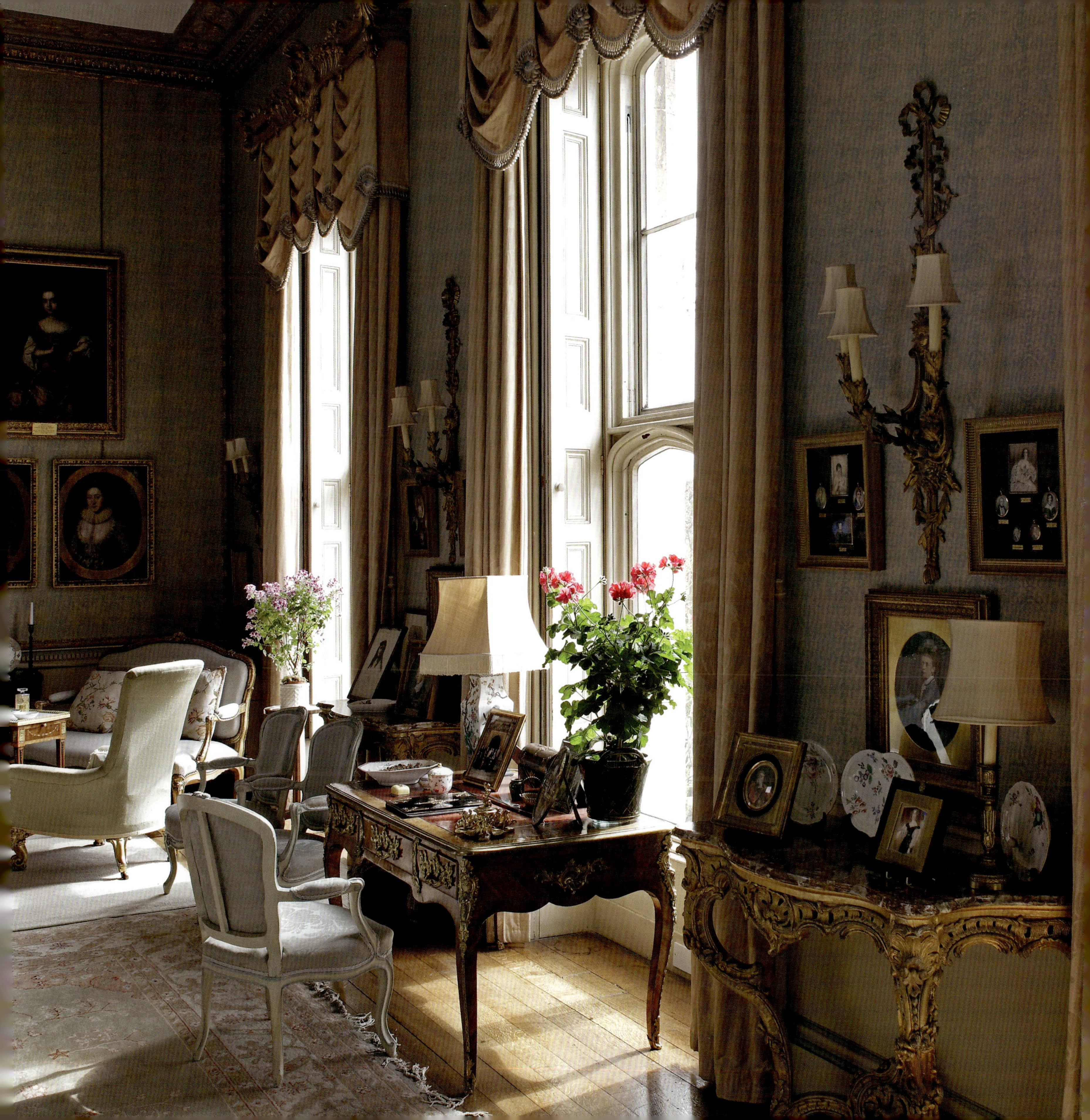

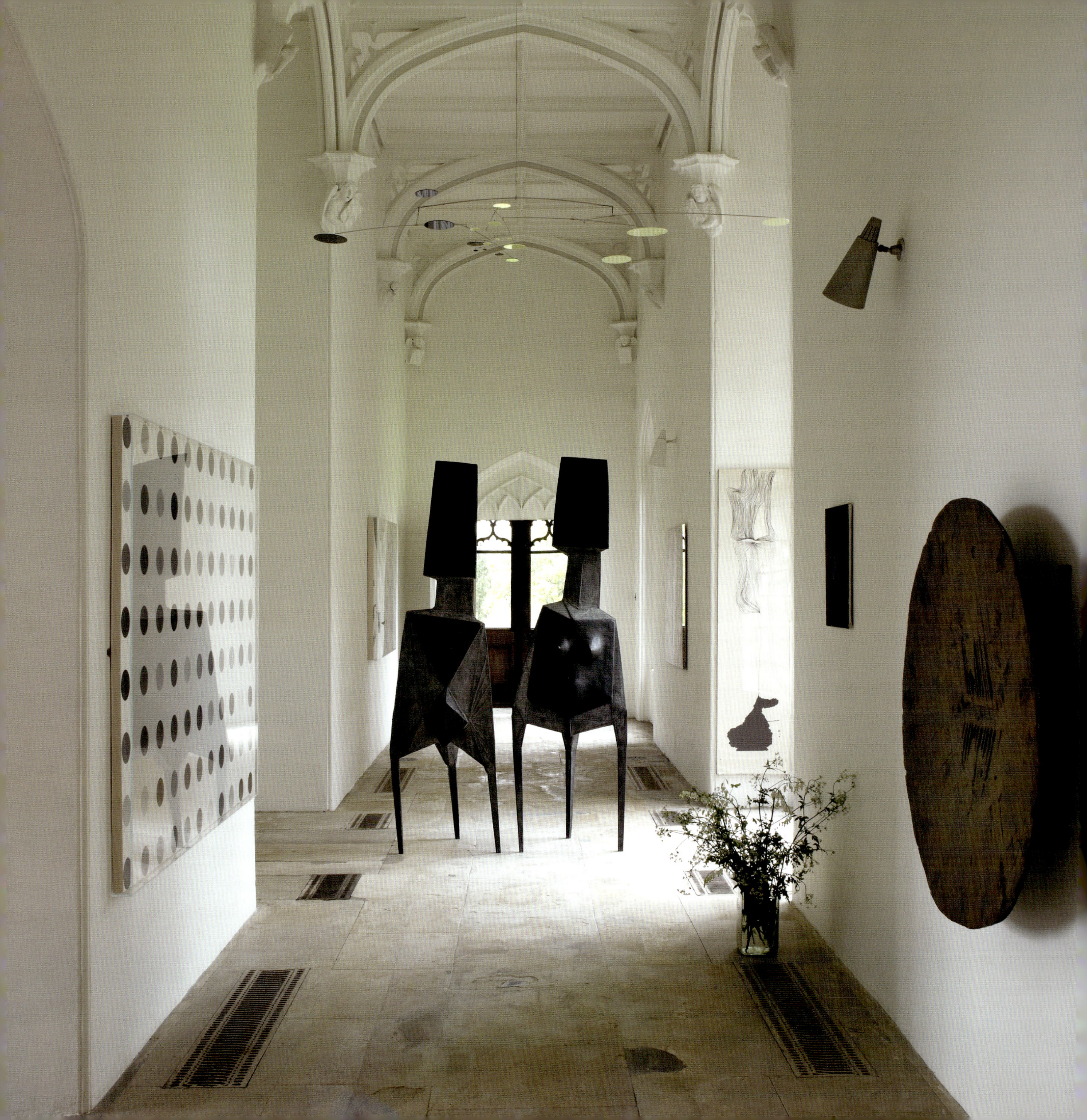

IV · TASTEMAKERS · THE TWENTIETH CENTURY

Lypiatt Park

The Modernist eye: artist Daniel Chadwick and the interiors his sculptor father Lynn white-washed in the 1950s.

There are those who come to historic houses with a mission to preserve them and their contents in an unbroken condition, and others who like to bring the aesthetic ideals of a new age. Sometimes these challenges can even become blurred—when, for instance, the interior to be preserved was a deliberate break with the past. One of the most memorable mid-twentieth-century drawing rooms in England must be that in historic Lypiatt Park, near Stroud, the home of artist-engineer Daniel Chadwick and his wife, Juliet.[1] The Picturesque house incorporates an ancient manor house, and the complex of buildings retains a fourteenth-century chapel still today. In 1624 Lypiatt Park was described as "a fair house of stone," and in 1710 as "a large ancient seat."[2]

For nineteenth-century owners, however, while the medieval house was steeped in romantic history, they nonetheless felt it needed updating. It was associated with the Gunpowder plot, as Catesby met with one of the conspirators here, and there was a room known as the Plot Room; the house had also been sacked and burned by royalist troops in 1645. In 1809 Lypiatt Park was remodeled and extended in a romantic Tudor Gothic style by Sir Jeffry Wyatville for Paul Wathen, who was later knighted and changed his name to Baghot.[3] In the late 1870s Thomas Henry Wyatt made further alterations for a later owner called J. E. Dorrington. The Dorringtons had built up a substantial estate, but the heir died in the First World War, so the estate was divided and sold in parts.

In 1958 the house was purchased by Daniel Chadwick's sculptor father, Lynn Chadwick, who, having lived for some time in a "tiny cottage without running water," had become well known after he was awarded the International Sculpture Prize for his exhibition at the 1956 Venice Biennale. The same exhibition toured Vienna, Munich, Paris, Amsterdam, Brussels, and London, bringing him to the attention of collectors and museums.[4] His new fame enabled him to buy this rambling Gloucestershire country house, which he gradually restored over the succeeding decades.

In the late 1950s Lypiatt Park had been empty for a decade and was in poor condition; most interior fittings such as chimneypieces had been removed. Daniel Chadwick recalls, "such houses were cheaper than a well maintained cottage, and indeed it had been scheduled for demolition, but my father was attracted by the thought that he could make use of these big rooms. We lived in a small part of the house and gradually opened up different rooms. As we opened them up, my father chose to paint them each white, as he wanted to be able to look at his own sculptures without distraction; they came and went, they were studied and looked at and then sold—always coming and going."[5]

The large, high-ceilinged room, with a towering Tudor-style oriel window, was added by Jeffry Wyatville (when he was still Jeffry Wyatt; he added the -ville in the 1820s, when he was working for King George IV, to distinguish himself from his prolific uncle, James Wyatt). It was designed as part of a suite of entertaining rooms typical of many remodellings of older houses during this period. This room was, in fact, first used by Lynn Chadwick as a working studio, as were several of the larger rooms in the house—there are still cherished burn marks on the floor from the welding of large sculptures in this room. The room is used today for display, invention, and parties, rather than as a traditional drawing room. The deliberate building up of architectural experience as you move through the rooms of the original design is enhanced by encounters with Lynn's sculptures and Daniel's mobiles: "his work is very rationalist,

THE DRAWING ROOM | 183

↓ The book shelving and catalogues installed by Daniel Chadwick.

→ The early-nineteenth-century drawing room was transformed in the 1950s by Lynn Chadwick into a place to work on art and display sculptures, and furnished in a modernist spirit, a style maintained by his son Daniel, also an artist and inventor.

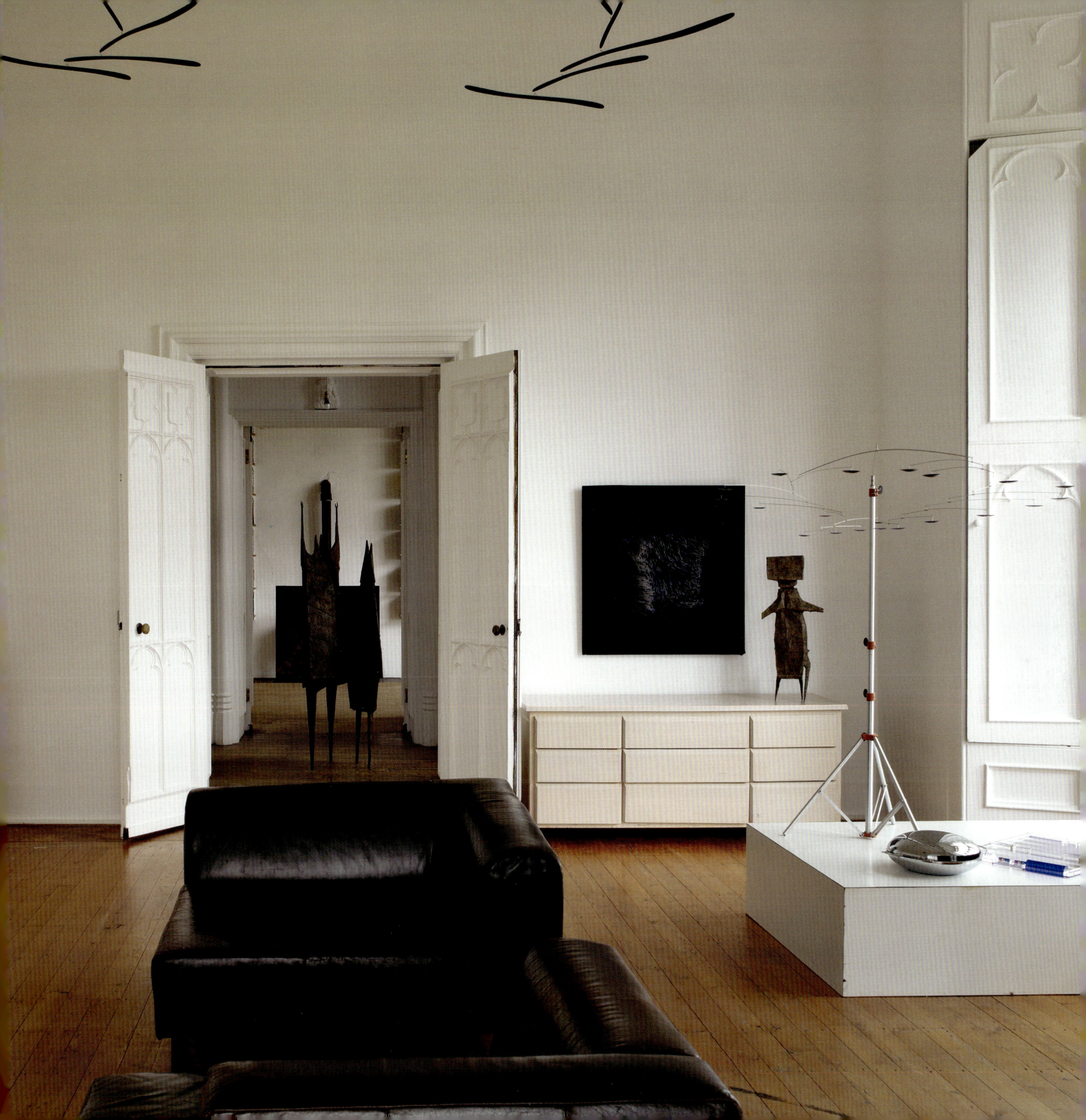

↓ *The simple spaciousness of the boldly scaled Gothic revival interior, and the curious dialogue of the arches and arcades which divide the main rooms provide a very effective backdrop to modern sculpture.*

→ *Lynn Chadwick's taut, crafted metal sculptures are seen here framed in the lobby separating the drawing room from the library; the Gothic fenestration belongs to the work by Jeffry Wyatville.*

about reducing things to lines and planes; Computers only see things as lines between points and planes so it is interesting to see modern computer-generated artwork echoing his work," observes Daniel Chadwick.

Lynn Chadwick was a leading sculptor in iron.[6] He had trained as a draughtsman in different architects' offices, and during the war he served as a pilot in the Fleet Air Arm from 1941 to 1944. He experimented with mobiles and had his first one-man exhibition in 1951. He executed three constructions for the 1951 South Bank Exhibition, received his Venice Biennale award in 1956, and won the Concorso Internazionale del Bronzetto held at Padua in 1959. Chadwick was widely regarded as the successor to Henry Moore as one of the most original British sculptors of his generation, and he is represented in most leading modern art museums, including the Tate and the Museum of Modern Art in New York. In 1951 Chadwick was commissioned by the Arts Council to exhibit at the Festival of Britain. His sculptures are probably seen nowhere as strikingly as they are in the uncluttered spaces of the Lypiatt Park, where they are placed carefully around the landscape surrounding the house. The 1950s whitewashed modernist-style interiors, with the simplified chimney spaces designed by Lynn Chadwick himself, have a curiously Arts and Crafts quality within the grandly proportioned room, as if intended to appeal to the more primitive barnlike qualities of these great rooms.

Lynn Chadwick died in 2003, and the house remains in family hands, occupied by his son, Daniel Chadwick, an artist, inventor, and engineer, who relishes the "new-old" qualities of Lypiatt Park. Trained in engineering, he worked at Zaha Hadid Architects between 1987 and 1991, has exhibited extensively in the UK and abroad, and has undertaken many prestigious installation commissions.[7] At Lypiatt, Daniel Chadwick maintains the 1950s aesthetic: "my father was a Modernist and so am I, but there is something extraordinary about the combination of modern white space and the historic qualities and craftsmanship of the older building which I am fully aware of."

Daniel Chadwick added the carefully stacked bookshelves in the adjoining room for the ranked exhibition and sale catalogues featuring his father's work from the 1950s to the early 2000s. This juxtaposition echoes the traditional relationship of a library connected to a drawing room. The huge dining room, transformed into a similar modernist space in the early 1960s, is hung with a large-scale spot painting by Damien Hirst, a friend of Daniel Chadwick's, who lives and works at nearby Toddington Manor; it is just another contemporary twist to these cherished and unexpected interiors.

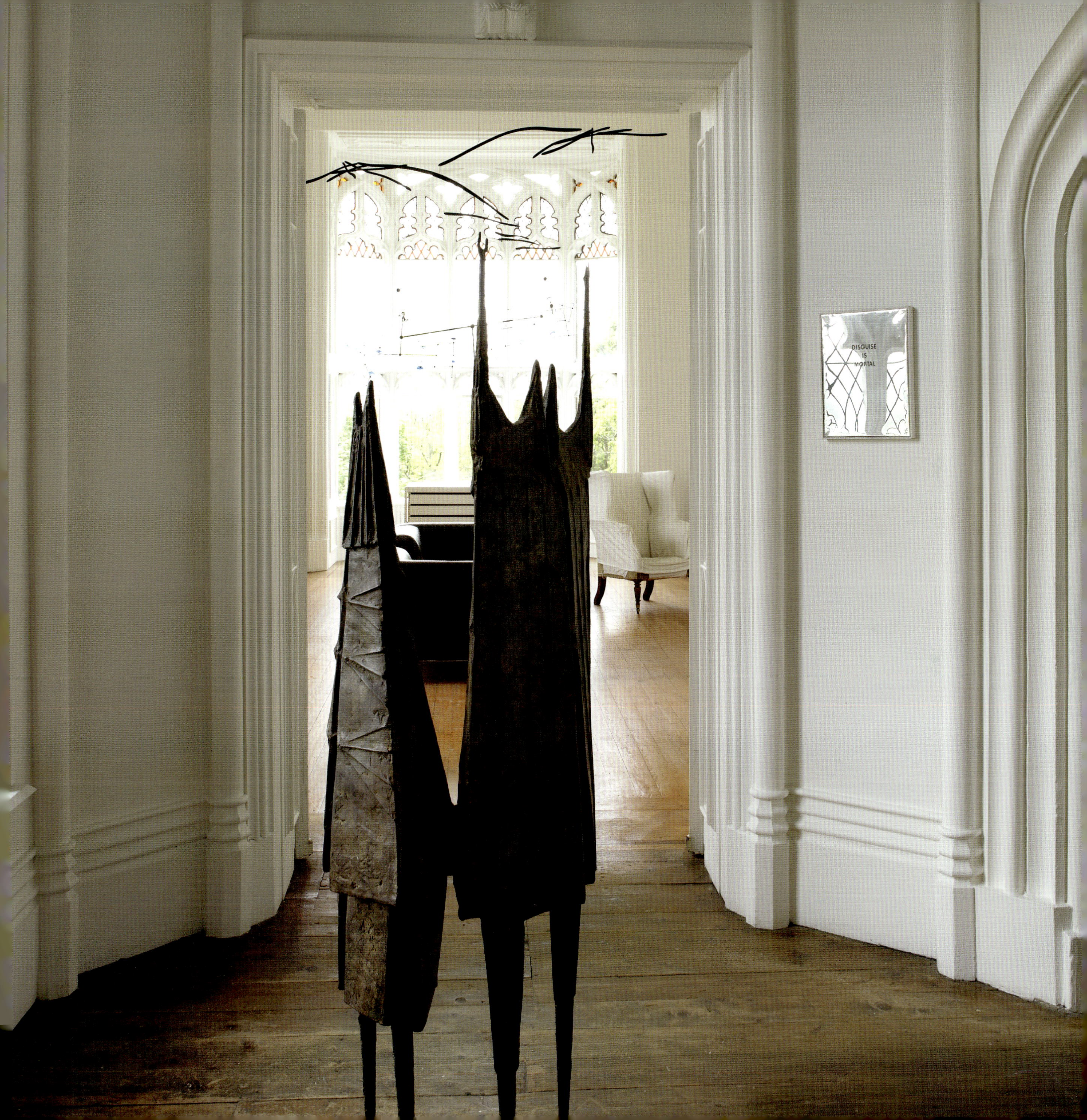
DISGUISE
IS
MORTAL

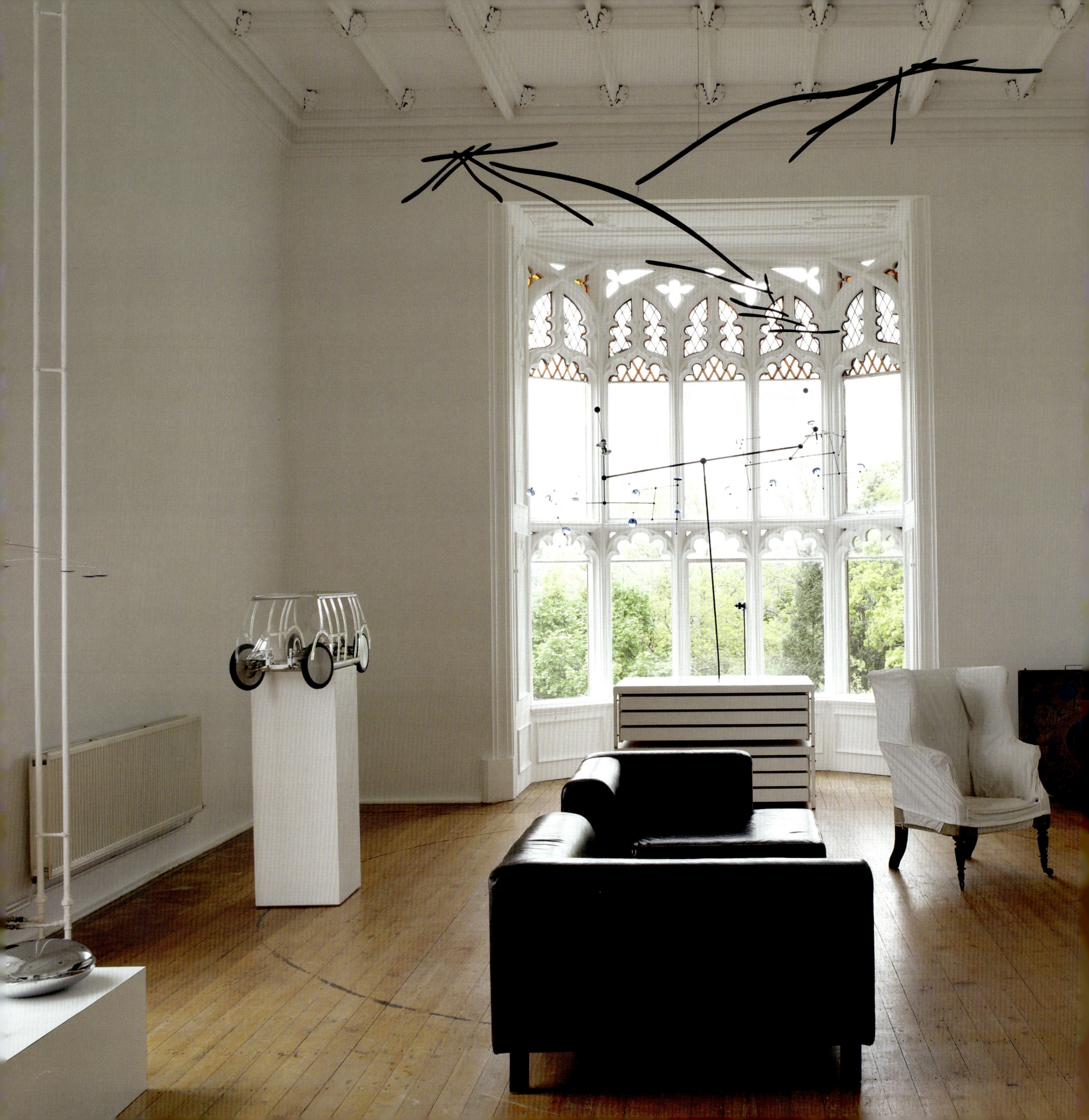

← A sleek, raised modernistic chimneypiece provides both a visual focus and a source of warmth in this cavernous and highly adaptable room, the floor is marked reflecting its use at one time as a studio by Lynn Chadwick; sculpture is also placed throughout the park and can be glimpsed from the full height bay windows of this room.

↓ Lypiatt Park is filled with inviting, brightly lit corners which suggest a house that is still much enjoyed by the artistic family who live there.

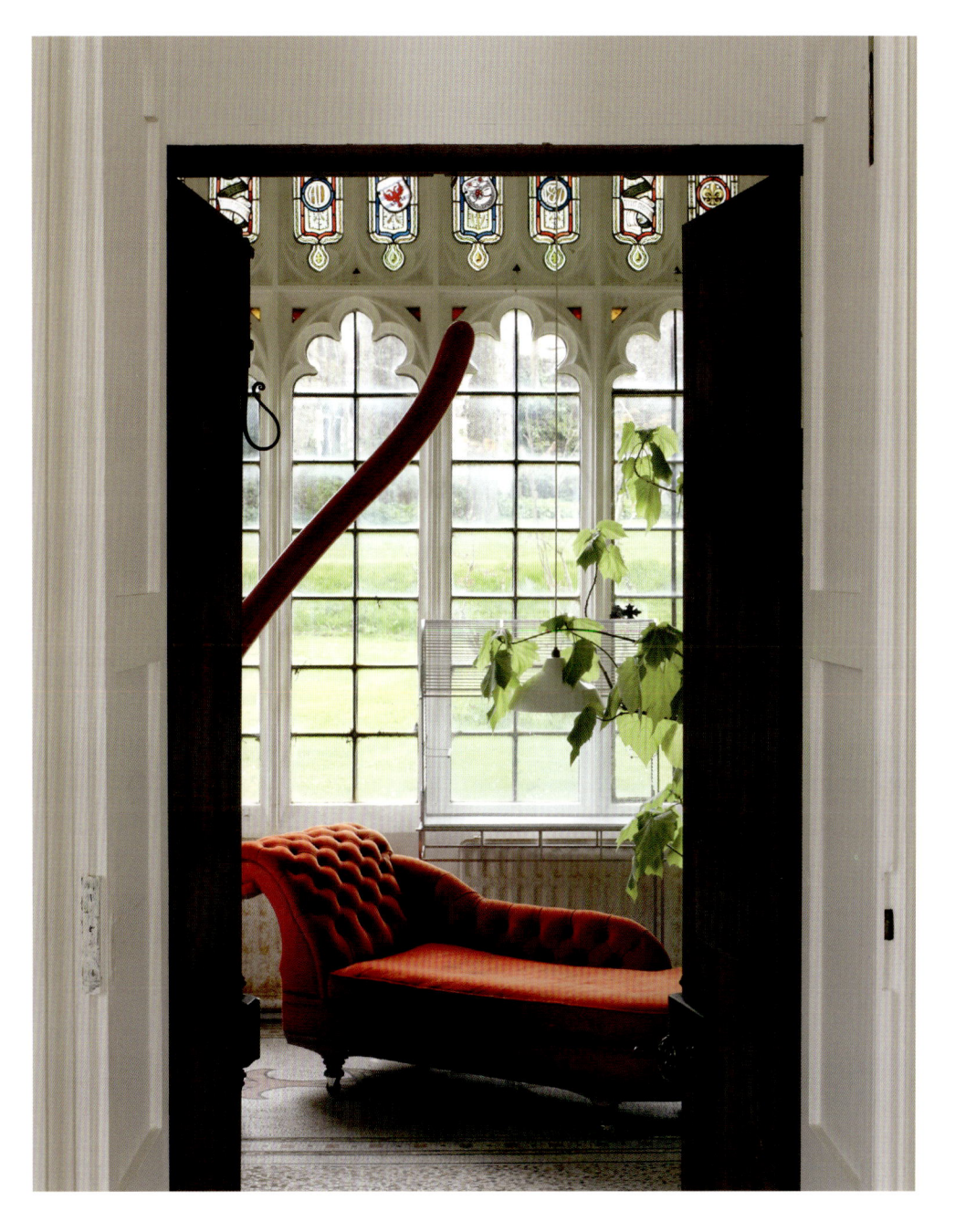

TASTEMAKERS | 189

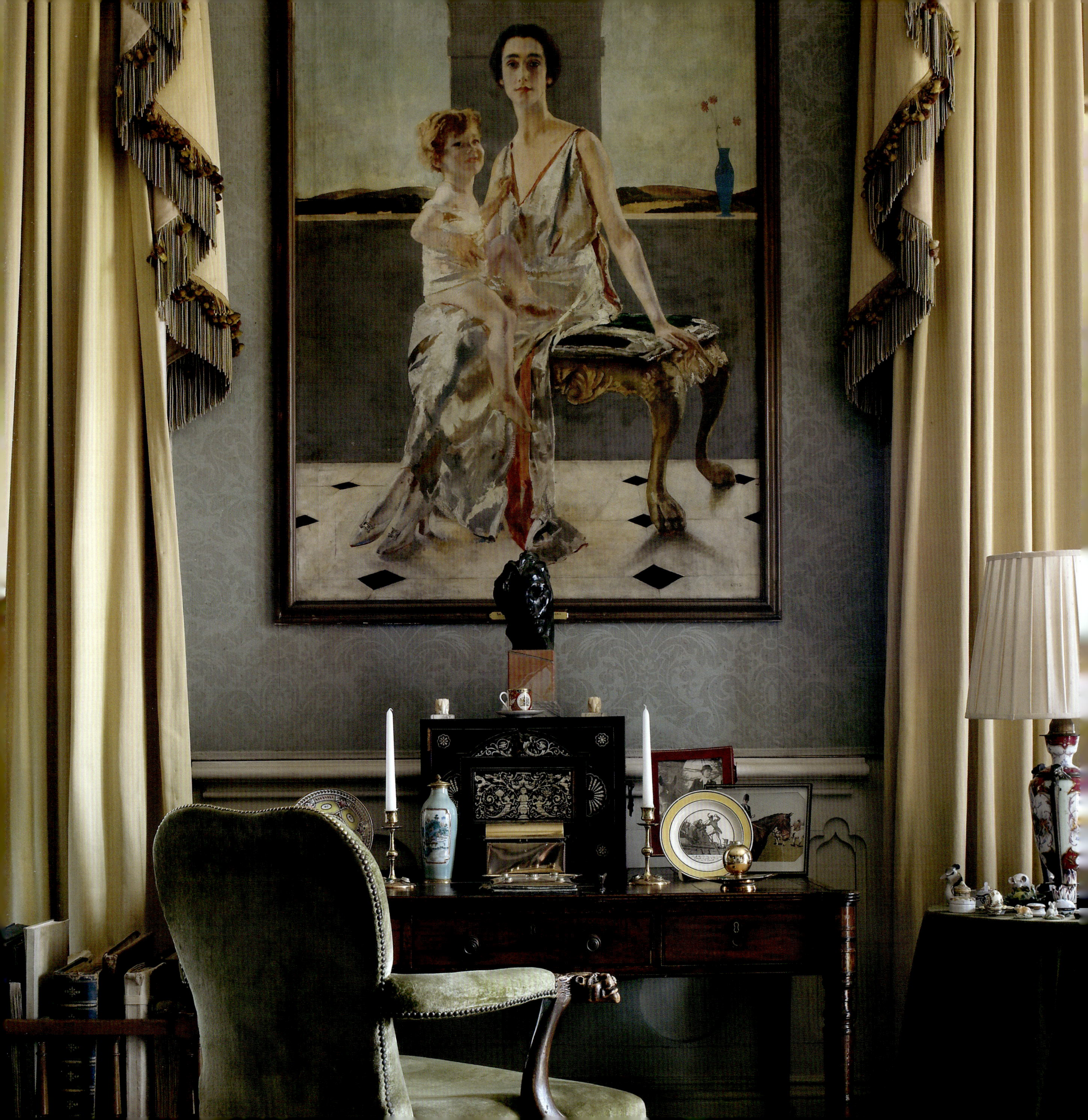

Cholmondeley Castle

Lordly magnificence: a room of Gothic inspiration decorated with the advice of John Fowler in the 1950s.

Few houses preserve the feeling of romantic Regency grandeur with such an air of familial enjoyment and comfort as Cholmondeley Castle, near Malpas in Cheshire. The sandstone Gothic-style house is beautifully sited, standing on a rise above a lake, surrounded by sweeping lawns and a variety of mature trees, including chestnut, cedars of Lebanon, and oak. The house itself is, in some senses, more of a grand Gothick villa than a castle proper, as mostly built in 1801–05 by George Cholmondeley, the first Marquis of Cholmondeley (1749–1827).[1] In 1797 he also inherited Houghton Hall in Norfolk from his Gothic-loving bachelor great-uncle Horace Walpole, who may well have encouraged in him an interest in the Gothic style. Lord Cholmondeley certainly wanted the appearance of "an old Gothic castle" and instructed his architect, William Turner of Whitchurch, "to exclude from both without & within *everything that is new fashioned*."[2] The Marquis is thought to have provided his own sketches of what he wanted, as Turner referred to having "contracted with the different Workers and Artificers for executing your Designs."[3] There is also evidence of Turner introducing his own ideas, especially modelled on his own observations and studies of Lancaster Castle. His father was the builder of the new Hawarden Castle in Flintshire in 1750–55, the seat of the Gladstone family. The old house at Cholmondeley, dated back to the sixteenth century, was remodelled by William Smith of Warwick (John Vanbrugh was also consulted at one time, but his proposals do not appear to have been executed).[4] In 1801 this house was entirely demolished, and the new work begun. The present, more convincingly castle-like appearance was the result of alterations carried out for the 2nd Marquess in around 1829 by architect Robert Smirke, who added a number of towers and turrets.

In typical late-Georgian fashion, the main rooms of reception are all articulated in one flowing and generous sequence, in this case on the west front of the house. This front is divided between a central salon, or anteroom, entered from the double-height entrance hall, and the dining and drawing rooms lie on either side of that room. The anteroom has a large canted bay with full-height Gothic windows (inserted by Smirke, it originally contained stained glass). The dining room lies on the north side, and the drawing room lies to the south.

The drawing room has its original "Strawberry Hill" Gothic-style chimneypiece and cornice, and dado panelling with quatrefoils, while the dining room has more Adamesque decoration. The drawing room also has a cornice of arrows pointing down, in what is sometimes referred to as "Lombard Frieze" form. As a room, it is dominated by three faded Teniers tapestries, which are said to have come from the old house, demolished in 1801. They have hung in this room since the early 1800s.[5] The tree-filled pastoral scenes of the tapestries are reflected through the tall windows facing west and south towards gardens, and the bosky parkland view from the tall Gothic windows from the other walls.

There are numerous portraits in the room: most notably over the chimneypiece is a John Wootton portrait of the Cholmondeleys' forebear Sir Robert Walpole (later 1st Earl of Orford) depicted surrounded by dogs, while a servant holds his horse. Facing this portrait, between the windows on the south front, hangs the beautiful 1920s portrait of the grandmother of the present Marquess, Sybil Sassoon by Charles Sims.[6] She is shown depicted with her young son, seated in an Italianate loggia. Framed photographs reflect the familial theme of the formal portraits on the walls and crowd the surface of the grand piano. On other side tables, old photo albums and Mughal

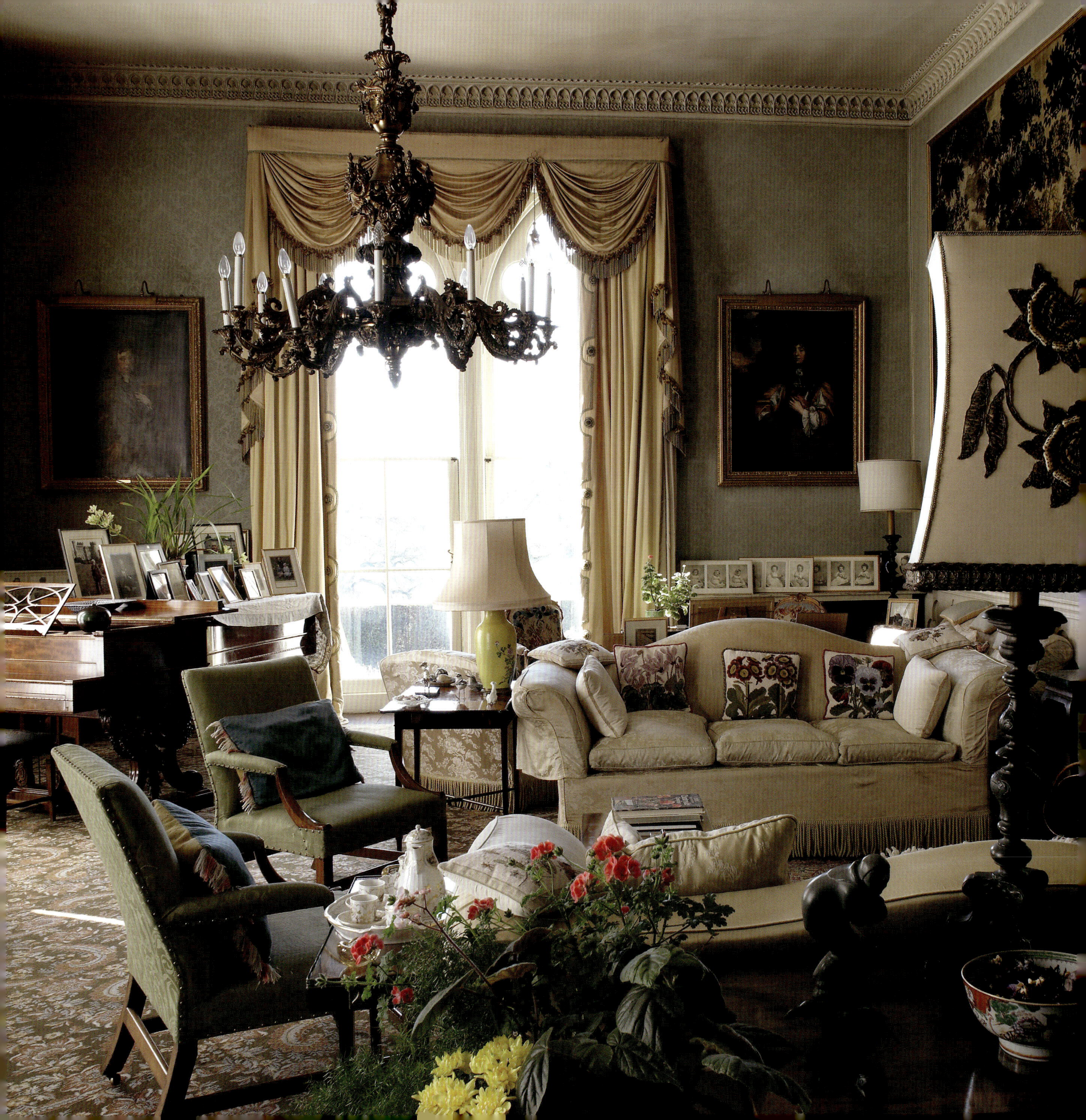

← A beloved family room: the Regency Gothic drawing room at Cholmondeley Castle in Cheshire was redecorated for the Dowager Marchioness of Cholmondeley in the 1950s with advice from John Fowler.

↓ Family portraits and miniatures add to the intimate character of the drawing room and anteroom at Cholmondeley Castle.

TASTEMAKERS | 193

↓ *The tall bay window of the anteroom at Cholmondeley Castle divides the drawing room and the dining room.*

→ *The chimneypiece in the anteroom: the group portrait is of sisters of the present Marquess of Cholmondeley.*

done in the 1950s and has been maintained in the same way for more than fifty years by Lavinia, now the Dowager Marchioness, who first moved here in 1949, wife of the 6th Marquess of Cholmondeley and mother of David Cholmondeley, the present marquess. In 1959 Lady Cholmondeley called on the advice of John Fowler, "the prince of decorators," for the redecoration of these main rooms and others. According to Martin Wood, Lady Cholmondeley recalled, "John always liked you to say what you wanted. Then he would adapt it to what it should be."[7]

The dining room walls were decorated in a warm Venetian red and hung densely with family portraits. The anteroom was hung in tapestries from the old house that were framed in 1803. John Fowler advised on various alterations to the room, including the insertion of a more classical chimneypiece and a modification to the cornice; he chose a small-patterned wallpaper and carpet, and apart from the sofa covers, this room remains as Fowler suggested.

Under Fowler's guidance, the drawing room walls were painted (or more accurately "dragged") in pale blue and are now hung in a pale blue linen in a flock pattern following the same colour scheme. The Gothic cornice was picked out in three colours: white, grey, and a soft green. The pale curtains were designed by Fowler in a simplified version of a Regency design, with yellow silk drapes with a pelmet of swags and tails, the curtain borders echoing the colours of the cornice. The dado and frieze throughout the room were painted in a simple stone colour with lines picked out in green and olive at Fowler's suggestion — this was to echo the greens and browns of the carpet, which was rewoven by Crossleys after the original. In 1976 Gervase Jackson-Stops described the effect in *Country Life* as "cool and soft," and it remains exactly so today.[8]

miniatures, books and places for drinks complete the family quality of the room. The armchairs and sofas are arranged for intimacy, and the anteroom provides another comfortable adjoining sitting room for larger parties.

The comfortable elegance of the room is not merely a matter of survival, however. The decorative scheme and furnishing was

194 | CHOLMONDELEY CASTLE

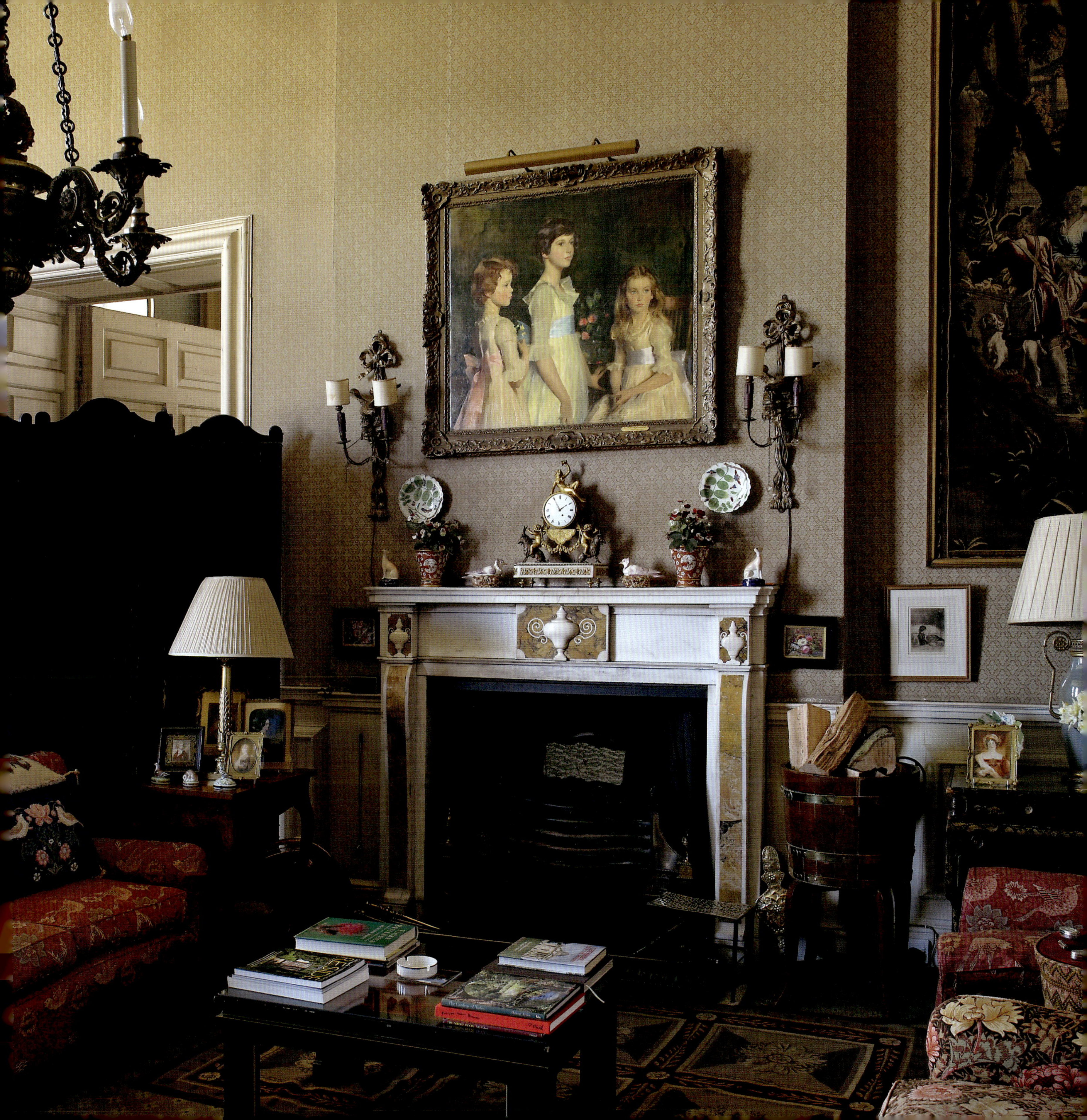

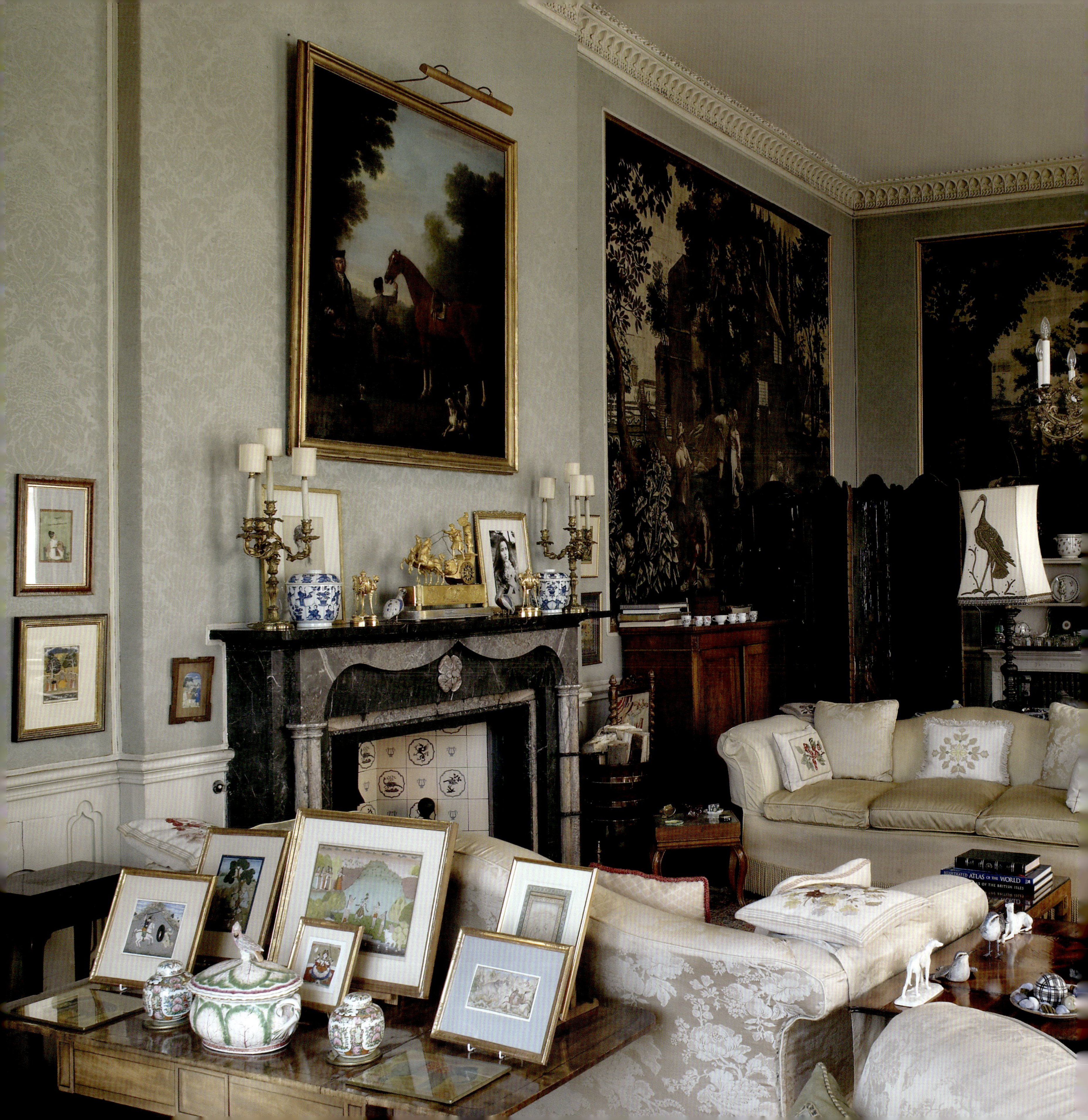
ATLAS OF THE WORLD

The tapestries came from the previous house on the estate. The detailing of the drawing room is consistently Gothic, while the dining room is entirely classical.

↓ The white curtains were designed by John Fowler. The grand piano top is crowded with framed photographs.

TASTEMAKERS | 197

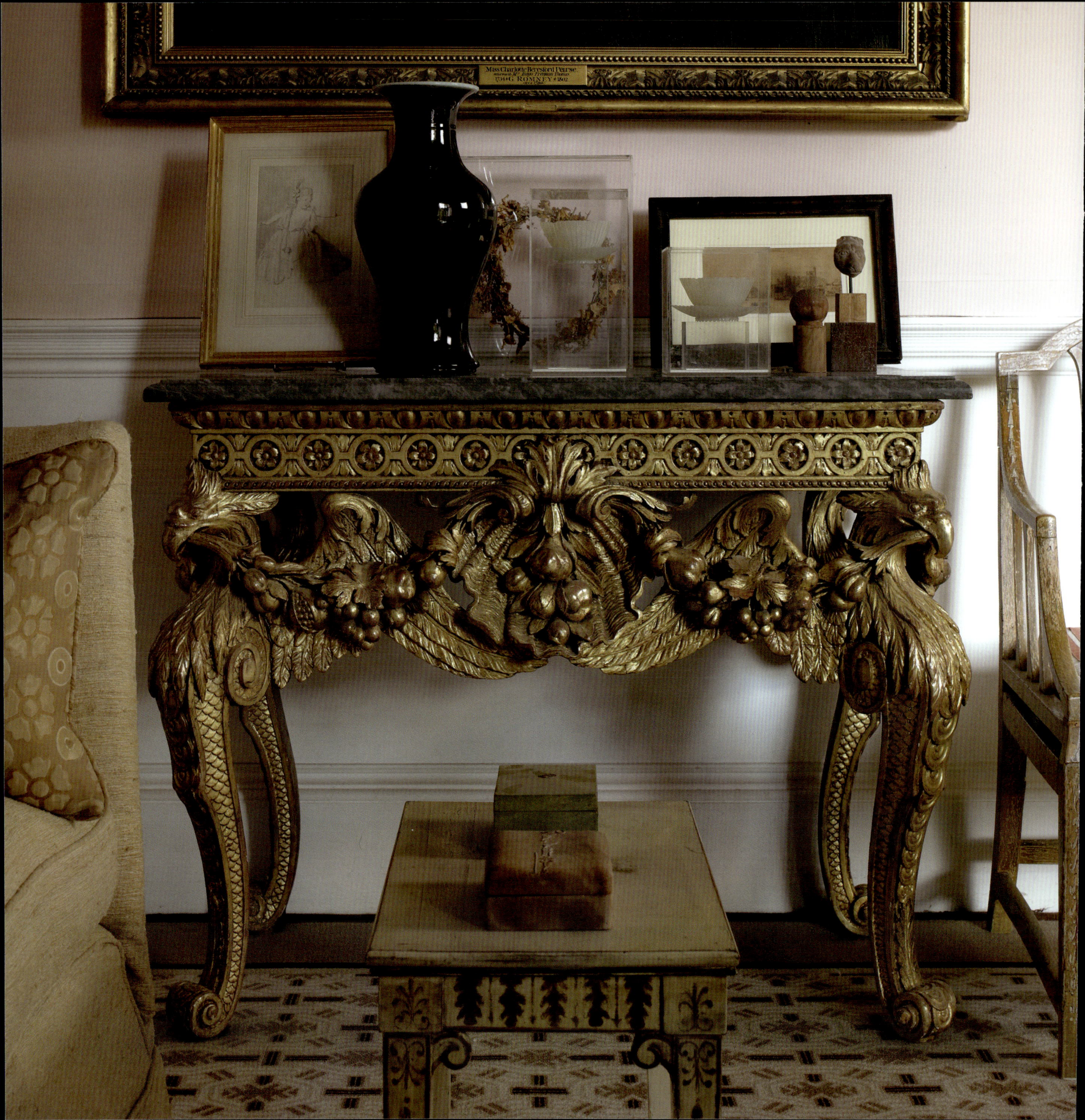
Miss Charlotte Beresford Pearse
G ROMNEY

IV · TASTEMAKERS · THE TWENTIETH CENTURY

The Grove

In the 1980s David Hicks made a comfortable room which demonstrates his skill at the arrangement of pieces.

David Hicks is one of the great names of English interior design. He led the field in the 1960s and '70s, combining a deep knowledge of the traditions of the great historic interiors with a rare originality. In *David Hicks on Living — With Taste*, Hicks himself observed that his "greatest contribution ... has been to show people how to use bold colour mixtures, how to use patterned carpets, how to light rooms and how to mix old with new."[1] Naturally, his own homes were the design laboratories for these style ideas that made him such an important figure (his clients included royalty, as well as figures from the world of fashion, such as Helena Rubinstein and Vidal Sassoon).

In 1960 Hicks married Lady Pamela, daughter of Earl Mountbatten of Burma. For twenty years, the couple lived in the eighteenth-century mansion Britwell Salome in Oxfordshire. That house has been well recorded in Ashley Hicks's books on his father.[2] They moved, in 1980, to a smaller house on the estate, The Grove, a farmhouse that had in the late Georgian period been occupied by the eldest son of the owner of neighbouring Brightwell Park, but on becoming a dower house was extended with a substantial new drawing room. Around this house David Hicks designed a garden, described by Rosemary Verey as "of theatrical proportions." The avenues, plantations, and sculpture of the garden were all intended to extend "the architecture" of the house and create diversion for the eye.[3]

Lady Pamela Hicks still lives at The Grove today and recalls that she was not expected to make any choices about decorating: David Hicks always planned everything out in his head within moments of applying himself to the task, and indeed had made a simple paper model with furnishings and paintings drawn out in ink (the sketch for The Grove's drawing room is illustrated in *David Hicks: A Life of Design*).[4] He did little to change the actual room but widened the chimney and blocked up two windows on either side of the chimney. The tall Regency looking glass over the chimneypiece was brought from David Hicks's library at Britwell. The room is attractively light with a tall French window giving a view framed by the formal gardens created by David Hicks; the door to the hall is also glazed.

Naturally most of the furnishings of The Grove drawing room came from their previous home but were all arranged in a new and original way. Mr. Hicks preferred to organize the rooms in unexpected ways. He did not, for instance, like to place a sofa and two chairs in the conventional horseshoe formation. Lady Pamela recalls how annoyed he got if the chairs were pulled out of his arrangement: "some guests who did this, were I am afraid, never invited back." He also forbade photographs and telephones in the drawing room.

The decoration of the drawing room takes some cue from the architectural character of the late Georgian room. Hicks chose a set of very fine eighteenth-century smaller portraits of women and children by George Romney. There is also a full-length Romney portrait of a family painted against the setting of the Colosseum in Rome: Sir George and Lady Warren, with Elizabeth, Sir George's child from his first marriage. The image of the daughter holding the small bird is particularly beguiling. The Romney portraits all came from the collection of Lady Pamela's great-grandfather, Sir Ernest Cassel, a great financier and friend of Edward VII and one of the great art collectors of the day. Some of these Romney portraits were loaned for a time to the Duke of Windsor while he lived at Fort Belvedere — in rooms decorated by Syrie Maugham.[5]

The walls of The Grove's drawing room are hung in a soft rose pink cotton, and the tall, centrally placed window is draped with ruched and bordered curtains of the same colour,

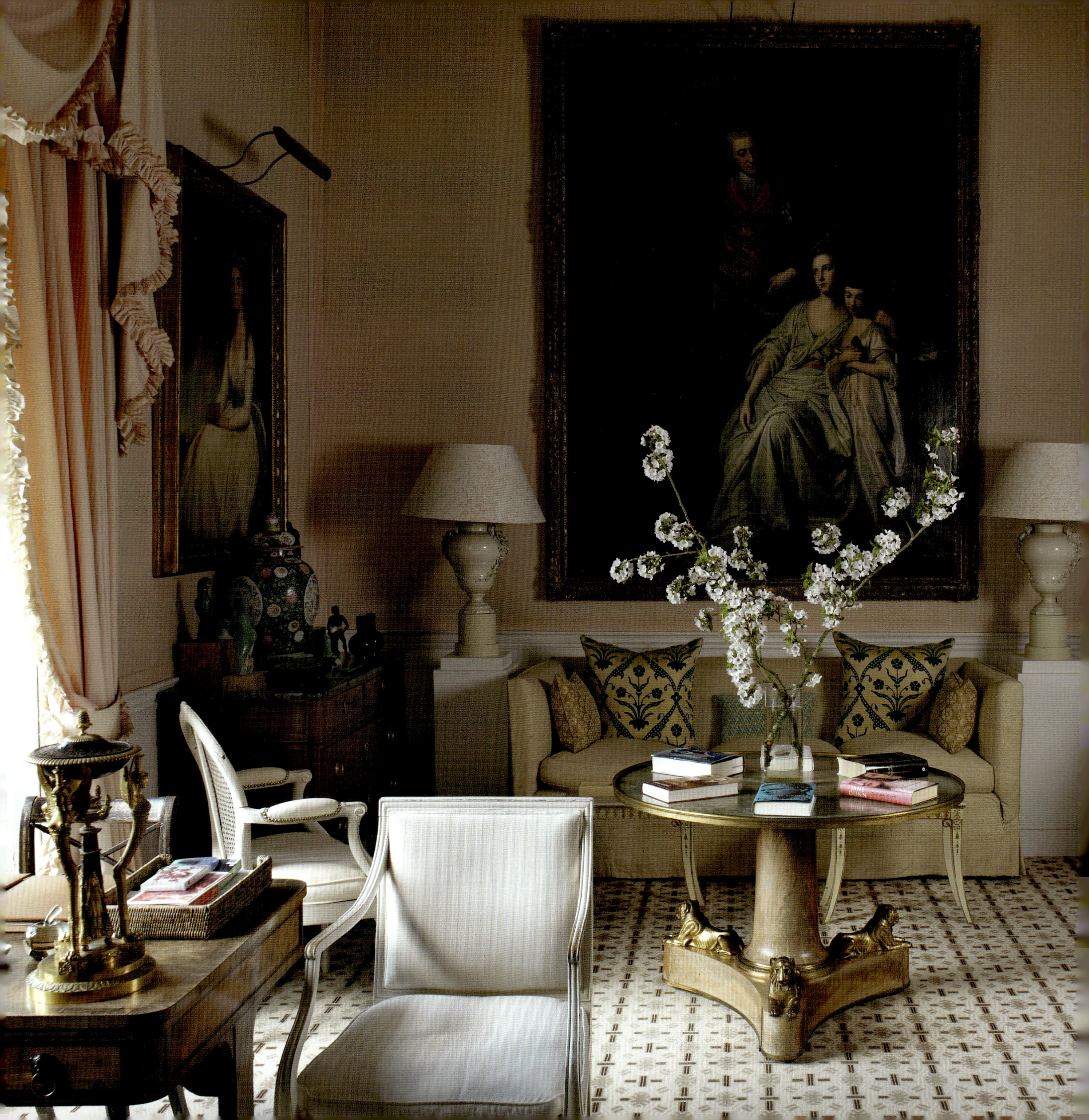

← The drawing room of The Grove, in Oxfordshire, to which the interior designer David Hicks and his wife, Lady Pamela, moved in 1980. The late Mr. Hicks planned the furnishing of the room in detail before they moved in. The Romney portraits were inherited from Lady Pamela's grandfather, Sir Ernest Cassel.

↓ The writing desk is placed at right angles to the window, to take advantage of the light and the view.

TASTEMAKERS | 201

↓ David Hicks took great care with the arrangement of objects and paintings on tabletops; such arrangements have become known as his "table-scapes."

→ David Hicks also designed and laid out extensive gardens, which lend a kind of borrowed architecture to the vistas from the house.

to David Hicks's own design. The style of the curtains was chosen to transmit an appropriately late-eighteenth-century feel to both the architecture and the dresses in the Romney portraits. Other pieces of furniture also come from Lady Pamela Mountbatten's parents' London home, Brook House, including the Regency round table and stools. The interior designer who advised the Mountbattens at Brook House was a New York friend, Mrs. Joshua Cosden, with whom they had stayed in Palm Beach. Brook House also contained the room painted for the Mountbattens by Rex Whistler, later moved to panel Lady Pamela's study at Britwell and then the dining room at The Grove.[6]

The geometric-pattern carpet designed by David Hicks was of a Brussels weave type that he particularly favoured. The sofa by the chimneypiece has been recovered in fabric by Ashley Hicks. The surfaces of tables and chests in the room each have their own arrangements of curios and vases, famously described as "tablescapes" by David Hicks.[7] Ashley Hicks recalls, "he was very keen on massing things by colour." David Hicks himself was quoted as saying: "It is perhaps I who have made tablescapes — objects arranged as landscapes on a horizontal surface — into an art form; indeed, I invented the word … What is important is not how valuable or inexpensive your objects are, but the care and feeling with which you arrange them." That idea must surely go for the furnishing of the entire room.[8]

The real delight of the drawing room of The Grove is perhaps its concentration of detail. The room is tall and elegant, but not overly large. Furniture, paintings, and objects are all arranged in a considered ensemble. Ashley Hicks also recalls a story his father used to tell about his own childhood, when an Italian lady moved into a grand house close to where his parents lived when he was a child. He watched the designers and workmen come and go, and when his parents were invited to drinks, they went to the house, and David Hicks remembered how everything seemed like a "magic spell; entire and perfect" and Ashley Hicks observes that "for the rest of his life, he always looked to re-create that sensation of complete perfection."[9]

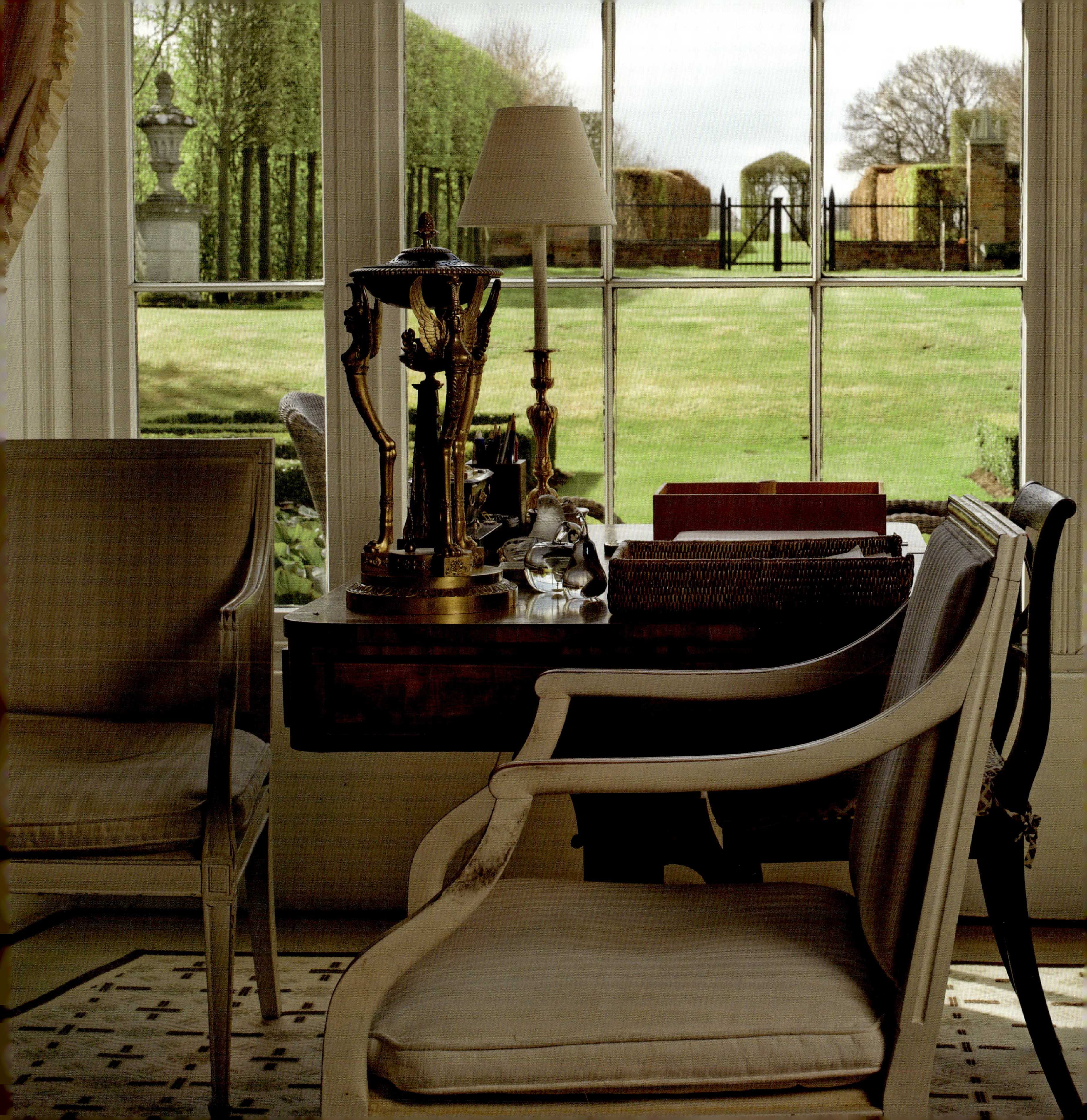

David Hicks enlarged the chimneypiece to take the overmantel mirror. The Romney portraits once hung at Brook House, the home of Lady Pamela's grandfather. The sofa to the left was designed by David Hicks's son, Ashley.

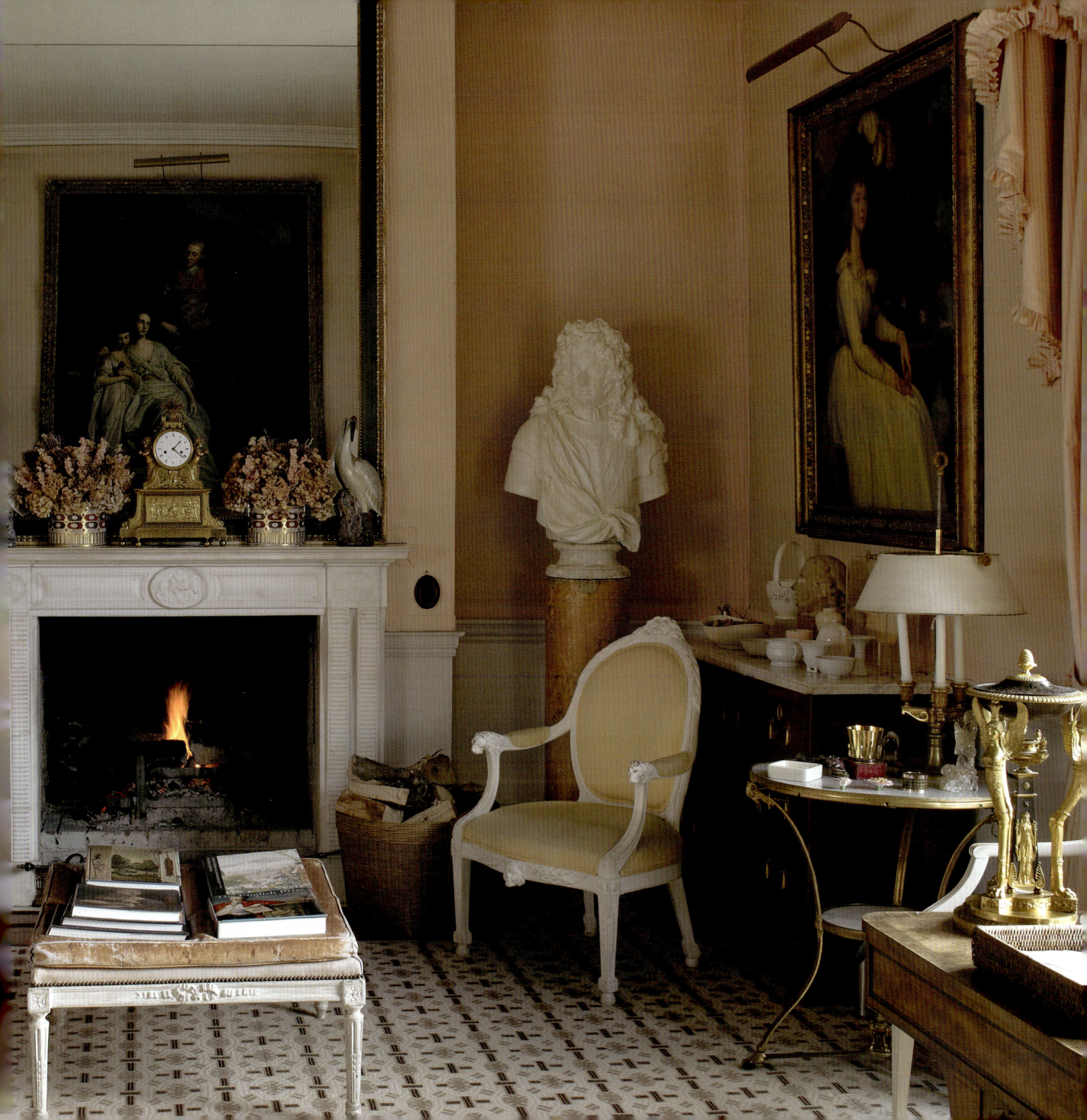

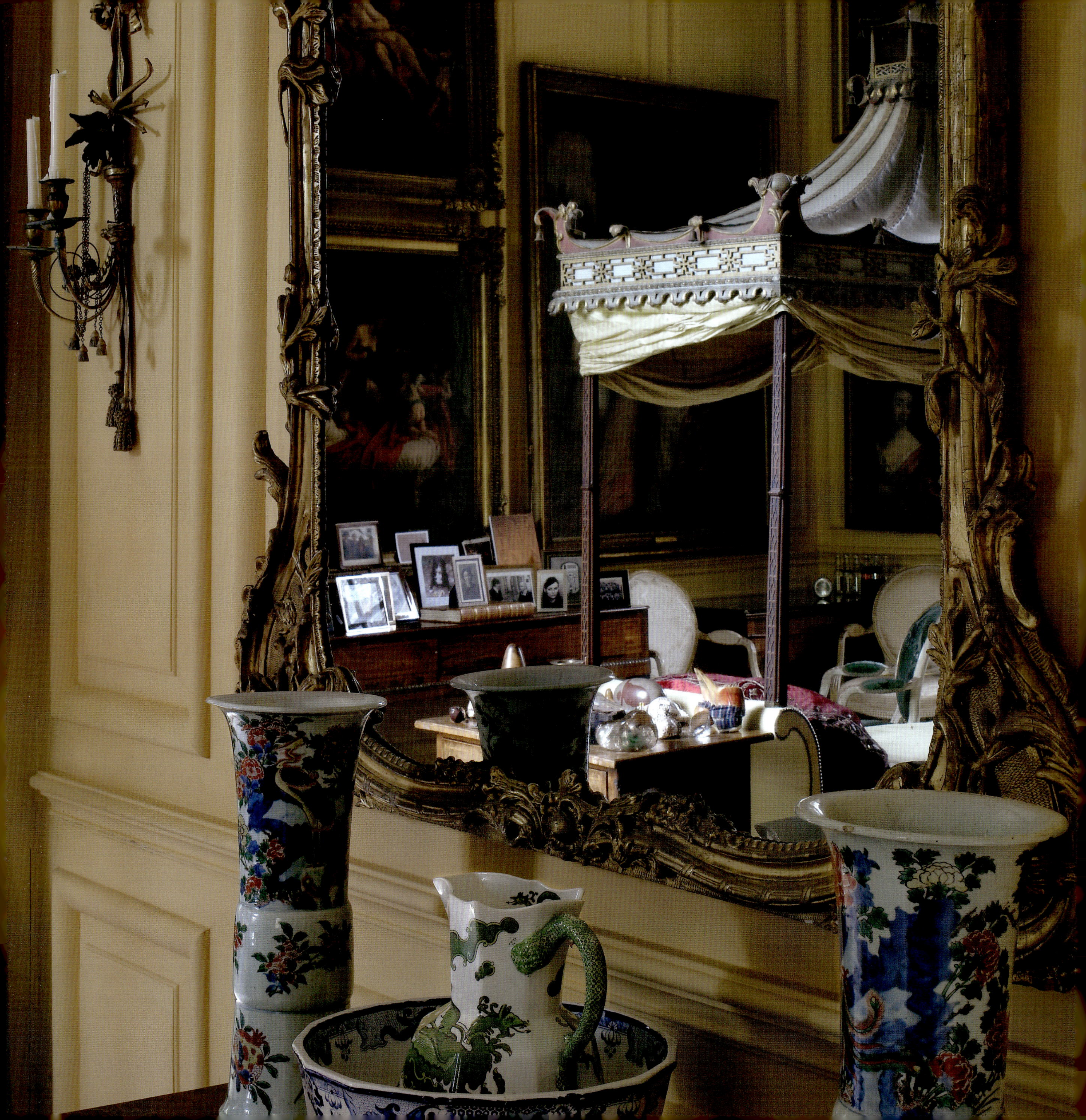

V · CONTINUITY · THE TIMELESS DRAWING ROOM

Stanway House

The triumph of the exotic: the Earl of Wemyss's drawing room is dominated by the Chippendale daybeds.

Stanway, in Gloucestershire, is one of the finest Jacobean manor houses in England, approached through a handsome gatehouse and built in the mellow Cotswold stone, which seems almost to glow in the sun. The house was altered in the later seventeenth and early eighteenth centuries, and was extended again by William Burn in the 1850s.[1] More significantly, Stanway was, in a sense, rediscovered at the end of the nineteenth century, as a building of beauty and historical association. Hugo Charteris, Lord Elcho, later the 11th Earl of Wemyss, and his wife, née Mary Wyndham, were at the centre of a group known as "the Souls," who were described by Consuelo, Duchess of Marlborough, as "a brilliant company, a select group in which a high degree of intelligence was to be found happily allied to aristocratic birth."[2] Many of this group took particular pleasure in reinhabiting the old manor houses that their eighteenth-century ancestors had often passed over to tenant farmers or given over to use as dower houses. They would then redecorate these houses in a way that enhanced their admired, aesthetic qualities of age and mellow beauty. Stanway still has a remarkable atmosphere, and is one of the homes of the present Earl of Wemyss.

The early twentieth century at Stanway was considered by some contemporary observers as a golden age, under the influence of Mary Elcho, later the Countess of Wemyss. H. G. Wells, for instance, referred to "the great days of Mary Elcho at Stanway."[3] Lady Wemyss was noted for her artistic taste and preserved the historic atmosphere of the house, while introducing William Morris papers and textiles into the bedrooms—one room is said by family tradition to have been papered by Morris himself. Mary's daughter, Lady Cynthia Asquith, wrote: "I cannot remember anyone who did not fall under the spell of Stanway. As a child I loved my home precisely as one loves a human being."[4] Lady Elcho also employed the Souls' favourite architect, Detmar Blow, to restore the house and make some additions in the form of a nursery wing. Blow's additions and the service wing added by William Burn in the mid-nineteenth century were largely removed in 1948.

The drawing room itself was probably built as the Great Parlour, part of the additions made to the house by Sir Humphrey Tracy, 3rd Bt., in the 1620s. The fielded panelling and dado rail are from the 1850s, but the Corinthian pilasters and moulded cornice were introduced in 1724 by John Tracy (1681–1735) and his wife, Anne Atkyns, sister of the county historian Sir Robert Atkyns of Sapperton (their arms appear carved over the gatehouse). These were designed by Francis Smith of Warwick, who also replaced the mullions with sash windows at the time, as part of a fairly modest and restrained programme to bring part of the old house into touch with contemporary fashions. The moulded early-seventeenth-century-style plaster ceiling in the room also dates from the 1850s and may be by William Burn.

Stanway passed by descent to John's granddaughter, Henrietta Tracy-Keck, who became Viscountess Hereford and lived at the house in her widowhood until 1817. At that point the house passed to her nephew, Francis, the 8th Earl of Wemyss (1772–1853), who was also a major Scottish landowner. This Lord Wemyss is shown as a child in the group portrait by Romney, which now hangs above the chimneypiece in the drawing room. His father's portrait by Henry Raeburn also hangs in the room, as does a Romney portrait of his mother, Susan, and his siblings. The family estates in Scotland included two great houses, Gosford, near Edinburgh, and Amisfield, near Haddington—the latter designed in 1756–59 by Isaac Ware.

THE DRAWING ROOM | 207

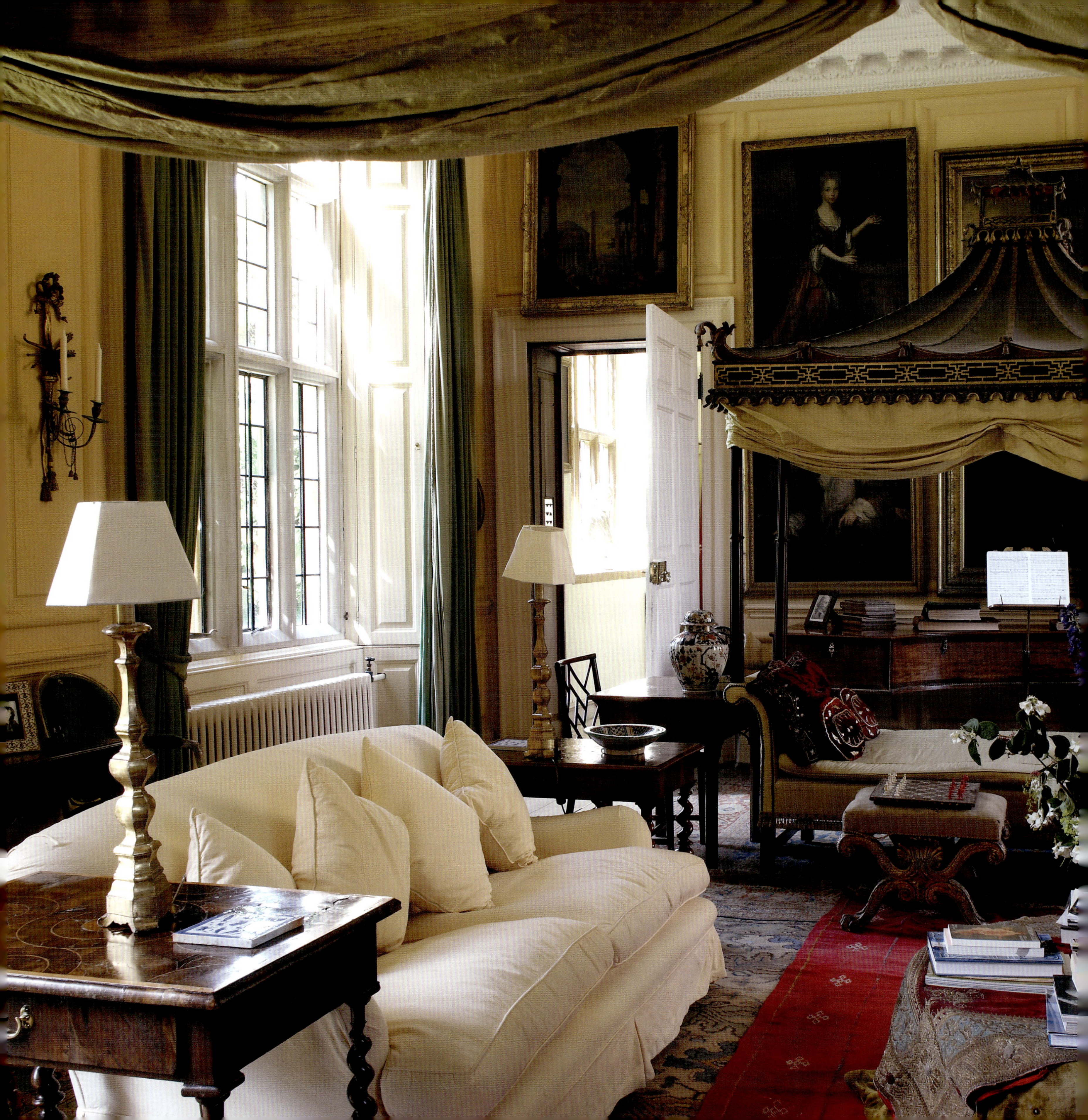

← The drawing room at Stanway House in Gloucestershire, the home of the Marquess of Wemyss, is dominated by a splendid pair of chinoiserie daybeds supplied to the family by Thomas Chippendale, originally for their home in Scotland.

↓ A series of paintings by Jean-Louis-François Lagrenée the Elder adds to the exuberance of this remarkable room.

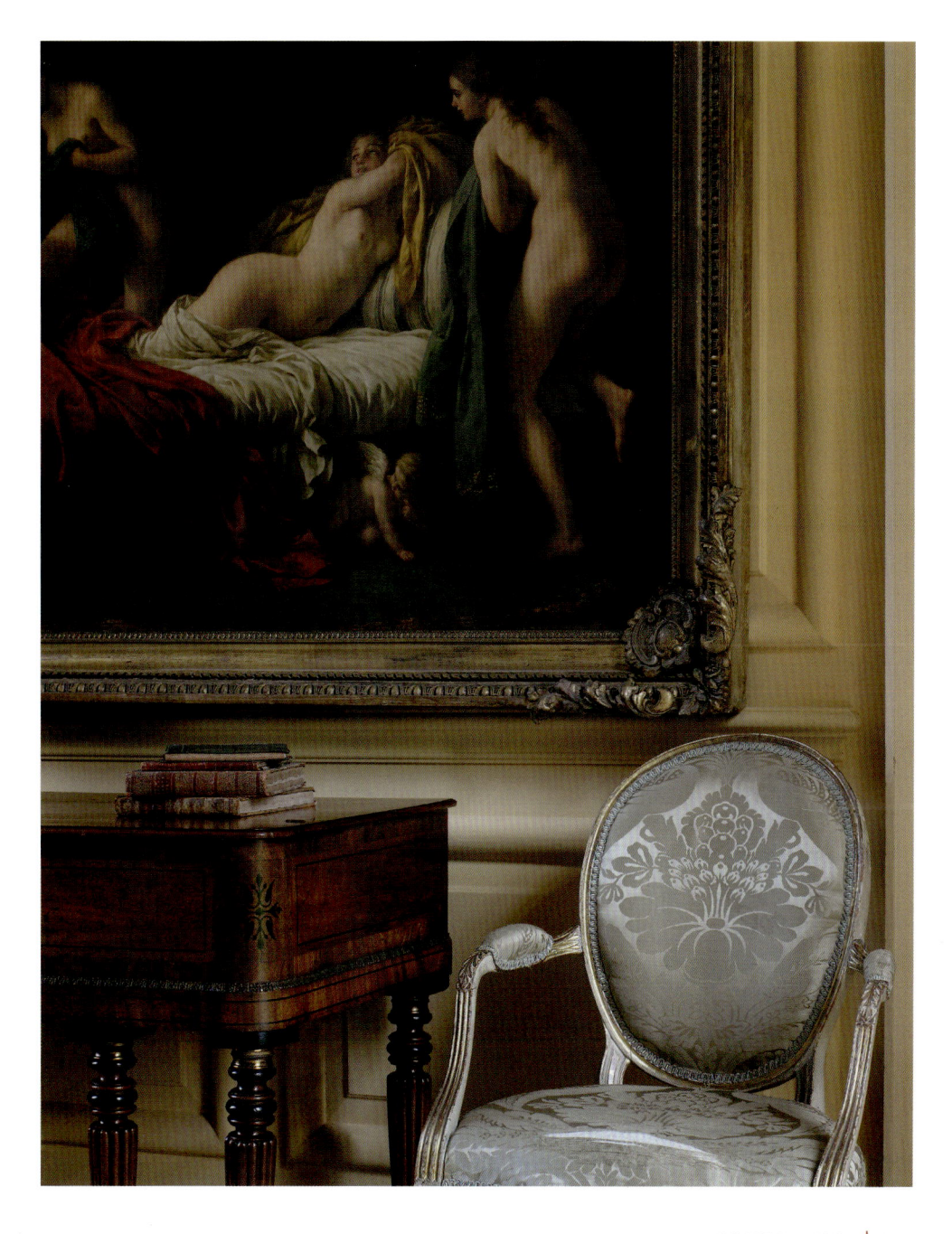

CONTINUITY | 209

The colour scheme of warm yellow was chosen by Lord and Lady Wemyss and executed in 2007. The windows on the north side of the room were reopened in 2006, dramatically improving the lighting of the room. The Jacobean ceiling plasterwork dates from the 1850s.

The remarkable chinoiserie daybeds seen in this room today were made in the mid-1750s for a dedicated Chinese Room at Amisfield for Francis Charteris, 7th Earl of Wemyss. Designed by the cabinetmaker Thomas Chippendale to evoke a Chinese wedding kiosk, they were naturally linked in the Georgian imagination to the service of tea and the receiving of company. The Chinese style was directly linked with the consumption of tea. Chinoiserie was an eighteenth-century style craze, which Horace Walpole summed up as having "a whimsical air of novelty that is very pleasing."[5] What is so extraordinary is to see it so vigorously combined with the model of the triclinium banqueting couch of the classical Roman world, framed by a vivid Chinese-style canopy. Originally the daybed would have had chintz curtains, which could be tied up at the sides or let down for further privacy, intimacy, and presumably warmth.

Such a glamorous piece of furniture should be imagined with a mid-eighteenth-century lady in a delicate silk dress, seated in the centre of the bed, framed by the sloped, painted roof and curtains, as if in a miniature theatre.[6] The design is full of visual diversion, and the pavilion-like roofs are crowned by miniature versions of themselves, the interior decorated with painted birds and bells. Chippendale included such daybeds in his famously lavish book The Gentleman and Cabinet Maker's Director, published in 1754 and illustrated with 161 engraved plates of "Elegant and Useful Designs of Household Furniture in the Gothic, Chinese and Modern Taste."[7]

The daybeds are arranged today at right angles to the chimneypiece and warmth of the hearth, as they would probably have been in the eighteenth century. These extraordinary and exotic pieces of furniture were brought to Stanway by the present Lord Wemyss's grandmother only in the early 1960s, but are part of an unforgettable ensemble today. The present Lord Wemyss has dramatically improved the light in this room by reopening two windows on the north side in 2006, having in 2003 altered one of the eastern windows on the south side to improve the view to the garden from the daybeds. Lord and Lady Wemyss chose the current colour scheme in 2007, with warm yellow walls, an off-white ceiling with gold-leafed beads on the fleur-de-lys, and gold leaf on window astragals.

The exuberance of the exotic daybeds is matched by a sumptuous pair of paintings: *Les Graces Lutinées Par Les Amours* by the French court painter Jean-Louis-François Lagrenée the Elder, completed for the Marquis de Verrey (Fragonard's patron) in the 1770s.[8] It is often these unexpected but imaginative juxtapositions that are so memorable in houses such as Stanway, which are much cherished and furnished with the contents of different family homes.

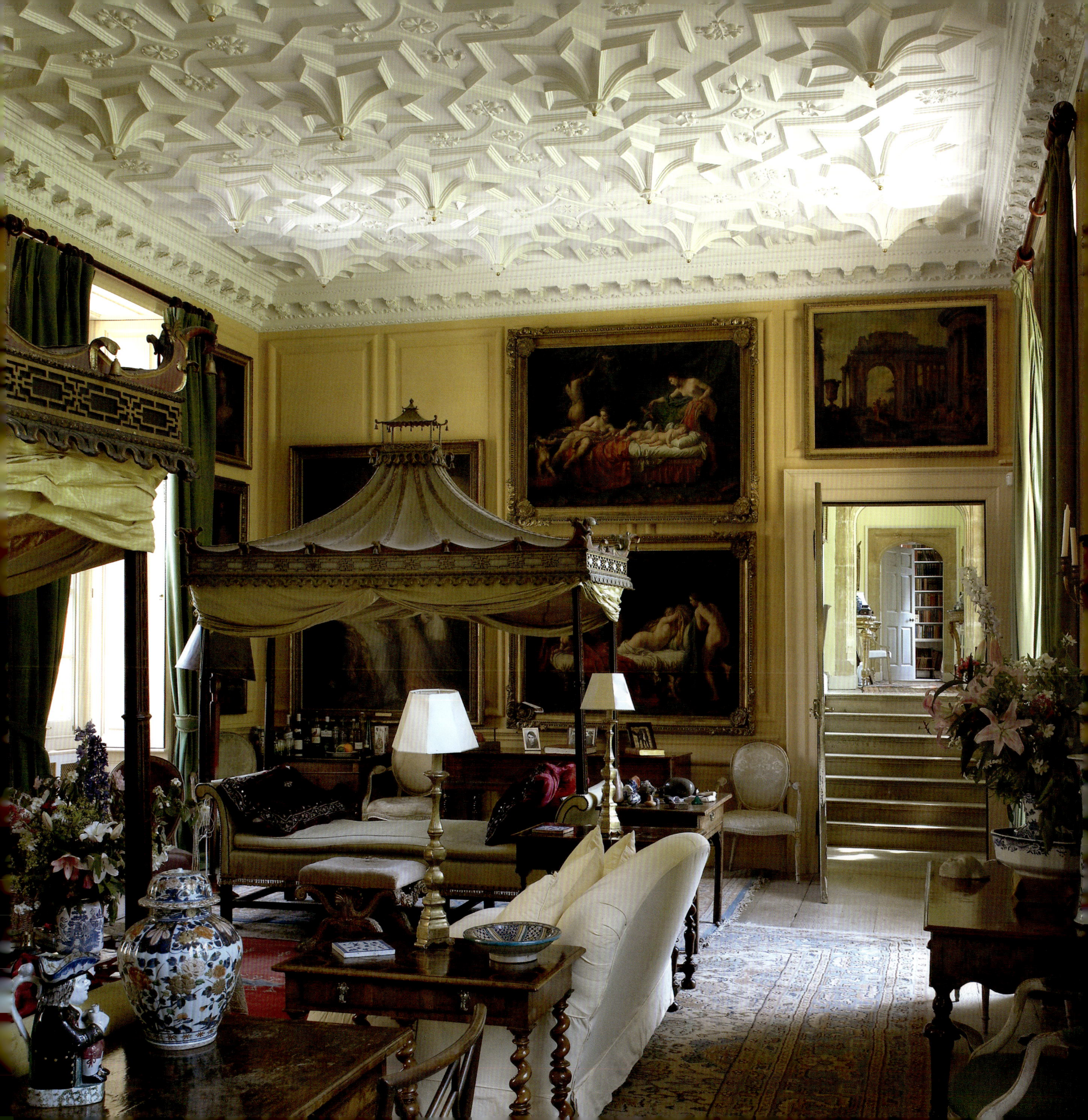

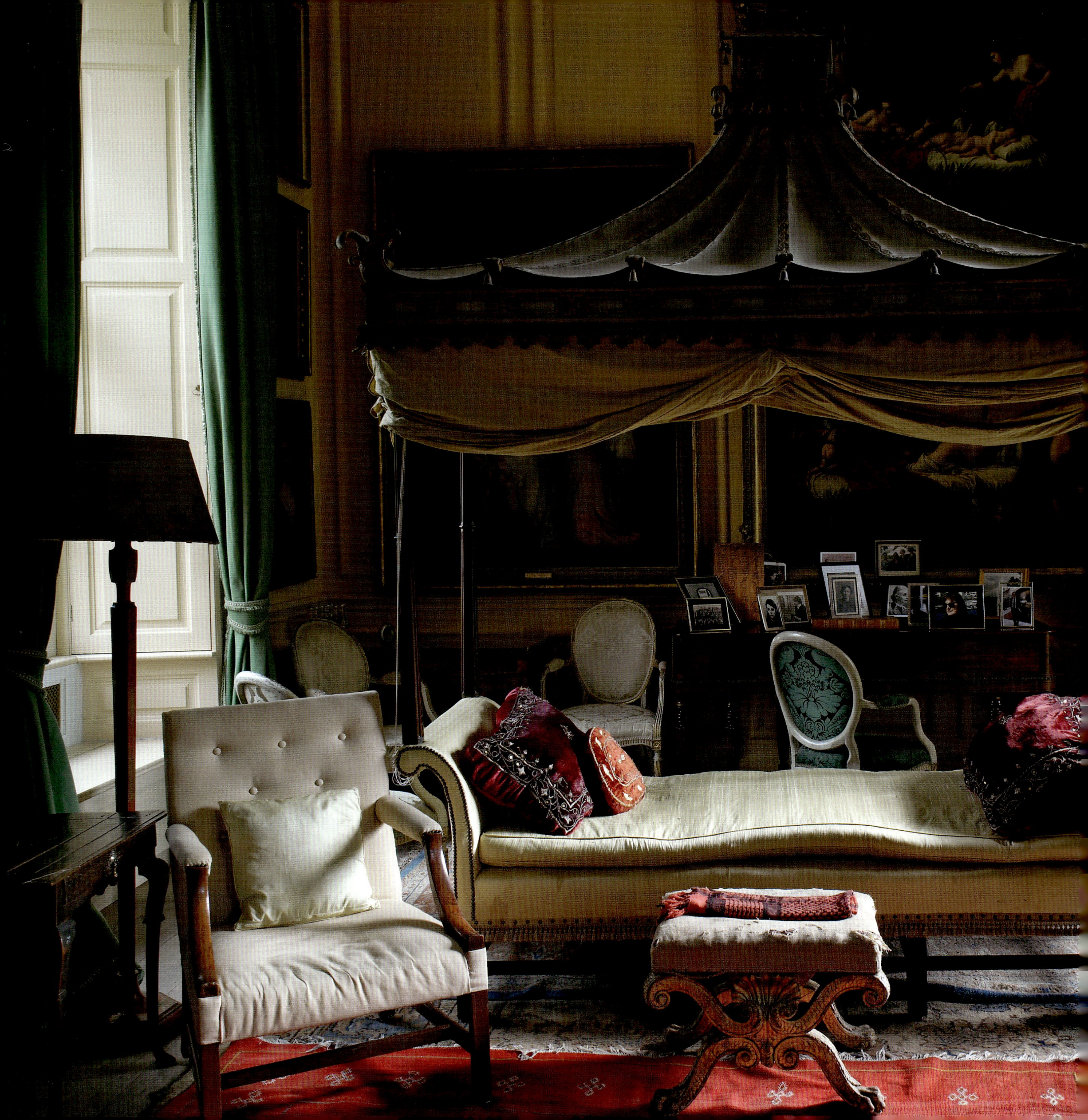

The chinoiserie daybed supplied by Chippendale in effect provided a stage within a room from which a hostess could receive her guests, framed against its exotic form and detail.

CONTINUITY | 213

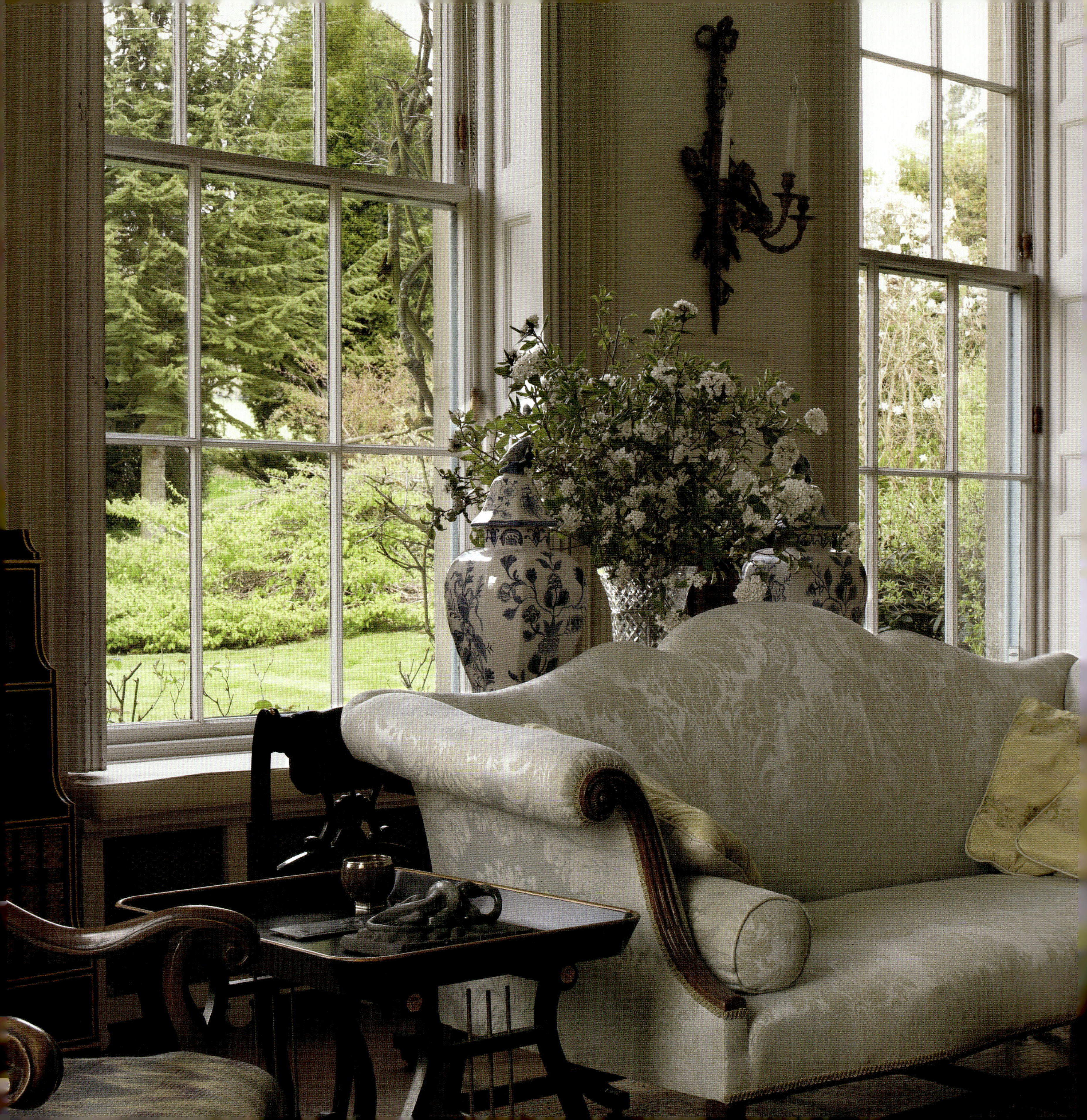

V · CONTINUITY · THE TIMELESS DRAWING ROOM

Bradley Court

Among the touches of humour and elegance here are sculptures and paintings by theatre designer Oliver Messel.

Bradley Court is a mellow Cotswold manor house, built for a branch of the Berkeley family of Berkeley Castle — there is a date stone of 1559 over the entrance. The house, which seems almost to grow out of the earth, is a handsome, many gabled structure, rendered in roughcast, with limestone window surrounds, under stone slate roofs.[1] It was altered slightly in the 1690s by a Bristol merchant, Thomas Dawes, who also laid out the formal gardens recorded in a view by Kipp in the early eighteenth century. In the 1790s, a two-storey addition was made to the north of the house, which included an elegant drawing room with tall sash windows looking over the garden, a fourteen-foot ceiling enriched with a central rose, and a cornice with a distinctive guilloche and acanthus leaf ornament, which the historian James Lees-Milne, who dined here regularly in the 1980s, suggested showed the hand of the Gloucester architect Anthony Keck.[2]

The proportions of the drawing room at Bradley Court, delightfully different in character to the sixteenth-century rooms of the house, capture precisely the importance of the one good room attached to an older house (echoing the first sentiment of Jane Austen's Mrs. Dashwood on seeing Barton Cottage in *Sense and Sensibility*, "this with a new a drawing room which may easily be added and a bedchamber and a garret above, will make a very snug little cottage" — in the Regency sense of the word).[3] Its style, however, belongs to a more twentieth-century story. The owners of the house, Thomas Messel, furniture maker and member of the creative Messel dynasty, and his artist wife, Pepe, have presented the room in a subtle mix of late Georgian and baroque.

Mr. Messel runs his own furniture workshop at Bradley Court, working in the great European traditions to create furniture for clients including the Earl and Countess of Derby, Alidad and Nicky Haslam. He has also made furniture for Windsor Castle and Kensington Palace.[4]

Over the past thirty years, Mrs. Messel has also entirely transformed and shaped the gardens, which can be seen from the drawing room — inspired by the woodlands garden of her own family home, Hazelmount in Cumbria. Thomas Messel himself grew up in Sussex and spent a good deal of time at Nymans, the romantic Picturesque manor house created in the 1920s around an older house by his grandparents, Leonard and Maud Messel, with its famous garden founded by his great-grandfather, Ludwig Messel (Maud was the daughter of Linley Sambourne, RA). Thomas Messel spent many summers at Nymans with his aunt, the Countess of Rosse.

Although his own career began as a guards officer, Thomas Messel was influenced to become a furniture designer by his uncle, Oliver Messel, one of the twentieth-century's foremost set designers, especially famous for his designs for Covent Garden and Glyndebourne.[5] Oliver Messel was also an important influence on another nephew, Tony, Earl of Snowdon. It was Lord Snowdon who recommended Bradley Court to Thomas and Pepe Messel when it was being sold by Polly and Adrian Garnett. Mrs. Garnett's brother-in-law, Seamus Heaney, wrote movingly of the view from Bradley Court in a poem: "Its prospects lie / Wooded and misty to my eye."[6]

There is an attractive touch of poetry about the Bradley Court drawing room, with everything carefully positioned and light, and touches of the wit and design skill of his uncle Oliver: the masks and miniature monkeys dressed in Mozartean dress. Thomas and Pepe Messel carefully restored the whole house with the help of stonemason Rory Young in 1984.

THE DRAWING ROOM | 215

↓ The tall windows of the drawing room at Bradley Court, Gloucestershire, were deliberately left without curtains to celebrate the views across the garden and the Cotswold country house.

→ The handsome, late-Georgian drawing room at Bradley Court, probably added to the sixteenth-century house by architect Anthony Keck, belongs to furniture maker Thomas Messel and his painter wife, Pepe. The credenza was designed by Mr. Messel.

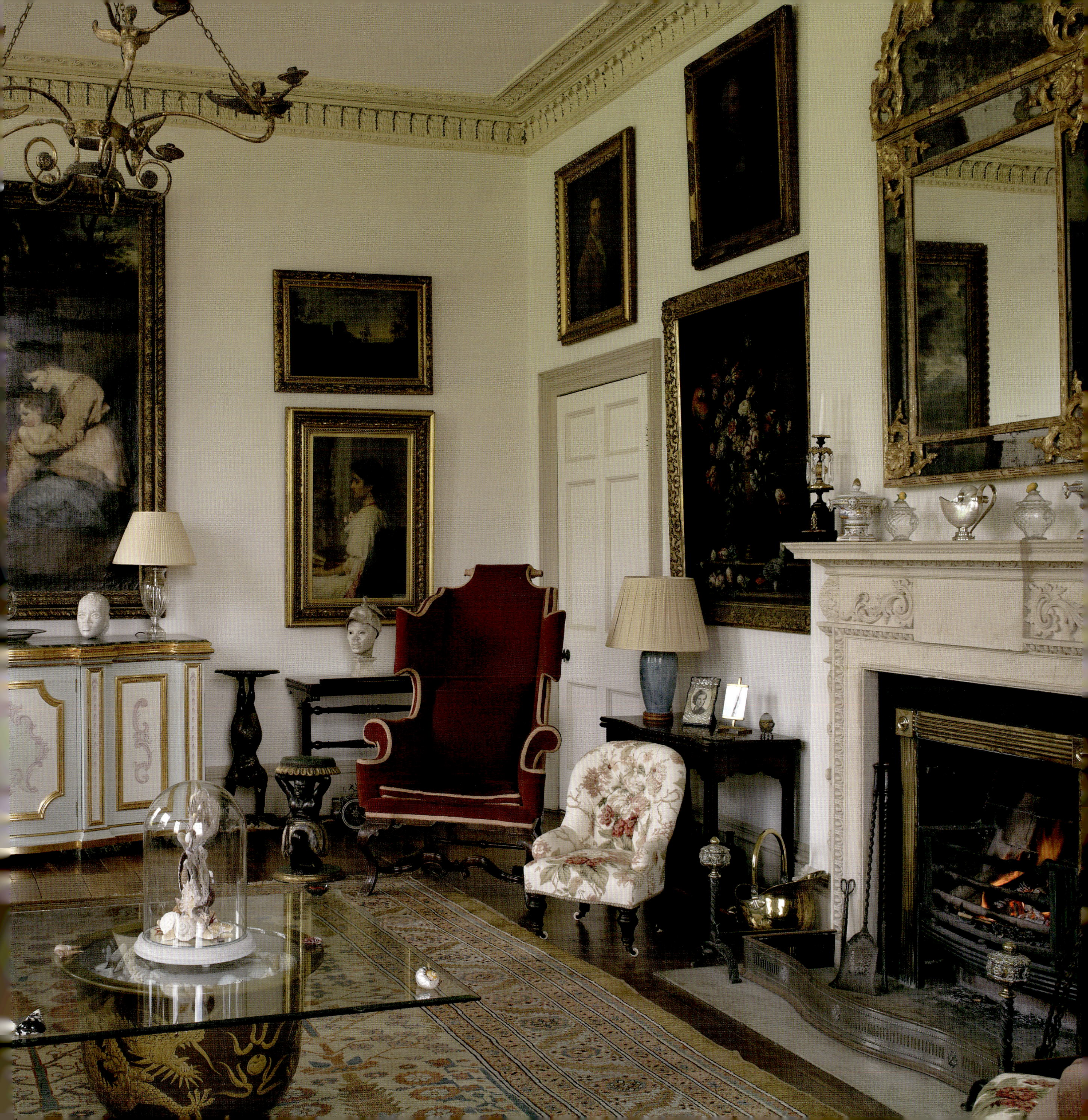

The drawing room at Bradley Court feels very connected with the garden on two sides and has the character of a pavilion in a beautiful garden. Floral arrangements bring the garden into the room.

The Messels introduced the rococo bath stone chimneypiece (restored by Rory Young) and furnished the room with pieces designed and made by Thomas Messel himself, as well as pictures and furniture inherited from his uncle Oliver, and from his father, Linley—some coming from his grandparents' home at Nymans in Sussex.[7]

The paintings include a Holy Family by Reynolds and an Italian landscape, as well as a portrait of a boy after Thomas Lawrence, a portrait of a toreador by Oliver Messel, and a portrait of Ottilie Messel by Marcus Stone. There is a portrait by Solomon J. Solomon of Mrs. Ludwig Messel, and paintings by Pepe Messel of the Ligurian hilltop village of Glori. The bold, Italian baroque-inspired credenza, on which sit masks by Oliver Messel, was made to Thomas Messel's own design and sits between two eighteenth-century architect's tables.

Lighting and mirrors are very important to the room, and on the architectural table are two large Delft ginger jars and a *Regence* mirror over the chimneypiece, a chandelier in giltwood and metal of five Nike (winged victories in the manner of James Cameron, the architect of Pavlosk), which once belonged to Oliver Messel.

There is a Broadwood boudoir grand piano, a pair of pier bookcases, and side tables in black lacquer by Thomas Messel. Among the comfortable set furniture pieces are an unusual late-seventeenth-century chair in the manner of Marot, an early eighteenth-century Venetian armchair, and a serpentine settee from Nymans. On the eighteenth-century sofa table is an elegant wine cooler from Nuremberg given to Lady Rosse by Harold Acton, and once borrowed and never returned by Oliver. (Thomas Messel recalls, "I took it back to my aunt, who gave it as a present to me.") The centre table is an antique Chinese egg vase covered with shells under a sheet of glass, put together by Pepe Messel.[8] Thomas Messel observes: "This is a dignified room, full of light and air, a delight after the more intimate rooms of the sixteenth-century house. We have never had any curtains in here, as during the day we like to see the views of the garden and in the night the immensely tall windows simply reflect like mirrors."

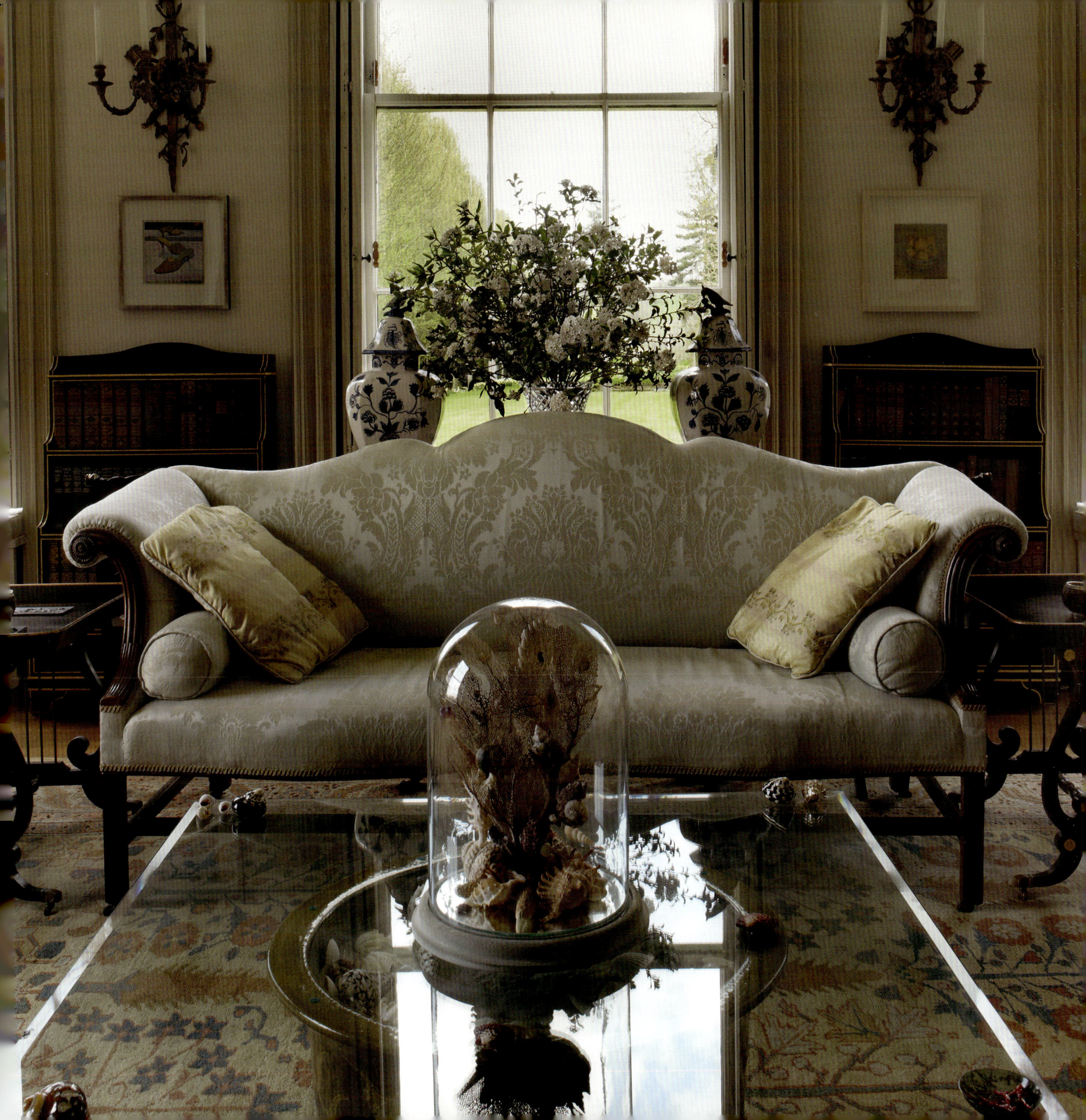

↓ Family portraits hang alongside decorative paintings by Oliver Messel.

→ A touch of fun: the well-dressed monkeys that adorn the grand piano were designed by Oliver Messel.

220 | BRADLEY COURT

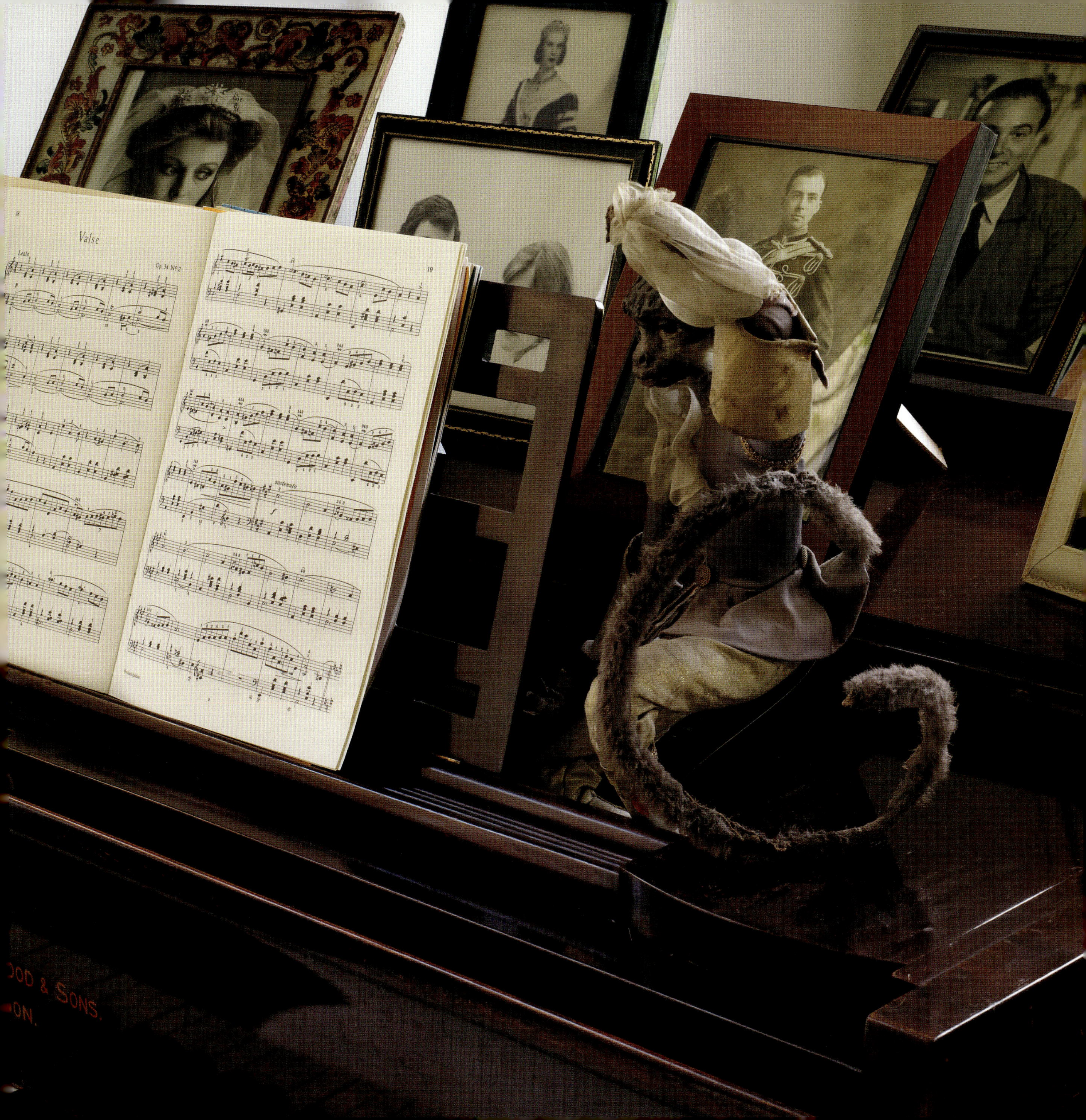
Valse
Op. 34 No 2
19
OOD & SONS.
ON.

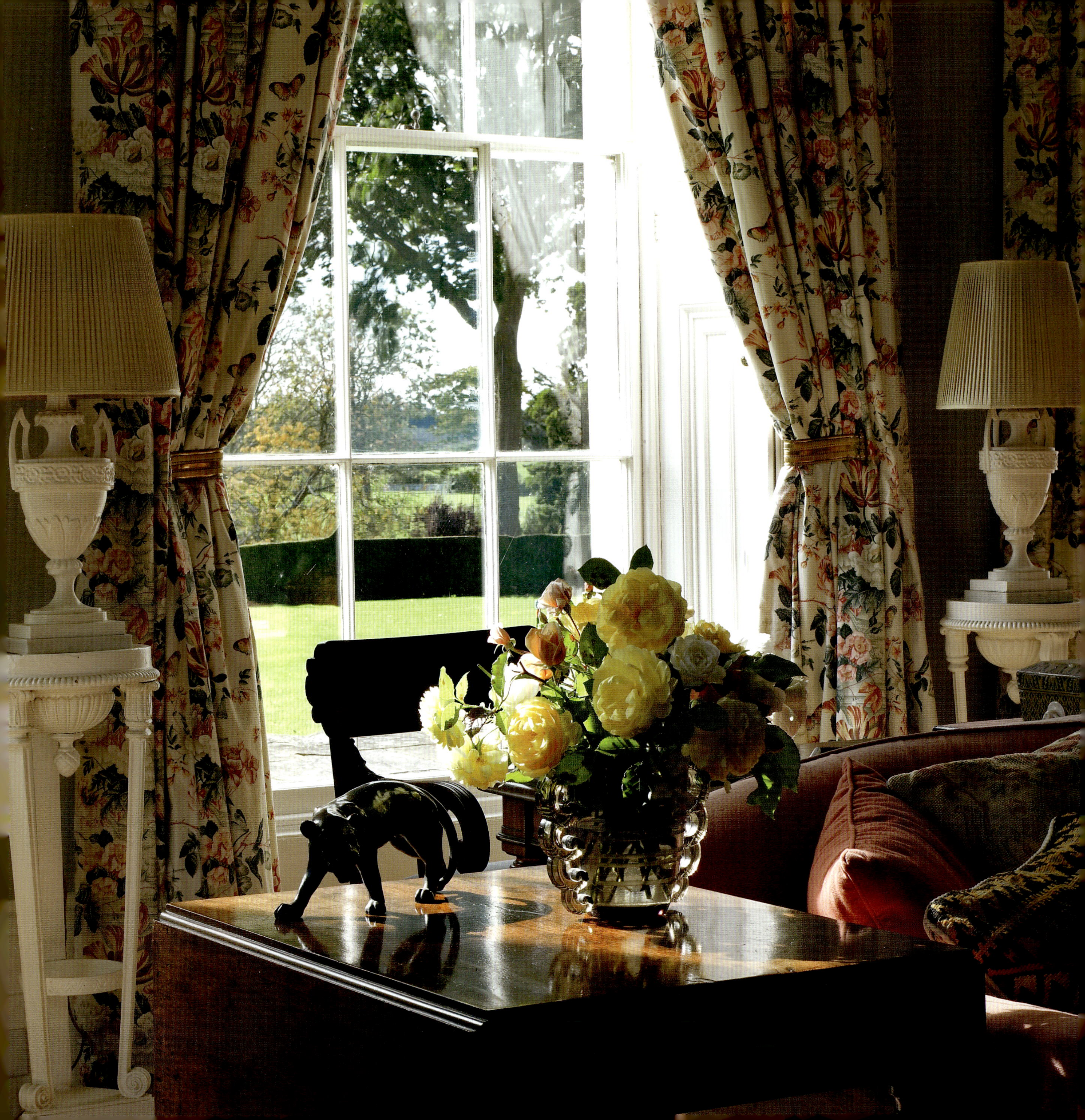

V · CONTINUITY · THE TIMELESS DRAWING ROOM

Wormington Grange

Simply English: this fine Regency drawing room has been decorated and furnished by John Evetts.

It is often the freshness of an English drawing room that appeals most to the eye: the relationship with the garden and landscape through tall windows, the cheerful floral curtains, comfortable sofas, and a certain cool reserve in colour and contents. Sometimes this is formed through accident of inherited history, and sometimes through careful design. When John Evetts took over his family home, Wormington Grange, near Tewkesbury, from his parents in the mid-1980s, the principal rooms were hardly furnished. These reception rooms — entrance hall, dining room, and drawing room — were all part of a new range added to an existing house in 1826–27 for Josiah Gist to designs by Henry Hakewill (1771–1830), a pupil of John Yenn who had won a silver medal at the Royal Academy.[1] This period of work transformed an elegant but not overly large house into a proper country house of much greater architectural dignity with appropriately spacious rooms of reception and circulation. Christopher Hussey visited Wormington Grange in the mid-1950s and suggested in his account of the house in *English Georgian Houses: Late Georgian* that Hakewill's principal assistant, John Goldicutt, who had studied in France and spent four years travelling in Italy, might be credited with much of the best finished detail. Goldicutt certainly published several books based on his travels, including *Specimens of Ancient Decoration from Pompeii* (1825), and would have been able to work up the rich but academically rigorous schemes of decoration that run through these principal rooms and have distinct echoes of the work of C. R. Cockerell.[2]

These 1820s reception rooms are all well proportioned and high ceilinged, with tall sash windows. They provided large rooms for entertainment of subtly different but related characters. Mr. Evetts's great-grandmother, Maud Clegg, who acquired the estate, was a niece of the Chicago department store owner and millionaire Marshall Field. Guy Dawber had designed Mr. and Mrs. Clegg a handsome house (Bibsworth House) on the edge of Broadway but, attracted by the position and space of Wormington Grange, they acquired the house and two thousand acres when they came on the market in 1920. Mrs. Clegg spent lavishly on furnishing the house then, as can be seen in prewar photographs, but these contents were largely dispersed in sales (and bequests) after the Second World War (as was most of the estate). But as a collector, enthusiast, and authority on Gillows furniture, Mr. Evetts has taken great pleasure in slowly refurnishing these 1820s room with pieces of suitable period feel and scale to create a classic English ensemble.[3] The drawing room has recently been painted in a Farrow and Ball French gray, but in the 1950s it was papered in a blue and white striped paper, as Mr. Evetts observes, "by a smart lady decorator who painted all the furniture white, and cut up Morris & Co. curtains and gave them to local churches." Only two things survived from pre-1950s schemes: the chandelier and the large looking glass. The lamp-stands came from another room.

The early-nineteenth-century classical detailing contributes to the overall dignity of the room. The plaster frieze of Grecian character was admired by Christopher Hussey as "at once bold and delicate."[4] Moulded fillets divide the ceiling into nine compartments containing enriched coffers, the central one with a large rosette from which the chandelier hangs. The cornice has an attractive combination of scrolls, anthemia, and palmettes, which are also present in the solid marble chimneypiece. An intriguing puzzle of Hakewill's design is that the sash window in the east wall reads as a single window on the inside, while reading as a tripartite window rather in the Wyatt manner from the outside. Intriguingly the original plans by Hakewill — which

THE DRAWING ROOM | 223

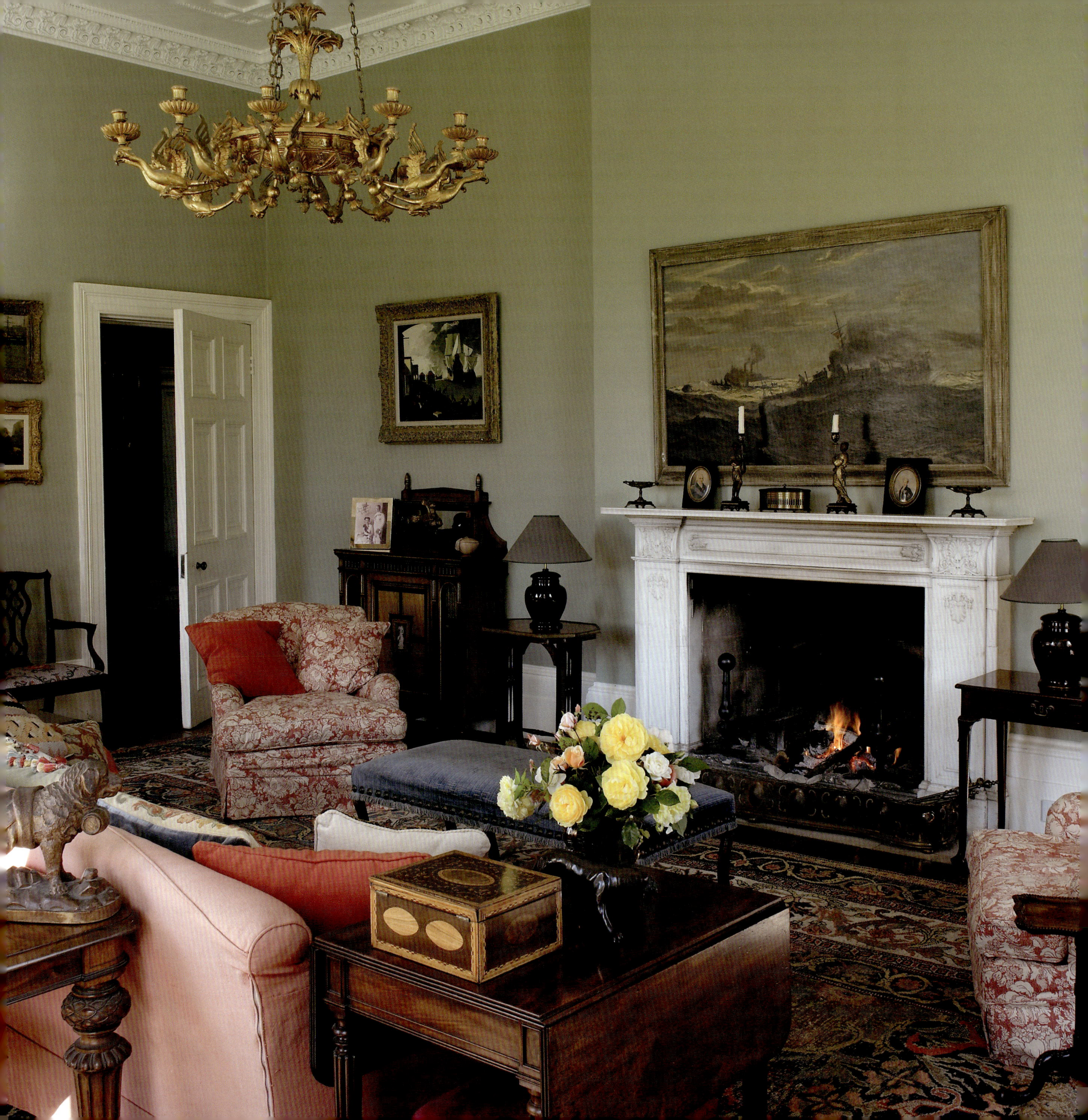

← The plain and stately early-nineteenth-century drawing room at Wormington Grange, Gloucestershire, is a quintessentially English room, designed by Henry Hakewill and John Goldicutt, and restored and redecorated by John Evetts.

↓ The ornately framed mirror is one of the few things John Evetts inherited with the house.

CONTINUITY | 225

↓ One of a pair of cabinets made by Manchester cabinetmaker John Lamb.

→ An early nineteenth-century writing table is placed against the main sofa in the traditional manner, evoking the pleasures of reading and letter writing.

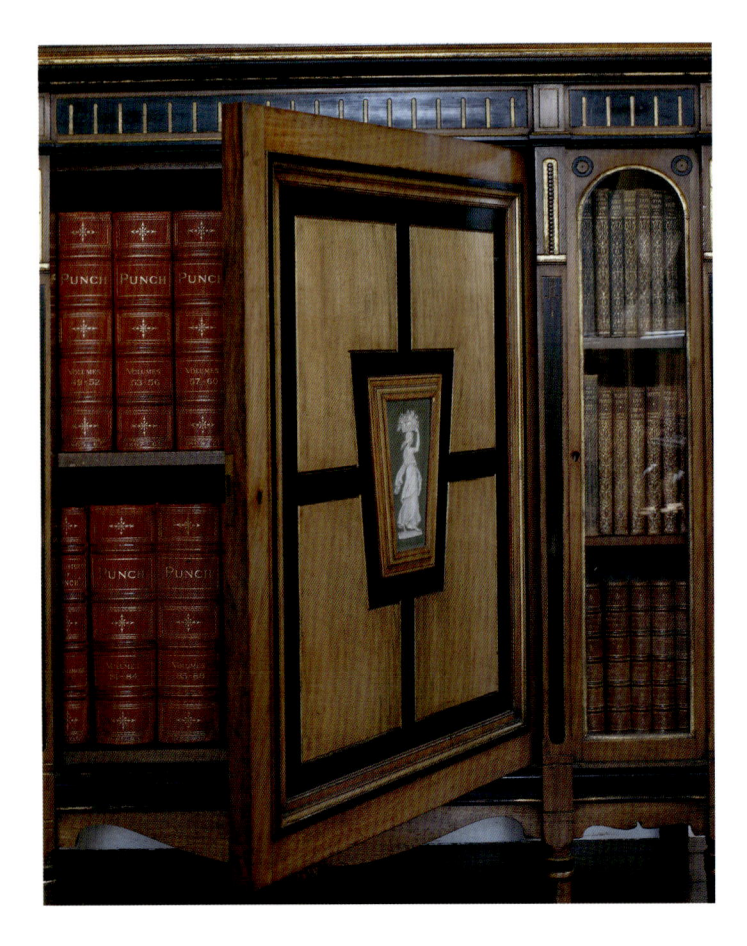

survive in the house — suggest that the drawing room was originally conceived with its chimneypiece on the south side of the room, with no windows on either side.

Mr. Evetts has collected early-twentieth-century oil paintings at auction to suit the character of the room, including a large oil painting of the two First World War naval war vessels on patrol by Norman Wilkinson, RA. He has also collected furniture of the scale and sort with which the room might have been decorated in its original period or within the first few decades after that, by makers such as Howard or Gillows. Mr.

Evetts recalls that he was very inspired by the early-nineteenth-century Gillows furnishings at Tatton Hall in Cheshire. The pair of cabinets on either side of the chimneypiece are good examples of the work of the mid-nineteenth-century Manchester cabinetmaker John Lamb. The curtains are of a traditional floral pattern. Photographs and portraits add a familial touch, including pictures of Mr. Evetts's grandparents, Lord and Lady Ismay. General Ismay was Churchill's personal representative on the Chiefs of Staff committee and the first secretary general of NATO.[5] He wrote his memoirs while in retirement at Wormington.

Despite a noticeable feeling of restraint in the decoration of the drawing room of Wormington Grange, the room is quite as comfortable as any. The clue perhaps comes in Mr. Evetts's career as the (principal) adviser on furniture for the Landmark Trust, planning and acquiring the furnishings for the many remarkable buildings restored by the trust, which was founded in 1965 by Sir John and Lady Smith.[6] At Wormington Grange, the drawing room shows all the tactful and deft choices made by Mr. Evetts and his partner, Annie, to make a large, high-ceilinged classical room both inviting and memorable and to allow the architecture to speak for itself. Mr. Evetts observes: "We use our drawing room on high days and holidays, as is the case with many drawing rooms I suspect. We live normally on the west side of the house."

In many ways the room presents a very English picture: tall windows onto well-maintained gardens, Regency furniture, bronzes and paintings, comfortable sofas and armchairs, a subtle colour scheme. But it also manages to have a fresh, modern, uncluttered feel. Mr. Evetts observes, "The vision of the Landmark has always been to have just enough to make the rooms work and for the architectural interest of the room itself to be properly appreciated. In some ways, it is about 'sculpting' the space."

EUROPEAN GARDEN DESIGN
FROM CLASSICAL ANTIQUITY TO THE PRESENT DAY
THE MARSHALL FIELDS
SACRED LEGACY EDWARD S. CURTIS
RANDOLPH CALDECOTT'S

↓ The curtains at Wormington Grange are in a traditional chintz, and the small painted stands are thought to be part of the original early-nineteenth-century furnishings.

→ John Evetts has hung the drawing room with a collection of twentieth-century oil paintings. The muted colours of the pictures and the velvet of the stool, and the different woods of the tables and cabinets all contribute to a mellow effect.

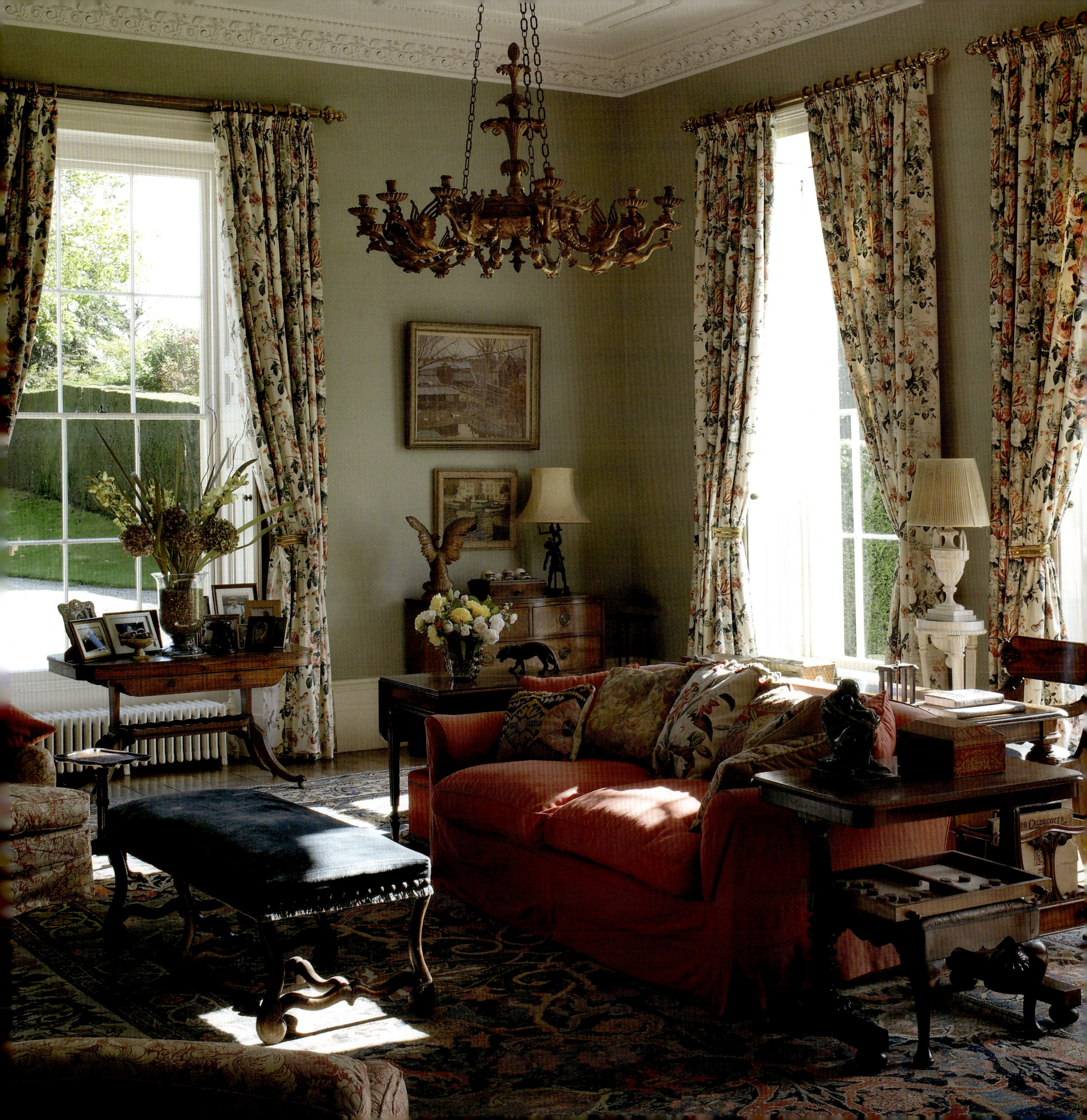

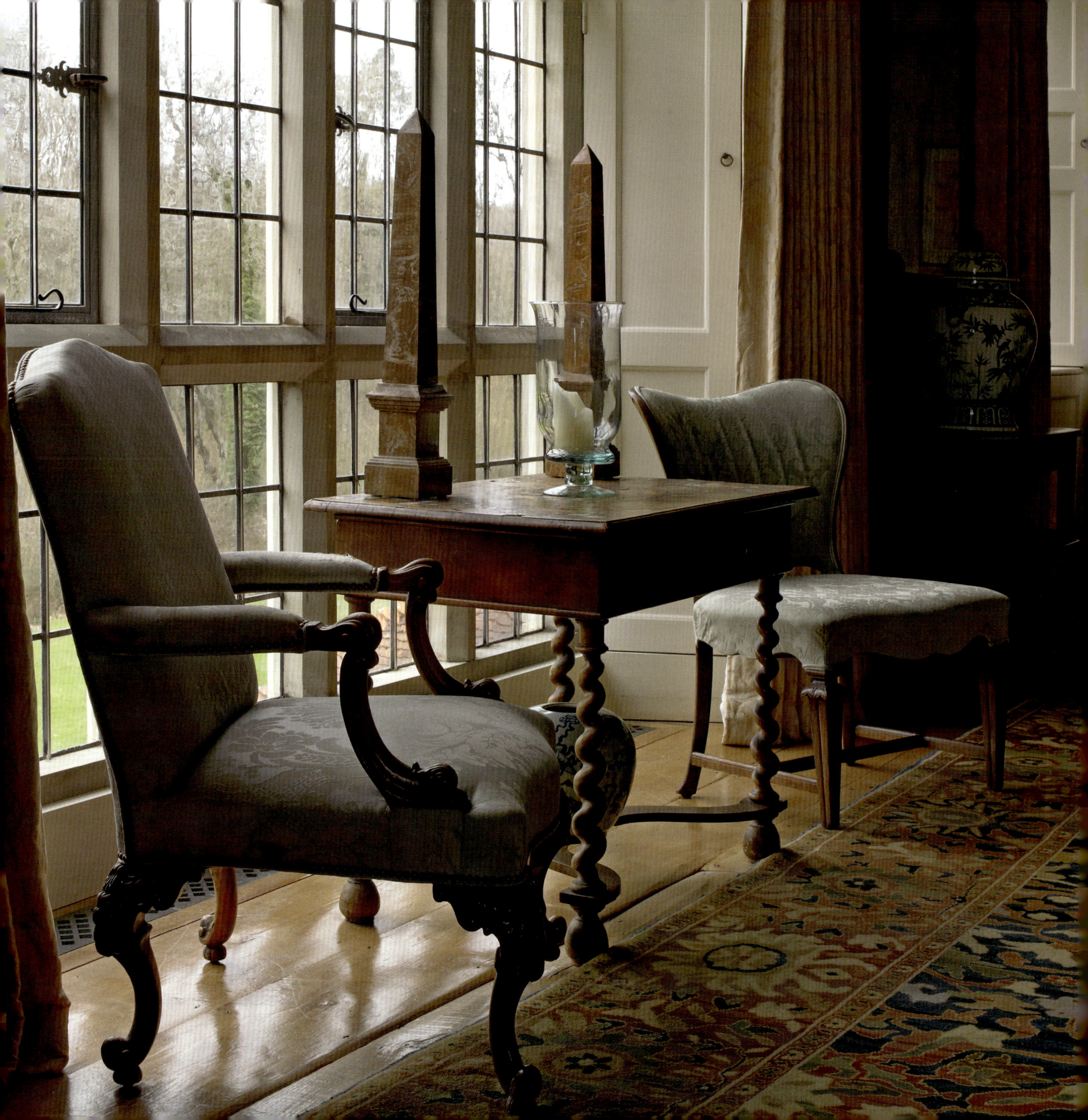

V · CONTINUITY · THE TIMELESS DRAWING ROOM

Whithurst House

In 2004 a room for entertaining in the spirit of the seventeenth century was designed by Christopher Rae-Scott.

Whithurst House in Sussex is a rare example of the determination to create a modern house in the tradition of the great Jacobean homes of England, with a strong emphasis on the emerging character of the classical tradition in that period.[1] In 1999 Richard Taylor and Rick Englert acquired the land with a 1950s cottage and spent a number of years planning the realisation of their architectural dream. They first demolished the cottage and built a new, barnlike lodge designed by London architect James Gorst. They then commissioned the Devon-based designer Christopher Rae-Scott, a friend of more than thirty years, to design the main house for the estate, which was completed in 2004. Mr. Taylor recalled, "we gave Mr. Rae-Scott a very vague brief: we wanted a big room for entertaining, a certain number of bedrooms on the same floor and a roof that you could give parties on. Kit Rae-Scott was almost immediately able to visualise the house and provided us with a design in a very short time which really could not be improved."

The historic nature of the surrounding landscape encouraged a different approach to the design of the main house. Mr. Rae-Scott made a careful reading of the historic character of the existing landscape.[2] The estate had been owned in the late eighteenth century by the 4th Earl of Newburgh, who is thought to have maintained a hunting lodge on the land. Mr. Rae-Scott argued that "the flavour of ancient establishment was an inescapably important factor in our consideration of the sort of house to build … there seemed no doubt that the only sympathetic answer was a traditional English building made of traditional English materials."

The house thus was designed in the manner of a symmetrical early-seventeenth-century hunting lodge and constructed in a warm red, handmade brick with stone dressings, and captures the essence of a traditional West Sussex house. The two towers on the entrance front have narrow windows, which give a solid, Vanbrughian quality to the house. Mr. Rae-Scott drew up highly detailed drawings of every aspect of the building for the guidance of the builders and craftsmen.

The result is a supremely well-crafted building of almost sculptural quality that sits handsomely in its setting. Mr. Taylor recalls, "with Kit Rae-Scott's input and advice we realised that what we wanted was a house that suited the historic landscape, and one which might have evolved over the centuries like the landscape. In my opinion, my house sits rather like a fort facing a four-acre lake." Like many smaller Jacobean country houses, the roof scape and the turrets are all part of the pleasure of the accommodation, viewpoints for enjoying the landscape around, and as well as the roof itself, there is an octagonal prospect room for entertaining. The forecourt has two single-storey wings that read as if they might have been late-seventeenth- or early-eighteenth-century additions.

In an illustration of the continuing attractions of a formal drawing room for entertaining, Mr. Taylor had specified that they wanted a first floor drawing room. Much of the pleasure of the design and planning of Whithurst House is in the spatial adventure inherent in the way that the house opens up from the entrance hall and staircase into different rooms—"a house full of surprises." The climax of all these progressions is the arrival in the drawing room, the largest single volume within the house. The drawing room in effect fills the depth of the west side of the house. Facing the chimneypiece is a long stone mullioned window in the centre of the western wall, which, with two smaller windows and the window on the south wall, gives wonderful views over the well-wooded parkland.

For the detailing of the interiors of the house, Mr. Rae-Scott

THE DRAWING ROOM | 231

↓ A painted bird's-eye view of Whithurst by William Pounds built to designs of Christopher Rae-Scott for Richard Taylor and Rick Englert.

→ The long drawing room at Whithurst is dominated by a seventeenth-century-style chimneypiece, around which the sofas are arranged; the ceiling is coved in the same period spirit; in this new house, the character of a traditional interior.

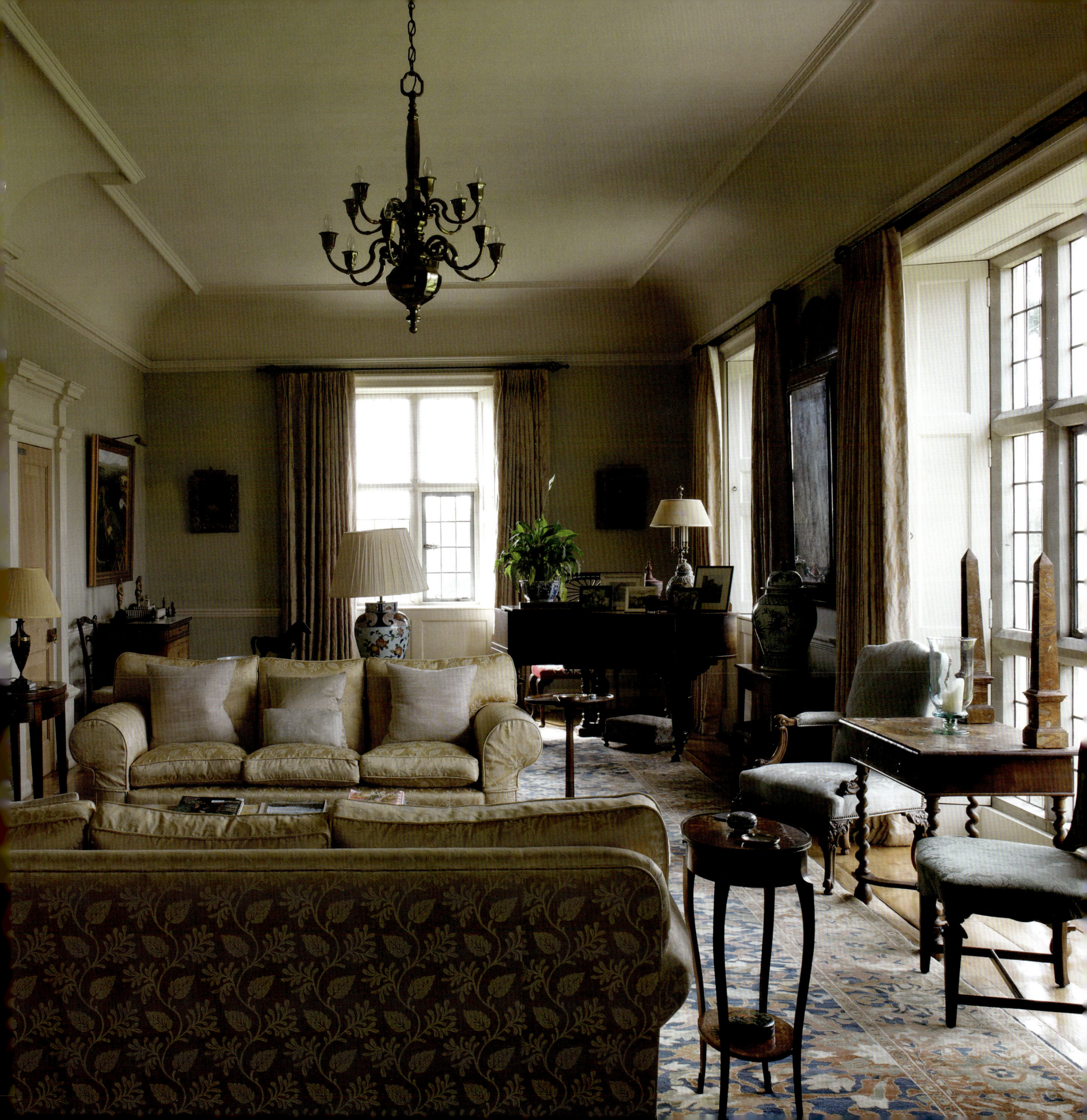

Despite Whithurst Park being a new building, the furnishings and collection of pictures are contrived to give the atmosphere of a mellow country house, with antique furniture, old rugs, and framed photographs crowded on the piano; the tall, seventeenth-century-style mirrors were designed by Christopher Rae-Scott and made up especially for the room.

recalled that they were guided by a "preference for solidity, sobriety and symmetry," and some of the more intimate living rooms, such as the ground floor dining room, are handsomely panelled in the later seventeenth-century manner. The drawing room is long and high ceilinged, combining the character of a great chamber and a spacious country-house Long Gallery designed for prospect. It is also well detailed, with a rough-hewn oak floor, oak doors, a stone chimneypiece, and leaded windows. The two door cases have a noticeably mannerist character as if they were an alteration of the late seventeenth century.

Mary Miers wrote in *Country Life* in 2005: "Whithurst's beautifully detailed craftsmanship is best appreciated in this handsome room, with its coved ceiling, hand-plastered *in situ*."[3] The stone chimneypiece speaks of the emerging classicism of the early seventeenth century, while the two tall William and Mary–style pier glasses were especially designed for the room by Mr. Rae-Scott and made up with antiqued mirror glass. The forty-foot-long carpet was woven especially for the house in Cairo. The central stool is an early work by David Linley. The rest of the furniture is a mixture of inherited and bought seventeenth- and eighteenth-century pieces, including portraits and drawings. A grand piano at the south end of the room shows that this is still a party room.

Mr. Taylor and Mr. Englert—entrepreneur and designer, respectively—have brought considerable visual awareness to creating their home; they also consider it "an Anglo-American project from the start."[4] They have carefully kept the long drawing room empty of clutter so it can be used for larger parties, while the key seat furniture is arranged so it can be enjoyed when they are alone in the house. A bird's-eye view painting of the house and park by William Pounds hangs at the northern end of the room. The drinks cabinet is wittily hidden in a small turret tower, as if an adapted garderobe. The long, light-filled drawing room has a calm, considered simplicity that has something of the familiar air of those much-admired seventeenth-century paintings of Dutch domestic interiors: the expression of a long-held ideal and a twenty-first-century dream.

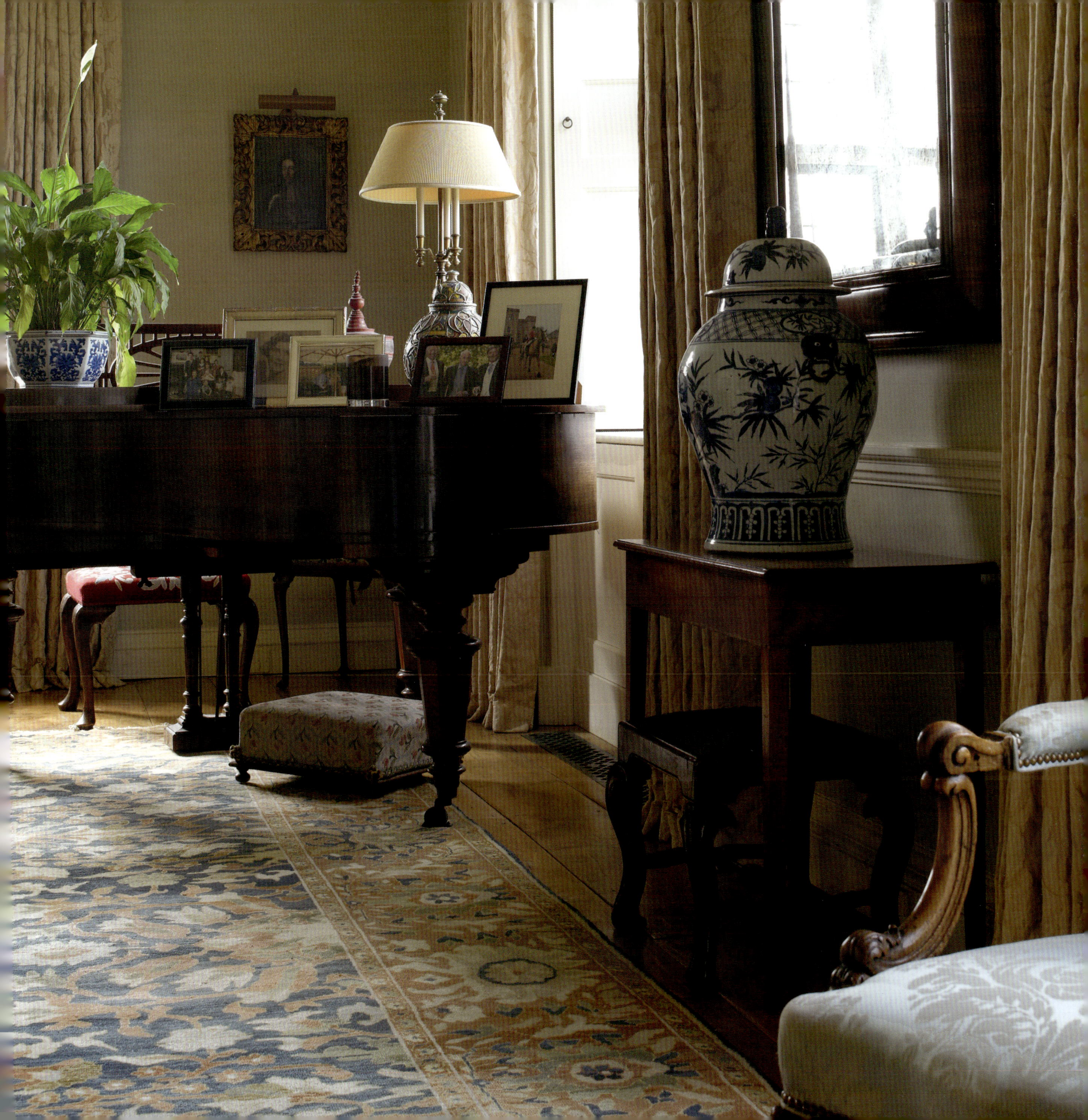

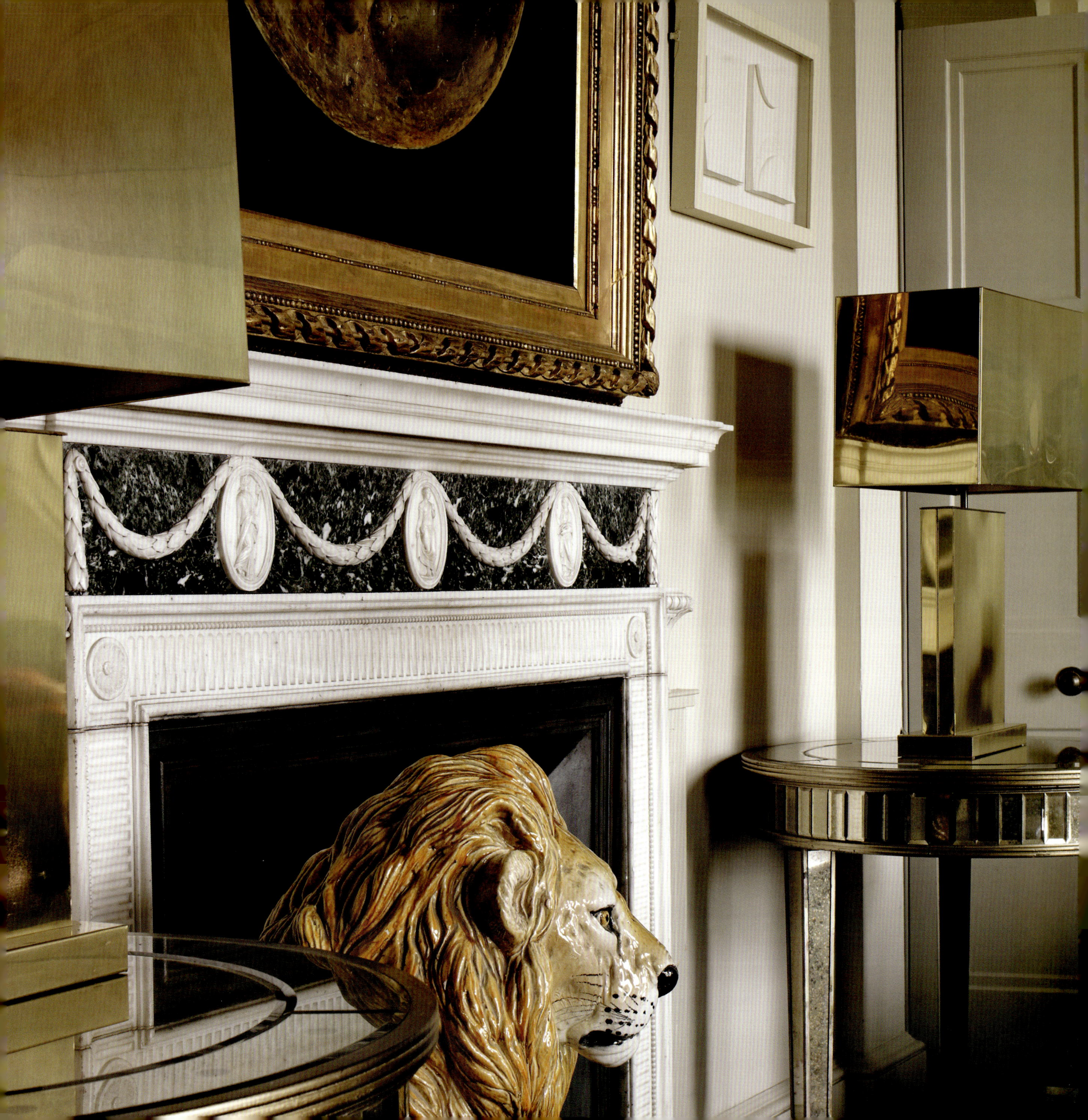

V · CONTINUITY · THE TIMELESS DRAWING ROOM

Aynhoe Park

Impresario James Perkins has furnished the Soane-designed drawing room in an homage to the 1970s.

The drawing room at Aynhoe lies at the centre of an elegant classical house of seventeenth-century origins.[1] Burnt down during the Civil War, it was rebuilt by the Cartwright family. In the early eighteenth century, Thomas Cartwright employed architect Thomas Archer to remodel the house in the baroque spirit, and he added the service wings to create a dramatic forecourt. The principal interiors of this house, however, belong entirely to the very early 1800s and were designed for William Ralph Cartwright (1771–1847) by the architect John Soane (1753–1837).

Between 1799 and 1805 Soane redesigned the principal reception rooms along the south front in an austere but playful neoclassical style, creating a subtle and sociable sweep of rooms for entertaining and more intimate family life. Soane also designed the brilliantly scaled triumphal arches that link the main house to Archer's service wings. The house remained in the hands of the Cartwright family until 1959, when it was sold and divided into apartments by the Country House Association. Aynhoe Park was sold by the Country House Association in 2005 and acquired by James Perkins, property dealer, designer, and impresario, who has restored it to a single dwelling and refurnished the rooms with confidence and originality.

The drawing room is at the centre of the house, and to the east lies what was known as the saloon and the orangery. To the west is the long dining room, an anteroom, and at the furthest end a high-ceilinged library, all connected by a long central enfilade.[2] Within this sequence Soane created an ingenious rhythm of subtly contrasting spaces. The drawing room is quite different in architectural character from the dining room and library, and this variation of spatial experience is very much part of the Regency country house ideal.

The drawing room itself is divided into three articulated parts and has shallow apsidal bays and a groin vault creating an unusual geometric effect. The dining room has a screen of paried Ionic columns framing the doors to the anteroom and screening a serving alcove with apsidal ends; the plaster cornice is a series of simple balls. The library, which fills the end of the house, has a series of recessed bookshelves under round-headed arches, and a highly unusual cornice of repeated miniature Gothic fan vaults.

The son of Soane's client was Sir Thomas Cartwright (d. 1850), who was British minister in Belgium (1830), minister in Frankfurt (1830–38), and ambassador to Sweden (1838–50). He married the daughter of a German count, who by virtue of her rank was styled Lady Elizabeth Cartwright. A talented amateur, she made a valuable series of watercolours of the interiors of the house in the 1830s. These include one of the drawing room furnished with comfortable sofas and armchairs, heavy purple curtains trimmed with gold fringes, and a grand piano.

Elizabeth Cartwright-Hignett, who grew up at Aynhoe before the Second World War, published the watercolours in a charming book, called *Lili at Aynhoe* (1989): "It was designed to be, and generally was used as, a music room because of the excellent acoustics imparted by its shape, although the two drawing rooms [the Soane drawing room and the French drawing room, as the saloon became known] were used together whenever there were visitors."[3] She also noted, "this room was used by the ladies in the evening, when they could get out their embroidery and work. There are three sewing boxes about the room and an embroidery frame on the table."

Having restored the integrity of the Soane design, Mr. Perkins has furnished these rooms with an eclectic collection

THE DRAWING ROOM | 237

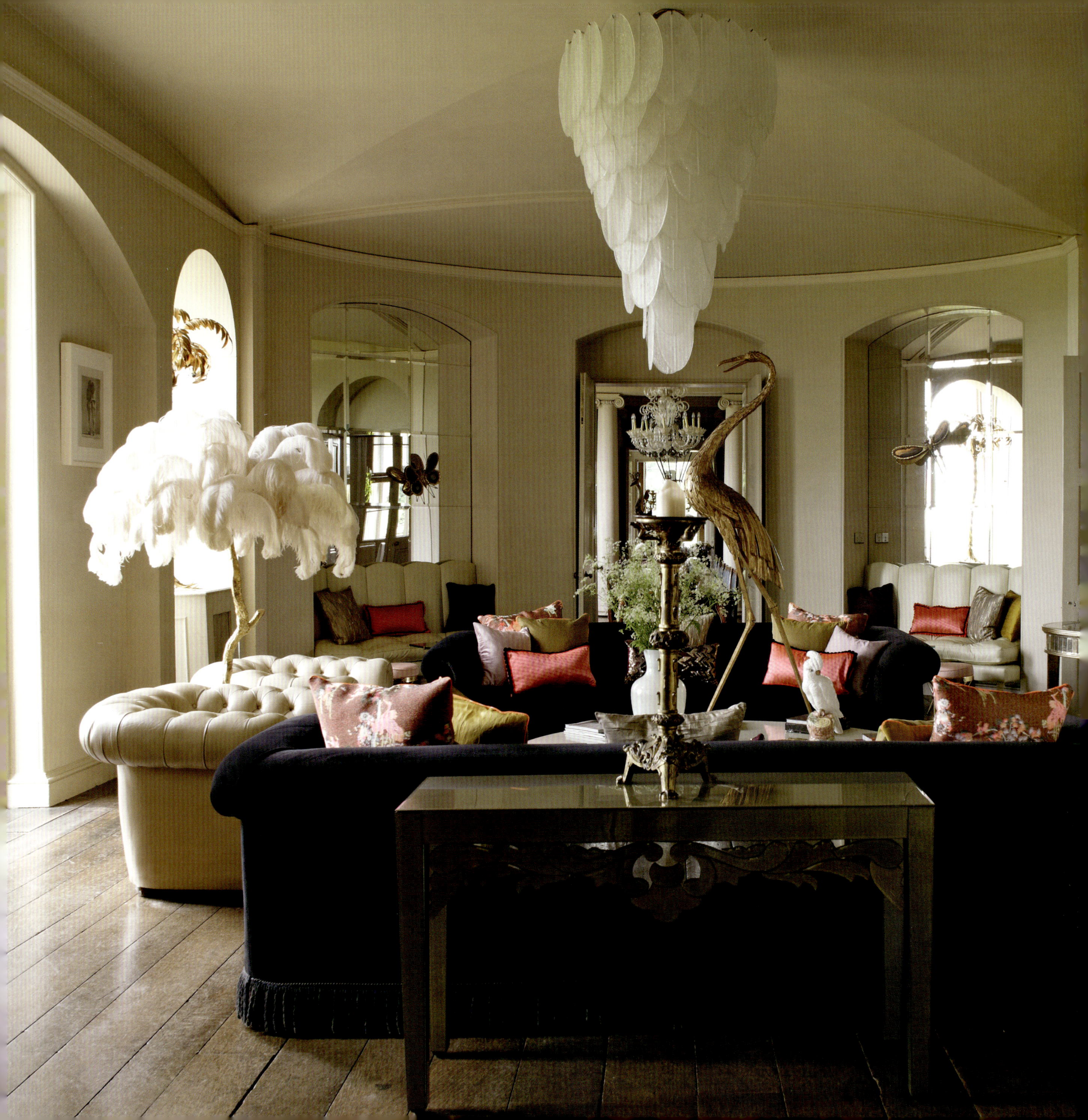

← The drawing room at Aynhoe, a masterpiece of a room designed by John Soane, looking through the dining room towards the library; the present owner James Perkins is an impresario and collector and has furnished the room with 1970s pieces.

↓ A gilded palm tree framed in the arched window. A vaulted ceiling and the canted ends of the room create a sense of unexpected drama in the drawing room, which would have been used for musical performance in the early nineteenth century.

CONTINUITY | 239

White leather banquettes fill the alcove under a faceted mirror, on which are mounted insect wall-lights designed by Jacques Duval Brasseur, originally designed for the Carlton Hotel at Cannes.

embracing classical plaster casts, surreally scaled taxidermy, antique furniture, and modern art. In a contemporary twist on the long tradition of the English country house, the drawing room has recently been re-presented as a "more feminine" space to balance the more overtly masculine character of the dining room and library. According to Mr. Perkins, "this is the most used room in the house."

The Christies catalogue for the 2012 sale of part of his collection described the impression made by Mr. Perkins's original placing of objects: "Aynhoe provides the perfect setting for James's skillfully arranged theatrical collection — an exotic story that unfolds piece by piece as one progresses through Soane's enfilade of rooms ... his eclectic tastes embrace everything from ancient marbles and taxidermy to bold modern design. He loves nothing more than to challenge the norm by juxtaposing from different periods and cultures." [4]

In a deliberate plan to continue the role of the country house as an inspiration to the arts, Mr. Perkins has also made the house popular with fashion designers and photographers, and it has been used in many fashion shoots for such magazines as *Vogue* and *Tatler*. The framed black and white photographs on the south wall of the drawing room were taken by leading fashion photographer John Swannell, who has done many shoots in the house, and include portraits of Helena Bonham Carter. The cushions on the main sofas were designed recently by the fashion designer Matthew Williamson especially for this room.[5]

Mr. Perkins says that "my new scheme here is inspired by the 1970s." To this end he has collected pieces of unusual decorative quality from that period and installed mirrors and white leather benches into the canted alcoves at either end of the room with mirrors. Mounted on the mirrors are insect wall lights designed by French designer Jacques Duval Brasseur (originally designed for the Carlton Hotel at Cannes). Duval Brasseur also designed the bronze-gilt, ostrich-feathered palm tree. The large frosted glass chandelier is Italian, and the glazed side tables were designed by Mr. Perkins himself. The painting of the mountains and the moon over the chimneypiece was also specially commissioned from the artist Mark Johnson. The abstract works on either side of the chimneypiece are by Oliver Lyon.

Through the open doors can be glimpsed the stuffed lion and giraffe of the dining room and the stuffed polar bear of the entrance hall — all of which strike a Dali-esque note. The combination of the faceted mirrors and the restrained classical detail of Soane's interior is almost art deco in spirit, and illustrates the near infinite variety of furnishing that can work with a space of this rigorous and original architectural character.

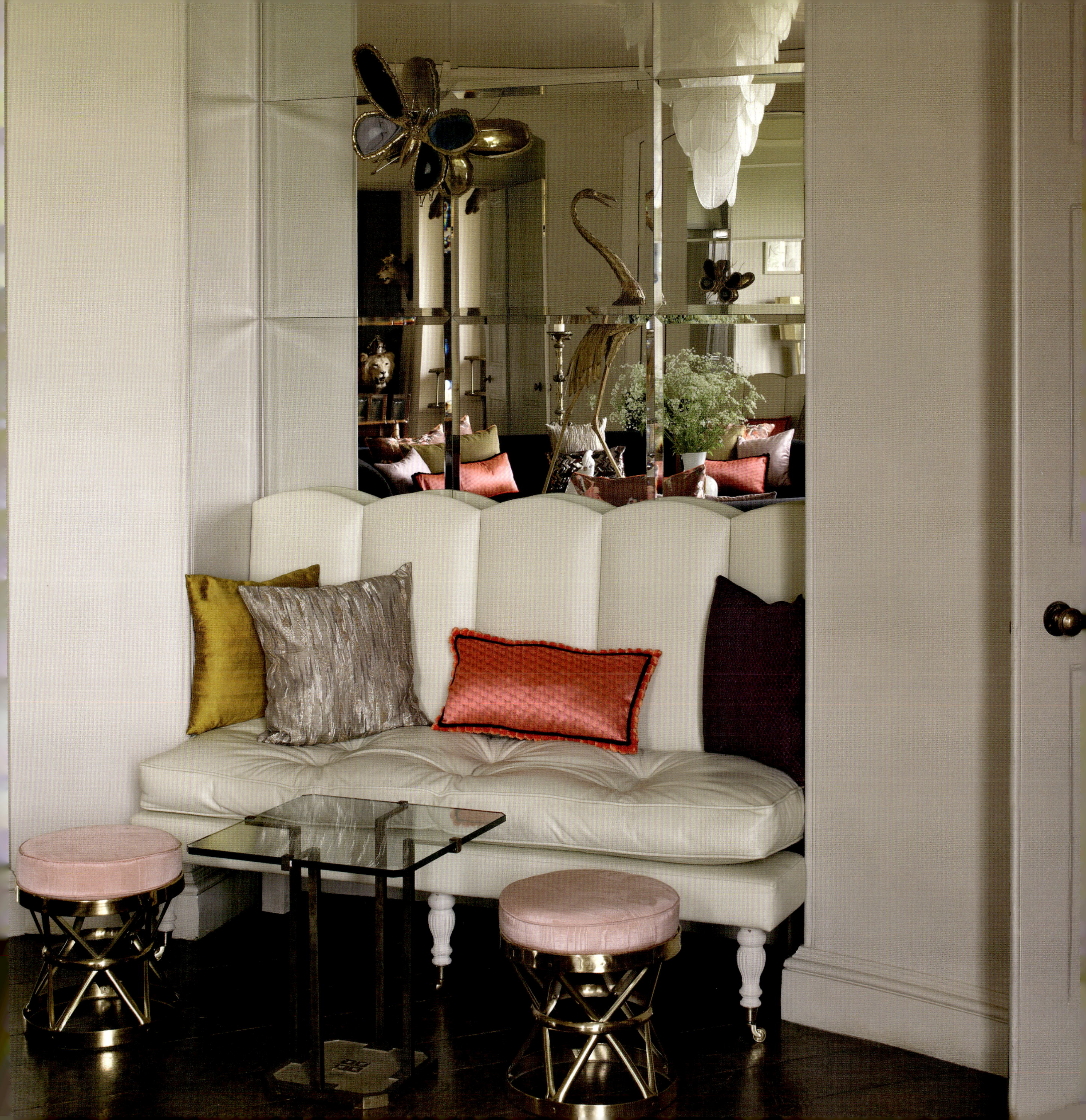

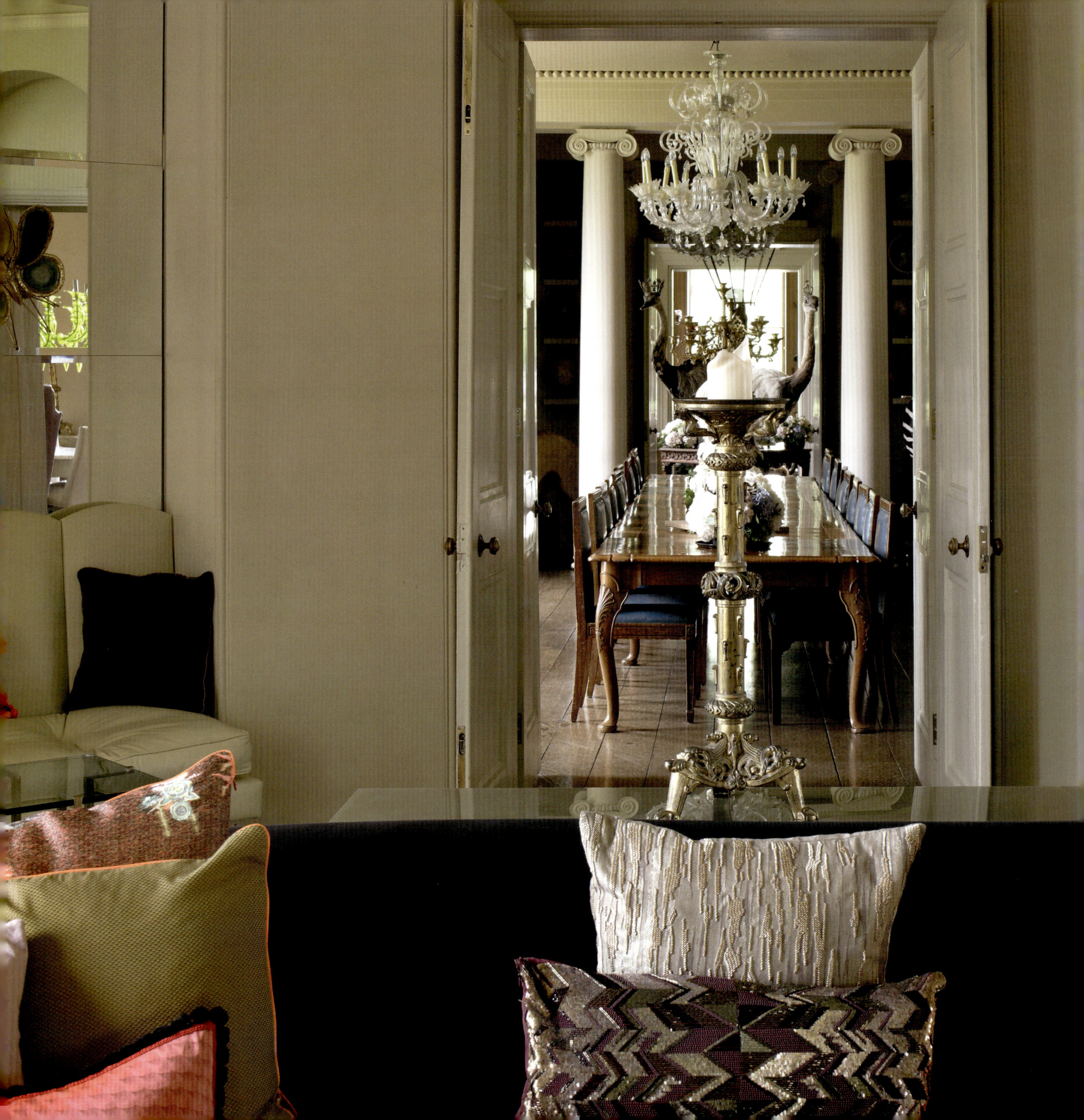

← Curious touches: stuffed ostriches tower over the dining table looking through towards the library; the boldly coloured cushions on the sofa were designed especially for the house by fashion designer Matthew Williamson, who has arranged fashion shoots of his collection here.

↓ The library at Aynhoe, also designed by Soane, furnished in a cheerful, eclectic spirit which recalls in some ways the interiors of the Sir John Soane's Museum.

CONTINUITY | 243

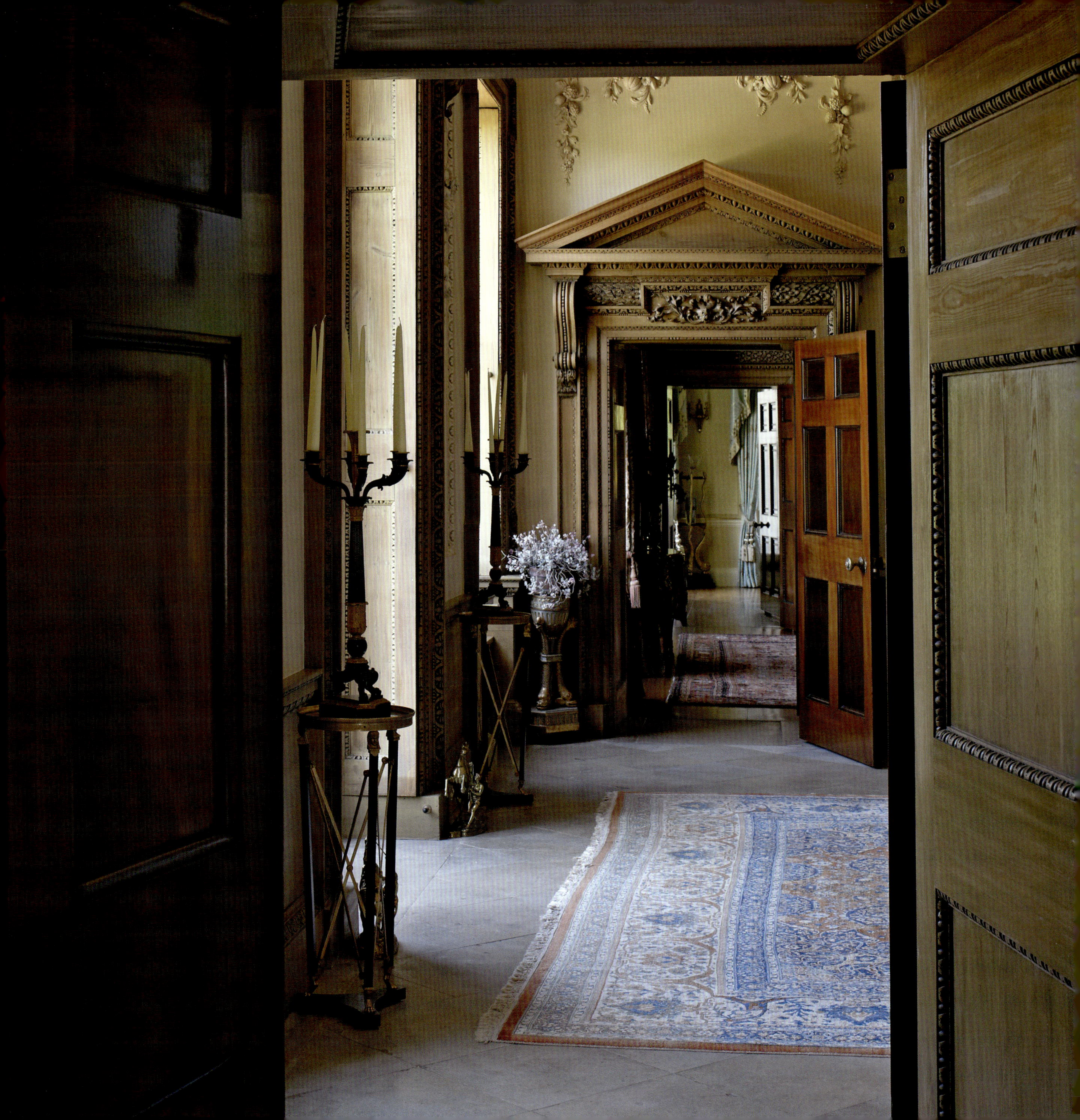

V · CONTINUITY · THE TIMELESS DRAWING ROOM

Thame Park

A Palladian house handsomely restored, with decoration advised by Henrietta Spencer-Churchill.

Thame Park in Oxfordshire is a handsome Palladian country house, incorporating part of the lodgings of a former Cistercian abbey.[1] It has been through a number of changes in the later twentieth century, and most recently was the subject of a thorough and sensitive restoration. The abbey was surrendered in the 1530s and granted to Sir John Williams, then passed to his daughter and her husband, Sir Richard Wenman. The estate remained in the hands of the Wenmans until the early twentieth century. The main west range of the house was built from 1745 to designs by William Smith of Warwick. His patron was Philip Wenman, 6th Viscount Wenman, who had succeeded to his title aged only ten in 1729. In 1741 he married Sophia Herbert, daughter of James Herbert of Tythrop — the marriage was probably the prompt for the rebuilding of the house. Thame Park has similarities with Kirtlington Park, in the same county where Smith also worked for the Dashwoods, who were cousins of Lord Wenman. The exuberant rococo plasterwork in the entrance hall at Thame Park is attributed to Thomas Roberts of Oxford.

The principal drawing room of Thame Park is a handsome double room on the west front, on the south side of the hall. On the north side is another sitting room and the main dining room. As with most major country houses, there has been a series of later remodellings, including work in the 1830s for Sophia Wickham, who entertained the Duke of Clarence (later William IV) at Thame Park. The Duke had wanted to marry her in 1818 but was refused permission — he later made her a baroness in her own right. The diarist Greville described her as "a half-crazed woman of large fortune."[2] Lady Wenman lived at Thame Park, unmarried, until her death in 1870. It may have been for Lady Wenman that the two rooms on the southwest corner were opened up into a single entertaining space. In the early 1920s the architect G. H. Berkeley Wills carried out a major overhaul for Mr. and Mrs. W. H. Gardiner, including reworking the opening between the two rooms.

The early 1920s was a key period for the "rediscovery" of Georgian style and the appreciation of plasterwork and carving of the period, evidenced by the many published studies of such work in the 1920s and 1930s. Berkeley Wills wrote admiringly of the house in the *Architectural Review* in 1922: "This western block, which was very accurately set out, and is a good example of simplicity and restraint, contains a fine range of reception rooms in the piano nobile."[3] The current drawing room was the billiard room in 1922, and the entire room was remodelled, given a wider central opening and a lower coved ceiling in the 1920s work. Berkeley Wills described the more general work of decorating the house to consist of "removing the nineteenth century work [including] some peculiarly repulsive decoration in the Louis XV style." According to Berkeley Wills, the finely carved 1740s pine chimneypiece in the drawing room was brought down from a bedroom in the house in 1922 and repositioned here. According to Wills, it was "pickled and the woodwork left slightly waxed."

Thame Park passed by descent to the Wykeham-Musgrave family, who lived more usually at their other property, Barnsley Park in Gloucestershire. There was a major sale of contents at Thame Park in 1919, and then the house itself was sold in 1928 to Sir Charles and Lady Forbes-Leith of Fyvie Castle. It was then sold by their son in 1938 to Sir Harold Bowden, the heir to Raleigh Bicycles, founded by his father, Sir Francis, the first baronet.[4] His son, Sir Frank, a collector of Japanese arms and armour, returned to live at Thame Park at the end of the Second World War, and remained there until 1982 when he sold up.

THE DRAWING ROOM | 245

↓ Thame Park, Oxfordshire: modern art sits comfortably with antique furniture.

→ The opening between the two sections of the drawing room was extended and detailed in the Ionic order in the 1920s; the recent decorative scheme was carried out on the advice of Henrietta Spencer-Churchill.

246 | THAME PARK

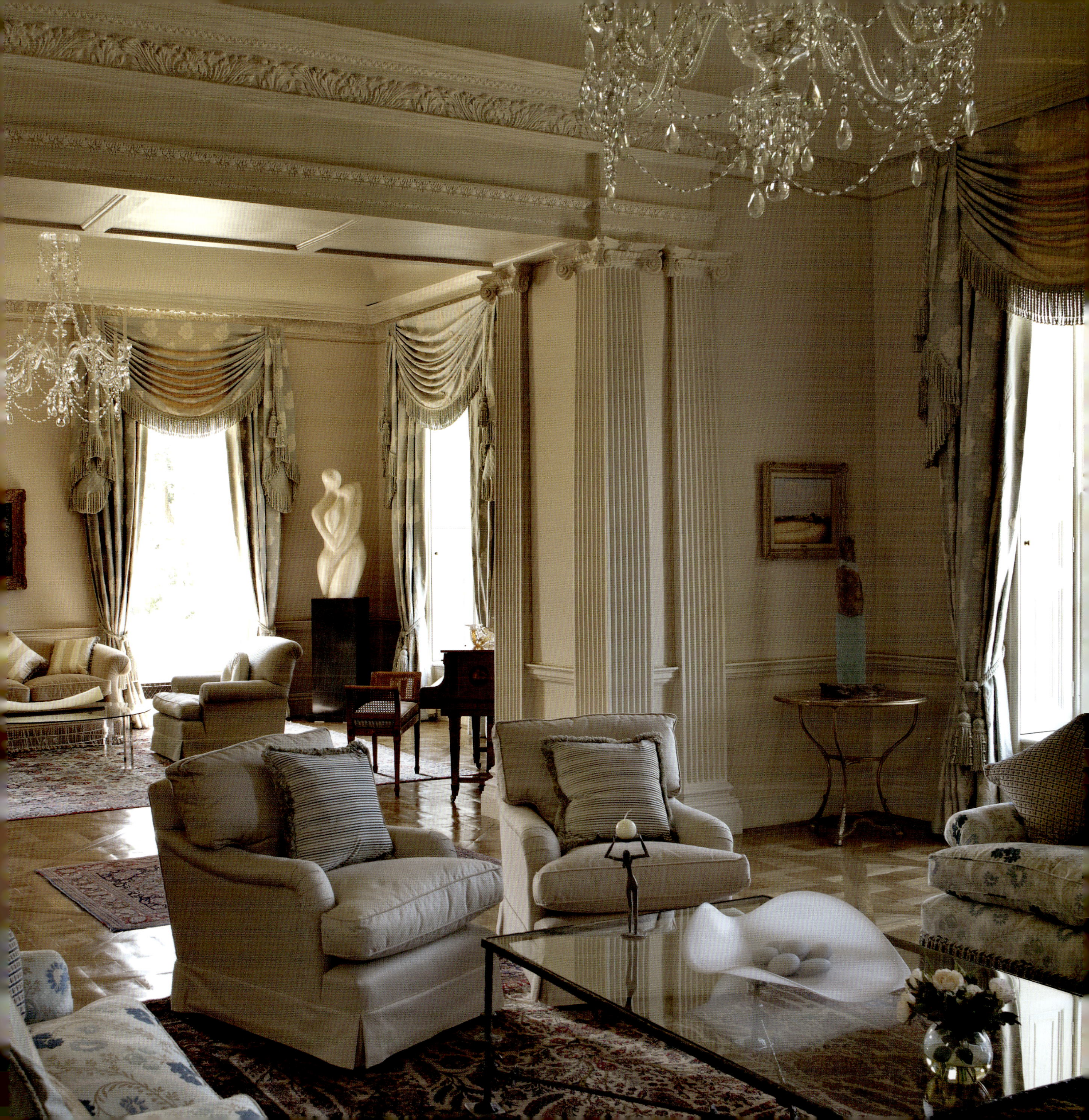

↓ A detail of the boldly scaled, specially made passementerie.

→ Modern sculptural pieces and glass-topped tables give a contemporary feel to the classical interior of Thame Park's drawing room.

The house was then acquired for use as a country house hotel, which was never fully realised. Nonetheless it was much used in this period as a film location, causing considerable damage to the historic interiors in the process.

Fortunately, Thame Park was bought in 2000 by Paul and Mina Matthews, who have carried out a sympathetic restoration of the whole house—first with architect John Simpson and subsequently with Purcell Miller Tritton. This has included the restoration of the rooms surviving from the historic abbot's lodgings. As an integral part of this refurbishment, the house has been decorated throughout with advice from interior designer Lady Henrietta Spencer-Churchill, in a comfortable and uncluttered, elegant modern style.[5] The Matthews appreciated that Lady Henrietta was content to work with furniture that they had already. They also had a clear idea that they wanted to mix modern and antique together—they have a collection of modern glass and own a number of pieces of significant modern sculpture, both of which feature in the main drawing room.

Overall, the drawing room was kept deliberately light, and a new oak parquet floor by Weldon was introduced and Persian rugs were used to good effect throughout. All the significant earlier details were retained in the restoration, and a new plasterwork ceiling was added to the central panel of the ceiling in the south end. The two large chandeliers were especially chosen to help knit the two spaces together visually. The walls are hung with a linen which, as Lady Henrietta observes, creates a surface that is "not completely flat, and this gives the room a kind of warmth and softness which works well with furniture and artworks from all periods."[6] The full curtains were chosen from an existing Colony design, which was recoloured especially for this room in a light blue-grey and detailed with fine passementerie. The upholstered furniture is arranged to accommodate guests while still retaining a good amount of circulation space. The overall achievement at Thame Park has been the highly effective recovery of the significant period architectural character of the principal rooms of this Palladian front, and the preservation of a fine balance between modern and traditional design in the presentation of the interiors.

248 | THAME PARK

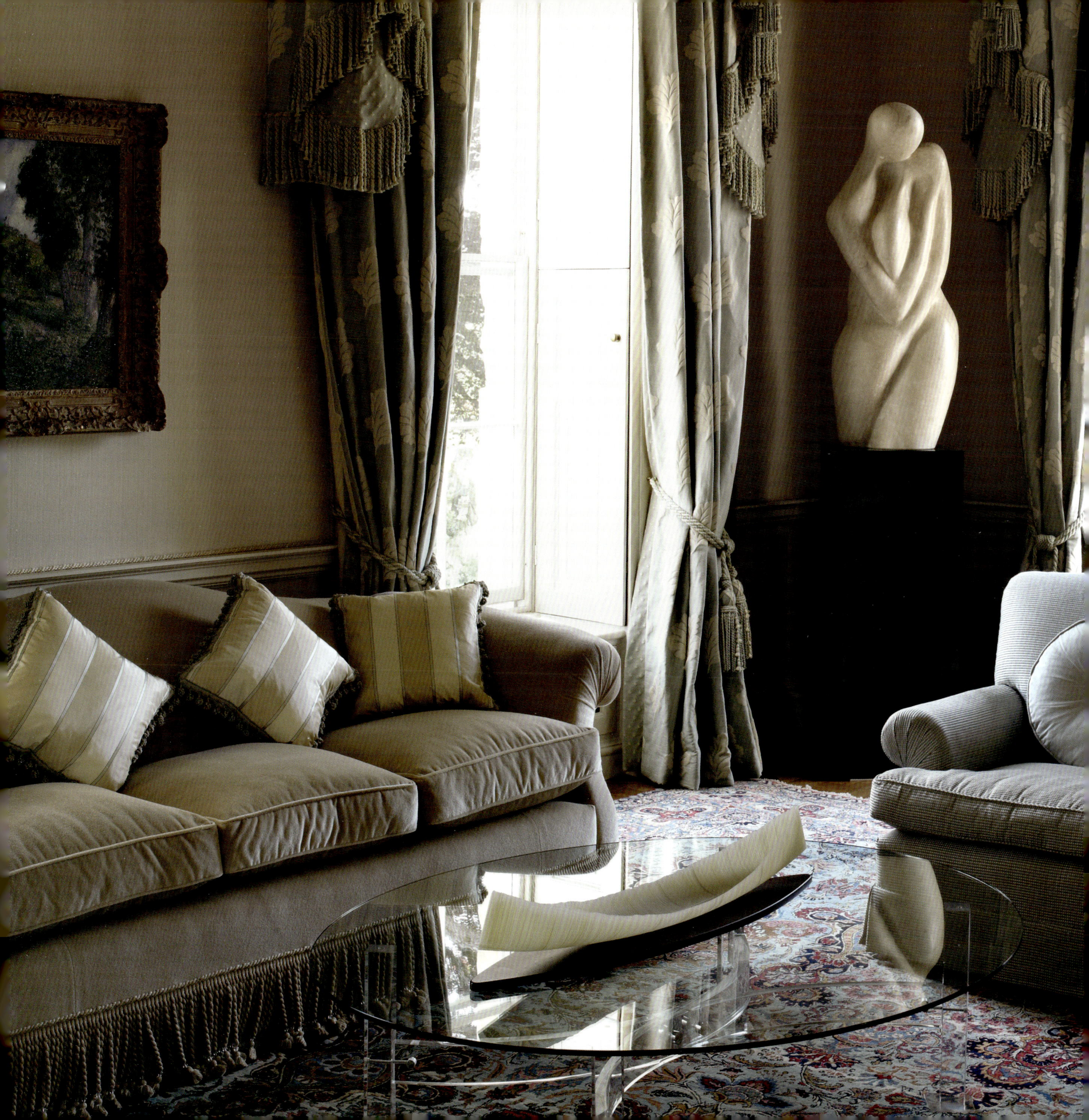

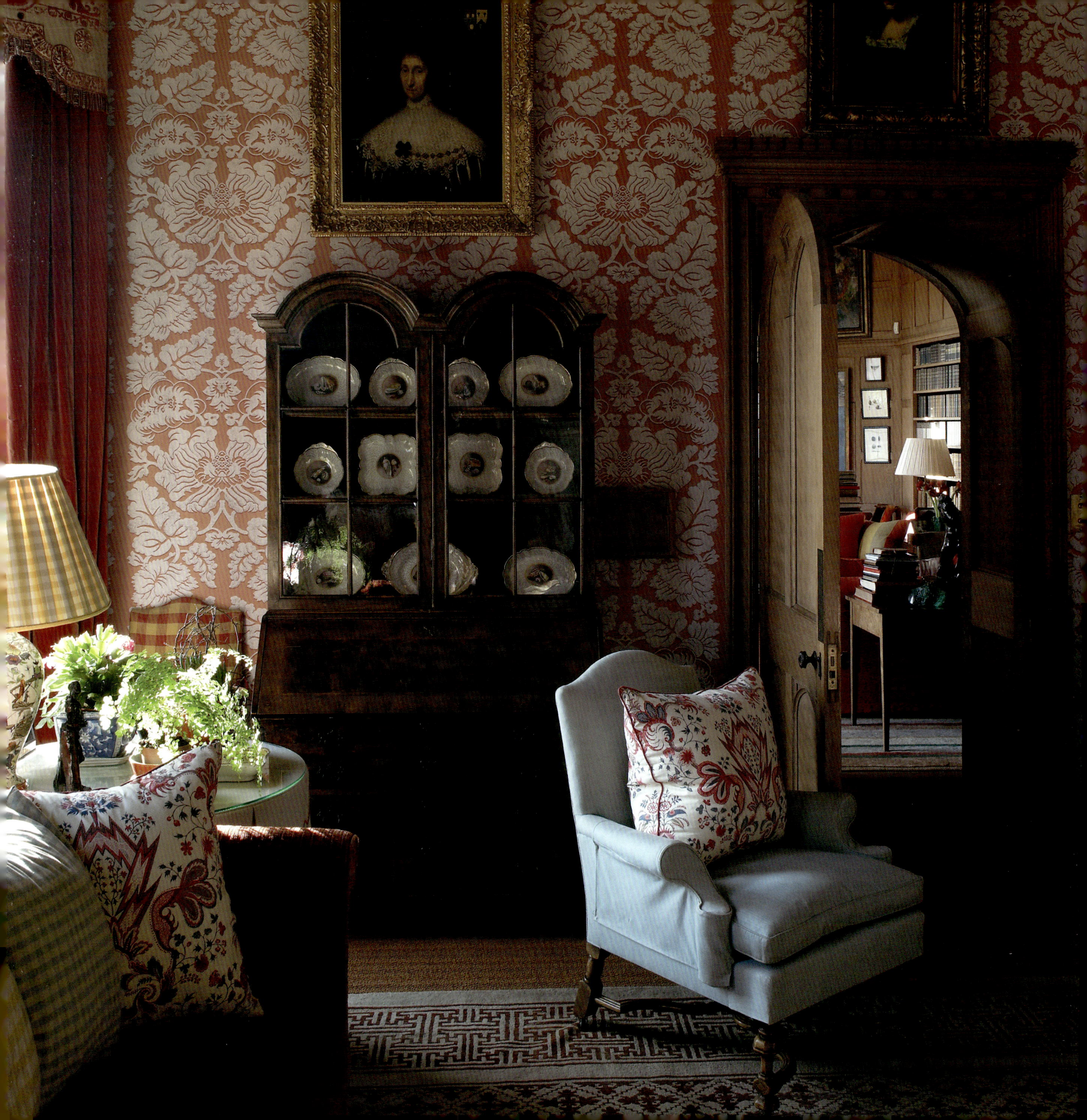

V · CONTINUITY · THE TIMELESS DRAWING ROOM

Knepp Castle

New generations: the Burrells have rearranged their drawing room with advice from Chester Jones.

The drawing room and library at Knepp Castle work as a pair. They would have been designed to do so in the Regency period, when Nash designed this romantic castellated house, and they do still in the twenty-first century, both connecting with the hall, across which lies the main dining room.[1] This is typical of the rational fluidity of spaces characterising the country houses of Nash that remains appealing in modern times too. The house suffered a fire in 1904 and thus the interiors were refitted with a restrained Arts and Crafts Tudor character, replacing much of the lost plasterwork and panelling. Sir Charles and Lady (Isabella) Burrell took the house twenty-five years ago and wanted to keep these rooms in the same kind of balance: a comfortable and elegant drawing room for drinks before and after meals, and a library which is more of an informal sitting room, but the two rooms open into each other so they can be used together.

Both the Burrells are creative, Sir Charles a sculptor and Isabella Burrell a biographer and travel writer, so visual decisions in these key rooms were important to both of them. Modern art was concentrated in the library, and family portraits in the drawing room. The latter include two attractive early-twentieth-century paintings. One is a portrait of Lady Burrell's grandmother, Nancy Lancaster (then Mrs. Ronald Tree) on horseback, with her son Michael on a pony, by Munnings, on the terrace at Cottesbrooke Hall in Northamptonshire, which they had rented for a hunting season. The pendant piece is a portrait, by Sir William Nicholson, of Thomas Denman, a great uncle of Sir Charles Burrell, also painted as a boy on horseback. In the library, there is also a fine portrait of Dame Laura Knight by Augustus John. Several works of art in the library are from the collection of a painter, Frank McEwen, acquired by Charlie Burrell's father.

Some years ago, Chester Jones advised on a major overhaul of the interiors throughout the house, while Isabella Burrell brought many of her own ideas to the project, influenced by memories of the homes of her grandmother, Nancy Lancaster, who leased and decorated a series of elegant Georgian country houses and also owned Colefax and Fowler (see page 167): "Chester's approach appealed to me because although he came from the Colefax stable he had a strong draw to the eclectic, to not being trapped in one period. We worked very closely together."[2]

The drawing room is tall, and in effect oblong, as it is canted at one end into a bay window looking over the park, and at the other around the door to the hall (the contrast between this and the spatial volume of the library is again typical of Nash's interior planning). The old hand-printed Colefax paper chosen for this room had "a big enough repeat pattern for a big room but subtle enough to put strong pictures on." The curtains and pelmets in the drawing room came from Isabella Burrell's childhood home, a domed Palladian house, Mereworth Castle in Kent, designed by Colen Campbell and inspired by the Villa Rotonda; according to Isabella Burrell, Nancy Lancaster "loved to use old tapestries and old fabrics in her interiors and hated using new stuff."[3]

The two huge sofas framing the area around the chimney-piece were copied from a pair that used to be at Ditchley Park in Oxfordshire, one of Nancy Lancaster's homes: "The sofas could have seemed too red and heavy so Chester suggested that acid lemon check which creates a very effective contrast."[4] The tablecloth is an exquisite piece of nineteenth-century needlework which belonged to Nancy Lancaster and was one

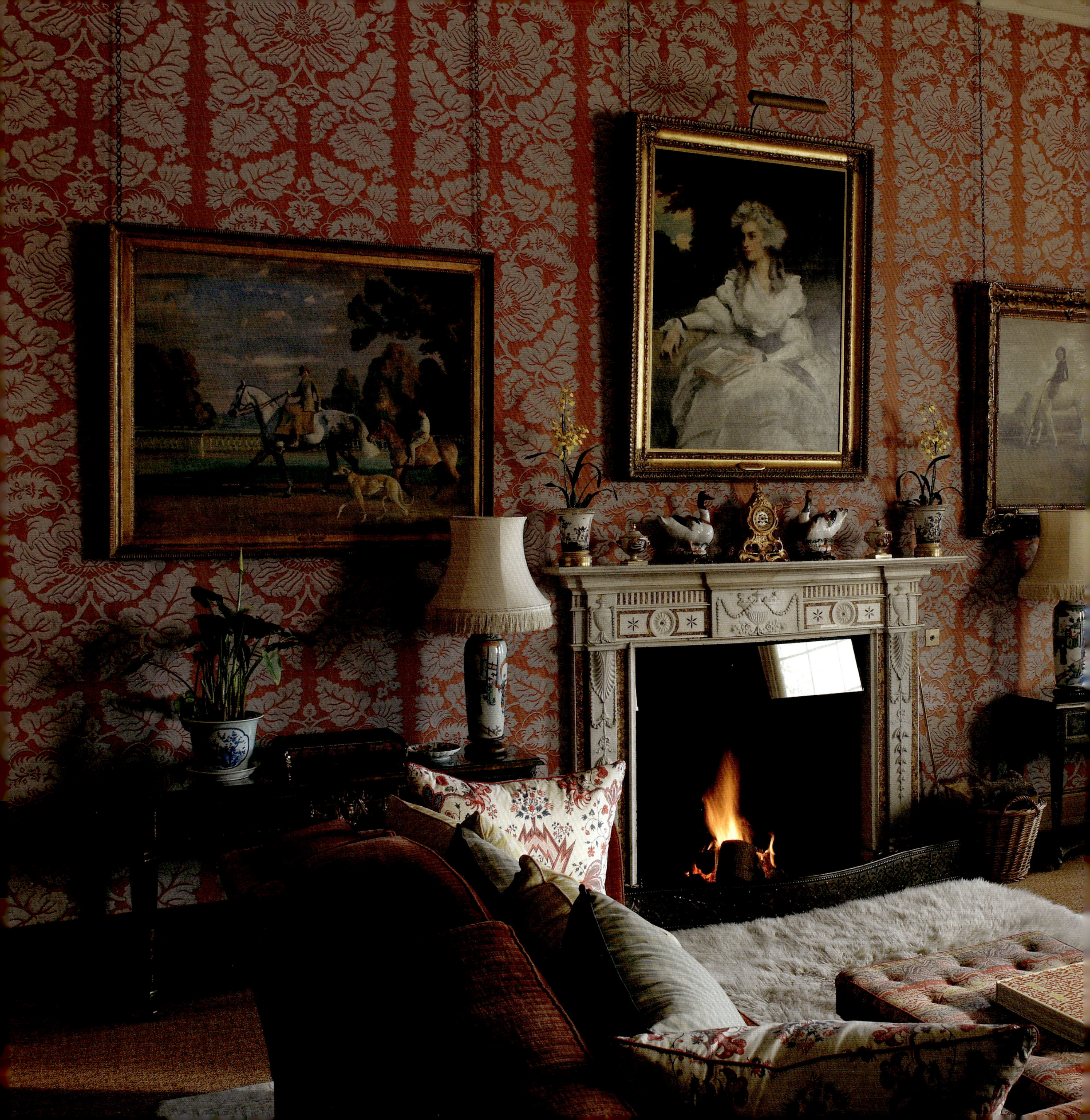

← A comfortable and well-considered room with views over the park. The portraits come from both the Burrell and the Tree families; the picture on the left hand side shows Nancy Tree (later Lancaster) with her son, painted by Munnings. The hand-printed Colefax paper was chosen for its bold pattern to suit the room and serve as a suitable backdrop to family portraits.

↓ The curtains and pelmets came from Lady Burrell's childhood home of Mereworth Castle in Kent; Chester Jones advised on the interiors at Knepp.

CONTINUITY | 253

↓ The original niches have been painted with trompe l'oeil panelling to suit the Regency Gothic plasterwork.

→ The boldly detailed paper contrasts with the crisp delicacy of the late eighteenth century inlaid marble chimneypiece

lighting is by table lamps and not overhead lighting. Both rooms have views over the park down to the lake, animated during the day by the slow progress of deer herds across the vista.

Isabella Burrell feels that she has been very influenced by the taste of her grandmother, although by no means does she follow her example slavishly: "Nancy Lancaster was always creating a kind of living nostalgia, something that recaptured for her the warmth, comfort and luxury of her childhood home in Virginia Mirador, with a big family who spent a great deal of time riding and hunting. She looked to bring something of that mix to all her houses. For her, and for me, the supreme definition of comfort is to feel at ease in a room. If you can't sink into the sofa and feel at ease in the room, it just hasn't worked. In terms of furniture and objects in a room, she liked every single thing to have a strong sense of its own identity, to have a personality. So a room never felt lonely even if you were alone in it. She liked the sense of provenance that came with an object with history. She also loved strong contrasts, to throw things together and see how they would get along — she was the same with her friends, I think."[5]

The drawing room is the more formal room of the house but it is a room set aside for conversation and pleasure — away from the technology that is present in other living spaces. At Knepp Castle, as in many country houses, the drawing room works in concert with the adjoining library, filled with interesting paintings, including a Graham Sutherland over the chimneypiece and an arresting portrait of Isabella Burrell's father, Michael Tree, by his friend Lucian Freud. Both rooms are full of colour, interest, and history, but they are also supremely comfortable with a modern streak that shoots through the colours and textiles in particular. Nancy Lancaster would have surely approved: things have been thrown together and seem to get along like old friends.

of her most treasured possessions. The alcoves on either side of the hall contained china cabinets, which were removed and replaced with *trompe l'oeil* painting of Gothic panelling.

The main carpet in the drawing room once belonged to Nancy Lancaster. The vast carpet in the adjoining library was designed especially by Chester and Sandy Jones and specially woven on large-scale looms in Turkey, with bold planes of colour, entirely derived from vegetable dyes. In both rooms

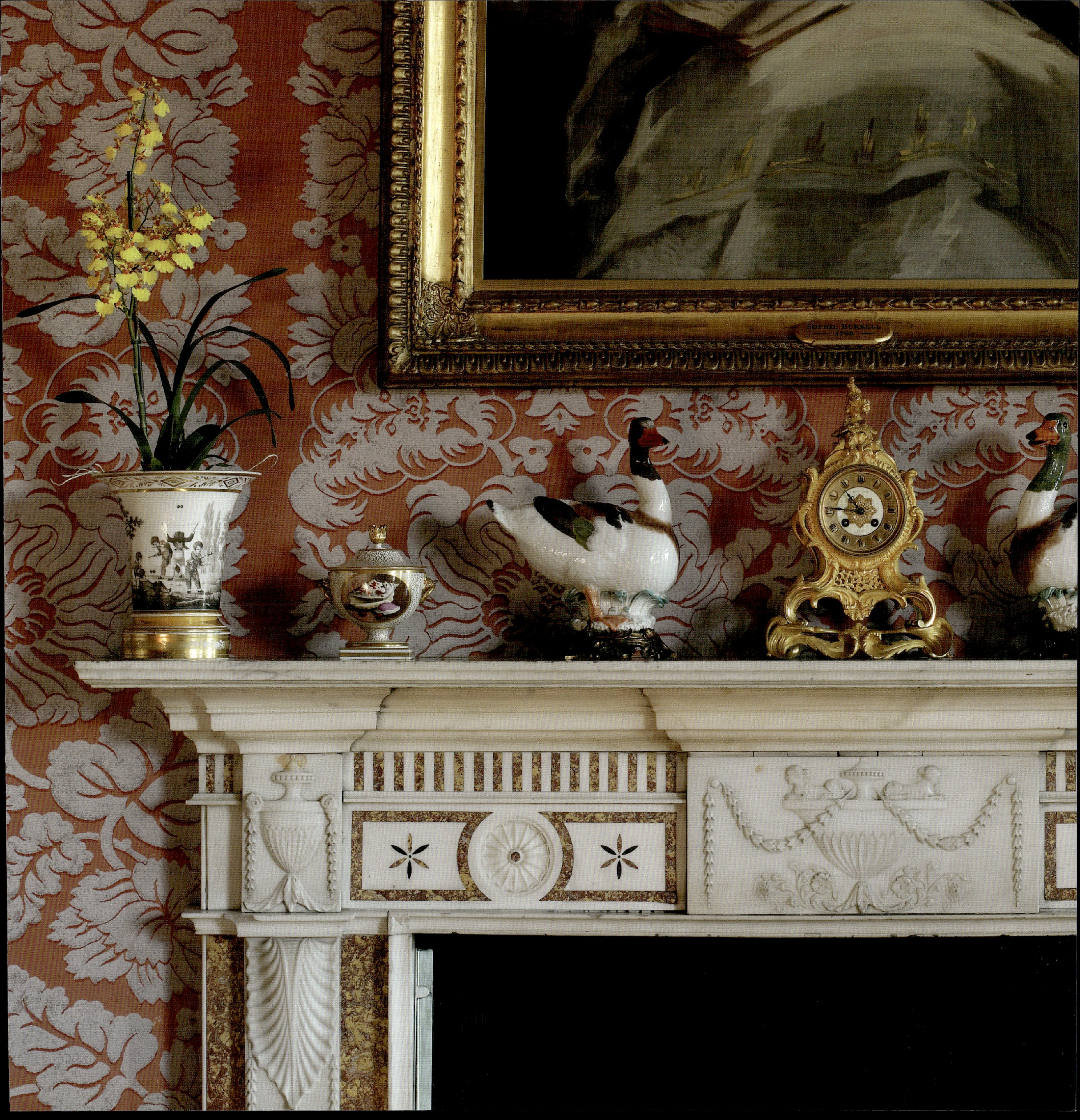
SOPHIE BURRELL
1760

↓ A portrait of Lady Burrell's father, Michael Tree, painted by Lucian Freud and hung over the Edwardian bookshelves in the library.

→ The oak panelled library adjoining the drawing room at Knepp; the rooms are used together for house parties. In previous generations the drawing room was considered the preserve of the lady of the house, and the library as the man's.

256 | KNEPP CASTLE

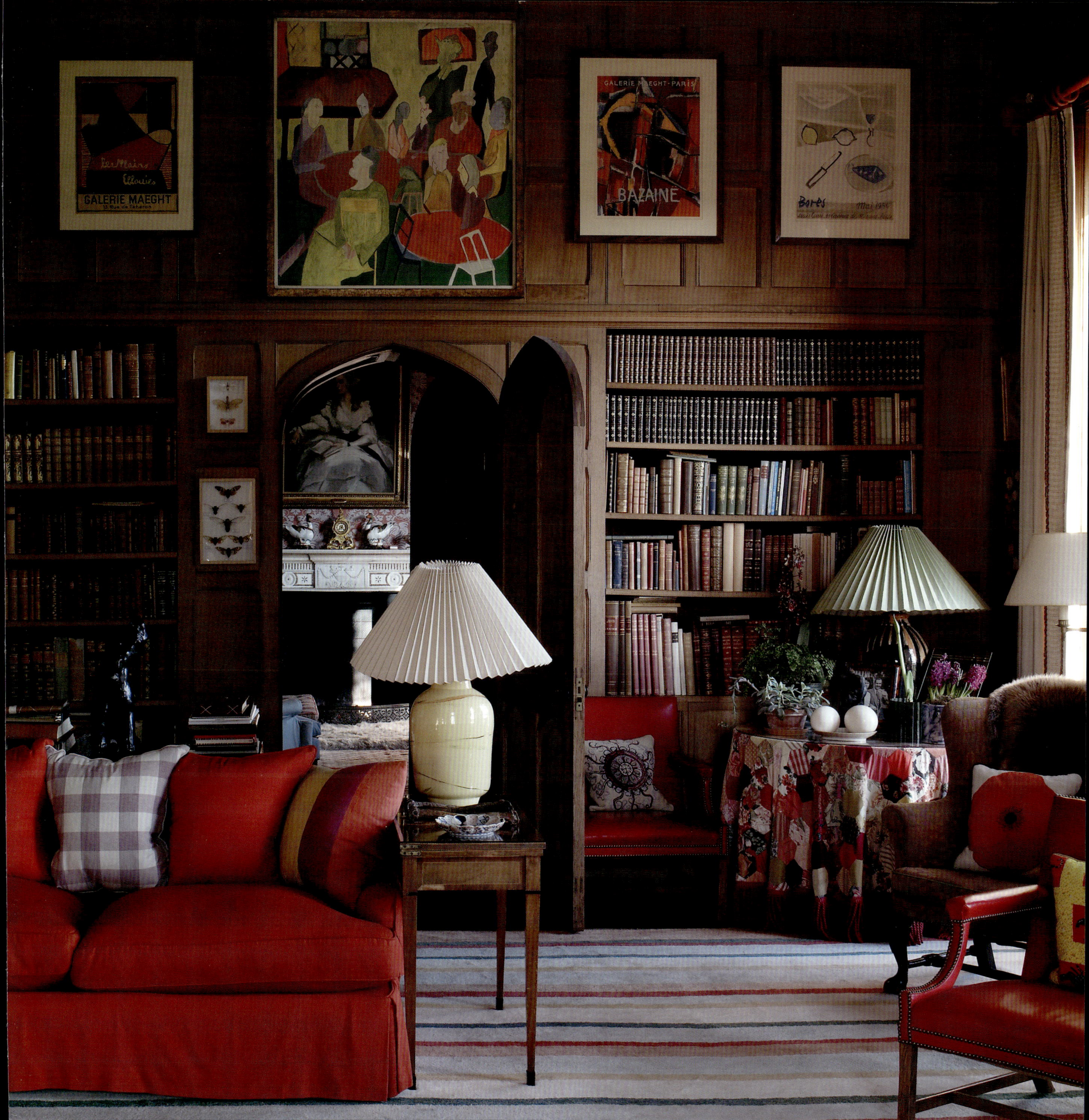
GALERIE MAEGHT
GALERIE MAEGHT · PARIS
BAZAINE

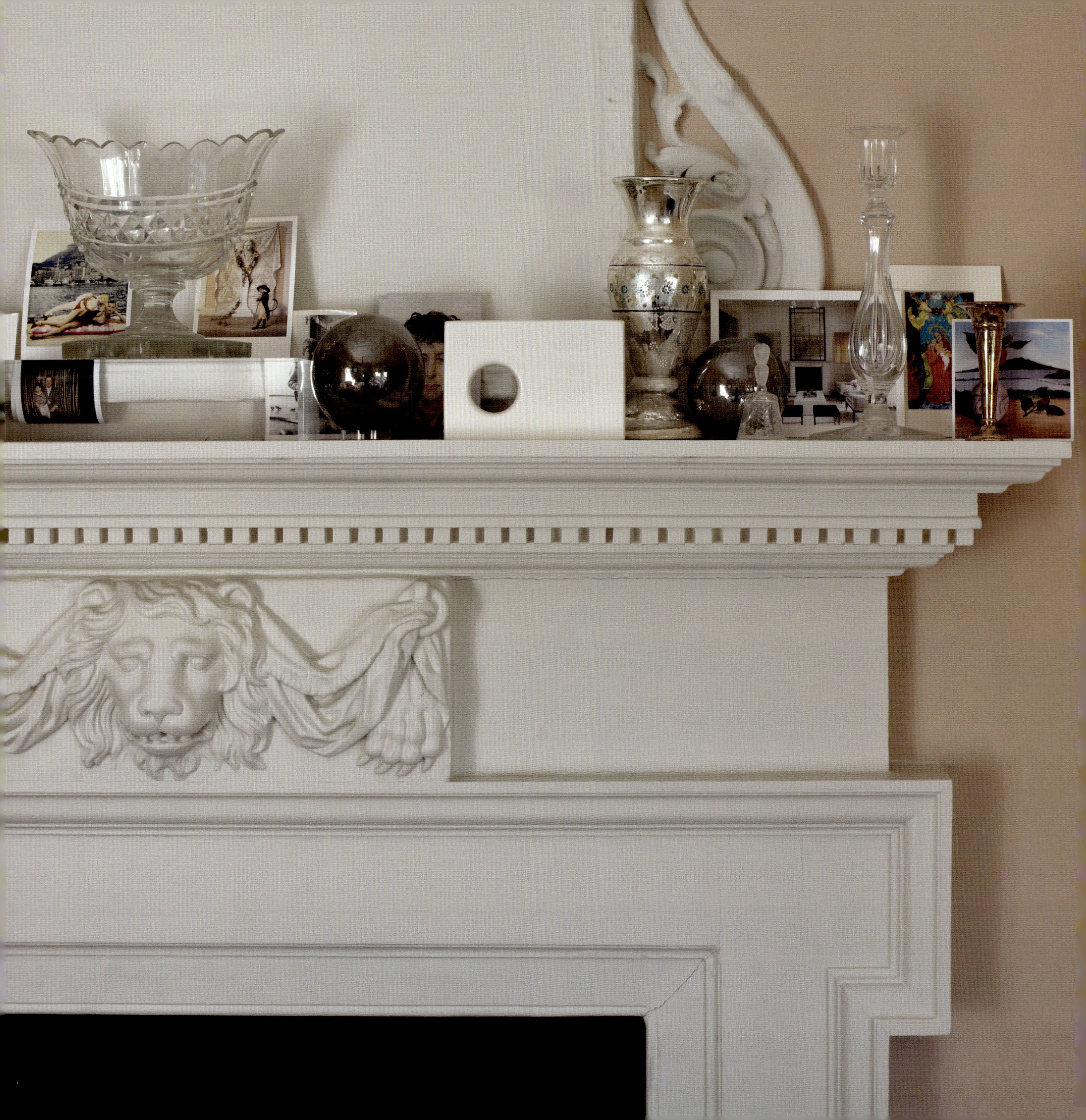

V · CONTINUITY · THE TIMELESS DRAWING ROOM

The Temple

Palace and cottage in one: a simple classical room in Veere Grenney's Georgian fishing lodge.

Some of the most attractive drawing rooms are some of the most unexpected. The drawing room of the Temple in Stoke by Nayland in Suffolk (right in the heart of Constable Country) is a delicious surprise. The room was originally the upper part of a mid-eighteenth-century fishing lodge or park temple built for the Tendring Hall estate to designs by Sir Robert Taylor. Taylor was a talented London architect who devised a new interpretation of the classical villa form for English country gentlemen and wealthy Londoners. Indeed, there are echoes in the form of the Temple that are reminiscent of his much admired Asgill House, which stands on the river Thames at Richmond in Surrey.[1]

The Temple was originally, in a sense, multipurpose, as it might have been used for fishing on the one side but was also used as a grandstand to watch coursing on the fields through the canted bay window to the west. It was also designed as a delightful retreat from ordinary day-to-day things. It was certainly a room to socialise in, to drink tea or wine, or to picnic on food brought out from the main house by liveried footmen. Fishing was a splendidly indolent, reflective pastime in the eighteenth century, as suggested in conversation pieces by Zoffany and others. Above all, the fishing lodge was a temple in the landscape and could be glimpsed from Tendring Hall, as an eye-catcher in the park.

Interior designer Veere Grenney, who has leased it since 1985 as his country retreat, observes that the Temple was in essence "a pleasure pavilion" and he likes to think this is still a defining feature. The drawing room—and it is the "essence" of an English drawing room in feel—occupies the whole of the first floor. The room is on an east-west axis and therefore enjoys both the rising and the setting sun. The rest of the rooms are all on the ground floor, and relatively small. A visiting duchess once dubbed the Temple an ideal kind of house: "a palace upstairs and a cottage downstairs."[2]

As is too often true, there is no longer a principal mansion house on the Tendring Hall estate, so the Temple is also a relic of a lost golden age. After the Temple was first built as a fishing lodge at the end of the eighteenth century, the Rowley family bought the Tendring estate and demolished the earlier mansion house. John Soane designed them an elegant new neoclassical country house, with a park landscaped by Humphry Repton, who tactfully preserved the earlier canal and fishing temple.[3] The handsome Soane house was sadly demolished in the 1950s, but the estate is still in the Rowley family hands today and the traditional landscape maintained with care. Since the late 1950s, the Temple has been leased by a series of interesting tenants, all with a deep interest in architecture and design, including David Hicks, the interior designer, and the dealer and designer Charles Beresford-Clark.

David Hicks leased the Temple from Sir Joshua Rowley, Bt, from 1957, and restored the roof and interior. Hicks planted the hornbeams that flank the house "like the wings of a stage set" and he commissioned Sir Raymond Erith to design the oeil de boeuf window on the ground floor.[4] Hicks himself designed the upper part of the Palladian-style chimneypiece, and Sir Joshua lent back the four busts which stand on the surviving brackets representing *The Four Ages of Man*. The large niches—which would originally have had sculptures of classical figures—are used by Mr. Grenney to display pots with flowering trees that are changed with the seasons of the year: mimosa, jasmine, orange, and limes. Mr. Grenney has also, with the Rowley family, restored the eighteenth-century canal and replanted more than two hundred sweet chestnuts in the avenue framing it. All

↓ The alcoves in the drawing room of the Temple, Suffolk, were originally designed for sculpture.

→ The drawing room of the Temple, home of designer Veere Grenney, originally one large room of a late-eighteenth-century fishing temple, with views to the east and west. The Palladian-style chimneypiece was designed by David Hicks in the 1950s. Veere Grenney painted the room this "potted shrimp" colour chosen by Nancy Lancaster at Kelmarsh Hall.

WORLD MURIEL BRANDOLINI
BE DAZZLED!
TWENTIETH CENTURY CASTLES IN BRITAIN
THE QUEEN'S DIAMONDS
MATISSEPICASSO

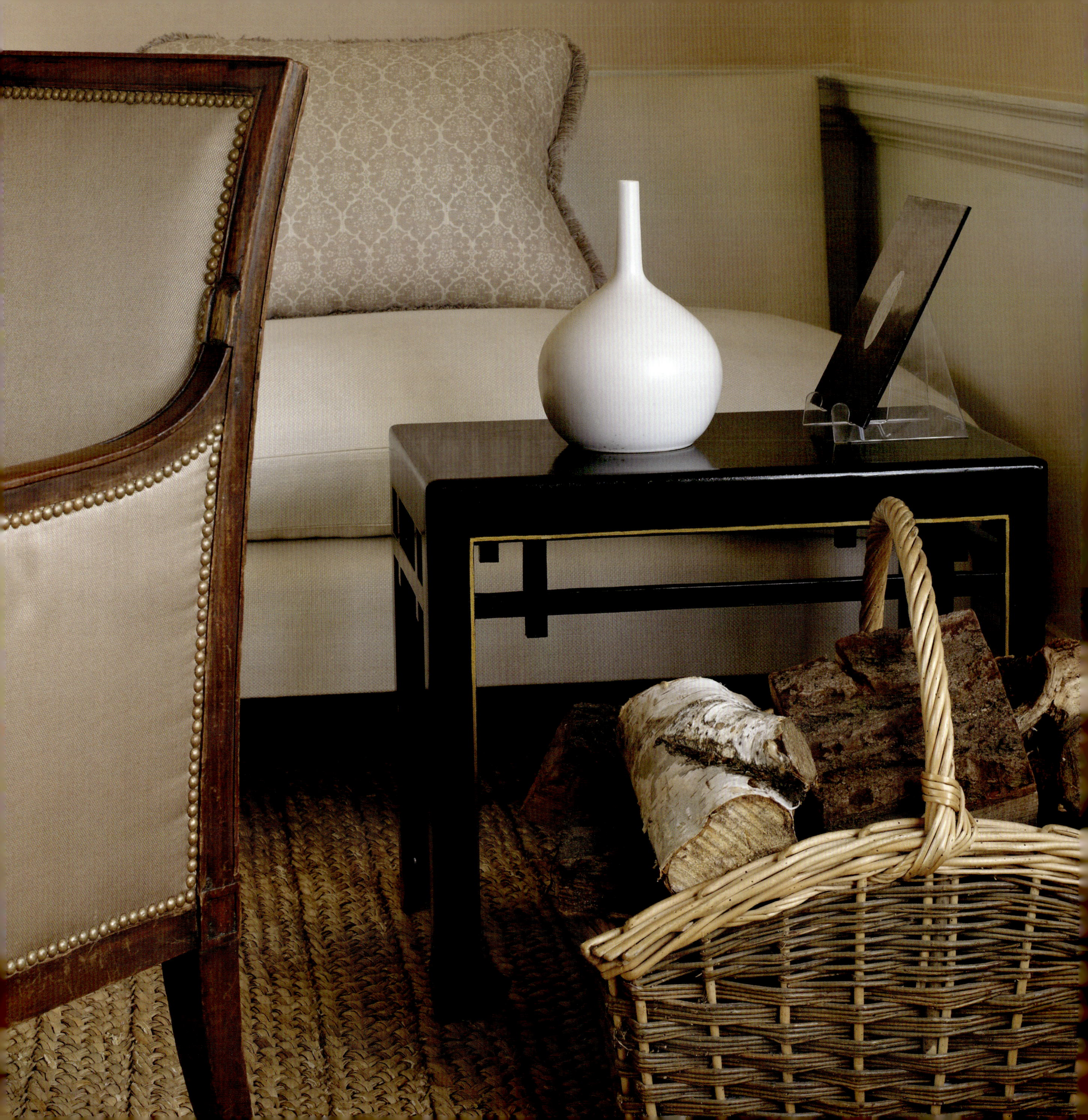

← *The banquettes designed by Veere Grenney were inspired by the work of designer Elsie de Woolf.*

↘ *The Temple, designed by Sir Robert Taylor and built for the Rowley family in the 1760s, has views over the park to the east and was used for watching coursing to the west.*

of this can be seen from the elevated viewpoint of the drawing room. Light also reflects off this expanse of water into the room.

The furnishing of the drawing room is deliberately restrained to make the most of the architecture itself and the fine proportions of the room, as well as the wonderful views out of the large sash windows. The main wall colour is a subtle but strong pink, inspired by the colour Nancy Lancaster painted the hall at Kelmarsh Hall in Northamptonshire, described as "crushed raspberry" by some and also dubbed "potted shrimp" by Nancy Lancaster's niece, Elizabeth Winn.[5] David Oliver, Grenney's partner, has developed a "Temple Pink" as part of the repertoire for his company, the Paint Library.[6] Charles Beresford-Clark's interior scheme was illustrated in *Vogue* in 1984, with a warm yellow on the walls.[7]

The flooring is a modern version of medieval rush matting laid by Hicks, which lasted fifty years until it was replaced two years ago. The banquettes on either side of the chimneypiece are inspired by ones from the 1930s designed by Elsie de Woolf (at the peak of her career she was known as Lady Mendl and was author of *The House in Good Taste*, 1913). The presence of Egyptian-inspired armchairs is one of Mr. Grenney's design hallmarks. Mr. Grenney was a director at Sibyl Colefax and John Fowler and spent time working for Mary Fox Linton before launching his own company based in Chelsea in London.[8]

Mr. Grenney has an intimate dining room and kitchen on the ground floor below, and a bedroom and guest bedroom in the side wings, with further guest bedrooms in a former garden building. He believes that a good drawing room should be, as at the Temple, "simply the best room in a house, but at the same time it should be comfortable and meant to be used and enjoyed." The drawing room here is used for drinks before lunch and coffee afterwards, when entertaining, but also for contemplation or reading in the light of the tall windows. Mr. Grenney adds, "Constable painted the view up Stoke by Nayland church from the side of the Temple and I think the views from both sides are framed almost in the manner of works of art."

The first floor drawing room at The Temple looks over the restored canal garden, framed by an avenue of trees.

Acknowledgements

This book is only possible through the vision of Charles Miers and David Morton of Rizzoli, to whom I am forever grateful; and to the wider Rizzoli team, especially Alexandra Tart, my patient and wise editor. The achievement of Paul Barker as a photographer is evident throughout all these pages, and we are both deeply grateful to Robert Dalrymple for his sensitive and bold design and for his instinctive understanding of the subject of the book. To Julian Fellowes, for his kindness in writing the foreword, and for celebrating the culture of the country house more widely, I am also hugely grateful.

From the writing point of view, numerous friends and colleagues have been sounding boards and invaluable sources of encouragement, ideas, critical advice and hospitality on my travels, and I would like to thank especially: Michael Ashby, Julian and Serena Barrow, Marcus Binney, John Bold, Simon Bradley, Jane Brown, Gabriel Byng, James Campbell, George Carter, Peter and Clare Clark, the Countess of Erroll, Leslie Geddes-Brown, John Goodall, the Hon. Desmond and Penny Guinness, John Hardy, Eileen and John Harris, Michael Hall, Richard Hewlings, Anna Keay, Tim Knox, Tessa Murdoch, Guy Oliver, Derek Matravers, Mary Miers, David Musson, Roger and Rosemary Musson, William Palin, Sue Palmer, Frank Salmon, Charles Sebag-Montefiore, Hew Stevenson, Patricia Smith, Simon Thurley, Jane Troughton, Rupert Uloth, Christopher and Lady Linda Vane-Percy, Susan Woodall, Melissa Wyndham; thanks too to all my friends and colleagues at *Country Life* magazine, and to the librarians of the University of Cambridge Library, the London Library, and the British Library. Special thanks to Justin Hobson of the *Country Life* Picture Library for his support with illustrations, and to Chris Rowlin and Harvey Edgington of the National Trust Picture Library for their arrangements for access to the houses in the care of the National Trust.

Paul Barker and I would like to warmly thank all owners, curators, and designers of the country houses featured for their generosity and encouragement, and for the work they do preserving these houses which are the pride of the nation: the Duke and Duchess of Northumberland, the Marquess and Marchioness of Cholmondeley and the Dowager Marchioness of Cholmondeley, Lady Henrietta Spencer-Churchill, Viscount and Viscountess Windsor, Lord and Lady Brabourne, Lord and Lady Inglewood, Sir Humphry Wakefield, Bt., and Lady Wakefield, Sir Charles Burrell, Bt., and Lady Isabella (Issy) Burrell, the late Hon. Marian Brudenell and Edmund Brudenell, the Hon. Henry and Martha Lytton-Cobbold, Alexandra and Rick Hayward, Richard and Lucinda Compton, Detmar Blow, Lucy and Jonathan Chenevix-Trench, John Evetts and Annie Dowty, Paul and Mina Matthews, Thomas and Pepe Messel, David Mlinaric, James Perkins, John Taylor and Gela Nash-Taylor, Richard Taylor and Rick Englert, and Lavinia Verney; as well as Eleanor Akinlade, Eilidh Auckland, Trudi Ballard, Andrew Barbour, Chloe Breenbank, Annabel Britton, Daniel Chadwick, Sue Edwards, Andrew Farquharson, Ffion George, Rhian Hentschel, Mia Herbert, Sally Hodgetts, Christopher Hunwick, Chester Jones, Roger Jones, Sarah Kay, Bob London, Barnie McIntyre, Lesley McDermott, Christopher Rae-Scott, Helen Royal, Aurelia Rupert, Helen Ryall, Daniel Slowik, Rebecca Young. Thanks also to all others not mentioned who helped with arrangements and facilitated the visits of myself and Paul Barker—and indeed to all who keep these houses shining and fine.

For myself, especial thanks to Sorrel May, Octavia Pollock, Neil Parker, and Harriet Salisbury for their help and support with the project; and to my wife, Sophie, and our daughters, Georgia and Miranda, for their patience and encouragement of the peripatetic life of the author, who might one day be on a long train journey to visit a room in distant parts, and on others, locked in his office for days on end, with only Archie, our Jack Russell, for company, besides an increasingly battered library.

JEREMY MUSSON

PAUL BARKER would also like to pay an especial tribute to his wife, Tracey Barker, whose involvement in post-production is vitally important to how the pictures look, an incredibly important job in the age of digital photography and one that requires many painstaking hours of work; and to thank his son, George, for his support and good company.

Select Bibliography and Sources

Abdy, Jane, and Charlotte Gere. *The Souls.* London: Sidgwick & Jackson, 1984.

Adam, Robert. *Works in Architecture.* London, 1778.

Aldrich, Megan. *The Craces: Royal Decorators: 1768–1899.* London: John Murray, 1990.

Allibone, Jill, *Anthony Salvin: Pioneer of Gothic Revival Architecture.* London: Lutterworth Press, 1988.

Aslet, Clive. "A Family's Idyll on the Hill," *Country Life* (February 1, 2012).

—. "Madresfield Court, Worcestershire, I, II and III." *Country Life* (October 16, 23, and 30, 1980).

—. *The Last Country Houses.* London and New Haven: Yale University Press, 1982.

Austen, Jane. *Emma.* Cambridge: Cambridge University Press, 2006 (first published 1815).

—. *Pride and Prejudice.* Cambridge: Cambridge University Press, 2005 (first published 1813).

—. *Sense and Sensibility.* Cambridge: Cambridge University Press, 2006 (first published 1811).

Beckwith, Lady Muriel. *When I Remember.* London: Nicholson & Watson, 1901.

Mrs. Beeton. *Mrs Beeton's Household Management.* London: Ward Lock, 1861.

Berkeley Wills, G. "Alterations to Thame Park." *Architectural Review* vol. 51 (1922).

Binney, Marcus. "Aynhoe, Northamptonshire." *Country Life* (January 22, 2004 and July 16, 2008).

—. *Sir Robert Taylor: From Rococo to Neo-Classicism.* London: Allen & Unwin, 1984.

Bold, John, and Edward Chaney. *English Architecture: Public and Private.* Cambridge: Cambridge University Press, 1993.

Brittain, Judy, and Patrick Kinmonth. *Living in Vogue.* London: Century, 1984.

Brittain-Catlin, Timothy. "True to Form." *World of Interiors* (October 2010).

Brown, Andrew. "Bulwer Lytton, Edward George Earle Lytton, (1803–1873)." In *Oxford Dictionary of National Biography*, edited by H.C.G. Matthew and Brian Harrison. Oxford and New York: Oxford University Press, 2004.

Burgess, Ruth. "Extravagant Abandon: The Life of Lady Ilsington." University of Buckingham Masters Thesis (2002–03).

Cartwright-Hignett, Elizabeth. *Lili at Aynhoe: Victorian Life in an English Country House.* London: Barrie & Jenkins, 1989.

Cecil, Mirabel, and Hugh Cecil. *In Search of Rex Whistler.* London: Frances Lincoln, 2012.

Chartier, Roger, ed. *A History of Private Life, III, Passions of the Renaissance.* Harvard: Belknap Press, 1993.

Chippendale, Thomas. *The Gentleman and Cabinetmaker's Director.* London, 1754.

Christie, Christopher. *The British Country House in the Eighteenth Century.* Manchester: Manchester University Press, 2000.

Cliffe, J. T. *The World of the Country House in Seventeenth-Century England.* London and New Haven: Yale University Press, 1999.

Cobbold, Lord. *Knebworth House, Hertfordshire: Home of the Lytton Family Since 1490.* Knebworth House, 2000.

Codman, Ogden, and Edith Wharton. *The Decoration of Houses.* New York: Charles Scribners and Sons, 1915 (first published 1897).

Cokayne, G. E, Vicary Gibbs and others. *The Complete Peerage* (revised edition), vol. XII. London: George Bell & Sons, 1910.

Colvin, H. M. *A Biographical Dictionary of British Architects 1600–1840.* London and New Haven: Yale University Press, 2007.

Colvin, H. M., and John Newman. *Of Building: Roger North's Writings on Architecture.* Oxford: Oxford University Press, 1981.

Cooper, Nicholas. *Aynho: A Northamptonshire Village.* Aynho: Leopard's Head Press, 1984.

—. *Houses of the Gentry: 1480–1680.* London and New Haven: Yale University Press, 1999.

Cornforth, John, and Gervase Jackson-Stops. *Attingham Park, Shropshire.* London: National Trust (1981).

Cornforth, John. "Deene Park, Northamptonshire." *Country Life* (March 11, 18, 25, April 1, 1972).

—. "Deene Park, Northamptonshire." Vol. 192 (November 12, 1998), 50–55.

—. *Early Georgian Interiors.* London and New Haven: Yale University Press, 2004.

—. *English Interiors 1790–1848: The Quest for Comfort.* London: Barrie & Jenkins, 1978.

—. "Felbrigg Hall, Norfolk." *Country Life*, vol.184 (April 5, 1990), 138–141, and (April 12, 1990) 102–15.

—. "Hutton in the Forest." *Country Life* (February 18, 1965).

—. "Newby Hall I." *Country Life* (June 7, 1979).

—. "Nymans, Sussex." *Country Life* (June 5, 1997).

—. 'The Key to the Drawing Room." *Country Life* (December 11, 2003)

Croft-Murray, Edward. *Decorative Painting in England, 1537–1837.* London: Country Life Books, 1971.

Cruickshank, Dan. *The Country House Revealed.* London: BBC Books, 2011.

Davidoff, Leonore, *The Best Circles.* London: Croom Helm, 1973.

Dean, Ptolemy. *Sir John Soane and the Country Estate.* Farnham: Ashgate Publishing, 1999.

Donaldson, Thomas. "Brief Memoir of the Late Commendatore Canina, Honorary and Corresponding Member of the Royal Institute of British Architects," *Papers read at the Opening Meeting of the Royal Institute of British Architects.* London: November 3, 1856.

—. "Some Description of Alnwick Castle," *Papers read at the Opening Meeting of the Royal Institute of British Architects.* London: November 3, 1856.

Eastlake, Charles. *A History of the Gothic Revival*, 1872 (reprinted Ulan Press, 2012).

—. *Hints on Household Taste* (1868).

Evans, Sian. *Mrs Ronnie.* Swindon: National Trust Books, 2013.

Faulkner, Rupert, ed. *Tea: East and West.* London: V&A Publishing, 2003.

Fay, Anna Maria. *Victorian Days in England: Letters Home of an American Girl 1851–1852* (Ludlow: Dog Rose Press, 2002).

Franklin, Jill. *The Gentleman's Country House and Its Plan, 1835–1914.* London: Routledge & Kegan, 1981.

Mrs. Garrett. *House Decoration.* London, 1876.

Gater, G. H., and E. P. Wheeler, eds. *Survey of London: St Martin in the Fields, II: The Strand,* vol. XVIII. London, 1937.

Girouard, Mark. "Dyrham Park, Gloucestershire." *Country Life* (February 15 and 22, 1962).

—. *Life in the English Country House.* London and New Haven: Yale University Press, 1993.

Goodall, John. "Baronial Bravura: Eastnor Castle, Herefordshire." *Country Life* (November 28, 2012).

Gore, Alan, and Ann Gore. *The History of English Interiors.* London: Phaidon, 1991.

Gunther, R. T. *The Architecture of Sir Roger Pratt.* Oxford: Oxford University Press, 1928.

Hall, Michael. *The English Country House.* London: Mitchell Beazley, 1994.

Hardy, John. Hayward, Helena. "Kedleston Hall, Derbyshire," *Country Life*, June 26, 194–197.

Hardy, John. "Robert Adam and the Furnishings of Kedleston Hall," *The Connoisseur*, July 1978, 196–207.

Harris, Eileen. *The Genius of Robert Adam.* London and New Haven: Yale University Press, 2001.

—. *The Country Houses of Robert Adam: His Interiors.* London: Aurum Press, 2007.

Haslam, Richard. "Oakly Park, Shropshire." *Country Life* (March, 22 1999).

—. "Shared enthusiasm: Oakly Park." *Country Life* (February 23, 2011).

Hervey-Bathurst, James, and Sarah Hervey-Bathurst. *Eastnor Castle*, 2001.

Hicks, Ashley. *David Hicks: A Life of Design.* New York: Rizzoli International Publications, Inc., 2009.

—. *David Hicks: Designer.* London: Scriptum Editions, 2002.

Hicks, David. *David Hicks on Living – With Taste.* London: Frewin, 1968.

Hill, Rosemary. *God's Architect: Pugin and the Building of Romantic Britain.* London: Penguin, 2007.

Home, J. A., ed. *Letters and Journal of Lady Mary Coke*, III, 1889, reprinted Bath: Kingsmead Books, 1970.

Hussey, Christopher. "Biddesden, Wiltshire." *Country Life* (April 2 and 9, 1938).

—. *English Country Houses: Mid Georgian, 1760–1800.* London: Country Life, 1955.

—. "Hilles, Gloucestershire." *Country Life* (September 7 and 14, 1940).

—. "Nymans, Sussex." *Country Life* (September 10 and 17, 1932).

—. "Stanway, Gloucestershire." *Country Life* (December 3, 1964).

Jackson, Alvin. "Walter Hume, first Viscount Long (1854–1924)." Oxford

Dictionary of National Biography, edited by H.C.G. Matthew and Brian Harrison. Oxford and New York: Oxford University Press, 2004.

Jackson-Stops, Gervase. "Broadlands, Hampshire." *Country Life* (December 4, 1980).

—. "Cholmondeley Castle." *Country Life* (July 19, 1973).

—. *The English Country House: A Grand Tour*. London: Weidenfeld & Nicholson, 1985.

—. *Treasure Houses of Britain*. New Haven: Yale University Press, 1985.

Jenkins, Simon. *England's Thousand Best Houses*. New York: Penguin, 2003.

Johnson, Samuel. *Dictionary*. London: printed by W. Strahan, For J. and P. Knapton; T. and T. Longman; C. Hitch and L. Hawes; A. Millar; and R. and J. Dodsley, 1775.

Kenworthy-Brown, John. *Dyrham Park, Gloucestershire: A Property of the National Trust*. London: The National Trust, 1961.

—. "The building of Dyrham Park, Gloucestershire for William Blathwayt" *The Connoisseur*, (March 1962) 149.

Kerr, Robert. *The Gentleman's House*. London: John Murray, 1865 (1873 edition).

Ketton-Cremer, R. Wyndham. *Felbrigg: The Story of a House*, revised edition. Swindon: National Trust, 2010 (first published 1962).

Kinmonth, Patrick. "South Wraxall Resurgent." *World of Interiors* (March 2010).

Knox, Tim. "Return of the Damask." *Country Life* (March 9, 2009).

Lawson-Dick, Oliver, ed., *Aubrey's Brief Lives*. New York: Penguin, 1962.

Lewin, Ronald. "Ismay, Hastings Lionel, Baron Ismay (1887–1965)." In *Oxford Dictionary of National Biography*, edited by H.C.G. Matthew and Brian Harrison. Oxford and New York: Oxford University Press, 2004.

Mcdonald, James. *Alnwick Castle: The Home of the Duke and Duchess of Northumberland*. London: Frances Lincoln, 2012.

Maddison, John. *Felbrigg Hall*. London: National Trust, 1995.

Mallock, William Hurrell. *Memoirs of Life and Literature*. London: Chapman and Hall, 1920.

Messel, Thomas, ed. *Oliver Messel: In the Theatre of Design*. New York: Rizzoli International Publications, Inc., 2010.

Metcalf, Pauline C. *Syrie Maugham*. New York: Acanthus Press, 2010.

Miers, Mary. "Knepp Castle, Sussex." *Country Life* (July 17, 2003).

—. "Whithurst Park, West Sussex." *Country Life* (May 25, 2005).

Millard, Andrew. "Sir Harold Bowden", second baronet (1880–1960)." In *Oxford Dictionary of National Biography*, edited by H.C.G. Matthew and Brian Harrison. Oxford and New York: Oxford University Press, 2004.

Miller, James. *Hidden Treasure Houses*. London: Macmillan, 2006.

More-Molyneux, James. *The Loseley Challenge*. London: Hodder & Stoughton, 1995.

More-Molyneux Family. *Loseley Park Near Guilford, Home of the More-Molyneux Family*. English Life Publications, 1968.

Morris, Christopher, ed. *The Illustrated Journeys of Celia Fiennes*. London: Macdonald, 1984.

Mulvagh, Jane. *Madresfield, One House, One Family, One Thousand Years*. London: Doubleday, 2009.

Murison, Barbara. "Blathwayt, William." In *Oxford Dictionary of National Biography*, edited by H.C.G. Matthew and Brian Harrison. Oxford and New York: Oxford University Press, 2004.

Murray Baillie, H. "Etiquette and the Planning of Baroque State Apartments." *Archaeologia*, vol. 101 (1967).

Musson, Jeremy. "Bradley Court, Gloucestershire." *Country Life* (September 15, 2005).

—. "Chillingham Castle, Northumberland," *Country Life* (April 22, 2004).

—. *English Country House Interiors*. New York: Rizzoli International Publications, Inc., 2011.

—. *The English Manor House*. London: Aurum Press, 1999.

—. "Knebworth House, Hertfordshire." *Country Life* (April 24, 2003).

—. "On My Chippendale Day Bed." *Country Life* (December 20 and 27, 2007).

—. "Rare Elizabethan Treasure: Loseley Park, Surrey." *Country Life* (May 9, 2012).

—. "Renishaw Hall, Derbyshire." *Country Life* (June 5, 2003).

Muthesius, Hermann. *The English House, 1904–05*, 3 vols (translation by Dennis Sharp). London: Frances Lincoln, 2007.

Northumberland, 8th Duke. *Alnwick Castle*. London and Edinburgh: William Blackwood, 1931.

Oman, Charles, and Jean Hamilton. *Wallpapers: A History and Illustrated Catalogue of the Collection of the Victoria and Albert Museum*. London: Sotheby's, 1982.

Mrs. Orrinsmith. *The Drawing Room: Its Decoration and Furnishing*. London: Macmillan & Co., 1878.

Oswald, Arthur. "Thame Park, Oxfordshire." *Country Life* (November 21, 1958).

Parissien, Steven. *The Georgian House*. London: Aurum Press, 1997.

Pettigrew, Jane. *A Social History of Tea*. London: National Trust, 2001.

Pevsner, Nikolaus, ed., and Bridget Cherry. *Buildings of England: Wiltshire*. London: Penguin UK, 1999.

Porter, Roy. *The Enlightenment*. London: Allen Lane, 2000.

Pugin, A. W. N. *Examples of Gothic Architecture*, vol. 1. London, 1838.

Rix, M. "Attingham Park, Shropshire." *Country Life* (October 21, 1954).

Robinson, John Martin. "Althorp, Northamptonshire." *Country Life* (May 13, 1999).

—. "A Return to Harmony: Broadlands." *Country Life* (September 5, 2012).

—. "Hutton in the Forest." *Country Life* (March 15, 2007).

Rock, Orlando. *Aynhoe Park: A Modern Grand Tour*. Christie's catalogue (October 9, 2012).

Scott, George Gilbert. *Remarks on Secular Domestic Architecture, Present and Future*. London, 1857.

Shapland, Henry. *Style Schemes in Antique Furnishing*. London: Simpkin, Marshall, Hamilton, Ken, 1909.

Sitwell, Osbert. *Left Hand! Right Hand!* London: Macmillan, 1946.

Smith, E. A. "Temple, Henry, second Viscount Palmerston, (1739–1802)." In *Oxford Dictionary of National Biography*, edited by H.C.G. Matthew and Brian Harrison. Oxford and New York: Oxford University Press, 2004.

Spencer, Charles. *Impressions of Althorp*. Spencer, 2012.

Stansky, Peter. *Sassoon: The Worlds of Philip and Sybil*. New Haven and London: Yale University Press, 2003.

Stevenson, J. J. *House Architecture*. London: Macmillan, 1880.

Sykes, Plum. "Country Couture." *Vogue* (September 2009).

Thornton, Peter. *Seventeenth-Century Interior Decoration in England, France and Holland*. London and New Haven: Yale University Press, 1981.

Lady Troubridge's Book of Etiquette, 1943.

Verey, David, and Alan Brooks. *Buildings of England: Gloucestershire*. Harmondsworth: Penguin, 1970.

Vickery, Amanda. *Behind Closed Doors: At Home in Georgian England*. London and New Haven, Yale University Press, 2010.

Walker, T. L., and A.W.N. Pugin. *Examples of Gothic Architecture Selected from Various Ancient Edifices*, vol. iii. London: Henry G. Bohn, 1838.

Watkin, David. *The Life and Work of C. R. Cockerell*. London: Zwemmer, 1974.

Waugh, Evelyn. *Brideshead Revisited*. London: Chapman and Hall, 1945.

—. *A Handful of Dust*. London: Chapman and Hall, 1934.

Wells-Cole, Anthony. *The Art of Decoration in Elizabethan and Jacobean England: The Influence of Continental Prints, 1558–1625*. London and New Haven: Yale University Press, 1997.

Wood, Martin. *Nancy Lancaster: English Country-House Style*. London: Frances Lincoln, 2005.

—. *John Fowler: Prince of Decorators*. London: Frances Lincoln, 2007.

Woollcombe, Tamsyn. "Chadwyck, Lynne (1914–2003)." In *Oxford Dictionary of National Biography*, edited by H.C.G. Matthew and Brian Harrison. Oxford and New York: Oxford University Press, 2004.

Woolf, Virginia. *Orlando*. London: The Hogarth Press, 1928.

Ziegler, Philip. *Osbert Sitwell*. London: Pimlico, 1999.

Notes and References

Introduction
1 Austen, *Pride and Prejudice*, 40–41.
2 Austen, *Sense and Sensibility*, 34.
3 Austen, *Emma*, 323.
4 For example, Austen, *Pride and Prejudice*, 40.
5 Girouard, *Life in the English Country House*, 57, 94, 99–100, 205–08; and Cornforth, "The Key to the Drawing Room," 44–47.
6 Adam, *Works in Architecture*, 3.
7 Vickery, *Behind Closed Doors*, 83–85; Cornforth, *Early Georgian Interiors*, 52–58.
8 Porter, *Enlightenment*, 35–37.
9 Parissien, *The Georgian House*, 43–44; Cornforth, *Eighteenth Century Interior Decoration*, 52–53.
10 Girouard, *Life*, 293–94.
11 Cooper, *Houses of the Gentry: 1480–1680*, 292–93. Cliffe, *The World of the Country House in the Seventeenth Century*, 27–30, refers to the "eclipse of the Great Chamber."
12 Girouard, *Life*, 93–95.
13 Pat Smith, "Interior Planning of the English Country House, 1660–1735"; I am very grateful to Dr. Smith for her helpful observations on this subject.
14 Thornton, *Seventeenth-Century Interior Decoration in England, France and Holland*, 58–59.
15 Gunther, *The Architecture of Sir Roger Pratt*, 65.
16 Colvin and Newman, *Of Building: Roger North's Writings on Architecture*, 74–77.
17 Morris (ed.), *The Illustrated Journeys of Celia Fiennes*, 170–71.
18 Girouard, *Life*, 204, quoting Congreve, *The Double Dealer* (although interestingly this does refer to the ladies at the end of the gallery).
19 Girouard, *Life*, 205.
20 Pettigrew, *Tea: A Social History*, 64–65; Faulkner (ed.), *Tea: East and West*, 90–91, 102–03.
21 Johnson, *Dictionary*, 1755.
22 Thurley, "The King in the Queen's Lodgings"; I am very grateful to Dr. Thurley for allowing me sight of his conference paper and Dr. Anna Keay for her advice; Baillie, "Etiquette and the Planning of Baroque State Apartments," 170–84.
23 Thurley, "The King in the Queen's Lodgings."
24 Home (ed.), *Letters and Journal of Lady Mary Coke*, III, 37.
25 Davidoff, *The Best Circles*, 24–25, 68–69.
26 Girouard, *Life*, 204.
27 Cornforth, *Early Georgian*, 83–85.
28 For Mrs. Delany, Jackson-Stops, *The English Country House*, 145; and Christie, *The British Country House in the Eighteenth Century*, 246, for Mrs. Lybbe Powys.
29 Repton, cited in Gore, *History of English Interiors*, 104.
30 Jackson-Stops, *The English Country House*, 157.
31 Cornforth, "Key to the Drawing Room," 47.
32 Fay, *Victorian Days in England*, 80–85.
33 Kerr, *The Gentleman's House*, 107–14; Franklin, *The Gentleman's Country House and Its Plan*, 43–48.
34 Kerr, III.
35 Stevenson, *House Architecture*, 56–61; thanks to Hew Stevenson for drawing this account of the drawing room to my attention.
36 Eastlake, *Hints on Household Taste*, 145–47.
37 Orrinsmith, *The Drawing-Room: Its Decorations and Furniture*, 8.
38 Ibid., 19 and 126–29.
39 Cornforth, *Quest for Comfort*, 70; Girouard, *Life*, 293, 300.
40 Beckwith, *When I Remember*, 108.
41 Aslet, *Last Country Houses*, 70–71.
42 Lady Troubridge, *Lady Troubridge's Book of Etiquette*, 241–42.
43 Beeton, *Household Management*, 963–70.
44 Muthesius, *The English Country House*, II, 36–38.
45 Ibid., II, 36.
46 Ibid., III, 189–90.
47 Wharton and Codman, *The Decoration of Houses*, 123–24.
48 Woolf, *Orlando*, 206.
49 Abdy and Gere, *The Souls*, 26–27, on Curzon; also, Musson, *The English Manor House*, 15–23.
50 Shapland, *Style Schemes in Antique Furnishing*, 29.
51 Girouard, *Life*, 310.
52 Nichols, quoted in Evans, *Mrs Ronnie*, 118–19.
53 Hall, *The English Country House*, 12–13.
54 Hussey, "Biddesden, Wiltshire,"; Musson, *The English Manor House*, 99–107.

Loseley Park
1 Musson, "Rare Elizabethan Treasure: Loseley Park, Surrey," 78–83; More-Molyneux, *The Loseley Challenge*, 21–23; More-Molyneux, *Loseley Park*, 10–12.
2 Musson, "Loseley Park, Surrey," 83.
3 Wells-Cole, *The Art of Decoration*, 35–38; cartouches from Virgil Solis; term figures from a plate by Du Cerceau.
4 More-Molyneux, interview with the author, 2012; More-Molyneux, *Loseley Park*, 10–12.

South Wraxall Manor
1 Cruickshank, *The Country House Revealed*, 48.
2 Aubrey in the 1670s spoke of it as a "dining Room," a word used interchangeably with "Great Parlour" (Aubrey, *Wiltshire*, 28–29; Cruickshank, *The Country House Revealed*, 28, also refers to as a "high dining room."
3 Walker and Pugin, *Examples of Gothic Architecture*, plate viii.
4 Information from Bob Loudon, estate manager, 2014; the date 1611, with the name John Sweetman.
5 Pevsner and Cherry, *Wiltshire*, 474–76.
6 Cruickshank, *The Country House Revealed*, 42–44.
7 Wells-Cole, *The Art of Decoration*, 143.
8 Ibid., 21, 60, 82, 142–4.
9 Lawson-Dick, *Aubrey's Brief Lives*, 317–19.
10 Jackson, "Long, Walter Hume."
11 Kinmonth, "South Wraxall Resurgent," 102–15.
12 Sykes, "Country Couture," 530–37; and interview with John Taylor.

Chillingham Castle
1 Musson, "Chillingham Castle," 130–35; and Sir Humphry Wakefield, Bt., interview with the author, 2012.
2 Cokayne and Gibbs, *The Complete Peerage*, 632–37; Musson, "Chillingham Castle," 133.
3 Ibid., and Information from Sir Humphry Wakefield, Bt., 2012.
4 Ibid.

Newby Hall
1 Harris, *The Genius of Robert Adam*, 212–31.
2 National Trust, www.nationaltrustcollections.org.uk/object/446663.
3 Harris, *The Country Houses of Robert Adam*, 110–11; the quote is included on the entry in the National Trust inventory, as in note 2.
4 Cornforth, "Newby Hall I," 1802–05.
5 For Syon, see Harris, *Genius of Robert Adam*, 64–83.
6 Ibid., 212–31.
7 Information from Richard and Lucinda Compton, January 2014: following recent cleaning an inspection of the reverse of the tapestry panels suggests that the tapestries' original colour was more of a pale rose pink rather than the crimson pink which the other versions of the *tenture de Boucher* were produced in.
8 Cornforth, "Newby Hall II," 1920.

Kedleston Hall
1 Harris, *The Genius of Robert Adam*, 19–39, esp. 26–29; Pevsner and Cherry: *Wiltshire*, 255–56.
2 I am grateful to John Hardy, scholar of eighteenth-century design, for drawing my attention to Scarsdale's verse, which was contained among Scarsdale's private papers. Cited in Hardy, "Kedleston Hall," (94–7).
3 Knox, "Return of the Damask, " 80–86, and advice from Ffion George and Andrew Barbour, 2013.
4 Harris, *The Genius of Robert Adam*, 108.
5 Harris, *Country Houses of Robert Adam*, 37.
6 Hardy and Hayward, "Robert Adam and the Furnishing of Kedleston Hall, 204–5.
7 Knox, "Return of the Damask," 82.
8 Ibid.

Althorp
1 Robinson, "Althorp, Northamptonshire," 151–55; Hussey, *Mid-Georgian*, 202–13.
2 Hussey, *Mid-Georgian*, 21.
3 Colvin, *A Biographical Dictionary*, 527–29.
4 Robinson, "Althorp," 152, for the Earl; Hussey, *Mid-Georgian*, 1202, for Walpole.
5 Robinson, "Althorp," 151; Spencer, *Impressions of Althorp*, 57.
6 Hussey, *Mid-Georgian*, 1202.
7 Ibid.
8 Spencer, *Impressions of Althorp*, 58.

Broadlands

1 Robinson, "A Return to Harmony," 56–61.
2 Smith, "Temple, Henry."
3 Jackson-Stops, "Broadlands," 2099–102.
4 Robinson, "A Return to Harmony," 159–60.
5 Colvin, *Biographical Dictionary of British Architects*, 529.
6 Lady Brabourne and David Mlinaric, interview with the author, 2013.
7 Ibid.; and Jackson-Stops, "Broadlands," 2100.

Oakly Park

1 Watkin, *C.R. Cockerell*, xix; Haslam, "Shared Enthusiasm," 36–41; Haslam, "Oakly Park," 152–59.
2 Haslam, "Oakly Park," 158.
3 Watkin, *C.R. Cockerell*, 162–63.
4 Ibid., 163–64, Cockerell disliked their neighbour, Lord Powis, whom he thought vulgar.
5 Fay, *Victorian Days in England*, 79–80.
6 Haslam, "Shared Enthusiasm," 36–41; Haslam, "Oakly Park," 152–59.

Attingham Park

1 Jackson-Stops, *The English Country House*, 57.
2 Cornforth and Jackson-Stops, *Attingham Park*, 9.
3 Ibid., 6, 28.
4 Bills from 1806 and 1812–13, now in the Shropshire Record offices; I am very grateful to Sarah Kay, curator of Attingham, for generously providing me with copies of these and the sale catalogue of 1827, and inventories of 1861 and 1913.
5 Howell, *The Stranger in Shrewsbury*, 1816, extract in NT files.
6 Leach, *The County Seats of Shropshire*, 1891, extract in NT files.
7 Letter written by Lady Berwick, dated July 27, 1920; I am grateful to Sarah Kay for generously providing me with copies.
8 Rix, "Attingham Park," 1350–53.

Renishaw Hall

1 Jeremy Musson, "Renishaw Hall," 148–53; for Badger, see Colvin, *Biographical Dictionary of British Architects*, 86–87.
2 Musson, "Renishaw Hall," 150.
3 Ibid., 150–51.
4 Sitwell, *Left Hand! Right Hand!*, 225–54.
5 Musson, "Renishaw Hall," 151.
6 Cornforth, *English Interiors*, 70–74.
7 Ibid., 70.
8 Musson, "Renishaw Hall," 152.
9 Information from Lady Sitwell.

Felbrigg Hall

1 Maddison, *Felbrigg Hall*, 4–5, 12–13; Cornforth, "Felbrigg Hall, Norfolk," 1990, 5 April, 138–141, 12 April, 102–05.
2 Maddison, 44–45; Ketton-Cremer, *Felbrigg: The Story of a House*, 112–29.
3 Ibid, 116.
4 Maddison, 12–13.
5 Ibid, 15.
6 Ibid, 52–53; Ketton-Cremer, 267–76.
7 Information from Elinor Akinlade of the National Trust.

Eastnor Castle

1 Goodall, "Baronial Bravura," 66–71; Hervey-Bathurst, *Eastnor Castle*.
2 Eastlake, *A History of Gothic Revival*, 147.
3 Aldrich, *The Craces*, 78–81.
4 Hervey-Bathurst, *Eastnor Castle*, 26.
5 Aldrich, 80.
6 Hill, *God's Architect*, 428.
7 Jackson-Stops, *Treasure Houses of Britain*, 609.
8 Aldrich, 141.
9 Jenkins, *Thousand Best Houses*, 313.
10 Information from James Henry, Bath, 2013.

Knebworth

1 Musson, "Knebworth," 102–07.
2 Brown, "Lytton."
3 Fitzgerald's remark is quoted in Mark Bence-Jones, *Ancestral Houses*, 1984, 139.
4 Aldrich, 71–72.
5 Bills, copies in the archives at Knebworth, originals in the Hertford Record Office, with thanks to Clare Fleck, the archivist at Knebworth House.
6 Aldrich, *The Craces*, 70–71.
7 Ibid., p. 72.
8 Maclise quoted in Cobbold, *Knebworth*, 39.
9 Mallock, *Memoirs of Life and Literature*, 261.

Alnwick Castle

1 Mcdonald, *Alnwick Castle*, 45, 67, 72, 79–86; Allibone, *Anthony Salvin*, 81–84.
2 Donaldson, "Brief Memoir"; with Donaldson, "Some Description of Alnwick Castle"; with contributions by Canina and Salvin, 14–26; all published in *Papers Read at the RIBA*, 1857.
3 *Papers Read at the RIBA*, 16.
4 Ibid., 1.
5 Ibid., 18.
6 Information from Christopher Hunwick, archivist, who has given generous advice.
7 *Papers Read at the RIBA*, 22
8 Ibid.
9 Northumberland, *Alnwick Castle*, 101.
10 Gater and Wheeler, *Survey of London*, 2–10.
11 Scott, *Remarks on Secular Domestic Architecture*, 232.
12 *Papers Read at the RIBA*, 16.
13 Mcdonald, *Alnwick Castle*, 79–86.

Hutton in the Forest

1 Cornforth, "Hutton in the Forest," 352–56; Robinson, "Hutton in the Forest," 78–83.
2 Lord Inglewood, interview with the author, 2013.
3 Cornforth, "Hutton in the Forest," 354.
4 Oman and Hamilton, *Wallpapers*, 381, Cat. No. 1067; I am grateful to Michael Hall for making this link.
5 www.hutton-in-the-forest.co.uk; sadly, Lady Vane's diary, known to have been once in the family papers, is currently untraced.
6 Lord Inglewood, interview with the author, 2013.

Madresfield Court

1 Aslet, "Madresfield Court," 1338–41, 1458–61, 1551–58.
2 Mulvagh, *Madresfield*, 27.
3 Waugh, *Handful of Dust*, 9.
4 Waugh, *Brideshead Revisited*, 198.
5 Aslet, "Madresfield Court," 1552.
6 Aslet, *The Last Country Houses*, 250–255
7 Lucy Chenevix-Trench, interview with the author, 2012.

Hilles House

1 Aslet, "A Family's Idyll," 58–63.

Alnwick Castle (cont.)

2 Abdy, *The Souls*, 9–15, 95, 101, 125.
3 Aslet, *The Last Country Houses*, 236–50; the break with the Duke of Westminster, 249–50.
4 Aslet, "A Family's Idyll," 63.
5 Detmar Blow II, interview with the author, 2013.
6 Hussey, "Hilles, Gloucestershire," 235 shows the adjoining room was screened off into a hall and dining room but is now treated as one room.

Dyrham Park

1 Kenworthy-Brown, *Dyrham Park, Gloucestershire*, 15–17; Girouard, "Dyrham Park," 335–39, 396–99; see also Kenworthy-Brown, "The Building of Dyrham Park," 138–44.
2 Murison, "Blathwayt, William."
3 Kenworthy-Brown, *Dyrham Park*, 16–17.
4 Information from National Trust internal report on decoration; thank you to Eilidh Auckland for sharing a copy of this material.
5 Ibid.
6 Burgess, "Extravagant Abandon"; Nancy Lancaster is quoted, 43
7 Ibid.
8 Kenworthy-Brown, *Dyrham Park*, 16–17.
9 Giroaurd, "Dyrham Park," 339.

The Yellow Room

1 Wood, *Nancy Lancaster*, 118–23.
2 Ibid., 106–12.
3 Lancaster, "22 Avery Row," typescript text written when Mrs. Lancaster gave up the flat in 1983; I am very grateful to Barrie McIntyre, archivist at Colefax and Fowler, for making this available and for other advice.
4 Wood, *Nancy Lancaster*, 118.
5 Lancaster, "22 Avery Row," 2.
6 Ibid.
7 Melissa Wyndham, interview with the author, 2013.
8 Roger Jones, interview with the author, 2013.

Deene Park

1 Cornforth, "Deene Park," 750–53 and 810–13; and "Deene Park, Northamptonshire," 50–55.

2 Miller, *Hidden Treasure Houses*, 102–20.
3 Cornforth, "Deene Park," 811.
4 The late Marian Brudenell, interview with the author, 2013.
5 Cornforth, "Deene Park," 811.
6 Miller, *Hidden Treasure Houses*, 120.
7 Ibid.

Lypiatt Park

1 Verey and Brooks, *Gloucestershire*, 466–67.
2 Ibid., 467.
3 Colvin, *A Biographical Dictionary of British Architects*, 1200.
4 Woollcombe, "Chadwick, Lynn."
5 Daniel Chadwick, interview with the author, 2013.
6 Woollcombe, "Chadwick, Lynn."
7 www.danielchadwick.com

Cholmondeley Castle

1 Jackson-Stops, "Cholmondeley Castle", 154–58, 226–30.
2 Ibid., 154.
3 Ibid., 227.
4 Colvin, *A Biographical Dictionary of British Architects*, 1061–62.
5 Jackson-Stops, "Cholmondeley Castle," 230.
6 For Sybil Sassoon, see Stansky, *Sassoon: The Worlds of Philip and Sybil*,
7 Wood, *John Fowler*, 184–89.
8 Jackson-Stops, "Cholmondeley Castle," 230.

The Grove

1 Quoted in his obituary by Mitchell Owens, in *The New York Times*, April 1998; from Hicks, *David Hicks on Living*.
2 Hicks, *A Life of Design*, 247–59; and Hicks, *David Hicks: Designer*, 20–27.
3 Verey, television broadcast, youtube.com, 1993.
4 Hicks, *A Life of Design*, 255; *David Hicks: Designer*, 68–99.
5 Metcalf, *Syrie Maugham*, 135–36.
6 Cecil, *In Search of Rex Whistler*, 170–77.
7 Hicks, *A Life of Design*, 254–53; and Lady Pamela Hicks, interview with the author, 2013.
8 Hicks, *A Life of Design*, 81.

9 Ashley Hicks, interview with the author, 2013.

Stanway House

1 Musson, "On My Chippendale Day Bed," 68–71; Hussey, "Stanway, Gloucestershire," 1490–94, 1646–49, 1708–71; and Miller, *Hidden Treasure Houses*, 235–53.
2 Abdy and Gere, *The Souls*, 9.
3 Ibid., 102.
4 Ibid.
5 Musson, "On My Chippendale Day Bed," 70.
6 Chippendale, The *Gentleman and Cabinetmaker's Director*, 1754, plate XXXIII, shows a Chinese "sopha."
7 Miller, *Hidden Treasure Houses*, 251–52.
8 Miller, *Treasure Houses*, 251–52, and information from Lord Wemyss.

Bradley Court

1 Musson, "Bradley Court," 130–35.
2 Advice to the author from Nicholas Kingsley, author of *Country Houses of Gloucestershire*, 2000.
3 Austen, *Sense and Sensibility*, 34.
4 Thomas Messel, interview with the author, 2012.
5 For Oliver Messel's design career more widely, see Messel, *Oliver Messel*.
6 Musson, "Bradley Court," 130–35.
7 Cornforth, "Nymans," 60–65; and for the collection, see Hussey, "Nymans," 292–97 and 320–25.
8 Thomas Messel, interview with the author, 2012.

Wormington Grange

1 Colvin, *A Biographical Dictionary of British Architects*, 86–87.
2 Hussey, *Mid-Georgian*, 175–80.
3 John Evetts, interview with the author, 2013.
4 Hussey, *Mid-Georgian*, 117.
5 Lewin, "Ismay, Hastings Lionel, Baron Ismay."
6 For the activities of the Landmark Trust, see www.landmarktrust.org.uk.

Whithurst House

1 Miers, "Whithurst Park," 115–19.

2 Ibid.; Christopher Rae-Scott, interview with the author, 2013; and letter to author, June 11, 2013. Mr. Rae-Scott kindly lent me his notes, which accompanied the original application.
3 Miers, "Whithurst Park," 116.
4 Richard Taylor, interview with the author, 2012.

Aynhoe Park

1 Cooper, *Aynho*, 193–96; Binney, "Aynho," 80–85.
2 Dean, *Sir John Soane*, 78–89.
3 Cartwright-Hignett, *Lili at Aynhoe*, 33–36.
4 Rock, *Aynhoe Park*, 6–7; for a description of Mr. Perkins's earlier collection, see Brittain-Catlin, "True to Form," 66–72.
5 James Perkins, interview with the author, 2013.

Thame Park

1 Oswald, "Thame Park," 1092–95.
2 Ibid., 1093.
3 Berkeley Wills, "Alterations to Thame Park," 16–19, the drawing room is illustrated on page 18.
4 Millard, "Sir Harold Bowden."
5 Mr. and Mrs. Paul Matthews, interview with the author, 2013.
6 Lady Henrietta Spencer-Churchill, interview with the author, 2013.

Knepp Castle

1 Miers, "Knepp Castle," 66–71.
2 www.chesterjones.com. Jones is also author of *Colefax and Fowler: The Best in English Interior Decoration*, 1989.
3 Isabella Burrell, interview with the author, 2013.
4 For Nancy Lancaster's former home, Ditchley Park, Oxfordshire, see Wood, *Nancy Lancaster*, 54–81.
5 Isabella Burrell, interview with the author, 2013.

The Temple

1 Brittan and Kinmonth, *Living in Vogue*, 66; the Temple is attributed to Robert Taylor, on stylistic grounds; for Taylor's work, see Binney, *Sir Robert Taylor*, especially Asgill House, 46–54.

2 Veere Grenney, interview with the author, 2012.
3 Dean, *Sir John Soane*, 24–25; 169–170
4 Grenney, interview with the author, 2012.
5 Ibid.
6 The Paint Library, David Oliver, see www.paint-library.co.uk.
7 Brittan and Kinmonth, *Living in Vogue*, 66–67.
8 Grenney, interview with the author, 2012.

Broadlands
1 Robinson, "A Return to Harmony," 56–61.
2 Smith, "Temple, Henry."
3 Jackson-Stops, "Broadlands," 2099–102.
4 Robinson, "A Return to Harmony," 159–60.
5 Colvin, *Biographical Dictionary of British Architects*, 529.
6 Lady Brabourne and David Mlinaric, interview with the author, 2013.
7 Ibid.; and Jackson-Stops, "Broadlands," 2100.

Oakly Park
1 Watkin, *C.R. Cockerell*, xix; Haslam, "Shared Enthusiasm," 36–41; Haslam, "Oakly Park," 152–59.
2 Haslam, "Oakly Park," 158.
3 Watkin, *C.R. Cockerell*, 162–63.
4 Ibid., 163–64, Cockerell disliked their neighbour, Lord Powis, whom he thought vulgar.
5 Fay, *Victorian Days in England*, 79–80.
6 Haslam, "Shared Enthusiasm," 36–41; Haslam, "Oakly Park," 152–59.

Attingham Park
1 Jackson-Stops, *The English Country House*, 57.
2 Cornforth and Jackson-Stops, *Attingham Park*, 9.
3 Ibid., 6, 28.
4 Bills from 1806 and 1812–13, now in the Shropshire Record offices; I am very grateful to Sarah Kay, curator of Attingham, for generously providing me with copies of these and the sale catalogue of 1827, and inventories of 1861 and 1913.
5 Howell, *The Stranger in Shrewsbury*, 1816, extract in NT files.
6 Leach, *The County Seats of Shropshire*, 1891, extract in NT files.
7 Letter written by Lady Berwick, dated July 27, 1920; I am grateful to Sarah Kay for generously providing me with copies.
8 Rix, "Attingham Park," 1350–53.

Renishaw Hall
1 Jeremy Musson, "Renishaw Hall," 148–53; for Badger, see Colvin, *Biographical Dictionary of British Architects*, 86–87.
2 Musson, "Renishaw Hall," 150.
3 Ibid., 150–51.
4 Sitwell, *Left Hand! Right Hand!*, 225–54.
5 Musson, "Renishaw Hall," 151.
6 Cornforth, *English Interiors*, 70–74.
7 Ibid., 70.
8 Musson, "Renishaw Hall," 152.
9 Information from Lady Sitwell.

Felbrigg Hall
1 Maddison, *Felbrigg Hall*, 4–5, 12–13; Cornforth, "Felbrigg Hall, Norfolk," 1990, 5 April, 138–141, 12 April, 102–05.
2 Maddison, 44–45; Ketton-Cremer, *Felbrigg: The Story of a House*, 112–29.
3 Ibid., 116.
4 Maddison, 12–13.
5 Ibid, 15.
6 Ibid, 52–53; Ketton-Cremer, 267–76.
7 Information from Elinor Akinlade of the National Trust.

Eastnor Castle
1 Goodall, "Baronial Bravura," 66–71; Hervey-Bathurst, *Eastnor Castle*.
2 Eastlake, *A History of Gothic Revival*, 147.
3 Aldrich, *The Craces*, 78–81.
4 Hervey-Bathurst, *Eastnor Castle*, 26.
5 Aldrich, 80.
6 Hill, *God's Architect*, 428.
7 Jackson-Stops, *Treasure Houses of Britain*, 609.
8 Aldrich, 141.
9 Jenkins, *Thousand Best Houses*, 313.
10 Information from James Henry, Bath, 2013.

Knebworth
1 Musson, "Knebworth," 102–07.
2 Brown, "Lytton."
3 Fitzgerald's remark is quoted in Mark Bence-Jones, *Ancestral Houses*, 1984, 139.
4 Aldrich, 71–72.
5 Bills, copies in the archives at Knebworth, originals in the Hertford Record Office, with thanks to Clare Fleck, the archivist at Knebworth House.
6 Aldrich, *The Craces*, 70–71.
7 Ibid., p. 72.
8 Maclise quoted in Cobbold, *Knebworth*, 39.
9 Mallock, *Memoirs of Life and Literature*, 261.

Alnwick Castle
1 Mcdonald, *Alnwick Castle*, 45, 67, 72, 79–86; Allibone, *Anthony Salvin*, 81–84.
2 Donaldson, "Brief Memoir"; with Donaldson, "Some Description of Alnwick Castle"; with contributions by Canina and Salvin, 14–26; all published in *Papers Read at the RIBA*, 1857.
3 *Papers Read at the RIBA*, 16.
4 Ibid., 1.
5 Ibid., 18.
6 Information from Christopher Hunwick, archivist, who has given generous advice.
7 *Papers Read at the RIBA*, 22
8 Ibid.
9 Northumberland, *Alnwick Castle*, 101.
10 Gater and Wheeler, *Survey of London*, 2–10.
11 Scott, *Remarks on Secular Domestic Architecture*, 232.
12 *Papers Read at the RIBA*, 16.
13 Mcdonald, *Alnwick Castle*, 79–86.

Hutton in the Forest
1 Cornforth, "Hutton in the Forest," 352–56; Robinson, "Hutton in the Forest," 78–83.
2 Lord Inglewood, interview with the author, 2013.
3 Cornforth, "Hutton in the Forest," 354.
4 Oman and Hamilton, *Wallpapers*, 381, Cat. No. 1067; I am grateful to Michael Hall for making this link.
5 www.hutton-in-the-forest.co.uk; sadly, Lady Vane's diary, known to have been once in the family papers, is currently untraced.
6 Lord Inglewood, interview with the author, 2013.

Madresfield Court
1 Aslet, "Madresfield Court," 1338–41, 1458–61, 1551–58.
2 Mulvagh, *Madresfield*, 27.
3 Waugh, *Handful of Dust*, 9.
4 Waugh, *Brideshead Revisited*, 198.
5 Aslet, "Madresfield Court," 1552.
6 Aslet, *The Last Country Houses*, 250–255.
7 Lucy Chenevix-Trench, interview with the author, 2012.

Hilles House
1 Aslet, "A Family's Idyll," 58–63.

2 Abdy, *The Souls*, 9–15, 95, 101, 125.
3 Aslet, *The Last Country Houses*, 236–50; the break with the Duke of Westminster, 249–50.
4 Aslet, "A Family's Idyll," 63.
5 Detmar Blow II, interview with the author, 2013.
6 Hussey, "Hilles, Gloucestershire," 235 shows the adjoining room was screened off into a hall and dining room but is now treated as one room.

Dyrham Park
1 Kenworthy-Brown, *Dyrham Park, Gloucestershire*, 15–17; Girouard, "Dyrham Park," 335–39, 396–99; see also Kenworthy-Brown, "The Building of Dyrham Park," 138–44.
2 Murison, "Blathwayt, William."
3 Kenworthy-Brown, *Dyrham Park*, 16–17.
4 Information from National Trust internal report on decoration; thank you to Eilidh Auckland for sharing a copy of this material.
5 Ibid.
6 Burgess, "Extravagant Abandon"; Nancy Lancaster is quoted, 43
7 Ibid.
8 Kenworthy-Brown, *Dyrham Park*, 16–17.
9 Girouard, "Dyrham Park," 339.

The Yellow Room
1 Wood, *Nancy Lancaster*, 118–23.
2 Ibid., 106–12.
3 Lancaster, "22 Avery Row," typescript text written when Mrs. Lancaster gave up the flat in 1983; I am very grateful to Barrie McIntyre, archivist at Colefax and Fowler, for making this available and for other advice.
4 Wood, *Nancy Lancaster*, 118.
5 Lancaster, "22 Avery Row," 2.
6 Ibid.
7 Melissa Wyndham, interview with the author, 2013.
8 Roger Jones, interview with the author, 2013.

Deene Park
1 Cornforth, "Deene Park," 750–53 and 810–13; and "Deene Park, Northamptonshire," 50–55.

NOTES AND REFERENCES | 269

2 Miller, *Hidden Treasure Houses*, 102–20.
3 Cornforth, "Deene Park," 811.
4 The late Marian Brudenell, interview with the author, 2013.
5 Cornforth, "Deene Park," 811.
6 Miller, *Hidden Treasure Houses*, 120.
7 Ibid.

Lypiatt Park

1 Verey and Brooks, *Gloucestershire*, 466–67.
2 Ibid., 467.
3 Colvin, *A Biographical Dictionary of British Architects*, 1200.
4 Woollcombe, "Chadwick, Lynn."
5 Daniel Chadwick, interview with the author, 2013.
6 Woollcombe, "Chadwick, Lynn."
7 www.danielchadwick.com

Cholmondeley Castle

1 Jackson-Stops, "Cholmondeley Castle", 154–58, 226–30.
2 Ibid., 154.
3 Ibid., 227.
4 Colvin, *A Biographical Dictionary of British Architects*, 1061–62.
5 Jackson-Stops, "Cholmondeley Castle," 230.
6 For Sybil Sassoon, see Stansky, *Sassoon: The Worlds of Philip and Sybil*,
7 Wood, *John Fowler*, 184–89.
8 Jackson-Stops, "Cholmondeley Castle," 230.

The Grove

1 Quoted in his obituary by Mitchell Owens, in *The New York Times*, April 1998; from Hicks, *David Hicks on Living*.
2 Hicks, *A Life of Design*, 247–59; and Hicks, *David Hicks: Designer*, 20–27.
3 Verey, television broadcast, youtube.com, 1993.
4 Hicks, *A Life of Design*, 255; *David Hicks: Designer*, 68–99.
5 Metcalf, *Syrie Maugham*, 135–36.
6 Cecil, *In Search of Rex Whistler*, 170–77.
7 Hicks, *A Life of Design*, 254–53; and Lady Pamela Hicks, interview with the author, 2013.
8 Hicks, *A Life of Design*, 81.

9 Ashley Hicks, interview with the author, 2013.

Stanway House

1 Musson, "On My Chippendale Day Bed," 68–71; Hussey, "Stanway, Gloucestershire," 1490–94, 1646–49, 1708–71; and Miller, *Hidden Treasure Houses*, 235–53.
2 Abdy and Gere, *The Souls*, 9.
3 Ibid., 102.
4 Ibid.
5 Musson, "On My Chippendale Day Bed," 70.
6 Chippendale, The *Gentleman and Cabinetmaker's Director*, 1754, plate XXXIII, shows a Chinese "sopha."
7 Miller, *Hidden Treasure Houses*, 251–52.
8 Miller, *Treasure Houses*, 251–52, and information from Lord Wemyss.

Bradley Court

1 Musson, "Bradley Court," 130–35.
2 Advice to the author from Nicholas Kingsley, author of *Country Houses of Gloucestershire*, 2000.
3 Austen, *Sense and Sensibility*, 34.
4 Thomas Messel, interview with the author, 2012.
5 For Oliver Messel's design career more widely, see Messel, *Oliver Messel*.
6 Musson, "Bradley Court," 130–35.
7 Cornforth, "Nymans," 60–65; and for the collection, see Hussey, "Nymans," 292–97 and 320–25.
8 Thomas Messel, interview with the author, 2012.

Wormington Grange

1 Colvin, *A Biographical Dictionary of British Architects*, 86–87.
2 Hussey, *Mid-Georgian*, 175–80.
3 John Evetts, interview with the author, 2013.
4 Hussey, *Mid-Georgian*, 117.
5 Lewin, "Ismay, Hastings Lionel, Baron Ismay."
6 For the activities of the Landmark Trust, see www.landmarktrust.org.uk.

Whithurst House

1 Miers, "Whithurst Park," 115–19.

2 Ibid.; Christopher Rae-Scott, interview with the author, 2013; and letter to author, June 11, 2013. Mr. Rae-Scott kindly lent me his notes, which accompanied the original application.
3 Miers, "Whithurst Park," 116.
4 Richard Taylor, interview with the author, 2012.

Aynhoe Park

1 Cooper, *Aynho*, 193–96; Binney, "Aynho," 80–85.
2 Dean, *Sir John Soane*, 78–89.
3 Cartwright-Hignett, *Lili at Aynhoe*, 33–36.
4 Rock, *Aynhoe Park*, 6–7; for a description of Mr. Perkins's earlier collection, see Brittain-Catlin, "True to Form," 66–72.
5 James Perkins, interview with the author, 2013.

Thame Park

1 Oswald, "Thame Park," 1092–95.
2 Ibid., 1093.
3 Berkeley Wills, "Alterations to Thame Park," 16–19, the drawing room is illustrated on page 18.
4 Millard, "Sir Harold Bowden."
5 Mr. and Mrs. Paul Matthews, interview with the author, 2013.
6 Lady Henrietta Spencer-Churchill, interview with the author, 2013.

Knepp Castle

1 Miers, "Knepp Castle," 66–71.
2 www.chesterjones.com. Jones is also author of *Colefax and Fowler: The Best in English Interior Decoration*, 1989.
3 Isabella Burrell, interview with the author, 2013.
4 For Nancy Lancaster's former home, Ditchley Park, Oxfordshire, see Wood, *Nancy Lancaster*, 54–81.
5 Isabella Burrell, interview with the author, 2013.

The Temple

1 Brittan and Kinmonth, *Living in Vogue*, 66; the Temple is attributed to Robert Taylor, on stylistic grounds; for Taylor's work, see Binney, *Sir Robert Taylor*, especially Asgill House, 46–54.

2 Veere Grenney, interview with the author, 2012.
3 Dean, *Sir John Soane*, 24–25; 169–170
4 Grenney, interview with the author, 2012.
5 Ibid.
6 The Paint Library, David Oliver, see www.paint-library.co.uk.
7 Brittan and Kinmonth, *Living in Vogue*, 66–67.
8 Grenney, interview with the author, 2012.

Index

A
Adam, Robert, 9–10, 15, 18, 23
— Kedleston Hall designed by, 56–63
— Newby Hall designed by, 48–55
Addison, Edward, 137
Aesthetic Movement, 19
Aldrich, Megan, 121
Alnwick Castle, 128–135
Althorp, 64–71
Anne (queen), 12
Arscott, Mary-Lou, 36
Arts and Crafts, 137, 145, 152–159
Ashbee, C. R., 145
Asquith, Cynthia, 207
Attingham Park, 88–95
Aubrey, John, 33, 36
Aubusson carpet, 22, 44–45
Austen, Jane, 9, 13, 215
Aynhoe Park, 236–243

B
Badger, Joseph, 97–99
Beauchamp, Countess of, 147–148
Beauchamp, Earl of, 145, 147–148
Beckwith, Muriel, 19
Beeton, Mrs., 20
Bennison, Geoffrey, 44
Beresford-Clark, Charles, 259, 263
Berkeley Wills, G. H., 245
Berwick, Lord, 89–90, 93, 95
Biddesden, 22–23
Blathwayt family, 161, 164
Blow, Detmar, 152–159, 207
Blow, Detmar, II, 156, 159
Blow, Issie, 156, 159
Brabourne, Lady, 73–76
Bradley Court, 214–221
Brettingham, Matthew, 57
Brideshead Revisited (Waugh), 145
Broadlands, 8, 10, 72–79
Brodsworth Hall, 17
Bromfield, Joseph, 81–83
Broughton Hall, 16–17
Brown, Capability, 65, 73
Brudenell family, 174–181
Bulletti, Signor, 129
Bulwer-Lytton, Edward, 121, 125
Burn, William, 207
Burrell family, 250–257
cabinets, 133–134, 226

C
Camuccini, Vincenzo, 130–131, 133
Canina, Commendatore, 129–131
Canova sculptures, 90, 93
Cardigan, Earl of, 175, 180
Carr, John, 49
Cartwright family, 237
Castilho, Mara, 156–157
ceiling decoration, 118–119, 124–125.
  See also plasterwork ceilings
Chadwick, Daniel, 182–189
Chadwick, Lynn, 182–189
Chamber, William, 49
Chenevix-Trench family, 145, 148
Chillingham Castle, 40–47
chimneypieces
— Alnwick Castle, 133
— Althorp, 65, 67
— Broadlands, 76–77
— Cholmondeley Castle, 191, 194–195
— Eastnor Castle, 113–115
— Felbrigg Hall, 105, 110
— The Grove, 204–205
— Kedleston Hall, 57
— Knebworth, 126–127
— Knepp Castle, 254–255
— Loseley Park, 25, 27
— Oakly Park, 81
— Renishaw Hall, 97, 102–103
— South Wraxall Manor, 33–35
— Temple, 260–261
— Whithurst House, 232–233
— Yellow Room, 168–169
chinoiserie, 207–213
Chippendale furniture, 49, 54–55, 97, 101, 207–213
Cholmondeley Castle, 190–197
Churchill, Winston, 22, 226
Clegg, Maud, 223
Clive, R. H., 81, 85
Cobbold, Henry Lytton, 121
Cockerell, C. R., 80–87, 129, 223
Cocks, Elizabeth Somers, 117
Codman, Ogden, 21
coffee, 12, 19
Coke, Mary, 12
Corey, Alex, 44
Cornforth, John, 54, 137, 175
Crace, John, 112–119, 121–125
Cragside, 18–19
Cruickshank, Dan, 33
Curzon, Nathaniel, 57, 61

D
Davenport, J. L., 97
daybeds, 207–213
decoration, of drawing rooms.
  See also ceiling decoration
— Aesthetic Movement, 19
— layered, 140–141
— from multiple periods, 28–29, 41, 44–45
— rich, 11–13, 108–109, 134–135
— stylistic restraint in, 22–23
The Decoration of Houses (Wharton and Codman), 21
Deene Park, 174–181
de Silva, Helga, 156, 159
De Vos tapestries, 97, 100–101
Dickens, Charles, 121
dining rooms, 9, 12, 15, 19, 81–83
Ditchley Park, 15, 167, 251
Donaldson, T. L., 73, 129, 133
Dorrington, J. E., 183
The Drawing-Room: Its Decoration and Furniture (Orrinsmith), 19
drawing rooms. *See also* decoration, of drawing rooms
— Alnwick Castle, 128–135
— Althorp, 64–71
— Attingham Park, 88–95
— Aynhoe Park, 236–243
— Biddesden, 22–23
— Bradley Court, 214–221
— Broadlands, 8, 10, 72–79
— Brodsworth Hall, 17
— Broughton Hall, 16–17
— Chillingham Castle, 40–47
— Cholmondeley Castle, 190–197
— Cragside, 18–19
— Deene Park, 174–181
— dining rooms and, 9, 12, 15, 19, 81–83
— Ditchley Park, 15
— Dyrham Park, 160–165
— Eastnor Castle, 112–119
— elegance of, 80–110
— evolution of, 24–79
— Felbrigg Hall, 104–111
— gender zoning in, 9, 20–21
— The Grove, 198–205
— Hagley Hall, 13–15
— Herstmonceux Castle, 10–11
— Hilles House, 152–159
— Hutton in the Forest, 136–143
— Kedleston Hall, 56–63
— Knebworth, 120–127
— Knepp Castle, 250–257
— Loseley Park, 24–31
— Lypiatt Park, 182–189
— Madresfield Court, 144–151
— naming of, 12–13
— Newby Hall, 48–55
— Oakly Park, 14, 80–87
— opulence of, 112–151
— origins of, 10–12
— Polesden Lacey, 22
— Renishaw Hall, 96–103
— role of, 9–23
— South Wraxall Manor, 32–39
— Stanway House, 206–213
— Syon House, 15
— tastemakers of, 152–205
— Temple, 258–264
— Thame Park, 244–249
— timeless, 206–264
— Whithurst House, 229–235
— Wormington Grange, 222–229
— Yellow Room, 166–173
Duval Brasseur, Jacques, 240
Dyrham Park, 160–165

E
Eastlake, Charles, 19, 113
Eastnor Castle, 112–119
eating rooms, 9–10
Elcho, Mary. *See* Wemyss, Countess of
Englert, Rick, 231–232, 234
English country house, 9–10. *See also* drawing rooms
The English Country House: A Grand Tour (Jackson-Stops), 89
Evetts, John, 222–229

F
Fay, Anna Maria, 14–15, 81, 85
Felbrigg Hall, 104–111
Fiennes, Celia, 12, 73
Finlay, James, 89
Fitzgerald, Edward, 121
Fletcher, George, 137
Fletcher, Henry, 137
floor, painted, 98–99, 101
Ford, Oliver, 175
Fowler, John, 82, 85, 166–173, 191–197
Fox, Hazel, 117
France, 9, 18
French boulle furniture, 107–108

G
Garrett, Daniel, 137
Garrett, Miss, 19
gender zoning, 9, 20–21
The Gentleman's House (Kerr), 15–16
Germany, 20–21
Gillows furniture, 140, 142–143, 161–164, 223, 226
Gilt Leather Parlour. *See* Dyrham Park
Girouard, Mark, 164
Gladstone, Margaret. *See* Vane, Lady
Glorious Revolution, 10
Gobelins tapestries, 49–54
Goldicutt, John, 223, 225
Gothic style
— at Cholmondeley Castle, 190–197
— at Eastnor Castle, 112–119
— at Hutton in the Forest, 137, 142
— at Knebworth, 120–127
— at Lypiatt Park, 186
Goudge, Edward, 105, 110–111
Great Chamber, 33
Great Parlour, 11–12, 33, 105–107, 161
Grenney, Veere, 258–264
Grey family, 41, 43–44
Griffin, William, 33
The Grove, 198–205
Guinness, Diana, 22–23

H
Hagley Hall, 13–15
Hakewill, Henry, 223, 225
Hampton Court, 12
Hardwick, P. C., 145–147
Haycock, John, 81–83
Hayward family, 101
Heaney, Seamus, 215
Henrietta Maria (queen), 12
Henry, Hugh, 74, 76
Herstmonceux Castle, 10–11
Hervey-Bathurst family, 114, 117
Hickman, Harriet, 81, 85
Hicks, Ashley, 199, 202, 204
Hicks, David, 198–205, 259–260, 263
Hicks, Pamela, 199, 201–202
Hilles House, 152–159
Hints on Household Taste (Eastlake), 19
Holland, Henry, 65–68, 73
House Architecture (Stevenson), 16
Household Management (Beeton), 20
Howell, Thomas, 89
Hulton, Teresa, 93
Hussey, Christopher, 65, 223
Hutton in the Forest, 136–143

THE DRAWING ROOM | 271

I

Inglewood, Lady, 140–141
Inglewood, Lord, 137, 140–141
Islington, Lady, 161–164
Islington, Lord, 164
Ismay, Lord, 226

J

Jackson-Stops, Gervase, 89
Jacobethan style, 145–147
James I (king), 41
Jenkins, Simon, 117
Jeune, Lady, 19–20
John Cornforth Memorial Fund, 61
Johnson, Samuel, 12
Jones, Chester, 250–257
Jones, Roger, 171

K

Keck, Anthony, 215–216
Kedleston Hall, 56–63
Kerr, Robert, 15–16, 18
Ketton, John, 108
Ketton-Cremer, Robert Wyndham, 108
Kime, Robert, 35–36
King James I Room. *See* Chillingham Castle
Kinmonth, Patrick, 35–36
Knebworth, 120–127
Knepp Castle, 250–257
Knox, Tim, 61

L

Lady Troubridge's Book of Etiquette, 20
Lamb, Emily, 73
Lancaster, Nancy, 161, 164, 180, 260, 263
— Knepp Castle and, 251–254
— Yellow Room and, 166–173
Lemere, Bedford, 85
libraries
— Aynhoe, 243
— Deene Park, 175–179
— Knepp Castle, 256
— Oakly Park, 81–83, 85–87
Linnell furniture, 57–61
Long, Robert, 33
Long, Walter, 33, 36
Long, Walter Hume, 36
Long Room. *See* Hilles House
Loseley Park, 24–31
Lowndes-Stone, Elizabeth, 28, 30–31
Lukin, William, 105
Lutyens, Edwin, 121, 153, 167

Lygon family, 145
Lypiatt Park, 182–189
Lytton, Elizabeth Bulwer, 121
Lytton, Lord, 120–127

M

Maclise, Daniel, 125
MacVicar Anderson, John, 65, 68
Madresfield Court, 144–151
Mallock, William Hurrell, 125
Martin, A. C., 36
Matthews family, 248
medieval house, 10
Messel family, 214–221
Miers, Mary, 234
Miller, James, 180
Mlinaric, David, 73–76
Montiroli, Signor, 129
More, George, 25, 28
More, Thomas, 28
More, William, 25
More-Molyneux family, 28
Morris & Co., 136–140, 207
Morrison, Lady, 148, 150
Murat, Caroline, 89, 93–95
Murray, Simon, 61
Muthesius, Hermann, 20–21

N

Napper, John, 85
Nash, John, 89–91, 93, 113, 167, 251
Nash-Taylor, Gela, 35–36
National Trust, 61, 93, 108, 164
Newby Hall, 48–55
Nichols, Beverley, 22
North, Roger, 12
Northumberland, Duke of, 128–135

O

Oakly Park, 14, 80–87
Oliver, David, 263
Orlando (Woolf), 21
Orrinsmith, Mrs., 19

P

Paine, James, 57, 105
paintings. *See also* portraits
— Alnwick Castle, 130–131, 133
— Bradley Court, 218, 220
— Dyrham Park, 163–164
— Felbrigg Hall, 105
— Oakly Park, 81, 84–85
— Stanway House, 209–210

— Wormington Grange, 226, 228–229
Palgrave, William, 49
Palmerston, Lord, 73
parlours, 9, 11–12, 33, 105–107, 161
passementerie, 248
Payne, Henry, 145
Perkins, James, 236–243
plasterwork ceilings
— Chillingham Castle, 41, 46–47
— Eastnor Castle, 113–114, 118–119
— Felbrigg Hall, 105, 110–111
— Hutton in the Forest, 137
— Loseley Park, 25, 28
— Oakly Park, 81–83
— South Wraxall Manor, 38–39
— Stanway House, 207, 210–211
Plymouth, Earl of, 85
Plymouth, Lady, 156
Pogmire, Alexander, 137
Polesden Lacey, 22
portraits
— Althorp, 65, 68–71
— Attingham Park, 89–91, 93
— Broadlands, 76–79
— Chillingham Castle, 44, 46–47
— Cholmondeley Castle, 191–193
— Deene Park, 175–180
— Felbrigg Hall, 105
— The Grove, 199–202, 204–205
— Hilles House, 154, 156
— Hutton in the Forest, 137, 140, 142
— Knebworth, 122–123
— Knepp Castle, 251–254, 256
— Loseley, 28, 30–31
— Madresfield Court, 148–151
— Oakly Park, 84–85
— Renishaw Hall, 97, 101
— Stanway House, 207
Powys, Lybbe, 13
Pratt, Roger, 11
Pugin, A. W. N., 33, 112–119, 121, 125

R

Rae-Scott, Christopher, 229–235
Raleigh, Walter, 36
Ramsden, Elizabeth, 54
Renishaw Hall, 96–103
rep, rose pink, 74–76
Repton, Humphry, 13
Richardson-Cox, Major, 36
Rowley family, 259, 263
Ruskin, John, 153, 156

S

Salvin, Anthony, 129, 133, 137
Samwell, William, 105
Sargent, John Singer, 93, 97, 101
Scarsdale, Baron. *See* Curzon, Nathaniel
Scott, G. G., 113, 133
sculptures, 49, 90, 93, 182–189
Sense and Sensibility (Austen), 9, 215
Shapland, Henry, 21
silk hangings, 43–44, 57–59, 61
Simond, Louis, 13–14
Sitwell family, 96–103
Smirke, Robert, 113, 191
Smith, Temple, 97
Soane, John, 236–243, 259
Somers, Earl, 113
The Souls, 153, 161, 164, 207
South Drawing Room. *See* Althorp
South Wraxall Manor, 32–39
Spencer, Lord, 65, 68
Spencer-Churchill, Henrietta, 244–249
stained glass, 125
Stanway House, 206–213
State Drawing Room. *See* Alnwick Castle; Kedleston Hall; Knebworth
Steuart, George, 89–90
Stevenson, J. J., 16, 18
The Stranger in Shrewsbury (Howell), 89
Stuart, James "Athenian," 73
— *Style Schemes in Antique Furnishing* (Shapland), 21
Swinton, Mrs. Campbell, 101
Sybil Colefax and John Fowler, 166–173, 263
Syon House, 9, 15, 49

T

tablescapes, 202
Talman, William, 137
tapestries
— De Vos, 97, 100–101
— Gobelins, 49–54
— Teniers, 194, 196–197
Tapestry Drawing Room. *See* Newby Hall
Taylor, John, 35–36
Taylor, Richard, 231–232, 234
Taylor, Robert, 259, 263
tea, 12, 19–20, 23, 101
Temple, Reggie, 93
the Temple, 258–264
Teniers tapestries, 194, 196–197

Thame Park, 244–249
Tollemache, Winifred, 153, 156
Tree, Nancy. *See* Lancaster, Nancy
Tudor house, 10–11
Turner, William, 191

V

Vane, Henry, 137, 140
Vane, Lady, 137, 142
Victorian design, 15–16, 21–22, 119
— at Hutton in the Forest, 140–141
— at Knebworth, 122–123
von Westenholz, Piers, 148

W

Wake, Joan, 180
Wakefield, Edward, 44
Wakefield, Humphry, 41, 43–44
Wakefield, Lady, 41, 43
Walker, T. L., 33
wallpaper, 253–355
— flock, 161, 164
— Morris & Co., 136–139
Walpole, Horace, 57, 61, 65, 191, 210
Warre-Cornish, Philip, 156
Wathen, Paul, 183
Waugh, Evelyn, 145
Webster, George, 137
Weddell, William, 49, 54
Wells-Cole, Anthony, 25, 33
Wemyss, Countess of, 207
Wemyss, Earl of, 206–213
Wenman family, 245
West, Benjamin, 81
Wharton, Edith, 21, 23
Whithurst House, 229–235
Williamson, Matthew, 240, 243
Windham family, 105–108
Windsor, Viscount, 85
withdrawing room, 11
Wood, Martin, 194
woodcarvings, 129, 132–133
Woolf, Virginia, 21
Wormington Grange, 222–229
Wyatt, James, 113, 183
Wyatt, M. D., 133
Wyatt, Thomas Henry, 183
Wyatville, Jeffry, 41, 167, 169, 183, 186
Wyndham, Melissa, 171
Yellow Room, 166–173
Young, Rory, 215, 218